DW Gibson has written for *The New York Times, The New York Observer, BOMB,* and *Tin House* and worked on documentaries for MSNBC and A&E. He lives in New York City.

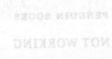

NOT WORKING

PEOPLE TALK ABOUT LOSING A JOB AND FINDING
THEIR WAY IN TODAY'S CHANGING ECONOMY

DW GIBSON

PENGUIN BOOKS

PENGUIN BOOKS

Published by the Penguin Group

Penguin Group (USA) Inc., 375 Hudson Street, New York, New York 10014, U.S.A.

Penguin Group (Canada), 90 Eglinton Avenue East, Suite 700, Toronto,
Ontario, Canada M4P 2Y3 (a division of Pearson Penguin Canada Inc.)

Penguin Books Ltd, 80 Strand, London WC2R 0RL, England

Penguin Ireland, 25 St Stephen's Green, Dublin 2, Ireland (a division of Penguin Books Ltd)

Penguin Group (Australia), 250 Camberwell Road, Camberwell,
Victoria 3124, Australia (a division of Pearson Australia Group Pty Ltd)

Penguin Books India Pvt Ltd, 11 Community Centre,
Panchsheel Park, New Delhi – 110 017, India

Penguin Group (NZ), 67 Apollo Drive, Rosedale, Auckland 0632,
New Zealand (a division of Pearson New Zealand Ltd)

Penguin Books (South Africa) (Pty) Ltd, 24 Sturdee Avenue,
Rosebank, Johannesburg 2196, South Africa

Penguin Books Ltd, Registered Offices:
80 Strand, London WC2R 0RL, England

First published in the United States of America by OR Books 2012
Published in Penguin Books 2012

1   3   5   7   9   10   8   6   4   2

ISBN 978-0-14-312255-5

Printed in the United States of America

ALWAYS LEARNING   PEARSON

To those who contributed to the story, with gratitude—
and to Tasha who makes each day a blessing, with love.

"All that each person is, and experiences, and shall never experience, in body and in mind, all these things are different expressions of himself and of one root, and are identical: and not one of these things nor one of these persons is ever quite to be duplicated, nor replaced, nor has it ever quite had precedent: but each is a new and incommunicably tender life, wounded in every breath, and almost as hardly killed as easily wounded: sustaining, for a while, without defense, the enormous assault of the universe..."

—James Agee

CONTENTS

BOOK FIVE   CORPORATE CITIZENS

BOOK SIX   PUBLIC DOMAIN

BOOK SEVEN   FRINGE

BOOK EIGHT   FAMILY

BOOK NINE   EVOLUTION

Acknowledgments

Vagabond Breakdown

Outside the collection of people I interviewed, there are various iterations of *we*, and I'll enumerate when necessary but in the end all that is important is *we*—again and again, and always. In the spirit of Agee, and in alignment with my never-ending pursuit of efficiency, here is a complete billing (in alphabetical order):

Mallery Avidon, collaborator, playwright, information fountain and haiku master.

Beluh, the Jeep: 1999 model, red, 140,000 miles and no air-conditioning, always questionable, mostly sturdy.

Ella, the dog (Pomeranian): honey colored and generally an accompaniment of Tasha Garcia Gibson.

Tasha Garcia Gibson, collaborator, wife, champion aesthete, shuttling back and forth between the road and a steady job.

DW Gibson, instigator.

MJ Sieber, collaborator and filmmaker, always finding light and depth.

Over the summer and fall of 2011 we drove across the country from Southern California to New York City. We occupied blistering hot sidewalks, trying to catch people outside unemployment offices; we attended church services where congregations provided guidance for the unemployed; we stalked business reporters, distant relatives, and recognizable facebook friends, trying to find those who were laid off in the five year span from 2007–2011, those who would be willing to tell the story of the day they lost that job, the circumstances that led up to it, and the consequences that followed.

We met these collaborators in libraries, parking lots, fast-food restaurants, homes, union halls, fellowship halls, cheap motel rooms, coffee shops and bars—wherever someone with a story preferred to sit and talk. The majority claimed that they or their particular experience—or both—were boring. And most people began with a 45-second version of their story. I'd ask a few questions and they'd tell a five-minute version. Then a few more questions and soon enough the most precise detail of the story had been reached—and it was often tethered to the biggest idea or strongest emotion or both. The unfurled version of each story lasted anywhere from 45 minutes to several days. Over the course of that time, a handful of generous collaborators invited us to eat and even sleep in their homes. Some did laundry—insisted on doing laundry. All of this and they were willing to tell a stranger a personal story they would likely prefer to forget.

Since it was work that had been lost, and work that was sought, I ended every conversation by asking each person how he or she defines the word "work." Here is a sample of what these Americans have lost—and what they seek:

Pride	Bread on the table	Results
Security	Adventure	Purpose
Self-worth	Labor	Nurture
Self-esteem	Blood, sweat & tears	Responsibility
A paycheck	A place to go	Fun
A career	Stability	Joy
A challenge	Life	Identity
A reward	Energy	Dignity
A roof overhead	Creativity	

The Precariat

This is the story of becoming unemployed through no fault of one's own, due to circumstances beyond one's control. That's an exact but twisty sentence designed to avoid all of these words and phrases: laid off, excessed, downsized, surplused, separated, sacked, terminated, reorganized, released, reallocated, managed out, fired, let go, discontinued, displaced, discharged, dissolved, RIF'd, canned, hosed, and blown out. This is the language used by the people who endured *it*, and none of the verbs fully serve the experience of having your work, identity, livelihood, and dignity swept out from underneath you. As one Human Resources manager put it, *"There is no way to say it so that anyone can hear anything but 'you don't want me here anymore.'"*

Layoff seems to be the most commonly used word despite—or maybe because of—a passivity that cheats the impact of the experience. As recently as 1989, the Oxford English Dictionary defined *layoff* as "a spell of relaxation; a period during which a workman is temporarily dismissed or allowed to leave his work." This book does not contain spells of relaxation, and not one person characterizes the event as something he or she was allowed to do. It is something new, *the layoff*, and something ubiquitous; as the writer Louis Uchitelle puts it, it has become "a mass phenomenon of American life."

Despite capitalism's propensity for exciting tension between ownership and labor, for much of the 20th century "the thrust of American labor practices had been toward lasting attachments of employers to workers and vice versa," Uchitelle writes in *The Disposable American.* "The direction was toward job security, not away from it. Efficiency seemed to require it." And to optimize productivity from both camps—risk-taking entrepreneurs and motivated workers—the American government embraced responsibility for providing rules and regulations. This philosophical approach—cultivated by an assortment of pre-New Deal progressives from Teddy Roosevelt to Al Smith—proved effective until the mid 1970s when the country experienced the worst economic conditions since the Great Depression, prompting corporations to abandon the more polite "early retirements" of the 1960s for outright layoffs. And in 1981, when President Regan awakened the slumbering Taft-Hartley Act to demand that striking air traffic controllers be fired and replaced, the new approach was vetted. A company's right to hire permanent replacement workers had been legal since the 1930s but major corporations did not aggressively exercise the right until Regan winked in that direction. And the governmental sanctioning of layoffs has continued through every administration since—Republican and Democratic—becoming not only accepted practice but also supported practice with programs like the Workforce Investment Act of 1998, which provides a purse to train those who have been unceremoniously dismissed. We have systematized the layoff, built up industry around it, written about it in movies and songs and novels: the layoff has become an integral part of the American experience.

We've accomplish this feat in almost the exact window of time—38 years—since Studs Terkel published *Working: People Talk About What They Do All Day and How They Feel About What They Do*, an oral history with an exemplarily expositional subtitle. The voices in *Working* confirm just how tied our work is to our sense of identity—an entanglement that goes back at least as far as the twelfth century when we began taking the name of our labor: Cooper, Smith, Weaver, Cook, Thatcher, Carpenter, Baker. What happens when that center post is yanked? Over the last four decades we have learned to prop up a revised identity often weighted by the experience of not working. As the cultural analyst Andrew Ross puts it: "Today's precarity[1] is, in large part, an exercise of capitalist control. Postindustrial capitalism thrives on actively disorganizing employment and socio-economic life in general so that it can profit from vulnerability, instability, and desperation."

This capitalist control—this vulnerability, instability and desperation—hit some kind of crescendo around 2007, when built houses didn't sell and planned houses stopped getting built; when 158-year-old financial intuitions imploded, and money started disappearing in $18 billion clumps.

It was sometime shortly thereafter that we crawled into the arms of this phrase, *The Great Recession*, initially blinded, then overcome, by the realities of the first—and here's to making it the last—depression of the 21st Century. The collapse of banking in the fall of 2008 created the conditions for a depression in economic terms—as underscored by Paul Krugman, a Nobel Prize-winner, and economist Elliot Parker, whom you'll meet in these pages—and a depression that functions on an visceral level. We the people, we the economic system, we the precariat are depressed. The only challenge to the depth of our depression is the strength of our character. They are both to be taken seriously.

From the beginning of 2007 to the summer of 2011 the national unemployment rate shot up from 4.6% to 9%. It reached 10% in October of 2009 and stayed well above 9% for 28 straight months (with the exception of March 2011, which was 8.9%). Two and a half years of increases and sustained high percentages demonstrate the only useful information yielded by the unemployment figures provided by the US Department of Labor: trends over time, measuring this year against that year. And it is safe to say that since 2007 we've climbed at a sharp angle in the wrong direction.

"First of all, it's a survey," says economist Elliot Parker when I ask him about the national unemployment rate. He looks slightly put out,

---

[1] Precarity is generated from the Latin verb *precor*, meaning to be forced to beg and pray to keep one's job.

as if disappointed by the incompleteness of the statistic. "'Cause we don't actually count all these people. In this monthly survey...if you've worked even a few hours, you're considered employed. If you stopped looking, you're not considered part of the labor force, you're 'discouraged.' And so the unemployment rates are always much higher than the official rates. Better estimates suggest that maybe a decent measurement would be closer to 17% unemployment. And that still does not capture the people who are underemployed, who are working at McDonalds when they used to be an engineer."

The national unemployment rate is an infamous underestimation. I'm inclined to believe that we stunt the number so severely only so we can keep calm and retain whatever will we still possess. Consider not only those who have downgraded jobs or lost jobs but also those married to, dependent on, responsible or concerned for someone who becomes unemployed. Consider those surrounded by vacated cubicles, absorbing the work of those who were let go, anticipating their own unkind fate. The sum total of these precarious circumstances is unknown. Whatever the number, it is our majority.

Beyond the limp statistics there are also endless variables—so ultimately there is nothing scientific about this book. It's all idiosyncrasy and particularity. The perspective is consistently lopsided, inclined toward the voice on any given page, and the speakers, en masse, stitch the narrative. Certain elements of the story couldn't fit in one clean section— and so run wild throughout the book:

Lists are everywhere, the names and numbers of those who are getting cut, or those who are being retained—or those who are waiting for the call from the union. Some lists are fiercely guarded, others secretly discovered. And for those who see the list before they are supposed to, or have a hunch, or realize they are excluded from next Thursday's meeting, there is always the experience of waiting. Waiting for the internal ring or the pop up request for a 4pm meeting. *Just drop the hammer. Do it. Tell me I'm here, or I'm not."*

Health concerns persist: routines are obliterated, not enough sleep, too much sleep, too much booze—insurance is skipped, roll the dice and hope for the best. Too much food, not enough food, trying to eat different food: *"I guess I don't need all that fat stuff I was eating to keep me going through the day."* Cooking instead of ordering; harvesting instead of consuming; gardens fill condominium patios and downtown rooftops. I met an architect-cum-horticulturist: *"I get a kick out of anything that grows."*

People are on the move, crossing borders into new counties and states and countries, chasing jobs and homes and schools: out-of-towners and immigrants from any place you could think to love or fear or envy or shun.

Age is rarely a positive factor. I'm too old. I'm too young; I don't have the experience, my skills are dated. Remove all dates from your resume. It is illegal to ask an interviewee his or her age but *"when they find out what year you graduated from high school, they figure it out."* Older people are replaced with younger people: *"Probably helped that the guy made about half of what I was making."*

The stakes are consistently high but varied in nature: debt, friendship, marriage, a newborn, health, shelter, food, identity, dignity. There are different types of sacrifice—there's giving up things you want, and giving up things you need—and it is not always easy to determine one's own location on the spectrum: *"I don't know how desperate I should be right now."*

Chance and timing always resurface: *"I got on the elevator at the county courthouse, and the door almost closed. It was about three inches, and this hand comes through, and this gal gets on…"*

There are multiple layoffs over multiple months or years. *"I've never had that 'we have bad news' talk. Here I am, within twelve months, getting it twice."*

Resumes are at the bottom of stacks, deleted from inboxes, and tossed across tables in half-hearted interviews. *"It's a buyer's market."* Don't try getting anyone on the phone. Human contact is diminished: filing for unemployment online—*"I thought there was an office you went to, like all the TV shows…they didn't even do unemployment offices anymore"*; eradicating Human Resource departments, ending employment by way of an emailed attachment. Proximity is minimized or avoided altogether: people are rarely told they are losing their job by the individual who made the decision. The decision comes from someone over there, in a corporate building two states or three continents away. *"It was sort of like that thing out there in the universe had done this to me."*

Capitalism not only prefers its labor to come without face or name but also that it be cheap. As one ex-banker pointed out to me, Jack Welch once floated the idea of building a giant factory on a giant ship so it could be docked around the world—wherever the wages are the lowest. The quest for cheap labor will travel to the farthest reaches of the world—and circle back around again when the opportunity presents itself.

Many people like to distance themselves from the severity of their circumstances. People tell stories of someone they know—someone even worse off. *They* really have it bad, not me. *"It's not like I can't buy groceries, you know?"* Even those who have gone without food or shelter speak of those who have done so for more time, or with less help from friends.

After talking, many people confessed anxiety—*"you know, I haven't been sleeping so well since you called me"*—and an unexpected gratitude, which I always seemed to share: whether speaking or listening, there is some strange edification in the expression of these experiences.

There was the wife who sat in the far corner of the coffee shop and waited for her husband to exit before darting over to hand me a small bill payment envelope with my name written next to the see-thru window. This is the typed note contained inside:

Dear Mr. Gibson:

Thank you for meeting with my husband H— today. He has been in quite a funk over the last couple of months, but his demeanor improves each time he has a conversation with you. I think it makes him feel better knowing that someone is finally giving his situation the attention it deserves. You have my best wishes for the great success in your latest endeavor and my gratitude for bringing out a bit of the H— who I fell in love with some 12 years ago.

Sincerely,

In a downtown St. Louis career services center, while I tried to connect with some of the people working on their resumes, one of the employees in the office tapped me on the shoulder and said, "I know why you're here. Come with me, I have something to show you." He had gray hair, a short sleeve white shirt and a dark tie. When he marched down the office hall, I followed. He led me all the way back to his cubicle where he did a Google search that yielded a page full of previously-clicked results, all the text had already shifted from blue to purple. The gray-haired man clicked one of the first hits, which led to video of a local news segment about a young dad who lost his high-paying job, endured months of unemployment, sold his house, downgraded to a job repairing highways, and got sideswiped by a driver—killed soon after he took the job. At one point in the news segment, the father of the deceased man is interviewed, and I can see this is the gray-haired gentleman standing behind me. He pulled me into his cubicle to show me his deceased son's story of unemployment. And then he gently shooed me away as soon as the video was finished playing—he didn't want me to have the chance to express condolences or sadness. He wanted his son's story to be told and he wanted to leave it at that.

No two conversations felt the same but still they all gathered around certain subjects—a sprawling Venn diagram. Some subjects resurfaced more than others, feeling central, and so they guided the organization of the voices in the book: those at the outset of careers comprise *Youth*; *Education* includes those who worked in the field or kept circling around to the subject in their own story; *Housing* brings together the people who built, sold, and bought the gluttonous amount of homes this country developed; *Community* details a couple of hollowed towns that once revolved around factories that have shuttered; *Corporate Citizens* are those who worked for large companies, sometimes for several decades; *Public Domain* gathers former civil servants; *Fringe* is made up of homelessness, hunger, illegal activity and various other extremities; *Family* is a collection of stories anchored by bloodlines; and *Evolution* is about disappearing professions and new pursuits.

In the end, all the voices are tangled, each finding a singular note while still echoing others. This story is told collectively and it confirms the community of those who share it: *"I can come home and say, 'Guess what? So-and-so came in today, and they're in the same boat, they just lost their job…I don't feel good about it, but it makes me feel better knowing that there's somebody else in the boat with me, I'm not paddling the canoe by myself anymore."*

BOOK ONE

YOUTH

"I had to work in the closet"

Wendy Hamilton

There's this joke that, from the day I was born, I was the boss. I came out with an agenda and budget, and I am not messing around here people, we've got stuff to do.

Wendy has great posture. She's been at attention for a long time because responsibility was demanded from her early in life. She's from a Midwest, middle-class family. Her dad was laid off in 2010: "…he was never really able to get back into his level, because he was now a 50-something overweight white man who didn't have maybe the most up-to-date training as the young kids."

After high school she did everything she was supposed to— went to college, got her Master's in Arts Management. I forgot to ask if she drinks coffee but if she doesn't I don't suggest she starts. Energy, she does not lack—nor brains. She is immediately likeable and I think it's because she's comfortable within her own skin, with the professional adult she's become. She's two months from her 33rd birthday and seems like someone who should be at the beginning of everything.

A fresh-out-of-grad-school 24 ½ year old, I got interviews all over the country. And I felt I was a really big deal and I actually had to turn down offers. I had an offer in Michigan, I had an offer in New York, I had two offers in DC.

I moved back here to Omaha in 2007. Thinking that, you know, my parents being in Omaha, aging a little bit, the Midwest is going to be lower cost of living, I'm going to be a big fish in a small pond, it won't be a problem to find a job.

I accepted a position with a museum of a very well respected pillar of artistic strength in the Midwest, and I was in fundraising, and I loved it. Things are going the way that I want: I'm here with my family, paying off the debt, I'm in my hometown—everything is going the way it's supposed to be going.

Then about 2 ½ years later, the dreaded executive consultant was brought in to review the management of the museum. And it started from the top down, and just about every week to ten days, more and more cuts were being made, and this was, whaddya know, September of 2008.

When the economy tanked, everybody panicked. We budget based on the quarter, and based on the giving history of the sponsor, or of the donor. In the fourth quarter, when so many of those donors lost funding, they weren't able to fulfill their pledges to us. We went from a staff of 79 to 40.

Over the course of four months, it was like walking on eggshells every day, and you never knew who it was gonna be. Job security didn't exist any more. It lasted so long—it was so belabored. It was just that feeling, you know, a constant…in the pit of your stomach…it's just like "I don't know what to do, I don't know if I should be looking for another job because I really like this job, but any minute this job could go away."

To be perfectly honest, I had kind of checked out, and I know that I was not performing the best that I could during those months, because you felt like it didn't matter. People who had been there for 25 years were being slashed. And they weren't getting notice. I had been there two and a half years.

And January 8, 2010, was the day of reckoning.

One of my colleagues called me the night before and told me that she was being let go. I was shocked. We thought—I thought—it was just going to be her that week. But when I got to work the next morning, I saw it in my boss's eyes. She kind of looked at me, she stood in the doorway and goes (using a sad, mopey voice:) "Hey…"

And I was like, (heavy sigh): "Is it my turn?"

"Uhm, I, I, er, can we, can we just talk?"

And I was like "We don't have to do that. (Sarcastic whisper:) It's OK, you can just say it."

And she was—this is my boss—she was crying and she was shaking. I guess I didn't think of it from her perspective, that she had to cut half her staff that day. And she was the one that had to stay. At that point I felt like I was comforting her, because she was having such a hard time with it.

It was a relief at that point. I mean, yes, I lost my job, I was 32, this was never supposed to happen to me. But, at the same time, I could not continue to live that way, every day. That day I wasn't emotional. I wasn't sad. My colleagues were sad, and my assistant, she was like, "What am I going to do now?" But that was a very strong day, I would say. I wasn't scared. I would say I was happy. Isn't that so weird? I felt an incredible burden had been lifted.

I was given severance, I was given the opportunity to keep my health insurance through COBRA[1]. And at the time Obama had passed a COBRA stimulus.[2] So, actually, when I was paying for my health insurance through COBRA, it was cheaper than when I was paying the group rate through the museum.

That was January 2010, and, again, based on my history, I thought, "Fine, I'm a fundraiser, I have a masters degree, I'm a big fish in a small

---

[1] Consolidated Omnibus Budget Reconciliation Act

[2] "COBRA continuation coverage assistance" under The American Recovery and Reinvestment Act (ARRA): an expired government program that is referenced with gratitude in more than one conversation.

pond…" I was laying in bed thinking, why do I feel so completely ok with this? And then I thought, I might not feel ok with this soon. I might start to freak out, I might start to panic.

I got a couple interviews, and they didn't go anywhere. And then I got a couple of more interviews and I was making it the third round, the fourth round, I was submitting writing samples, my references were being called, and then I was being told that I was not the successful candidate. And that went on for eight months. Which is not even that long in the grand scope of how long some people have been out of work. But again, that wasn't supposed to happen to me. I did everything I was supposed to do, and I'm type A, and I'm a pleaser, and I know Excel spreadsheets, and I'm funny—I was all of these things.

I must have done something wrong…it's my fault.

I believe it doesn't matter how confident you are, how old you are, what class you're in, when you get laid off, that's going to get into your mind, at some point. Even if it's only for five seconds, there will be a moment of…it's my fault.

I had made it through to the fourth round of interviews, with a non-profit human services organization, and I just knew I had that job. And then I got an email that said "We really appreciate your skills, and everything that you bring to the table, but we'd like to go with someone who has more experience." I was rejected in an email after four interviews. They knew what my experience was. What was the point of all of that?

I started panicking. And then I thought, everything that I thought was marketable about me, or what is an asset about me, is false, because this is a different world.

In the Fall of 2010, I was financially freaking out. All these months of not being fully employed, so trying to keep up with everything and living with my parents, who are amazing. Love my parents. But there's, again, I don't care how confident you are. There is a piece of you that is like, "I'm living with my parents," you know? And I love my parents—but I live with my parents!

Finally I got a call from S—.

You know when you feel like something's about to happen and all of a sudden, like, the sky is bluer and music on the radio is better and you don't care that you ate junk food last night? Everything is just better. That's how I felt when S— called me. It was like, okay: this is why I went through everything. This is my dream job. Right away, they sent me to a national conference in Las Vegas, and I met hundreds of people from S— all over the world, and it was like, I described it as orientation week in college, when you're like, "Oh my god, I just met so many people, and they're so cool, and we're gonna be best friends, and I'm gonna change the world." That's how it felt. And I was like, "God, finally. This is why I had to lose my job and feel like a loser face."

I didn't even want to decorate my office. Because I was so scared. Even though in my heart, I was like, 'I'm going to be with S— forever.' I waited probably four months, and I finally started putting things on the walls.

Little did I know I'd be taking them down a couple months later.

I was in the middle of writing a $125,000 grant, and got a schedule request from the CEO, and it was a four o'clock meeting, and I was like, "Hmm. That's weird." And I accepted the request, and I said, "Hey, what are we talking about? Are we going to go over the grant?"

And she wrote back and said, "Yep. And some other stuff."

Okay.

This was at about noon. I was like, "What other stuff could there be?" You know, at four o'clock, what are we talking about? So I went through the rest of my afternoon, and I'm just trying to get through the day. Four o'clock rolls around, and I just thought I was going to go into her office and we were going to go over the grant and look at the narrative, because it was due the next day. Massive grant.

Well, she went into the conference room, and I was like, that's also weird. Why aren't we just meeting in her office? So I go in the conference room, and then HR walks in.

My heart's racing. My stomach is flipping. My mouth goes dry.

This is still very fresh, because it was exactly one month ago today.

My CEO said, "How's it going with the grant?"

And just like it was a year and a half ago, I said, "You don't have to do that." I was like, "What's going on?"

And she's like, "Well…" And she kind of danced around it. She danced around it a lot. And this whole time I'm thinking maybe I'm going to be put on probation, because the budget, you know, we're not quite at budget yet, or maybe I'm gonna have to do a review. But then the words "We're restructuring the department. We're going to have to let you go" came.

The difference this time was no severance, no notice, and it was you're gone today.

I was so calm. I was freakishly calm. And I just said, "Why? Why me?"

And again, she danced around it. "Well, there's only so many positions…"

All of a sudden without warning I go from having a perfectly normal day to being let go. That happens in big corporations. That doesn't happy in tiny little nonprofits who make pennies for human services.

I have all of these things in my head like what did I do wrong, how did I fail? In my mind, I'm like, panicking. Like, "No. You're wrong. You're wrong. You've got the wrong person," or "this isn't the position you want to cut, because I'm doing this, this and this." I had never even been given a 90-day review, a six month review. I had only been there seven months. In my dream job. And then I was being told that it was going away. This is going to sound so cliché—but I don't think they cared that they just completely changed my life at all.

It was humiliating.

I had to have somebody there watch me pack up my office and watch me go through files. She and I became very, very close colleagues, and she was crying. And she just kept saying, "I'm so sorry." And she even said, "I don't agree with this decision. I wish it didn't have to happen." And she said all these wonderful things about how, you know, my passion and my energy and my positivity and all that, but you know, in that moment, you don't hear anything at all. At that point, I cried. I cried a lot. Like full-body weeping, like, "Oh my god. What am I going to do?"

That's what I did that night was I cried. I had Taco Bell. Because who doesn't want Taco Bell when they're sad? But I don't think I ate it all. I think

I thought, "This burrito will solve all of my problems," and sure enough, that burrito did not solve my problems.

And I thought, "God, I have to start telling people, and what am I going to say?" And they're going to say, "Again? Again you lost your job?" I was ashamed, and I was sad, and I was humiliated. I remember I was crying and crying and crying and crying to my parents, and then I just kept saying, "I am so embarrassed. I am so embarrassed."

My sister came over with pie, and cried it out a little bit, and she was very sweet. She made all of these to-do lists for me for the immediate five days. And one of them was "you have to remember to shower." And one of them was "please don't forget to eat." And then one of them was, one of my to-dos was "think about going to yoga, and maybe even go." You know, stuff like that. My to-do for Monday, the following Monday, the only thing it said was, "Fight the blues."

I did not make it facebook official for a few days. I did shower. And I did think about going to yoga, but I had ice cream instead. And I got in a fury of cleaning one day. I was like, "I will clean this house until it doesn't ever need to be cleaned again." You know it's a good cleaning day when your back gets sore the next day.

And then I stayed in bed the following week. I got really, really sad, and those were the days that I didn't eat. And those were the days that I didn't get up. And those were the days that I was humiliated and really just felt like a loser. This is not supposed to happen to me.

It was so draining. I didn't have anything left. I had no energy. I had no motivation. I was like, how am I going to do this again? I'm going to write cover letters again. I gotta go online again. I gotta file for unemployment again and go through the waiting period and the adjudicator and the phone calls and the questions and—oh my god, what am I going to do?

I was like, I think I have to grieve. I think I have to go through all of the stages of this, because I feel like I did something wrong. I feel like I've been a bad girl. And ultimately, it's that little girl, it's that little child in you that's like, "What did I do wrong? I'm so sorry."

I'm still getting over it. It was like a horrible, horrible, horrible break-up. I was telling my parents, "You know, it's like a new relationship.

Against my better judgment, I have fallen fast, and I have fallen hard. And I am in love with S—." Then when this happened, it felt like I had been living a lie or something.

So twice in 18 months, two very different experiences, and yet I'm right back here feeling like I got it wrong. There's something that I'm not doing right 'cause I keep losing jobs.

This time I don't feel creative, and this time I don't feel refreshed, and this time I don't feel revitalized. I feel like a loser. And the same thing, I'm applying for jobs, and I'm not getting calls even though everybody loves me, and everybody knows me, and everybody knows I have this great work ethic and I'm a good writer, and da da da da da. I'm not getting calls.

I'm still going through it now, you know, when I go out. I'm very involved in my community. I volunteer at everything you can think of, and I go to art openings, and I go to shows, and everything, and so when I see people... "Hey! How's S—?"

I have to go, "Well..."

Then I have to go through it all over again. And it's that again that is now hanging over me. Because these people that knew what I had gone through before, they just... "Not again." And then it's that same thing. I have to comfort them through it. Which is fine, because it helps me get over it too, but, you know, then I have to go through the editing. What am I going to say? What am I going to not say? How am I going to make it sound like I'm okay so they don't worry about me? When inside I'm just so sad.

My mom has a very difficult time coping with big life stuff. She's very black and white existence, and grey is like—I mean it just rocks her world. My mom has Asperger's Syndrome. Basically, if you think about a very awkward 12-year old who kind of just never really gets social situations and empathy, that's my mom. Another way that I explain it is that it's kind of like being bilingual. So you've got this other thing in your household that maybe everybody in that household understands and can speak and relate to, but in the outside world, it's kind of like, how do you bring someone from the outside in?

In addition to that, she has several other disorders. She has very profound obsessive-compulsive disorder. She has anxiety and paranoia.

She has really serious learning disorders. But she's amazing. She's funny. She's really, really smart, and she would never admit that.

The museum layoff, I had some time to prepare her and say, "You know, mom. Things might be changing." But with S—, I was so devastated that I knew that I had to get stronger in order to help her through it, and so I waited a week to tell her. And she completely spazzed, just like I thought she would. And her reaction was, "Well, great. Now I have to worry about you. Anyway, I went to the store and the ice cream was on sale, and then I went and got some peanut butter…"

Okay…Which is fine.

A lot of people have asked me if I would consider relocating. And that's a really difficult question, because I'm responsible for the care of my mom. I need a job. So it's not that I'm not looking outside of non-profit, but I don't know what else I can do. It's very confusing, because I don't know how desperate I should be right now. I don't know if I should just take the first job that comes up regardless of the salary and the title and all of that because it's a job and it maybe has health insurance, or I don't know if I should wait.

I did everything you are supposed to do, I had my job, I had my health insurance, I was a big time grownup at 25, I had tons of credit cards and I thought I'd be ok, and I just figured that's what everybody does, that's how you survive.

Love my parents, though I do, I did not have any money going into college. I never had a savings account, and I always worked for arts organizations or non-profits.

Sometime around 27 it occurred to me that those credit cards have to be paid back…ha ha…(nervous laughter)…based on the fact that I had been using credit cards since I was 18…No judging, right?…

She takes a moment, not really a deep breath or anything just sort of settling into herself.

…in the past five years, I've paid off $36,000 in credit card debt.

After releasing the number she belts the highest note she can hit,
vibrato and all, like an opera star. I give her a moment then ask if
she's completely finished paying off her debts.

Is anyone ever done dealing with their debt? I am so close. I am so close I can taste it. I had this five-year plan of how I was going to whittle down the credit card debt, pay off my car. Rather than going into bankruptcy and being mortified at 27, I did one of those credit consolidation programs. I got down to the last $1,000 that I owed. There's like two cards left, and I think I had ten credit cards enrolled.

I started in 2005, so it's taken about six years to pay that off, but that was instead of bankruptcy, and I just have to believe that I made the right decision not doing bankruptcy as a young, unmarried...talk about shame.

I really could've had that paid off probably by this month, but then my income drastically changed, and so I've been doing that.

My car is like this close, and there's all these things that are so close, and I just keep getting pushed back. Because I spent so many months in 2010 as a self-employed consultant, I owe taxes. Not too much. But I owe. Okay, so I'm on a payment plan for that. That's about $1,000. Credit card's about $1,000. Car's about $1,000. Then I had a horrible shoulder injury. Guess how much I owe on that? About $1,300. I've got all these little things, and it's like, how does anybody do it?—with children! Here I am, just me, and I'm trying so hard to pay for life, and then I lose my job on top of it, and it's really difficult.

Yeah, probably I shopped too much here and there, but really, what I was charging was bills. Gas, groceries, anytime I needed to come back to Omaha for something, whether it was a happy time or a sad time, I had to charge it. My paychecks were going to rent. I should've gotten a roommate sooner. I lived above my means for too long, and so my entire paycheck was going to rent. And it took me a really long time to have that financial epiphany of like, "This isn't good anymore."

So that's where I'm at. And then there's student loans on top of that, but those don't count.

She smiles a worried smile and holds it for a moment.

When you're 18 and it's your first day of college and you're at orientation and you sit there and they tell you how to sign your papers for financial aid, they don't really explain interest, and they don't really explain credit cards, and they don't really explain living above your means. And I take responsibility for maybe not researching that as well as I should have. I didn't have a super great role model for that kind of thing, and I was single, so I didn't have anybody like, "You're spending too much on gas." It was all just me. I only had to answer to myself. So that's part of it is just trying to forgive myself for letting it get that far. I'm taking responsibility for it.

I actually had terrible sleep last night, and I had nightmares all night that they hired me back, only I couldn't work in my office. I had to work in the closet. And like, I wasn't allowed to tell anyone that they hired me back.

You know, it's still really fresh right now. I still have to figure out what this means, what I'm supposed to do, how I'm going to pay my bills, how I'm going to be a responsible person and get a job. I'm obviously still reeling…and really bitter. Not bitter. Trying not to be bitter.

I'm sorry if I'm a little bit Polyanna, but weren't we taught that good behavior gets rewarded? Weren't we taught that "be all you can be" and "live the American dream" and go and get a job and be good at it?

"I just try not to do anything crazy"

Justin Fiedler

Outside his home there is a crate filled with a heap of empty beer bottles. It's a daily routine observed by Justin and many of his Reno contemporaries: leaving the glass for the early morning recyclers who collect them—also drinking all the beers.

Justin is 25. His skin is ghostly pale and his bushy, dark beard makes him look like someone from 1849, thinking about heading west next month. In fact, he has already made the journey. Born and raised in Mobile, Alabama, Justin moved to Reno in 2007. He left Alabama because there was "nothing really keeping me there... I didn't have many friends and I just wanted to get out on my own."

His father, still in Alabama, recently lost a twenty-five year job at a ceiling tile plant. His mom lost her job with a regional office supply store when it was sold to a national corporation.

Justin says he followed a friend who wanted to come west: he seems to enjoy many things and initiate few. He is slow-moving this early in the morning—and I can't say I blame him: it is bright and

*hot and all parties involved in this conversation, Mallery and MJ
included, are, safe to say, creatures of the night. The world is a bit
sluggish and subdued.*

*Justin sits under the protection of shade on the steps outside his
one-bedroom portion of a small duplex. There aren't many things
inside. A foosball table and drum set occupy most of the place,
separated by an empty space left for jam session participants and
amplifiers. Above the kitchen entry there's a cartoon drawing of a
pin-up girl on a torn piece of paper that could almost be mistaken
for a patch of shoulder stolen from a sailor. On one wall there
is a collage of photos, ticket stubs and handwritten notes—all
assembled by Jason's mom after a visit: "I had a really good time
with you...Love you. Miss You. Come home soon. Mom"*

*Back in Alabama Justin attended college but says he couldn't
afford to continue after moving to Reno. "I wanna finish school
eventually. I don't really know when that's gonna be; I don't know
how I'll know when that's gonna be, but I feel like that's something
internal."*

*While he was still in school he worked part-time in retail for a
nationwide electronics store. He stayed with company in Nevada,
working full time and excelling with multiple promotions.*

*He enjoys building his own computers but he's hesitant to
pursue a career in that direction. He's unfamiliar with—and so a
little fearful of—identifying something he enjoys as work "because
I don't know if it would still be fun for me to do."*

About a year and eight months I was a manager. I made $38,000. They
offer quarterly bonuses and I'd made a bonus every three months for
performance. Two weeks before I was let go they gave me a raise, a $2500
a year raise for performance. For the new year, you were given a bonus
based on how you did against your store's previous year and certain things
like that, and I was still beating my store's previous year but they had
jacked the numbers so much between the two years that it was almost
impossible to compensate. It went from about $36,000–$35,000 a month

to $51,000–$52,000 a month. The previous year they were at $40,000 a month—the actual sales.

Usually you could expect a 10% growth from year to year, that's normal for most sales, but the sales in those few months or so when the economy was doing really bad were not going up. Some places were going down in sales. It was really tough to turn a gain on the year before at that point.

They extended our store hours I guess in an attempt to make more money; they kept us open for an hour a day every day longer, and they cut our payroll hours by about 15 hours a week. The person who came in to close would have to come in an hour or even two hours later, so it would be a person by themselves from open until two o'clock in the afternoon or so and you'd miss a lot of customers between there. I did it most days a week and would do as best I could, but with one person and four, five customers you really can't make sales. You can check people out, it's hard to make sale and spend any real time with a customer.

My boss told me, "If you don't get your numbers up, we're going to have to let you go." And he would say that for probably a year…leading up to the actual event he would say it more and more, asking me if I'd been looking for other jobs and stuff. He wasn't malicious, I know he was under a lot of pressure to make it look like he was trying to do something to make the district do better. I was doing everything I could, there was no way really to…I dunno, I think I was doomed to failure.

I got let go about a year and a month ago.

I wasn't due in until the afternoon. My boss called me that morning and said he needed me to come in early. It happened in the back room. He said that I needed to turn over my keys and everything that I had from work, and said that they weren't going to need me anymore. He said there was nothing he could do about that.

I gathered my things and then said bye to all of my employees who were there. They knew what had happened too; I had pressured them saying you know, we have to help our sales or you know…I didn't necessarily want to fire any of them because there was nothing really that they were doing wrong that I could see, but I told them that my job was on the line because my boss's job was on the line. And he actually got laid off the week after I did. (Laughs.)

I think only one or two of the fifteen stores in the district were hitting their goals, and so that pretty much gave them a right to fire thirteen out of the fifteen of the managers if they wanted to. It seems like they were firing all the old managers and replacing them with new managers... inexperienced, outside hire managers that they were paying a lot less. And I know this because I trained one of them. She was my assistant manager and she was offered a position at another store and we talked about what she could expect to make and things like that. And she got shafted— almost half of what I was making. They told her she could either take the position or she was going to be let go. And so she took that position.

It was just kind of a turning point in my life, because I've had a job since I was about 16 or 17 I think was my first job, and I worked since then, and that was when I was 24, so—seven solid years and I moved here on my own, I've got no family or anything, I'm no longer friends with the person I moved out here to live with...So I really have no fallback now. I didn't know if I was going to be able to get unemployment or anything like that, so it was really kind of scary, that day.

I went home and I made some phone calls and stuff about unemployment and how to file for it and everything. I do it online. It takes like thirty seconds. I put in my social security number and my pin, I was available to work, I didn't work—then hit submit. That's pretty much it. They've never even asked me to go down there and talk to anyone or anything.

I started looking for jobs but nothing really offered me what I was making on unemployment—not even close. I've been looking for jobs that pay well, but eventually, I'm just going to have to take a job that pays less. I mean I always keep my ear to the ground, if something worthwhile was to come up to my friends, or someone told me about. I look on Craigslist maybe once every two weeks just to look through like job openings and stuff, but for the most part, not a whole lot until it's time to get an extension.

Unemployment is four percent of your highest quarter per week. So if you made like, $30,000 a year, and you made just $7,500 every quarter, then it'd be four percent of $7,500, which would be $300 a week. So that's that. Even four percent of my highest quarter is more than I would make working at ten dollars an hour for forty hours a week. And that sounds like a pretty decent job, ten dollars an hour and forty hours a week, but that wouldn't be any different than what I'm doing now. Unless I can find something significantly better than that, then I'm not gonna take shit. The only thing that worries me still is no health insurance. So that's a little bit scary but I just try not to do anything crazy.

"They call me their butterfly"

Tina Hall

She grew up as a military kid. By the age of five her dad put her in the boxing ring and out on the shooting range. A paternal grandmother was a full-blooded Cherokee Indian. She passed when Tina was 15. "Beautiful lady. I loved her."

Tina lives in Maryville, Tennessee, and knows exactly how beautiful this part of the country is: "You go on up to 441 and out towards the lake...oh my gosh, just gorgeous. Beautiful mountains. Little waterfalls. There's even creeks where you can take your jugs and get fresh water."

At 33, her dark hair is died a dark red; she has a nose ring and, as she puts it, "psychedelic colors on my nails." She was a straight A student who "completely followed all the parents' rules. I was one of those kids that whippings didn't work, grounding didn't work. It was the disappointment. I couldn't stand disappointing anybody."

She did have one lapse. Late one night, at the age of 18, Tina and a friend decided on the spur of the moment to move to Florida.

"We packed up my little bitty Hyundai with my little $300 check, and we drove down to Jacksonville." But after six months Tina was homesick so she returned to Tennessee. "That was my big adventure."

In 2009, she escaped an abusive relationship with the help of a good friend: "She walked in on him choking me to the point I was turning blue. He had busted my head through the front door... it was a two-month planning to get me out." She has resiliency that traverses the personal and professional. Her experience with unemployment begins with a career in the mortgage business in Knoxville, 15 miles north of Maryville.

I was a senior supervisor at C— Mortgage for seven years, made $100,000 a year.

It started out as father and son, very family-oriented company. We were used to $2500, $3000 dollar bonuses. Once B— bought out our company, it went all to hell. It really did. They took my seven teams and slammed me with somebody else, and came to me on Christmas Eve: "You have to fire this person or it's going to be you."

I mean, honestly. On Christmas Eve I had to fire a lady, or it was going to be me. And I just don't agree with that. I had to finally stand up for myself and be like, "I don't believe in this and I can't honestly in good conscience do that."

A few months later, we were all in a meeting discussing the bonuses that they were taking away from us and the extra work we were going to have to do. I was already working to one, two o'clock in the morning. There were 12 of us supervisors that walked out that day.

I went through a really bad divorce and kind of lost everything. And mentally just broke down. After ten years of us being married...all of a sudden a lady showed up at my door with a six-month old baby.

$495 later, it wasn't his baby. But it was already done.

So he needed to sow his wild oats and move back home to mommy. I put him through college and everything, got him a corporate job and...

he needed to move on. My ex did a lot to me, and he wiped out my bank account, pretty much. And it's been a struggle since trying to find anything else.

My real mother is dying, and through the years of her medication and stuff...doesn't want anybody around. When she wants to see me is when she wants me to pay her mortgage—and that's very hard for me. You know, I'm barely getting gas. There's days I don't eat. And that's very hard. And I'm not used to that either. I'm used to being able to stop somewhere and get me something to eat—and provide for people. So her and I haven't even spoken in a couple years.

My real father went through a midlife crisis after my parents divorced and my grandmother died, and basically got with this lady that's 23 years younger, and she was very jealous of me because I was his only real child. She made him choose, and he chose.

I haven't spoken to him in four years.

My brother was the troublemaker. That's why I had custody of his daughter for eight years. He went to prison, and I don't agree with his lifestyle and just couldn't involve myself in that. I helped him as much as I could. I had my niece for eight years, and I raised her. She's almost 11. She's with my mom. It's two streets over from her school. It was just something for my mom to live for. She's dying and going through all that, she had no will to live. So I let her live with my mom for the last two years. I'll go and visit her. I'll usually go to the school and visit her, or I'll pick her up and take her away because, like I said, my mother and I...

I have no family. I've actually spent the last three Thanksgivings, Christmases and birthdays on my own. I haven't even had a birthday card. (Laughs.) I was like, "Somebody, please at least just draw a little birthday card for me." It's not about having gifts. It's just that family thing, and I don't have that.

I've worked since I was 14 years old. I got a hardship license. My grandmother was sick. My little $300 Chevette was my first car, and I drove to work and I've worked ever since. And like I said, I put myself through two college degrees and paid it all by myself.

After Tina left the mortgage business and got divorced in 2007 she decided it was time for a drastic career change: "I was just over the whole corporate America thing, and I wanted to help people."

I was with a company called O—, and I had worked with adults there. They were just precious. I loved them to death. They were a bit violent because they were schizophrenic. Severe MR[1] patients. A lot of health problems. We had water restrictions, fluid restrictions, food restrictions. You had to be very strict with them. One of them I caught with my lunchbox, sitting. I mean, this is like a 6'2" man, sitting in the middle of the kitchen, eating my lunch and drinking both of my sodas—had both of them!—and he was just ecstatic. But I had to take them from him because he would go into diabetic shock. So he became distressed and came after me with a frying pan.

I have a companionship license. And I also was certified in prescription administration for disabled persons. First aid, CPR, I did all of that.

The individuals I was with, they don't have the ability to set controls. I had one that was a food hoarder, and it was almost to the point of being very dangerous, because he would go into diabetic shocks. It was so eyes-on, I would go check the mail, and I would see him running through the house with hot dogs, bologna, anything he could get. And he would hide them, and we would have to do daily room checks, and whole entire packs of hot dogs were eaten through the night. You know, whole entire packs of bologna and stuff. And you know, there's no telling how long he had hid what where. Then you got the food poisoning aspect of it. We eventually had to end up locking the refrigerator because he was just such a hoarder. He was a precious guy, but he was obsessed. These individuals could never have touched their own medications.

We had several houses, and then we put two to three of them in each house. This particular house had a man that was blind, deaf and mute, and he was severe MR. In one of our other houses, there was a man that was in a wheelchair. They were just incredible. One of the men that I

---

[1]   Professionally designated as "Mentally Retarded"

worked with, nobody had actually ever sat down and taught him to write his alphabet or his name. And in the period of time I was there, he was writing his name. They would let him sign his disability checks with an X. And I'm like, "No." That's not okay. You know, he has rights. You need to let him be able to sign his own name. So I taught him how to do that.

The company felt that we were in danger, because nobody could handle them. I was already working 16 hours a day, and that's legally all you can work. They just had nobody else that could handle them—or would. They just came to us one day and it was like, "We're shutting down the house."

I was like, "It just takes patience, and you have to have the right attitude about it."

And she was like, "I don't have any more of you…"

I think it was a week or two later, and we were without a job.

You're already heart-attached to these people. I mean, they're beautiful, wonderful people that don't have anybody. I cried for so long, because I fell in love with them. They were great.

Were you given the responsibility of explaining the situation to them?

Nope. We couldn't talk to them about it. So it was kind of…we were there and they were used to us, and then we were gone.

Once that house shut down, I went through a really bad year and just slowly kind of lost everything. My divorce. I was trying to get rid of the house, because he left me with everything. We physically had six cars. And that was just because that was his obsession. And slowly I tried to get rid of everything, and I finally got down to a one-bedroom apartment, and when my dad walked out on me and couldn't help me anymore, I lost everything. Ended up sleeping in the rain one night. I found myself sitting in my truck, broke down on the side of the road, and I had nowhere to go. I called an ex-coworker of mine and she had actually come and got me, and that's when I moved out here a little over three years ago. Just kind of built and picked myself back up.

I ran into a lady. She was a preschool director over at Maryville city schools, and the superintendent of special education. She kind of took me in, in a sense. She fell in love with me as soon as she met me, and she was just like, "You are smiling no matter what you go through. You're just like a ray of sunshine." Matter of fact, they call me their butterfly. And she was like, I just can't believe everything that you've been through. And she just kind of took me in from there.

I started working for Maryville city schools. I got into the TA* work. Loved it, loved it, loved it. And then they asked me...Really, they were kind of fighting over me at the different schools because I had a lot of progress with my kids, and I love it so much. It's just absolutely heartwarming to me.

We knew that the school was going to be shutting down...but we had no idea in the middle of the school year. It was "We don't need you today." I mean, I literally had my lunch in my little bag, and my purse, and walked into work and had to give my badge, my key and walk right back out.

"...You're off until next year. You've got a job next year."

You know—supposedly. I don't know how much I believe in that. And it's a part-time job versus my full-time that had benefits.

The way that they did it is that they terminated the positions for the rest of the year, so they didn't even have to pay our insurance benefits. We've lost our benefits.

The COBRA was $673 a month. And I'm like, how do you expect me to pay $673 a month for insurance, and I'm not employed—and you're fighting my unemployment?

My kids were devastated. One of them's still kind of going through adjustments and has been restrained several times. I never had to restrain him. Never once. I had one lady come up to me at Wal-Mart after the school, bawling her eyes out, and she said, "Daniel has not been the same." She said, "He cried for two weeks and refused to go to school. He wants his Miss Hall." And she asked me for my number and she said, "I would like for you to come visit."

---

*   Teacher's Aide

I taught swimming lessons to four of my seven kids, and then I kept two of them after school. I was just the kind of different, cool kind of teacher, you know? I've got the red hair. I've got the nose ring. You know, I always have these psychedelic colors on my nails.

I have my breakdown moments…I have my days I just want to sleep and bawl my eyes out and nobody talks to me. But for the most part, through everything that I've been through…I was kidnapped as a teenager and kept for six hours in a truck. And ever since that happened, it's just been a thought of: I'm so happy to even be alive. And I have such a need in my heart that I want to help people. So I figure if I smile…it's eventually going to work out. It's eventually going to be better. And when I made it through that day, I just…No matter what I've been through, I can handle a lot. I can get through it, and being a grouch or mean to people doesn't make it any easier, you know? I've noticed smiling and greeting people that you don't know, your day just seems to go better. It just kind of makes you a little bit happier. The word "thank-you" is just so powerful.

I've kind of been cleaning houses. I also run a camp, a two-week camp during the summer—Camp Chickababa[1]—for disabled persons. But it's only two weeks in the summer. My swimming lessons are up now until the summer. So I'm just, like, stuck.

The only thing that I have left right now is I also had an afterschool program with a couple of my kids, and I have one that I keep from 3:00p.m. to 5:15p.m. The kid's mom died a year ago. I mean, it's less than $6 an hour I keep him for. Dad's a single parent trying everything he can. He had promised months ago that he was supposed to be getting state funding. Well, state funding says that, even with autism, children are not considered MR, so therefore they don't get the funding. But they're just as disabled as an MR patient because he's non-functioning as far as doing everything on his own. He doesn't comprehend. So he's having a really hard time getting state funding, being able to get to where he can pay

---

[1] "It was called 'Camp Chickababa 'cause a little kid that they started it for many, many years ago loved chicken pot pies. And he couldn't say 'chicken pot pie.' It was 'chicken baba.'"

me at least minimum wage, you know? So that's basically all that I have right now. I'm looking at $65 a week…

Today my friend and I were talking, and she said, "Go to Target. Go to Wal-Mart. Go to every fast food restaurant," you know. But when I go there, they'll all say three or four times, you're overqualified and we can't afford you. And I'm like, you don't understand. I'll clean poop off toilets right now. You know? Whatever it takes. I don't care how much. I'm overqualified, so they won't hire me. So I'm just like, you know what? I don't care what it is. I just need some form of income.

As a single, young female, there's nothing to help us. I have no children. And I'm like, "Okay, well, I was smart enough to not have children in a bad situation…" You know? I've put in a lot of work and paid a lot of taxes for everybody else. Help me.

I have to provide for myself, and it's really hard. I have my little puppy, and we're sharing food. She saved my whole sanity. And she's such a mama's girl. She's everywhere I am. My dog will not have it without sitting beside me. And most of the time, she goes everywhere I go in my truck.

Lord knows, I have every reason in the world to have hatred in my heart, but I just…it's not worth it. I'm only 33, and I have many more years, and I figure eventually, I'm going to pay my dues and something's going to break. I'm actually a workaholic. When I'm working, that's when I'm focused. It's the most important thing. I can't even put that into words. It becomes a lifestyle for me once I'm working, if that makes sense. Because I want everything in my heart into it, because I want everybody to see, "Wow. Not only does she work, she's good at it."

"Yell about it and maybe try to fix it"

Jessica Smith

One set of grandparents came over from Germany in the 1880s or something, right in time for a recession. I guess it was better than being in Germany. And then the other set of grandparents have been here since before the American Revolution, so I'm half-immigrant and half-American. Not that everybody's not an immigrant. But immigration is a huge issue right now in Alabama.

Jessica is referring to yesterday's news: a Mercedes Benz executive from Germany was visiting a plant in Tuscaloosa. A cop pulled him over and because the 46-year-old executive didn't have sufficient paperwork to prove his status, he was arrested. "He was driving without his papers," Jessica says, shaking her head. "He's the head of one of our largest state employers."

Alabama's history with discrimination had been a long-time sticking point for foreign corporations looking to do business in the state. Mercedes Benz waited until the Confederate flag was removed from the state capitol building in 1993 before opening the plant. At the time, the director of the Alabama Development Office, Billy Joe Camp, said "I don't believe we ever would have gotten this plant if the Confederate flag was atop the Capitol."

Eighteen years after taking down the flag, Alabama has reincarnated discrimination with its 2011 immigration law that required the Tuscaloosa officer to arrest the Mercedes employee. And it's threatening the region's proven ability to build its economy through international partnerships: a copper products company from China, which had announced plans to build a 300-job plant in the black belt town of Thomasville, is suddenly reconsidering the move because of the 2011 immigration law.

Jessica, 32, was born and raised in Alabama. She speaks of her home state with much authority, frankness, and hope. After stints in other states (New York and Virginia) and another country (Sweden), she moved back to Alabama in 2010 with her fiancé, Nick, and this is where they've made a home. They have a newborn and Jessica wants to be near her family.

Her own mom was laid off in 2007. "She was really depressed. She had never been depressed. She came home crying. It was probably one of three times I've ever seen my mother cry."

Her dad sells municipal uniforms for police, sanitation workers, fireman. It's a small business with about a dozen employees. He's surviving but things have slowed: "He hasn't taken a paycheck in over a year now."

And he hasn't laid off anyone.

Jessica has two Master's degrees, the most recent is from the state university in Buffalo, New York. She operates in many spheres of art and literature. She has written for several years, mostly poetry, with some significant publications, but she's on hiatus these days: "I have a job and a kid, and it's just not going to happen."

Recently she was hired as a librarian at a nearby private boarding school. "Nick and I got jobs within a year of being here, even though we have no connections. And I think that if I was

not white, that would not have happened," Jessica says, circling
back to the issue of discrimination. She's sure to point out that
discrimination is by no means unique to Alabama: Buffalo, too,
was "highly segregated and still very racist."

It's in Buffalo where her story of unemployment—and
underemployment—begins. That's where she and Nick were both
working at a high profile classical music organization. She was
also an adjunct professor at the state university.

I received a letter that said I wouldn't be able to adjunct in the spring.
I got that letter, and then around Thanksgiving, I was laid off from the —
Orchestra for the fourth time since I'd been working there. They just kept
laying people off because they didn't have enough money to pay them.
Basically, they can't make payroll, so you get laid off for two weeks. It was
really stressful.

I got a call, and it was actually my fiancé, but we were not dating then.
And he was like, "So we're gonna have y'all not come in for the next couple
of weeks, and we're still trying to figure out how to restructure, and we're
just going to take a couple of weeks to figure this out."

I knew that Nick was just the messenger. When he was calling me to
lay me off, he was just the pawn of the system. I wasn't mad at him.

This was right around Christmas. I actually ran into the Executive
Director in the hallway and I was like, "You can't lay off people at Christmas.
You can do it any other time. You can do it in January. But it's just not right
to lay somebody off at Christmas."

I had nothing to lose, you know?

He was like, "Mm-hmm." He was so far removed from the process. He
didn't even know who I was, really.

Two weeks later, I found out that I was pregnant. So I was like, "This
isn't good." I didn't plan to be pregnant, so I was really freaked out. And I
didn't know whether I could afford to be pregnant.

And two weeks later I went back to work. They had cut everybody's
hours based on their sales. So this was really horrible, emotionally, because
if you're a salesperson, you need a lot of emotional support from your

organization to keep getting out there and getting rejected and still going out there and trying to sell stuff. I can't make better sales if I'm constantly under this pressure of you're going to get laid off or your hours reduced if you don't make sales.

I think basically we all kind of scurried around and tried to find sort of our Hail Mary leads. Happily, this was a month before our subscriptions renewal period, which is when you call all of your members who are probably going to give you money so basically I was just totally like, ballsy. I would call people, and I would be like, "Hey, this is the — Orchestra. We're calling for your yearly subscription renewal. It's going to be $1,158. What kind of credit card do you want to put it on? We take MasterCard, Discover, Visa." The lead sales guy was like, "You have to read that script," and I was like, "I'm not going to read the script. I'm just going to get the money."

Late February, early March…it was cold. It's Buffalo. It's cold and dreary, and there's snow on your car you have to wipe off every morning. And the last thing that you need is somebody laying you off.

The final one was a little different.

I was working with Nick and I was like, you know, I can't handle working here anymore. It's just gotten too insane. They were working with a really skeletal crew. It was like there were so many demands on this very skeletal crew that I just wanted to go home and drink afterwards. And I was like, "I don't want to be at a job where all I want to do is go home and drink. That's not healthy." So I was like, you know, "The next time there are layoffs, just lay me off." And he did. Because at that point he was my direct supervisor— not to be confused with having any actual control over me. (Laughs.)

He emailed me so that it was official, so that it was in writing.

And then we were like, "Okay, who's going to pay for groceries?"

This was around the time that I found out I was having this child, so I had a lot of clout. (She smiles, mischievous.) What it did for me is give me unemployment benefits during my pregnancy and after.

That's where I was when I started back to school for library science. I went back to get student loans so I would have this couple thousand dollars in the bank if anything went wrong. Every time anything came up, like a car repair of whatever, I was just shit out of luck. Like, anytime anything over $100 came up that month, then I would either have to ask my parents, put it on a credit card or ask for money from a friend. And it was just really eating at me, because I could never get ahead.

Then I was like, "I could just apply for unemployment, like everybody else." I just never thought of myself as somebody who was unemployed. Who would take unemployment? That's what other people do when they're unemployed. Like those guys down there working on the construction site...

She motions to a work crew in the parking lot outside the windows of the quiet library reading room where we sit.

...when they get laid off, they apply for unemployment. If you're a failed graduate student working as an adjunct, you don't apply for unemployment, because that's not, like, a real job. So you don't deserve, like, real unemployment. I had trouble thinking of myself as a worker when I was initially laid off, because I was sort of stringing these part-time jobs together in order to do my real work, which was the artistic work that I do, which is a totally different kind of work, because it's not on any sort of economical grid. I can't get unemployment for not being able to write a poem for a couple of months.

I'm an artist, my ideal is to work as little as possible so I have as much time as possible for my art, which is every artist's ideal. So I had been stringing together these little part-time jobs, actually putting myself in this situation where I was really stressed out all the time, because I didn't know if I was going to get laid off. It was actually more hours and more stress than having a real job.

A lot of people who go into academia, their parents are like, "When are you going to get a real job?" You know, and stop fucking around with this little project that you're working on. If you start going to school when you're 18, and you go straight through, you're still, like, 30 before you have a PhD and can be on the job market. And let's say you get a job your first year on the job market, which would be miraculous. Then you've still gotta defend those 12 years you spent out of the workforce.

My dad didn't go to college. My mom went to college but they're both people who go into office buildings and do work that is set out, like there's a specific thing that you do. It's not going to a coffee shop and working on a major writing project.

But the state of New York thought that I was gainfully employed, and thus gave me gainful unemployment, so, I mean, they weren't like, "You were just an adjunct? That's not a real job." They were like, "Here's your $270 a week." So I was really grateful that those things were in place, and that I had been paying into them. I felt guilty for taking unemployment, because I felt like there were people who really needed it more than I did, but that turned out not to be true, because it was like 15 months until I found a job.

I thought, unemployment: you have to really prove that you're unemployed and that you're looking for a job. So I went downtown to the unemployment office, and stood in line. I thought these were things that they required. It was basically a career center where they taught you to use a computer and how to put your resume online if you needed to. Of course, I already had a resume. It was already online, etcetera. The career center was really not aimed for people looking for jobs of the type that I was looking for. It's really for people who are looking for jobs where all the workers are basically expendable. Like, you plug one in, and you take one out, and then you plug the next one in. And I was looking for jobs where I as an individual would be able to make a contribution.

The reason that I finally got a job had nothing to do with my resume. I had left my normal signature on the bottom of my email, which has my website on it. My boss read my blog, which, under ordinary circumstances, I would never want my employer to read. Decided he liked me, and hired me. It was just a personal connection. I didn't know anyone there. He just decided that I, based on my personality, fit in with the people at my current job. And he was right. But that had nothing to do with how I formatted my resume.

Librarians are not stupid. They know that public library branches are closing, mainly due to funding, due to tax revenue, due to nobody has a job. I mean, with the rest of the economy, public libraries suffer. Which is really a bad thing, because public libraries are also one of the few places that can provide career advice for people who are unemployed. So it becomes a vicious circle where you can't get advice about being employed, so you can't get employed, so you can't pay tax revenue, so the libraries go out of the business. And you can't get information about any career that you might be interested in. But we understand that. We, the librarians, understand that and that public libraries are endangered, and so the library profession has evolved into what's sometimes termed a knowledge management profession, so there are a lot more librarians in the private sector working to organize the information and the knowledge that is in companies. So you would go into a company and sort of interview all of the people that have been there all their lives, figure out what they know that has never been written down for the company and organize it into usable information for people coming in.

I mean, basically I just lucked into getting a job. And so did Nick. I mean, we were both very lucky. But the other thing that unemployment reveals is how people who are employed basically are very just lucky, you know? Unemployed people get a lot of flack, but you can apply for literally hundreds of jobs, and it has nothing to do with you, whether you get it or not, and it's very hard to learn that lesson. You just have to keep pulling the lever and hoping the quarters come out.

I have health insurance, and my baby has health insurance through my job. But Nick and I aren't married, so he doesn't have health insurance—even though he's the father of my child. I don't know...the politics of who gets health insurance and what a family is and how people are related is just a mess.

It must be better to be unemployed in New York, because you get Medicaid when you're unemployed. There's no questions. It just goes along with your unemployment. And so I had health coverage when I was pregnant, and I had the baby, and I had a total of, like, a $20 co-pay for something along the way. It was all covered. I never had to worry about anything. When I moved down here, my New York Medicaid didn't work anymore, and you can't get Medicaid in Alabama unless your monthly income is below $175 dollars. If you're that poor, then you get benefits.

But what about all of the people that are not that poor? I can imagine that there would be part-time employed who would make a lot more than that and not be eligible for any of the benefits for the poor in Alabama. It's a story too of the underemployed.

I think the great tragedy of the current recession is how much untapped talent there is. How people like my fiancé, working 35 hours a week in basically a job that an intern could do is not meeting his potential in terms of his skill levels and his educational background, and I know that's true for a lot of my friends, and it makes me really sad, because I think my whole generation is just under-utilized. Like, there's all this great talent. I mean, really not everybody went to college, but pretty much everybody I know went to college, and most people went to grad school, and there's all this knowledge…all this unharnessed energy and desire to give back to the community, to help other people, to really exercise all of your individual talent, and it's just dumped.

I think we feel that something has to be done, which is why everybody's at Occupy Wall Street. I mean, something has to be done. We're not sure what. We know that the system is really not working, and that it's systemic. There's no one thing that's going to help. But there's hundreds of things that, if tweaked, might help. And since you got all of these great, talented people that are underemployed or unemployed, and they have time to go down to places like Occupy Wall Street and yell about it and maybe try to fix it.

It really makes me cry thinking about how much wasted talent is out there.

It's not like, you know, "The system is fucked up, and we're angry." I mean, they are angry, but they want to fix it. It's not like throw out the baby with the bathwater. It's like, how can we help this baby, you know?

"There has to be a floor"
Tobias Elmore

After the conversation with Jessica in the tranquil Mountain Brook section of Birmingham, Tasha and I drive downtown to walk along the designated path for the historic marches to Kelly Ingram Park and the Sixteenth Street Baptist Church where four girls were killed in a 1963 bombing.

It's my first time standing in this park, across the street from this church. A funeral service has just ended. The casket is brought down the steps, put into the hearse and driven away. The crowd files out of the building in conversation and embrace, swelling with energy. Tasha aptly points out: "Whoever died was certainly well-loved." There is a celebratory feel to the clusters of black suits and black dresses. We sit across the street and several people come over to meet Ella, who is spinning and dancing, trying to get someone's attention.

Eventually everyone is gone and we start back toward our car, walking along a second designated path—this one for marches to city hall.

It is a bright sunny weekend and downtown Birmingham is empty and quiet. When there is an occasional sound—a car engine or construction site—it echoes, filling a hollow.

Just a few blocks removed from Kelly Ingram Park, Tasha says, "Here it is." I turn back toward her voice and it's only then that I see Occupy Birmingham. I had already walked a few feet into the street past the quaint, well-organized encampment. It dominates one of four corners at the broad intersection shadowed by towering buildings tagged by banks.

Tobias Elmore is sitting in a canvas chair at the edge of the sloping sidewalk. He is a 34-year-old African American and a cane rests against his leg. He graduated from Troy University in 2001 and works in video production and graphic design. His protest poster features a pyramid of champagne glasses. The top three glasses are filled with bubbly; the rest remain empty. The emptied bottle is lying nearby, on its side beneath the words "Trickle-Down Economics."

I think I've gotten more people to pause at a green light and look at the picture. They have to try and stop and think about it for a second. That's my goal.

Tobias's attention turns toward a fellow occupier who has just arrived with lunch and a mic check:

WHOSE STREETS?
Our streets!

WHOSE TOWN?
Our town!

WHOSE ECONOMY?
Our economy!

WE ARE
The 99%!

Over the course of the afternoon there's a core group of half a dozen protesters, continually accompanied, more or less, by another half dozen or so dropping in for five minutes or an hour to support the effort. One guy pulls up in his car just long enough to drop off a box of bottled water. He gives a thumbs-up through his windshield.

It was a Baptist church, mostly African-American. I was basically an independent contractor for them. They had a TV show on local access channel type of thing, and they wanted to keep that going. So I produced their show.

I saw the writing on the wall. It felt like the economy was going to tank. And that wasn't much before the presidential election in '08, you know, where Obama started to come on the scene, and I think everybody was feeling the economy starting to crater a little bit. That was probably not long after the time where the banks collapsed. When people have less money, they contribute less money, and then the church didn't have the money to pay me anymore.

I used to take all payments in cash for a while. I didn't accept a check. Because I didn't know what was going to go down with the bank. I didn't know if they were going to fold, or what.

It was April '09—April, May, sometime in there. Before summer.

The church has the sanctuary and then there's…it almost looks like a school on the side. They've got this whole building attached. My office was in the back. One of the deacons came back there. I think we went to his office and talked.

"Well," you know, "We gotta let you go. Money's drying up, and we can't do it anymore. It's too big of an expense." They were up front about it, and there were no hard feelings.

I just shook my head, and I was like, "Okay." Because, like I said, I saw it coming, and I felt like maybe I would be okay. I had a lot of my own equipment at the time. And I still do. I was like, maybe I can drum up, you know, more business. But it just didn't work out that way.

Being disabled, I'm luckier than most people. I get Medicare and the VA benefit covers a lot of stuff that has to do with my disability, so more or less, I'm covered on all that stuff. My father served—I think he got drafted—he went to Vietnam. When he came back, he was not well. I met him once. I was born with a specific disability that qualified for a specific benefit under the VA, which is more or less their confession that something he was exposed to probably caused it.

Sometimes I feel guilty about the benefits. I feel like they should be an option for everybody, like it shouldn't be just me. So it's about priorities. Is it our priority to take care of our citizens, or is it our priority to make sure that health insurance companies keep making cash off keeping everybody healthy?

The whole If-you-just-work-hard, American dream, it'll-all-come-together stuff is a bunch of ra-ra nonsense. Maybe it will. Maybe it won't. I think if you work hard and you educate yourself, you've got a much better chance. But that ain't no guarantee. And that's why there has to be a floor. You can only fall so far. That includes you're not on the streets, eating out of a trash can somewhere. So that's what I believe. And they say that we don't have the money, but that's nonsense. I try to explain it to people: when they say the 1% owns 40% of the wealth that means of every single penny that exists on a ledger inside of the United States somewhere, 40% of that is in somebody's pocket. They own it. It's not available to be made. And therein lies the problem. And they tell you they don't have enough for you to get food stamps, to get unemployment, to get all of this. But it's a lie. They do have it. That's just not their priority.

My mom is a 20 plus year veteran of the Navy. She joined probably a couple years after I was born, I think to get me healthcare and to get herself educated. She got her Master's degree while she was in there. And even she has a hard time finding a job at this point. I think she's a little disappointed about lack of opportunities, especially with all the work you put in. Again, it's that "if I just work real hard and I educate myself, it'll all work out."

Maybe. We'll see what happens.

Martin Luther King was in, what, Memphis? He was there to support a march of sanitation workers. He was there on his poor people's campaign. That's what it was about. He conquered race with the idea that…Well, let me put it this way. When people talk about education, and they're like, "Oh, these minorities, they get all of the favors and blah blah blah, we need to go with income-based." I'm like, okay. 'Cause guess what? The shocking correlation, you'll find out, it turns out when you're of color, a lot of times you don't have any money! Who knew? Shocking. Shocking.

My grandmother moved up here from Greenville. I'm not sure when they moved, but they were in the city when the marches happened when people got blown over with water hoses and dogs just down that way.

Tobias motions to the empty city blocks behind him.

They weren't there, as my aunt famously tells the story. My grandma was like, "Don't you take your ass down there."

"Because why?"

"Because Bull Connor[1] would split your goddamn head open. That's why!"

It was dangerous at the time, so I understand why people didn't do it. It's like any movement. Not everybody is going to participate. Everybody who does is like a proxy for the people who don't. That's what I hope I'm doing.

---

[1] Birmingham's Commissioner of Public Safety during civil rights movement.

BOOK TWO

EDUCATION

"I could just teach like that my entire life"

Ryan

I meet Ryan in the living room of the small house that he shares with his girlfriend in Columbus, Ohio. It's a dark space with a dog roaming in and out; shades cover the windows, blocking out the bright morning outside. Late last night, Ryan said he would get up early and tell me the story of losing his job. When he agreed to it we had all consumed several drinks and everything was a-okay. Now it's pre-coffee and he's a bit guarded. He worked as a high school teacher—and there's a chance that he might do so again. He doesn't want to burn bridges in the district. So Ryan is not his real name. Not that he is being overly provocative with what he says; it's more an inherent guard that sometimes comes up when I ask to hear about a layoff. Some who give an initial promise to tell about their experience end up backing out at the last minute. A completely fair decision and—having thought about it daily—one I think I might make if the tables were turned. I know that willingness to talk

about being laid off is not to be taken for granted. I am thankful
that even this early in morning, Ryan remains willing.

He's 29, and even this early in the morning when no eyes are fully
opened he looks like a leading man, a la Val Kilmer circa "Top Gun."
He has an undergraduate degree in aquatic biology from Ohio State.
"I didn't know that I wanted to do that, it was more like...you can get
a degree in fish? Wow, ok, yeah, that sounds like a good idea. I'm a
huge fisherman and outdoorsman...went fishing my whole life with
my dad..." For four years Ryan conducted research on Wall-eyed
perch, then came a transition.

I went and taught at this little research lab where they also taught
middle schoolers and high schoolers that came over for field trips for
one or two days. And I realized that I really like teaching, I think I have
the personality for it. I would have students engaged with me and get
excited and tell me that I did a good job, and I could sense that I had their
attention, and those are easy classes to teach, too, it wasn't like there was
a test or standards or something, it was like, look at this snake, look at this
bird, look at this big fish we caught, you know? So it was easy to engage
them. I wish I could just teach like that my entire life. I was making crap
money; if I could just somehow support myself on that crap money, I
would do that every single year, I could go live in a tent somewhere and
be fine. That was the easiest form of teaching.

My dad was a teacher, most of that one side of the family were
teachers. I used to teach in high school, like little middle school weekend
classes, it was this little school program, and I was good at it then, too, but
it was one of those, I'm not gonna be a teacher because everyone else in
my family is a teacher thing. And then I actually did and was like, crap, I'm
good at it, so I was like, OK, fine, I'll do it too.

Got my Master's in education and found a job at a school district for
a year. I guess I was in a very diverse neighborhood but the school itself
I would definitely say trended to the poorer side. I was doing biology
and environmental science. I moved from classroom to classroom. That
happens a lot of times where you kind of cart around everything you need

and you're put in different classrooms based on what the need is. That's obviously for first year teachers but you can be a third year teacher and have that happen to you as well. It'd be nice to have one classroom but it doesn't work out that way. I liked my school. I had to break up fights or altercations occasionally, but I don't think that's much different from that many schools.

Once the levy didn't pass it was one of those things where from that moment...I basically taught the entire year thinking that there was a chance that we wouldn't have a job next year. It was one of those things I have no control over whatsoever. I could be the best teacher in the world and that really has no effect on whether I keep my job or not. So I just tried to do the best I could and went on about my business. Pretty much certain that I was going to not have a job, I just kind of cleared out my locker before I really needed to.

It's usually the young teachers, that are gonna be the ones that go. I think a lot of younger teachers probably feel this way...I mean, I have mixed feelings about tenure, because there are a lot of crappy teachers and they've just been doing it too long, and teachers hate a lot of their kids, they're bitter about these kids. Some teachers would be in the break room and just be like, "This kid's an asshole, and he's a piece of shit." It felt like a toxic environment to the point where I didn't like to hang out with a lot of the teachers. Every school is like that, you have good teachers and bad teachers, but if you're a good teacher, sometimes you don't want to listen to the other teachers bitch about how much these kids are horrible. There's usually an explanation for why a kid's an asshole—background, bad parents...that kid gets abused by his mom, and yeah that's why he's an asshole, you know, he's not—and he's a kid. High schoolers—they might look like adults, some look 25, but as soon as they open their mouths, they're still kids in my mind. It's like oh yeah, you're a child. you're 6'4", 260, but you're a child. So I try and give them the benefit of the doubt.

It was early in the summer where they were like "shooooop"...

He makes the sound—and motion—of sweeping something out of the room.

...can't let you come back.

Principal called me. It was just...

He holds up "hang loose" sign as an imaginary phone.

On the phone?

Mmhmm. That was it.

Did you know instantly?

Yeah, yeah. Pretty much, I mean like I said I was kind of in limbo. As it got close to the end of the year it seemed pretty likely that that was going to occur, it just hadn't become official yet. It was a pretty brief conversation, really. Kind of one of those, sorry, wish we could keep you, you did a good job...

I don't really have a summer break. I've been doing lots of other work, trying to make sure I have enough money to pay the bills and everything else. I've got a buddy who owns a farm, and I work with him. I got a marketing job, and playing online poker, which hopefully won't take away my money, which is possible. (Laughs.) I've got a bunch of brain-dead jobs, but I'm fine with it. Pays the bills.

And what's your healthcare situation? Do you have...

None. I walk around very carefully.

I've kind of floated through life always...seeming to find the right job at the right time so I guess I haven't been screwed long enough yet to really freak out about being fired. Maybe in a year or something when I'm still landscaping or something like that...Maybe it'll hit me later, but it just doesn't really hit me now.

I basically don't spend any money. We bought this house but it was my girlfriend's purchase 'cause she had been saving up and even as a teaching thing, with my student loans, I don't have anything saved up, I'm terrible at that, so it's her purchase. I'm paying my part of the mortgage but it's my rent essentially. She stressed that I won't be able to throw in my chunk for it, which I've been able to do, but—that's probably the most stressful part to me, is her being stressed out about me supposedly supposed to be stressed out. She's certainly supportive, but she wants me to find something.

I just focus on making sure that I can pay the bills because even with all these little random jobs I'm not making that much money. I basically haven't left Columbus. Used to spend a lot of time going to random places, going finishing—I haven't done anything. 'Cause it's too much gas, so that part definitely sucks.

I still kind of miss it, but at this point I've kind of stopped looking for teaching jobs because it's a pretty toxic market right now. Most of those people that were let go aren't looking to go back into teaching, which sucks, cause there are a lot of smart, good people that were good teachers.

I've just been looking for research jobs, trying to find something. I just applied a week ago, there's a research position for studying biograss for fuel. Took my resume in by hand and tried to suck up to them to see if they'll give me a call back. So who knows.

I love teaching too but I want to see where the education system is in the next year or two. The way that Ohio is right now...pay is being slashed, we're getting fired, and the worst thing for me personally, what was frustrating is you can't teach kids how to think anymore, you have to teach them to the test. Every teacher in the world essentially hates No Child Left Behind. There are certain grade levels where they're given this standard test. It drove me nuts, basically. I think it drives most teachers nuts that they have to teach the test. You just have to work so hard to teach some of this memorization, that you're not really teaching them. I personally, as a science teacher, don't really care if you know every step of photosynthesis—I care about your understanding of how the world relates to each other, 'cause that's how science works, everything is connected to everything else, and you can get your kids to kind of see the big picture— whether they go into business or art or whatever, if your brain functions like that, you're going to be a better person. But in ten years...I don't care if you know the little details of ADP, ATP, and all those little things. I mean, you should still learn it, but the fact that that's what I have to solely focus on, and then teachers now are rewarded or punished based on how well those kids do on those tests, so, you get paid better if those kids do well, or you get paid worse—you get your pay cut, or you don't get a bonus, or you get fired—if your kids do poorly. So it's not like you can try and say well screw the test, and try to teach them that way anyway. It's frustrating.

And now school systems are rewarded based on how everybody does on these tests, like how the whole school district does. But basically what that means is that the poor districts do poorer and they're punished by getting less federal funding and the school districts that are generally doing really well are going to continue doing really well and they get more and more money. Realistically the school districts that are going to do poorer are poorer neighborhoods, so basically we're like ok now the poor neighborhoods get even less money, and these neighborhoods that are always well-to-do are going to get more of the federal funding. It's ridiculous. You can't expect kids from the ghetto to do as well as kids that have like two parents and it's just those socio-economic conditions for two different worlds and you can't expect the kids to do the same.

Part of teaching in a poor neighborhood is that you have to spend half your time teaching the kids that they're loved, like let them know that you care about them, that's half your job so you can't spend as much time teaching them. And a lot of the times they're farther behind in the material anyways, so you can't teach to the level that you want to. You may want to teach at that level but some of those kids can barely read. And then you're expected to…that they should all do just as well on the test as some kid whose parents make, on average, $300,000 a year. That's ridiculous.

I had a friend who was fired and she got a new job and her new job is basically teaching the misfits in the school, those classes designated for kids that are troublemakers basically. And her class size I think it was 36, 38 kids per class. You can't teach a class size that big. The research says, I think it's anything over 18 or 21 and you degrade your quality of teaching and the quality of learning, no matter what kind of teacher you are or who the kids are, there's a cutoff point. And almost every class in America is over that ideal size that you want.

They showed a video—I was in grad school when I saw this—where they pick the kids at random, and they'd pick them out in the lunchroom, and there are some lunchrooms in America where the kids are making fun of them and laughing at them like "Ohhhh you gotta go take a test." And the kids would be so pissed off that they had to waste their time taking some test, and they showed South Korea and every kid that was picked was applauded and encouraged and the whole place was erupting like, "You can do it, do the best you can!" It was just a cultural difference, where they care about their education, every kids cares about their education. It'd be nice if our kids thought that way, it'd be a lot easier to teach them. Here, you're a dork or you're a tool or whatever if you like to learn. It's a cultural thing. We have a lot of problems with our schools. Funding is slashed and we're falling behind in the world, but part of it is our lack of interest to learn, which is too bad. Our country is not where we would like it to be, that's for sure, and anyone that thinks we're going to be the elite superpower the next twenty years, they're kidding ourselves. There's going to have to be a lot of drastic changes. Not just in education, in everything. It'll be interesting to see where we go.

"Let's just share this teacher"

Kent Jackson

Kent Jackson, 45, is from the town of Valley Falls, Kansas: "...super small town...thirty-six kids in my high school class. It's a place where those that stay, are high school educated or maybe dropped out, have a job being a waitress—stuff like that. They're good people. And of course they have no health insurance."

Kent's parents are retired mail carriers. He and his siblings were the first generation in the family to go to college. "My dad wanted to be a farmer...It would have been nice for my dad to have a son who was a farmer but, whatever, that wasn't my ball of wax."

We meet early on a July morning, just days after he's received a job for the fall. He'll be teaching in the Kansas City Public School District. "It's an inner-city school district...for most teachers it's tougher but, whatever, doesn't matter to me—they're kids." He has an electricity about him, still riding the good news, and he confesses he would not have given me an hour of his time a year ago. Or the

year before. Or the year before that. "It would have been too difficult,"
he says, rubbing his graying stubble, "Too difficult in so many ways."

I got into Special Ed, taught two and a half years in middle school and high school. Then my professor's like, you need to keep going, get your PhD. I went and got one at KU[1] in Special Ed. I would go back to my hometown, go to the bar or whatever, and people would joke around, "Oh, Doctor Jackson."

I was like, "No no no. I'm from Valley Falls, please do not do that."

I went through the program in two years, graduated, got the dream job for most professors—being a tenured-track position. I was back in Pennsylvania, I could have been there forever—I mean, to tell you the truth it's pretty hard to not keep a professor job.

I taught college students that wanted to be teachers, both General Ed and Special Ed. As a college that prepared those people, it was hard for us to justify the fact that it was a good major because our graduates weren't getting jobs.

I was at the point—I could take a sabbatical and sit on my rear for a year and then go back and teach there. I kinda made a deal. I said just give me a year pay and I'll leave, and I'll start finding a job back here in Kansas and go back into K-12, high school—I really liked it.

Nothing came up last year until the last minute, end of July. The organization I worked for, they survive by sub-contracting with school districts that work with real troubled kids, like kids with behavior things going on, taken out of the home because parents are messing around illegally or whatever. Almost at the bottom of the rung are these kids. When school districts don't want to—or can't—figure out something, they contract. And so if you're new to the district, or you don't have many years, you're going to be at a place like this. I mean, you can spend a whole day being called an F-word, and it's draining and it is the position that you have the most— what's the word...burnout. Usually BD[2] teachers last four to five years.

[1]   Kansas University
[2]   Behavior Disorder

In January, I said, "How about the job for next year?"

My boss goes, "You're doing fine, if you weren't doing fine with these BD kids you would know it by now...you're fine."

It wasn't a month later, I heard on the intercom—ten minutes after the kids left, by the way—we're having a faculty meeting. As soon as the director showed up with the principal, I was like, "This isn't gonna be good."

They just said, "We've lost it. We were blindsided, start finding a job—start looking."

The district just decided, we don't have the money to sub-contract, therefore, the school isn't going to be run by you, we're gonna take it back.

We were shocked.

Everybody went home sort of demoralized. I figured all of the teachers would call in sick the next day. 'Cause heck, I had ten days of sick leave just like everybody else, what in the heck, the organization isn't committed to us. And there were a couple of people that did say screw it. The gal across the hall said, "I was physically sick, I couldn't go to work the next day, I wouldn't be good with the kids."

The morale was not good. I mean, I was so excited, I loved my job, and I was preparing for next fall, I was gonna make enhancements, I was gonna improve stuff. And once that happened, it's like, screw this.

They kept telling us, guys, we're here for the kids, guys, we're here for the kids. And the administration tried. They had breakfast layouts on Fridays like, "C'mon, we can make it through, we can make it through."

You gotta put on a smile for eight hours, and you can't be telling the kids, because that's gonna wreak havoc. I tried my best to keep a positive attitude...and I felt like I did, and I think the principal felt like I did. But it was hard.

All of us were essentially Special Ed teachers and we were competing for the same jobs. At lunch, some of them stayed in their rooms and filled out applications. Before we were happy and telling each other what we did over the weekend. After, it's not that it didn't happen at all, but it wasn't near as often. There was one teacher that sticks out in my mind, she goes, we've got to just support each other, we've got to write letters, she was kind of a churchy person, she goes, "I'm praying for all of us," and whatever. We tried to hang in there, but in reality, we were hunting the same jobs, so that was just—the work climate wasn't fun. It wasn't like we were slicing each other's tires. (Laughs.) It was really hard. We were scrambling. The gal across the hall, we were good colleagues, but we were competing. She got a job probably 45 minutes away where she was gonna have to go move in with her boyfriend, which she wasn't ready to do, but she needed a job.

What school districts now are doing is collaboration with each other and saying, "Ok, you're a small district, you're a small district, let's just share this teacher." One of the school districts, this is past year because of budget crunch, they had a principal in elementary school, a principal in the high school, and a superintendent. Budget cuts, they said let's get rid of the principals, and now we're gonna have two administrators and find some lead teacher to get by without this administrator.

Our principal had to sit down with a flow chart and decide, "Do we want to keep him, can we transfer him to another location or not?" I found out they would like to keep me, but they wanted to stick me in a web-based school where the teacher sat there and made sure the kids looked at their computer and did their diploma online. And I'm like, I can't do that, I will substitute teach, I can't do that. Number one, I don't believe in that education. I thought, man, in a year, if I sit in front of a computer and make sure kids are awake, that is just…a downward spiral. A lot of my colleagues—4-5 of them—decided to go that route because they needed it, they needed a job and they weren't getting interviews.

I got panicked for the month of June. I was working at a theater popping popcorn with high school kids…at $7.25 an hour. My boss was a high school kid—it was terribly demoralizing. But I was like, I have to do it.

I had a teacher tell me, oh yeah, if you're out at the bar and meet somebody that doesn't know what you do, almost immediately, the response: "…Oh, I love that, I love people that care for kids, oh I'm so glad that there are people like you."

Well then, freaking pay me! But whatever. (Laughs.)

"Same thing, just younger"

Barbara & Raul

They've been married for a year and a half. Barbara's from Puerto Rico so they had the ceremony there. They're giving me visiting tips for the archipelago: $10 camp sites on the smaller islands, the smaller beaches—away from the cruiseliners and murky water—hiding in a cell phone reception hole, one of the world's most rapidly disappearing features.

The beach breezes they describe are too far to feel from the Pittsburg coffee shop where we sit. They've been in this city for the past four years, migrants from Philadelphia. "I like Philadelphia 'cause it's a bigger city," says Raul, "but I like Pittsburgh because it's a more livable city. I think it looks nice, especially at night."

Barbara and Raul want to tell me their story but ask that I don't use their real names. They are open and willing, yes, but respectfully insist on privacy as a central right. I can't argue with that.

They have two children, a ten-year-old boy and an eleven-year-old girl.

Barbara has spent most of her thirty-three years moving back and forth between the US and Puerto Rico. Her father went to college, and so did she—majoring in Latin American Studies.

She's had a career teaching in schools, many Catholic. She was raised in Catholic schools—"zero to twelve"—but confesses she "barely passed religion...even though I'm a practicing Catholic I don't really follow it because there's a lot of things I don't agree with. Like gay marriage, I don't see what's the point of not letting them get married. I kind of respect the bible, I respect the Koran, I respect all those books, but some things, I'm like 'nahhhh, I'm not following it.' I don't think that God wants you to deny a person a liberty."

Raul, 31, was born in the mountainous Peruvian city of Arequipa, the son of a college professor. He was brought to the US as a child and ended up studying mathematics.

So it sounds like you might have brought her this way.

Raul: Oh yeah definitely. We met in Philadelphia actually, at Temple University. When we were in college we were teaching in North Philly in the Badlands in public schools. We were in the local communities, which is a predominantly Latino neighborhood that's very very run down. So a lot of these kids don't focus on education, and they're not used to seeing other Latinos teaching them. They bond to you quickly for whatever reason. They attach themselves. And they actually will listen to you if you give them the right messages.

Barbara: These are kids that are in the system...they come in literally without a book bag on them, they walk in just for breakfast and lunch to hang out. Somehow you have to engrain the curriculum, and you have to make sure they don't go crazy and throw chairs or anything around. And try to find a way where maybe they'd like to learn. They were young kids, they were the byproduct of the bigger kids: they weren't taught something essential and then it kind of gets passed down. It's like a cycle, a vicious cycle. Same thing, just younger. I have a lot of family members that go the same route, they want to do something better but sometimes things happen, you know, they have kids when they're too young, they have to maintain the kids, and—things happen.

I loved the job. I love the kids and when I told them I was leaving they were really sad and upset.

Raul: We would listen to the news and hey, people are getting laid off here, laid off here, laid off here. But it hit us in 2010, so I guess it hit us relatively late.

When I came to Pittsburgh in 2003, I started working for the school for adjudicated juveniles. Students from Philadelphia that get arrested, the judge sends them to my school here in Pittsburgh. Some males, mostly females. I understand how they work 'cause I was already in the school systems in Philadelphia, I understood the neighborhood cause we lived in that neighborhood—we could relate. So I started teaching math. It was mostly in high school and they were 14–18 year olds.

They had money problems forever. Since I was there, we'd gone through maybe four, five six principals. They couldn't manage the money.

And this is a for-profit school?

Raul: Yeah, yeah, it's a private for-profit school. The company has the school, the residential facility, they have various programs—a lot of correctional facilities throughout the nation. Late 2009 they were talking about the school shutting down, the school going somewhere else, we're losing population. 'Cause we were dependent on clients coming from other counties like Philadelphia—mostly from Philadelphia, very few from Allegheny County.

There were talks about, you know, if we increase our population… so we always knew that it was unstable. People were constantly looking for other jobs, people were constantly applying to other school districts. Maybe two, three times a week we had a morning meeting. And various issues came up, usually about how to benefit the students, but towards the end, when I was there, it was more like, what's happening with us, are we moving, are we staying, are we shutting down the school?

It came down that they were going to let go a number—I think they said 10 to 12 people were gonna be let go—in a week or two weeks, we'll let you know who it is.

For the most part, it was a great work environment, we got along with the students, but there was definitely resentment among teachers, like, OK, there's no stability here, there's no room for growth here, we could shut down at any time. People aren't as dedicated as they would be, they resent having to go to work.

They called us out to the office one by one. And we kinda all knew, ok, you're being called to the office…When anybody goes to the principal's office, they're in trouble. Any time. It's never a good thing to be called—even as teachers.

When I went down, they were like, "It was beyond our control that we have to shut down and release some of the faculty, so we're not holding any grudge against you."

And then on my part, I didn't hold any grudge against them because I knew it wasn't on their level either, it was someone above them that made the decision to shut down our school.

They go over your severance, your package, and then you walk back upstairs with a yellow envelope, so everybody knows that you've been separated. And we were supposed to teach for the day. (Laughs.) I knew that was the last day of my instruction with them, so I didn't like "instruct," I just helped them. I didn't come out to every single class and say, "Today's my last day." But I had my envelope and I laid it in plain sight so whoever made that inference and asked me about it, I would talk to them about. They knew, even the students, that this was the day when a lot of the staff were gonna leave. So they see you going to the office, they see you coming back with that envelope.

Some of them, they were sad to see me leaving so they were crying and I would talk to them, like, it's really not that bad, it's just a new opportunity to do something else. But they develop that attachment to you, and all students do. So you try to talk to them and counsel them.

When I engaged them I tried not to be too personal with them. I didn't try to give them too much information 'cause I don't think it was appropriate for them to know something personal like that. But I would let them know that today is my last day.

They laid off one from every department, and it was only a two-person department. When I left, that other teacher that was left was stuck teaching all my classes. Since it's for-profit...education was never really a priority, it was mostly to make money: let's get more clients from Philly, they were talking about getting more clients from Detroit—anybody at risk that's adjudicated by the court system and their county would pay for them to come to our school, they would try to get.

The population that we dealt with was very needy, they were very combative. So knowing that we were gonna leave upset a lot of them...they had fights and they wouldn't listen to the new teacher 'cause they attach themselves to somebody, they like that stability and that consistency.

Barbara: When I came here in '08, I didn't come here with a job, but I'm like, "I'm a teacher, I can get one anywhere." But my emergency certification from Philly wouldn't transfer to this public school system here. So I went to private. I couldn't find one school that took me all five days. But two schools took me: three days in one school, two days in the other school. Perfect, ok. No health insurance but whatever.

In '09, the school that had me for two days announced they were closing in March. Apparently, on a Friday, they called all the kids and everybody to the auditorium. I wasn't there, it was the day I was in the other school. So when I came back, I had a nice little letter in my mailbox saying, "As per our conversation or our meeting that we had last week, the school is closing, make sure you start taking down your posters, and all these things."

I should have had a clue because the school was also downsizing. Instead of having second, third grade, fourth grade, we had second and third in one room, fourth and fifth in the other room. And the school was quite empty, but I never thought it was gonna close.

I told my principal of the other school, and she was like, "Don't worry, I can get you for the whole five days because I'm gonna get rid of somebody and you're gonna be the homeroom teacher."

I'm like ok—I'm in the swing of things. Everything was wonderful—until March.

Our school's Father came in the classroom and he was like, "We're doing a meeting in the school's church, can you please bring your students down?" And that was weird because he never came up. If he came up, it was like, "Hey how you doin'?" The kids loved him and he left. To call us for a meeting, it was weird.

We're going down the stairs…and the kids are asking what's going on, and I'm like, "I'm in the same boat, I have no clue, I'm sorry. Let's just go downstairs, stop talking…" The teachers were all looking at each other like "What's going on?" We all were like, "No clue—let's go downstairs."

The school was not that big. Our church was the auditorium too. While we're doing the rosaries, the principal was looking at us…and somebody said, "Look over there." And I looked over there and the principal was like, "Come." I'm like, ok…And then somebody would come and stay with our kids. It was a parent of one of my students. My kids are like, "Where you going?" and I'm like, "I don't know, give me a second, let me figure that out."

I noticed we were all getting called. We went to a classroom that was cleaned out and we had chairs in a circle, and we all sat down and the Father came in and one teacher was like, "I think I know what it is."

And Father has this paper and first it's like, well, it's a Catholic school so we gotta pray. And we're all praying and he referenced when Jesus fell the three times with the crucifix. He was like, "Jesus fell once, like the school fell once, and then we came back up. And Jesus fell a second time and the school fell a second time, and we came up. Jesus fell a third time— we cannot get up."

Raul: That's what he said to you?

Barbara: Yeah! We were like, "REALLY?" It was like you had to really read and hear what he was saying. And I didn't like that. And then he was like, "I'm sorry to say, there's no budget for the next year." And that's when everybody started crying.

I remember looking at this other teacher, and we were all like, no, there's no way—and then we looked at our principal, she's crying, so we're like, it has to be true. I was trying not to cry, I was holding it in, but I really got close to this one teacher, and she really helped me out 'cause I was only there as a full-time one year and part-time the year before, and she was like, "Don't worry, we'll meet again," and she hugged me, and that's when everything came out. And we were all just crying.

And then Father was so dry, he was like, "You need to stop your crying because you have to pick up the kids again."

And we're like, what?!? Dude, we can't even like breathe...we're not picking up the kids—I don't want to. And so he let us...you know, like calm down. Then he said, "How should we tell the kids? Should I tell them now, or should I send a letter?"

And we said, "It's better that it comes out of you because if we give them a letter, somebody will give the letter to their parent—others are gonna open them on the bus, so might as well get the news from the source instead of the classmates opening letters on the bus."

My eyes were red, my cheeks were puffy. I had one kid, oh he was a handful, I always had him next to me in church because I couldn't trust him a foot away, that's how he was. He was like, "What happened to you?"

And I'm like, "Oh, I hurt myself on my knee, I twisted my knee..." or something.

So Father came back, and read the same thing, "Jesus fell once, and the school..." The same thing. And the kids...they were all crying—even kids that got into fights, even kids that would tell you you're the worst teacher ever, even the kids that hated school, are the ones that were crying. It was very sad. One kid in particular, he was also another—we had a handful of kids that were handfuls. I was taking him to the bathroom...'cause he was hyperventilating. He was like, "Well, how long did you know?"

And I'm like, "I just learned ten minutes ago."

And he was like, "It can't be."

"I'm thinking the same way too."

"I lost my school."

"Dude, I lost my job."

We were in the bathroom hugging and he was just crying hysterically—he's a big boy too, so I'm trying to like help him. By helping him, it made me stop crying, 'cause I had to be stronger for him.

I took my kids upstairs, and they were crying hysterically, we had kids hugging each other and saying "I love you, man" and "We gotta exchange emails" and all these things, and it was an hour before school closed, before the bell rang. We had an hour and we couldn't teach. The counselor would walk around to see what we needed. And I'm like, "We need everything—I don't even know what to tell you."

The kids were asking the questions like "What's gonna happen next?" and I'm like, "I don't know." Afterwards, for like a month…they were on like their best behavior, you know? They were constantly coming up to you and hugging you; they wanted to see what you were doing at lunch. And I'm like, you know, I don't know what to tell you. We had parents who were trying to raise money, but the school was already in the hole for I think a quarter of a million dollars, something like that. There was no way we were gonna make that money that quickly.

When you're a teacher, you take everything from the walls and there's lockers or whatever. This time we had to take the whole school out, like literally the room was just walls and carpet. And the other schools nearby were coming in and just picking stuff from it. I'm like, it's like vultures picking from a carcass. I organized these books for a year and these are my stuff.

This was my stable place—I saw myself being there for years. My mom's a teacher and she's been teaching for 30-something years, she's retired herself. I felt like, that's a place I could have stayed at for a long time. And to just get that pulled under you, it's just like…It's really hard to accept that. And then, not only that—the relationships with your coworkers. When you guys are talking and doing lunch and venting frustrations about the time you had to work with a student, and sharing recipes, you know, baby showers, we would have baby showers in the teachers' lounge. And we hung out, you know? And just to have that pulled away…

(She looks at Raul.)

It not only happened to both of us, but I also had a family member that lost his job too, so it's not just…it's everywhere. Any person you talk to, either they got laid off or they know a family member that got laid off.

Raul: We kinda knew that it was gonna happen so we were just like, well, "What are we gonna do now?" And you know, "Well, we'll figure it out. We'll do something."

Barbara: We don't splurge…

Raul: Yeah we don't spend money on…

Barbara: The thing is, we don't go out to eat, we cook at home…

Raul: We don't have health insurance. Neither one of us. I know they offered me COBRA—'cause I had full health insurance while I was employed with them…but from what I understand, it's…

Barbara: Very expensive.

Raul: It's very expensive and doesn't cover too much. We don't have health insurance, we haven't had it for years. Well—I haven't had it since 2010 and—

Barbara: —I haven't had it since before that.

Raul: 'Cause her job never offered that to her.

Barbara: I'm fine. I mean, I had pneumonia but my dad took me to— he works part-time in a hospital so he took me to his hospital. Luckily. But other than that…we're kind of healthy.

Raul: Our kids don't have health insurance—yeah we haven't had insurance in a while. We try to eat healthy, we try to exercise. We try to live within our means; we know we don't have health insurance so we're not gonna do risky things. We don't go snowboarding and try to break our legs.

I had some money saved up, so we were financially stable 'cause she was working so that would supplement some of the savings that we had. I actually had to cash my 401K in to pay bills this year. For pretty much a whole year, since April of last year till January of this year, I didn't touch that money, but earlier this year I had to, just to, you know, maintain financial stability.

Barbara: The whole summer, I'm looking for jobs. Schools start in August and I felt weird, because normally, August you're in a room getting things ready.

I don't wanna be in another school that closes.

Raul: There was a joke between her co-workers that was like, "Whatever school she goes to, the school's gonna shut down by the end of that school year." She was in two schools that shut down…

Barbara: I was "The Closer."

Raul: As soon as she went there…

Barbara: That was the nickname, whatever.

Raul: So her co-workers were like, "Not you! We don't want you here."

He laughs. He's teasing her and she takes it well; they smile together.

Barbara: It's emotionally hard to be in a school that closes. I want something more stable. I'm going back to school and changing careers, I'm thinking of going to medicine, to nursing. I mean, they can't close a hospital, really. (Laughs.) I'm thinking of changing because I'm just tired of being in the school and closing.

Raul: I've been unemployed for a year—I'm actually getting into a different field. I no longer want to teach. I was thinking about going into either law enforcement or IT, cause my master's is in computers and networking. So I was looking into that, and I'm looking into a program that has computer forensics. So it's like the law enforcement-computer aspect put together. I'm probably gonna go back to school too, you know, get that degree and then go into that workforce.

You have to move on. So now you make the best of it. It can happen, it happened, so now you do something about it.

Barbara: You can't just hide and cry, or anything. Eventually you have to...

Raul: Right, you have to help yourself, to get yourself out of the situation. As hard as it may be.

Barbara: And as a parent you can't just be downtrodden in front of your kids, you have to still have that front...

Raul: Yeah, we haven't told our kids. Boy and girl. Ten and eleven. So they're not babies, but they're not grown, either. I think this is a grown-up situation and I don't want them to think...I think they kind of lose some of their innocence if they're exposed to a lot of grown up issues, so we haven't told our kids, they still think that we are going to work. I don't think it would be right to tell them, because in their life, nothing has changed— they're going to the same schools, they're doing the same activities that they were doing. I just don't want to expose them to grown-up issues if we can avoid it, so we haven't told them.

Barbara: Let me worry about money.

Raul: Yeah, "You don't have to worry about money." I don't want them to worry about money.

"I ran into the white guys"
Manuel Aguirre

We meet inside a Fresno mall. Half the shop spaces are unoccupied; many are filled with discount merchandise stores. There is a carousel with dim lighting. Mallery and I sit with Manuel in an empty food court, highlighted by an Orange Julius. The air-conditioning feels like a rescue from Fresno's unspeakable heat.

Manuel, 61, sits at attention in his collared, pressed shirt. He talks calmly, in a distinctive, majestic voice: it manages to be gritty and silky all at once. Radio, come find Manuel Aguirre. He's been out of work for sixteen months.

I grew up as a migrant kid, so I never expected to actually do the things I've done. So I got fortunate, I wound up in the military—they paid for my schooling. So I got an undergraduate degree in finance and marketing, then I got an MBA.

I wound up in Sacramento and got hired by P—. So I spent the next twenty-four years in telecommunications. I got exposed to a whole lot of things in the corporate world. I moved around a lot. Every two and a half years I changed jobs. We're just not as loyal to employers as we used to be, because employers are not as loyal to us as they used to be. So it's a give and take, or…take and take.

When I left P—, I left on an early retirement offer that they had. So I was only fifty at the time; I retired at the age of 50, got my benefits. I was playing my guitar, playing golf, doing those things—then I realized I was too young to not work. So I went to work for a company that publishes the yellow pages book here in town. They've been around for twenty years, they've been successful, and I think that position was created—my suspicion—at a time when they had a good year. And then they realized that, I think as a result of the economy, they couldn't afford it anymore. And the bottom line is, they had been successful without it before.

There was no indication, it came as a surprise. I was with family up in the East Bay, we had an emergency going on, so while I was up there I kept calling my bosses saying, you know, "Is everything ok? I'm still here, do you need me to come back?"

And all indications were, from my boss, "Family's important, you stay up there, we'll get by without you, everything is fine." So I kept checking in from time to time and all the indications were that it was fine.

Then I got a call one day to let me know that they were going to let go of a couple of our new people so my first thought was—it was interesting—I must really be important, for them to be calling me to let me know what the executive staff is going to be doing in terms of their workforce. (Laughs.) Then they told me, "Oh, by the way, your job is one of the ones that that's being cut."

I'm old enough to know…I've been around long enough to know that it's business. If you can't support a position, you can't support it, and you've gotta let it go. So, it came as a surprise, but I understand that that's the way it is…

I came back the following week. I cleaned out my office, some friends came by, we talked a little bit about it, I think they were surprised as well that that had happened; all of them were very supportive. They said you don't have to worry, with your background—I have a master's in organizational management as well.

I come from a family of twelve, twelve children, and only three of us actually went to college. But the amount of education we've gotten, those three of us, I consider it to be substantial. When I look at other people, yeah, I think we've done well for ourselves.

My mom died in '81 and my father died fifteen years later. They're from Mexico. I was the first one in our family to be born in the States. We were in El Paso, in Texas at the time. My father was from the state of Durango, and my mom was from Chihuahua. They always seemed to know the value of an education, even though they were migrant workers themselves, my mom went to third grade. My dad never saw the inside of a school.

He told us, he told us early on, the reason I brought you from Mexico to the States, is because in Mexico, the education was for the rich, and the poor, you just couldn't get educated. That's why he brought his family here.

Everybody has monsters in their lives, and the monsters being the people that always told you you couldn't do it—you were not good enough. My monsters were my counselors in high school, who should have been encouraging me, who always kept telling me, you know what, you're just not college material, you should go off and find yourself a trade. That leads to a lot of ignorance—ignorance not being derogatory, it's just a lack of exposure. When I got out of high school, I didn't even know that I could apply for scholarships, nobody had ever explained that to me. So it wasn't until I joined the air force during the Vietnam War and I ran into the white guys. (Laughs). That's not intended to be derogatory, but I ran into the white guys who knew so much more about all of this...Who actually knew that there were scholarships out there, who knew the value of the GI Bill, who came from families whose parents were educated, who knew the value of an education. Even though my father always knew the value of the education, I don't think he could see beyond getting out of high school—if you got out of high school, as far as he's concerned, you're an educated man. So I never had expected to go to college.

These white guys that I had come to know were taking night classes and asking me if I wanted to go with them. And so I did...got the undergraduate degree, got my MBA, and then came out here, started to go to work. So I know the value of school, it's done a whole lot for me. It's done a whole lot for us.

Who's "us"?

Myself, my brothers...

I was sharing a story with one of my friends who works for a foundation here in town about a conversation that I overheard my father have—we were actually in Livingston, up north, picking grapes for G—Winery. I was a freshman in high school; it was a set routine, you go to school, you get out of school, you come home, you go out and pick grapes for a couple of hours and then come home and do your homework and do that. So typical routine was that the parents would end their workday, would come home, have dinner. We all lived in this labor camp that was kind of u-shaped and we all had one room, so the parents would grab their chairs, bring them outside to enjoy the breeze and the evening, and then have conversations with their neighbors. And so there was a part of the conversation that was, how much money did you guys make today? It seemed to always come up. So one day I happened to be playing with my friends there, and I was right in the area where my father was talking to this man, this neighbor. So my dad asked this man, "How much money did you guys make?"

And he said, "Oh, we made"—I forget the amount, but it was a good amount—"$250–300 dollars."

And I remember my father saying, "You know what? That's good money but the thing you should be concerned about is not how much money you make today to buy that new truck to come back and do this every single year, but how much money you're keeping from your children by keeping them out of school when school is in season."

That's when I realized how strongly my dad felt about education. For some reason it stuck to me. It came back to mind when I was writing a paper for my second Master's, one of my economics classes, and we were talking about this notion of opportunity cost, that's when I realized opportunity cost was not whether I bought mutual stocks or buy CDs or whatever, it applies everywhere. Like in the migrant help, there's gains and losses depending on the choices that you make.

I've had to rely on my savings to a point, and because of the downturn of the economy, the investments that I had, 401Ks all of that, took a huge hit.

Soon after I got laid off it was a pretty quick realization: I'd bought the house at the peak of the market, unfortunately, so it was obviously worth less than what I owed on it. I basically said, you know what, if you can get it down to half of what it is—and the payments were about 3000 a month— then I can probably work this out somehow, and they looked at it and looked at it and said, "We can't do this, we recommend that you do the short sale." So...I had to sell my house on a short sale. That was, I think, probably—you can call it trauma. And I don't consider myself to be traumatized by the experience, but that was probably the most traumatizing thing that I had to do as a result of that.

And so what are you doing now, where are you living now?

I have an apartment. It's ok, but you know what? I'm accustomed to living in a home, I'm accustomed to have the backyard, go and sit around and do the things that I need to do, and actually be outside. I don't like apartments. If I have one goal, it's to get a job, apply for another VA loan, and get out of there, and get back to feeling...I hope this doesn't demean individuals who live in an apartment, but that's not my feeling of being normal. My feeling of being normal is being in a home, so my goal is to get back to being normal. That's why a job is so important.

BOOK THREE
HOUSING

"We had our economy tied to a couple horses, and they're dead"

Prof. Elliott Parker

So you want to know about Nevada....

Elliot Parker is a professor of Economics, chair of the department at the state university in Reno. We meet in a small garden on campus known as Honor Court, the place where the school engraves your name in stone if you give $50,000 or more. We stick to the shade while the professor's ten-year-old daughter waits, patiently, for me to stop talking to her dad so they can play catch on the lawn in the middle of the big quadrangle behind us.

The son of a military man, Elliot grew up all over the world, "lived in Germany and Turkey and Iran, few places around the US." Most of his family goes way back in the south—Texas and Georgia. His maternal great-grandfather "was a deputy Sheriff in Indian territory when he was sober, and when he wasn't, he was a cowpuncher," the

professor says with a big grin emerging from his salt and pepper
goatee. A cowpuncher is—I had to ask—apparently just that.

Nevada's an interesting case. We are the economy with the largest number of foreclosures[1], where the economy—housing prices—have fallen more than anywhere, we're the economy with the highest unemployment rate, and we're the economy least prepared to get out of it. It starts with a couple things.

One, our proximity to California. We're a little bitty state right next to a great big state. And this part of our history goes back a long time—Nevada was created by the overflow of the forty-niners who went looking for gold, and then came back here looking for gold and found silver. And that's what made us. So we had mining and that didn't last but a decade or two and then there was a long decline for us. And in the 30s we realized if we could legalize gambling—it was our engine of growth. And especially after World War II with the growth of the LA area, and all the people who started coming to Vegas, Nevada took off that way.

So Nevada looked like it was a model that worked, but it's sort of like a curse. In the same way you have a petroleum curse in developing countries, where they rely on petroleum for their exports and their income and they don't bother getting educated and they don't want other investing—Nevada's been like that for a long time. We've been using our monopoly on gambling.

Well, about 20 years ago, a lot of other states decided that they wanted that revenue too, and so they started having casinos there. You started having Indian casinos develop and, for example, in Reno there's a lot of closed casinos. Well, those closed casinos were closing before this recession, 'cause in Northern Nevada we've got some Indian casinos on the other side of the mountains, and those mountains, you know, the pass is something like 7–8,000 feet. In the winter, that's hard to get over.[2] And

---

[1]   June 2011

[2]   The "pass" that the professor refers to is known as the Donnor Pass, and is indeed, very hard to get over. It runs into California, known as the Golden State, not the Silver State.

so those Indian casinos have drawn off about two-thirds of our business. Which is a lot.

We can't raise taxes on casinos without forcing more of them over the edge because so many of them are already teetering. Even the companies like Harrah's, which started here in Reno—Harrah's got bought out by Caesar's and they relocated their headquarters out of state. So basically, our own casinos are making their investments in places like Macao, and along the Mississippi—they're not putting their money here anymore, even though this is where they got their start.

The decline in that sector has been covered up by the fact that California went through a housing boom, you know, those housing prices started rising...de-regulation led banks to lend more, and so roughly a third of all mortgage-backed securities were in California alone. The housing bubble that we saw was primarily a coastal phenomenon. So California housing prices, which were never low, all of a sudden are just rising through the roof. And you've got all these Californians, who are able to sell their house to somebody else at insane prices, get a lot of equity and then look somewhere for cheaper housing. Well, where's the best place to come? They can come here where we don't charge much in tax and they can buy a house for much cheaper. And so after a while, we were building houses for them. Now, that's not a bad thing if it doesn't get out of control, but our construction sector was the largest construction sector in the entire country as a share of our economy. After a while we get to the point where we're building houses for construction workers who are moving here to build houses for other construction workers. And somehow we thought that was a sustainable model. That can't go on for very long.

One estimate was if you took the amount of construction workers who were unemployed in Nevada out of the picture, our unemployment rate would have been about average. But we had a huge number of people who had moved here—we were the fastest growing state in the several decades before this crisis happened. And now all of a sudden those people move here, many of them have bought houses themselves, now can't sell them, it's hard to leave, and they're stuck. And so we have high unemployment and falling state revenues and things just downward spiral.

No nation counts unemployment perfectly. Every nation counts it a little differently. In China—back in the old days, I used to be a China scholar—China twenty, thirty years ago didn't even have any official unemployment. They called it "waiting for employment"—you were in the system but hadn't yet gotten a job.

The way the US counts it—first of all, it's a survey, 'cause we don't actually count all these people. In this monthly survey what they count are people who have not worked at all in the last couple weeks and are looking. So if you've worked even a few hours, you're considered employed. If you stopped looking, you're not considered part of the labor force, you're discouraged. And so the unemployment rates are always much higher than the official rates.

There are some questions about which measure we should use—better estimates suggest that maybe a decent measurement would be closer to 17% unemployment. And that still does not capture the people who are underemployed, who are working at McDonalds when they used to be an engineer.

Human cost is huge in this. Human cost is hard to measure. I mean, what does it do to someone's self-esteem? What does it do to the way you feel about yourself, what does it do to your tendency to abuse your body, through drugs or alcohol? What does it do to the long run possibilities in your life? All of a sudden your opportunities are foreclosed on, you stop investing, and just like real capital, human capital depreciates if you don't use it—people become less skilled the longer they're out of the workforce, and this is a huge impact not only on the overall economy, but on the individuals. Some people lose their jobs and for the rest of their life they'll never get back to where they were. Yeah, some people lose their jobs and it becomes a call to re-invent themselves, but I would argue that for every one of those, there's probably five people where the consequences of losing their jobs long run are huge. Maybe they wind up losing their wife, they lose their home, they lose their self-respect. Just looking at the raw numbers like an economist doesn't quite do it.

Some states decided to do the frugal thing by cutting their budgets, and what that does of course is slow their economic recovery, because now what they're doing is laying people off, and ironically in a state like Nevada, the people we're laying off are the state employees who tend to be relatively more educated. And so we're going the wrong way—we're shutting down the university, closing departments and other things, at a time when we should be trying to re-educate Nevadans so that they can move into new areas.

Governor Gibbons advocated cutting our state support at the university by 50%, wound up only cutting it by 20%. This time we were supposed to cut it by another 29%.

For the first couple years, what we tried to do was invisible to most people. We didn't want to impact classes in particular. So we wound up cutting student services...we cut a lot of administrative services, a lot of things like maintaining the website so we could attract more students, a lot of information services. We cut the library; we stopped buying new books and new journals. We stopped hiring people. So there's ways we've tried to do it with the least impact. Nonetheless, there are a number of departments that have been cut and tenured faculty let go. In the department of resource economics, which was in the College of Agriculture, we shut down the entire department, and it was a fairly productive department with a PhD program, brought in a lot of grants and did lots of research, fairly well ranked, and they're gone.

There's been a huge demoralization. This was a university on the rise. This is a university that most of us were proud to be at, where we really thought, we're on a trajectory to become a really good university.

Somebody once said about being a professor, "it's the greatest job in the world, you have the freedom to work all the time." With professor, the line between work and the rest of your life is not very clear, 'cause for the most part, you do what you like to do, you do it all the time, and there is really not a segmentation between professional and private in that sense. I mean, most people come up and say, "Hi, my name's Joe"— not "Hi, my name is Joe and I work at a restaurant." But professors walk up and they'll tell you what they do long before they tell you their name. 'Cause it's who they are. But for many other people, work is what they do simply to earn a living, and for those people I feel sad. Of course it's even worse if you can't earn a living 'cause you can't find a job, because even just working to earn a living and meet your bills, buy food and all the rest, even that gives you a sense of self-esteem. So there's a sense of self-worth that comes with work. And I don't think you can underestimate that.

So what's the prognosis? The optimist in me says, if you push people to the wall enough they can really get creative and from that crisis, as they say, comes opportunity. Maybe eventually people will start trying to figure out how to reinvent this place, but for right now, we had our economy tied to a couple horses, and they're dead.

Reno has to totally reinvent itself from a casino town to a university town, and that is really where I think the city has to go. I don't see Carson City[1] doing the things necessary to build the infrastructure or attract businesses here. So the idea that we're going to have all this wonderful economic diversification now that the casinos are dying isn't right. I worry about the economy in that sense, and I don't see people flocking here for investment purposes once we've lost our monopoly over gaming, and I don't see them moving here with insane amounts of equity to buy houses, 'cause we have lots of houses underwater and housing prices are still declining.

I don't know if you're familiar with the story of the Great Depression, but in 1936, there was an effort both by the Federal Reserve bank and the federal government to tighten up. The federal government started worrying about the deficit and they tried to tighten up on that, the Federal Reserve worried about how much money the banks had and they tried to tighten up the reserve ratios. And what happened is, we double dipped. I think right now we're about 1935. And I'm hoping that 1936 doesn't happen.

Before the 30s, maybe one out of every three recessions was a depression because financial crises used to be a lot more common before the Roosevelt period where we started regulating. People have forgotten that, and they think somehow that the government created this, that it wasn't the private sector. But the history doesn't tell us that story.

---

[1]   State Capital of Nevada

What most people don't understand is: this is not your typical recession. And when people say it's a 'depression,' they're not just using hyperbole. The president doesn't want to say it, other people don't want to say it, because they don't want to do things to undermine confidence because an economy works on confidence. The fact that we did something about it a few years ago, the fact that the Fed acted even though there was limited amount they could do, the fact that the Obama administration—and the Bush administration before that—intervened, is what kept it from becoming a great depression, but it's still a depression.

The Crew

"We're not living like kings no longer"

Jim

In Reno, Mallery, MJ, and I crash on the floor of a small house, hosted by the good Jeff Mitchell, and his housemates on Sinclair Street, just a five-minute walk from the casinos clustered around Virginia Avenue. Jeff, 25, was raised in the suburbs and moved into the heart of the city for college. He shares the home with Andrew and Tony and various guests—it's always open, there's always some sense of activity—somebody's strumming a guitar, somebody's getting off, somebody's reading a book or a magazine or a blog or a post. Last night I saw only the silhouette of someone—a roommate? another guest like me?—rummaging around for a guitar pick at 3:30AM, saying he needed to get that "riff out of my head." I'm willing to bet that at any given minute of any day or night, there is always someone awake in the house. I'd say between the three housemates they hold no fewer than half a dozen jobs collectively.

Jeff waits tables at a casino restaurant and also works with the Reno Bike Project, a non-profit that, among other activities, provides the unemployed with bikes so that they have transportation for interviews and, eventually, employment. Jeff recently graduated with a sociology degree from the UNR. When he heard we were coming to town he volunteered to take us around the city whose name is inked into his left inner bicep. His kneecaps jointly bear the state's motto: "Battle Born."

"Reno has a big exodus problem of its youth." Jeff underscores this at least once a day. "And that, I think, presents one of the largest problems for the city on a cultural level—so many artists go to Portland, Seattle, San Francisco and New York. If everybody keeps leaving, this place will never get better, and I want it to get better because I really love it here, I love my friends. It's my home."

Jeff shows us what he loves about Reno: the serene banks of the Truckee River, which runs from Lake Tahoe and stops on Pyramid Lake: "It's one of the few rivers in the world that doesn't terminate at an ocean."

He also shows us what he does not love about Reno: The motels along Fourth Street, where, in an empty parking lot, a young woman, probably a teenager, stands alone, gaunt and sunburned, with one finger tugging at the belt loop on her shorts and another finger summoning men who pass in cars. A toddler wobbles across the next parking lot, toward a motel laundry room.

We walk with Jeff along Virginia Avenue, past the mega casinos, several completely abandoned, a drag defined by padlocked doors and blank, unlit marquees.

"You can't have the first and foremost pillar of your infrastructure with an intrinsic incentive to disenfranchise the community that it is trying to propagate," says Jeff. "So if your workers get their paycheck and turn it over into the casino again, that is not sustainable for an economic system."

We drive out to Jeff's mom's house for iced tea. She lives twenty miles north of Reno, near Lemon Valley. Out this way there are rows and rows of tiered, weed-infested retaining walls, which were supposed to separate new homes that were never finished. Some didn't even begin: floor plans are indicated merely by clustered utility lines coming out of the earth.

At Jeff's request, Jim, a neighbor, comes over to talk to me because he is currently unemployed.

I believe that it's time for the president to go. He's a nice guy but... there was too much for him to have to tackle, and he's not used to this. My advice would be get out before you get shot, you know. Somebody's gonna get mad. I liked him, but...he keeps talking about the economy—well, I don't see anything.

Jim is not so sure about this conversation, this request to talk with a friend of a neighbor's son about not having a job. Jeff and his mom drift in and out of the room, joking with Jim, and eventually he settles into our conversation. The television runs in the back of the den where we sit.

Jim has always lived in Nevada, and traveled just about everywhere in the west for work. He is the son of a butcher and the grandson of a plumber. His great-grandfather: "he was a roaming preacher. He was a Chinese guy. He had come from China, came over to here. Married. It was back in Kentucky...that's where the family kind of started." I check to see if Jim looks at all Chinese but he doesn't. He is as he was before with coarse skin, which seems permanently tan. Various drops and smudges mark his t-shirt and jeans. He's a union-eschewing, last-name-concealing, 43-year-old drywall man.

Boom was everywhere. Vegas, here. Most of these people that bought these homes actually came from California. They had sold their house and they made bank, $600,000. Came here, paid cash. $300,000, you know?

We just got overzealous about everything. Everybody saw it coming, but who cared? The money was coming in. We all thought we were going to live like kings. Well, we're not living like kings no longer. It finally caught up with us. All of a sudden, we started seeing the custom homes just stopping. Left and right. Nobody was building nothing, you know. People with money didn't want to get involved. They were scared.

I mean, you can only build so much. It was just house after house after house after house, which was great, but it got crazy. It was insane. You were working six days a week and couldn't keep up with it. Mexicans came in—don't care, they have to work too—but they drove our wages down, because everybody's coming in. They'll come in cheaper. I do a lot of hand texture, I was getting 45 cents a square foot. By the time it was over with, I was down to 15 cents a square foot, and I'm having to split it. And it takes a good week to do a house. A lot of work, you know, ten-hour days in there. By the time you get paid, there's not much money.

Most've those guys are gone. Immigration's already gone through these big companies. They hit us. We got fined, I think, $25,000, because we had people that weren't legit. They went back to Mexico, California, San Diego. That's where they're from. I knew a lot of them. Great guys, hard workers. But they brought the price down on us. The boom was going. Nobody cared. Now look at everything: foreclosures everywhere.

It started about four years ago. It just all came to a halt. You go out to some of these tracks where the lots are cut, they're ready to go. Power's there. Nobody building, you know?

I've been with my company for 23 years. We have a big shop. We're not just a garage. It's a nice building, you know. Most of the guys have been there as long as I have. We all know each other.

We got to the point, there was nothing. The company came in that morning: 'We're not union no more.' They dropped it because it was costing too much. We were all union, and it just stopped. The company just stopped it.

There was no union work you could see. Hotels, nothing's going. There might be one or two jobs in this town that might be union. You've got probably six hundred guys sitting on the list down at the union hall.

Then they might get a job. That job might last you 30 days, 60 days, and then you're back down on the list.

I was a company man. I'm staying with the company. Been with the company forever. I'm going to stay with the company. If you're with a company, you're a lot safer. When the work's there, you're going to have it. With the union, you don't know what's going to happen. You may not get called for that job.

The union is good, and the union is bad. You got your pension. You're taken care of. You've got your insurances and stuff. Being non-union our company can give you insurance, but you have to pay for it. I'm not going to pay for it, because I'm not going to go ahead and spend $65 out of my check every fricking week or every ten weeks—however it's broke down. That's $65 that I could use. Am I taking a risk? Maybe so. But how many people actually got insurance in this town? You're lucky if you do. And the insurance isn't all that great anymore anyway. You know, it's almost a joke.

I'm doing okay now. But who's to say next month what's gonna happen? Three times I've almost lost the house.

How did you salvage those three situations?

Drink a lot of beer. (Laughs.) No, just try to survive day-to-day. I just made it work. I went through hell. Power would be off one week. Cable would be off. I'm like, "Damn! I can never catch up." You gotta pay one thing, you gotta try to pay the other thing. You get used to it. I mean, you can't go out. You can't do anything. You gotta sit at home, which gets fricking boring. Can't afford to go anywhere, why spend money that you don't need to?

You see the gas. It might drop one week to $3.65, but next week, it might be right back to $3.99 again. When you're not getting a full check and stuff, you gotta watch where you drive. And I have to drive to Lake Tahoe quite a bit, South Shore, so that's, you know, almost $45 to get up there and back. I've gone to Sacramento. I go all over the place. Wherever there's work, I'll go.

"Oh shit, you came here for what?"

John Jerome Welshans Jr.

My father and mother broke up when I was nine years old. My father went to California. I went out there and lived with him, saw California before it became the California that it is. Then I went ahead and went to California three times after that, trying to make my mark out there. I was there before, it was all orchards and vineyards, and it was heaven. Then the job market started expanding, so I ended up with Hewlitt-Packard out there, welding for the ironworkers. It went on and on until finally it just turned into a California that you couldn't stand. So the last time I thought I was gonna be able to make it out there, and I said "No." I came back, I said "I need West Virginia. I need the hills."

I meet John at his church in Wheeling. It is a small congregation, about 50 families. We sit in the second floor fellowship hall where the sun breaks through the stained glass windows on either side of the table where we sit. There are voices outside, coming from the street below where a Saturday fundraiser is wrapping up—a car wash and bake sale for a family that lost a home in recent floods.

Wheeling, like many other rustbelt cities, exemplifies the decline of manufacturing in America. It has endured heavy unemployment for decades; its losses began generations before Lehman Brothers went bankrupt or the housing market evaporated. At the height of the city's steel industry—1930s—the population was over 61,000. In 2010 it was just at 28,000.

In the last decade there was an attempt to bring retail development downtown: local businesses were cleared out of buildings to make room for an outlet mall. The deal for the mall fell through, and the commercial spaces that were emptied remain so.

John was born and raised in West Virginia. The 57-year-old is a self-proclaimed naturalist: "I'm a four seasons person. The anticipation of new." He is short and appears to be very strong. He has a firm handshake, his booming voice and laughter fill the fellowship hall. "This is the church I went to when I was young, and the Lord done brought me back here after three different churches."

He is a Civil War re-enactor who once got laid off while in the middle of battle at Gettysburg. When I ask about his family history he does not hesitate: "Family tree-wise, we came up from the South after the Civil War. My grandfather, Ruben Howard, he was a salesperson, but he was also an alcoholic. He was cursed with the sin. My pap, he was a run-of-the-mill man, did everything he could but he was also cursed with the sin of alcoholism. A lot of that went through my family...a lot of us have been able to handle it, but my wife's family also had a lot of the curse of that sin."

What's the best thing about this state of yours?

I was not born a prideful man. I am proud of my country beyond belief. But state pride is not something that I was raised in because of the fact that we all have to be it together, and if you start dividing, then you got problems. So I don't divide at all.

I'm an electrician. Jack-of-all-trades, ace-of-a-none. I suffered from a lot of depression when I was younger, so I bounced around a lot. I was mixed up in life: didn't know what I wanted to do, how I wanted to do it, who I wanted to do it with or anything. The only thing I had that was good was my wife, who I've been married to for 38 years. She's the one that kept me on the quick and narrow. We made it through all of our hardships.

I'm always laid off, because that's my work, but it's only like two or three months a year. Most of my 22 years have been—I've just been going from here to there to find work. The farthest I've ever worked was Utah. I was forty-some miles away and found out the job got shut down. That was back in '98 or '99, I think. I went and they said, "Oh, shit, you came here for what?"

I went, "You're kidding me, I just burned a thousand dollars to get out here!" So I turned around and come back.

At 37, I think it was, I got into the electrician's unit in Wheeling, Local 141, and they changed my life. They really straightened me out. They cared enough to worry about who was joining them, and if they weren't doing what they were supposed to, they were going to teach them how to do it. They really brought my life around to be the man I am today. They helped out a lot on that. Pride in your work, doing the job right, not tearing out the pocketbook of the people you're working for, the people you're working with. I'm a union man, and it's a situation where you're always trying to look out for each other. That's why I was saying this layoff thing is really something. Construction union is the last strong union there is, and it's getting its guts ripped out now.

You think about it, the coalmines back here, the rednecks started fighting against the coalmines because they had to work so many hours in such hazardous conditions and we're back there right now. Men are mandatory six days a week, twelve hour days. So here we are. History repeats itself. We'll be back.

That's greed that does that. If you're not a greedy person, that won't happen, because the natural good things will take the course. They'll take over.

There are so many things that you watch on the trickle-down part that you just see going to the wayside, and then they go, "Well, we have to raise the fuel bills," but yet in the newspaper you see that Exxon made record profits last quarter—they have the gall to say that even in the newspaper? And they're wondering why we're so upset about things, and wondering why we wanna do something about it. I think they need a part on the ballot: none of the above. Let's redo, man. If we gotta redo it, why don't they have to redo it?

Have you ever been caught-off guard by a layoff?

Oh, yeah. Oh, definitely. The C— power plant was getting ready to put in auto-burning coal, but their conveyers can't feed fast enough. So they were getting ready to put in a new conveyer system. This was going to be a lot of work but it just stopped. They said, "Everybody's laid off. Sorry, boys, here's your check." It was all 'cause Bush said don't worry about all your clean air acts and all this kind of stuff, and he gave them extensions to put in the new systems. You get a Republican, you're gonna have weapons. If you get a Democrat, you're gonna have work. Those are the bottom lines right there.

Previously there's been other work to go to. Now there's none. And there's a lot of closed unions where they have 2,000 men to employ, so they can't bring a lot of guys in to do the job. We did a job at a powerhouse that they built down south here. They were working guys two months, rotating them in and out of the job so they could give them some cash.

Sharing the work between all the guys?

Yes, yes, yes.

It's construction. You know this when you get into the trade. You know to expect it. You have to bank accordingly. You have to finance accordingly. And this is something over the years you learn to do, so that's fine. I've been out of finances three times in my career. But it's not as bad as what's happening now. I mean, I've been laid off for three years; I work sporadically. I'm with a contractor that's kept me for the last three years.

They've been real good to me, and they've been helping me out a lot. But it's only been like a year's worth of work in the past three years. I've worked as little as three days: going to work for three days, then laid off for another two months.

So I knew this time when I come on unemployment, things were gonna be bad. That I was not going to be able to make ends meet. And in fact, I don't make ends meet now. I do whatever I can.

I'm working out at the Good Zoo. I drive the train out there. I'm a big train buff. I love anything to do with trains, and children just...I'm just absolutely nuts about the job. It's the most positive job you could ever work. Everybody comes out there, they're happy. And if they're not happy, they fall asleep on the train, so everything's good. (Laughs.)

I started out with $440 unemployment. They said, "Well, if you fit the criteria, you're going to be able to go ahead and get an extension." So they looked at and they said, "Even though you're part-time, you work more than 40 hours, you can't get any more money."

And I says, "Are you kidding me?" I says, "...I'm working 40 hours and I make $240..."

And they says, "You're working full-time."

I said, "You're forcing me to stay laid off, you realize that. I'm going to make more money being unemployed than I am working...That doesn't make any sense. I make more on unemployment. It's stupid. I could go ahead and stretch the unemployment dollars out by working and you paying me less." But no. That's not what it's about. It's about the red tape.

They says, "We have rules and regulations we have to follow." So that helps their numbers. "This guy's fully employed; we don't have to give him unemployment."

How would you define the word 'work'? What does it mean to you?

Security.

Pride.

Something we don't have.

The Hustlers

"I don't see it, I didn't spend it, I don't owe it"

Fresno James

This was all before I grew a conscience.

I meet Fresno James because I decide to buy beer. While checking out with provisions at Trader Joe's on North Blackstone in Fresno, he cards me at the register, noting my New York driver's license and the fact that I am on the wrong side of the country. It's early in the journey, the first time I'm called upon—by a stranger—to explain the purpose for driving across the country. I do, clumsily, and as fate would have it, Fresno James was, in fact, laid off in 2007.

His real name is James Morrison but between our initial meeting at the register and later learning his family name—which is worth noting on its own—Mallery, MJ and I have already taken to calling him Fresno James—maybe it was the mustache? We confess this, and he enthusiastically grants permission to continue.

Fresno James, 25, grew up in Santa Barbara and roamed around a bit on the west coast. He attended some college classes but prefers not to pursue a degree. "I'm just not a huge fan of higher education. I've never really been good with constraints. I've never liked being told there's a certain way to do...anything. Especially now, the idea of going back to school is preposterous to me. Tuition is outrageous, especially in California."

He will not be found on Facebook—not under his given name, nor under any aliases. He doesn't like the idea of endless connectivity. He doesn't like ending arguments by finding the answer on a pocket-sized touch pad: "I don't want to settle this right now. I want to grab another beer and keep talking about it because that's fun."

He's been in Fresno for seven and a half years. He rents a house with his wife in the tower district, not far from the teashop where we meet when he's off work.

He tells me a string of entirely engaging employment stories, and as Fresno James is a writer, a collection of short stories therein resides.

In high school he blackmailed an extra week of pay from a movie theater manager who he caught looking at porn.

He used to work as a telemarketer, selling magazines. After the entire staff was laid off and the office closed, Fresno James received one last opportunity to return to work: "They actually offered to pay people to come back and clean shit up, like to help break the place down, to get all the computers packed up, to get everything done. I went! I went! It was like $10 an hour or something like that. The managers, the head honchos were there for that too, kind of overseeing that whole thing, probably to make sure that nothing got destroyed. And I think that they actually ended up going into another room or something because there were people being pretty vocal."

After losing that job he joined a national mortgage company that specialized in subprime lending.

The funny thing about being a loan officer is that there's no "officer" to it at all, you're just a salesperson. I didn't really have any training at all, they said, ok just call them and ask these questions and fill out this application—and I'm doing loans for these people and I have no idea... Like, I've rented apartments my whole life, I have no idea what goes into having a mortgage, what goes into having a loan or any of that stuff, so they sort of just throw you in there and I was supposed to have training but it never happened.

It's on the telephone all day, getting leads to people, you know like all those internet things? "You could own a home...you could do this... you could to that"...whatever. So people go online and put in their information and the company pays big bucks for these leads. And you start out the day with a couple of leads, they give you the leads, you make your call, you fill out a lot of applications. That was the day, just making telephone calls for eight hours, essentially.

With sub-prime mortgage, it's definitely a more narrow market. They're not looking for people who can go to the bank and get a good rate. Obviously if you're online, filling out applications to get a re-finance on your home or to purchase a home—whatever—you probably don't have very good credit. That's just a given—why wouldn't you just call your bank and be like, "Hey can I get a decent loan with decent rates and terms and everything's clear?"

People were definitely being duped into taking these crappy, horrible loans. And they didn't know any better. And a lot of these people were either in dire straits, like in desperate need of a re-finance, or just so pumped that someone was gonna finance them at all—they had probably been turned down everywhere; they were finally gonna pay off their credit cards or whatever it was. Besides, the loan officers were lying to them, and telling them this is a fixed rate loan...fixed for a year, fixed for two years, and then it adjusts at the highest interest rate, so...I couldn't tell them things that weren't true. But the ballers at the office were—the people that were making, you know, five, ten thousand dollars in commissions a month—were definitely lying all day, every day.

It was a salary of like $2,000, or $2500 dollars a month, which to me was a shitload of money. I was like, hell yeah, even if I don't make any loans, I get this money? Awesome. So that's why I took the job, and probably why I was less motivated to lie. They had kind of warned me that I needed to pick up, get more loans or whatever, and I'm like, well, I'm trying, you guys haven't given me any formal training that you promised me so I don't really know what you want from me here.

It almost felt like things were just falling apart. I think the market was kind of at the start of the decline. Like it was one of those things were you would expect to come in and have like no desks and just phones on the floor, just like everybody out, some huge indictment—I was always expecting that.

My boss just pulled me outside to have a cigarette. I wanna say it was morning. Like ten or eleven probably. She said, "I need to talk to you."

And I was like, "Alright, yeah."

Right outside the building she told me, what did she say to me...I'm trying to remember her name, kinda weird old lady—Wanda—yeah she was nuts, always looking disheveled. She told me that they were gonna have to let me go, that I was being laid off. I think that was pretty much it.

She felt really bad, I think she knew she had to fire other people too, so I think she was having a hard time. It was a lot of apologizing on her part, she just said that she really liked me and she was sorry and she thought I was really good at what I did and it was nothing personal. And you know, I understand that. I was nice to her about it, I get it. I always know it's not middle management that's doing this to people, that's fine, I'm not mad at you. I think she was worried that I was gonna be mad at her. But it's like, I'm not mad at you, I get it.

I just went home. We had just moved out into an apartment, our first apartment together. So that was just kinda the crappy part about it. Rent was way more than we were both paying before, so the money was definitely needed. I just said, "It's gonna be fine, I get unemployment." What I collected on unemployment was enough to keep us afloat. I'm always really good at saying it's gonna be alright; she just believes me, 'cause it always is. There's really not much—financially speaking—that gets me down. It's always gonna be alright. As a young person who hasn't accumulated much stuff, I think the people I feel the worst for who lose their job are, you know: twenty years, house payment, cars—like all this stuff. I didn't have any of that. I own my car. When I first got the job, with one of my commission checks, I bought my computer straight-up, I didn't owe any money on that, I didn't have any credit cards, I didn't have any of that.

It's just insane the way we live in general. I find myself tripped out by society all the time.

Funny thing talking to my dad about all this, is how disenfranchised he's become. He lived during America's golden time, you know? Like post-industrial technology, all that stuff, there was that Golden era, between post World War II to right before Reagan or something, or even through Reagan, for a little while. Talking to him about that stuff is interesting to me. He used to be a pretty hard-nosed Republican...but he's so fed up, too. I think for any reasonable person, Bush just demolished it for any real free-thinking individual. Of course, that's the standard refrain, but it's so true. I think that that's where the line is drawn. If you continue to believe that bullshit after Bush, then you're one of the sheep people, you will gobble up absolutely anything.

I mean, I do tons of research, I just love to inform myself. At a certain point, though, I do have to step back just because I get so impassioned with things that my wife will be like, "I can't hear about this shit anymore." I understand, I get it. She does a great job—she's a smart woman, I love her to death—she does a great job of keeping it localized, just like, to herself and immediate people that we love. All my friends are really great at it too, I'm really one of the only ones that is kind of like, look at the overall spectrum of things, and they're like, "Why does that matter to us locally?"

It does and it doesn't, and I get so pissed and that's the thing I just kind of step back from it.

I was in one of the industries that helped cause all this crap to happen, and actually had a point of reference when I heard them talking about the subprime…Like the thing that got me the most was the way they placed the blame on the consumer…these people really didn't know any better. I think they really didn't understand the way this stuff worked.

Credit used to be such a different thing. To get it, you had to be tight. You had to have money and be able to pay back, and all this stuff, and then over the years, I think, just with credit cards and everything else, people started looking at virtual money in a different perspective—as just that. It didn't become credit any longer, it became virtual money: I don't see it, I didn't spend it, I don't owe it. I have a brother that's been bankrupt twice. And he's like one of those people who still has unopened boxes from crap off TV in the corner of his house, and I see the sickness that is American consumerism, and it's gross—and it's unreal. But I guess that's America.

The way things have come down this time…there's just no consequences for anything. People always say like oh, America's been through this before, America's been through a depression. And just in the back of my mind, and as someone who is not—I mean, I'm aware of what happened with the depression and how we got out of it and all that stuff, but it seems to me that they changed a ton of stuff after the depression to ensure that that stuff doesn't happen anymore. And it seems to me that we've changed nothing. That we've gone…right back to the same practices we had before. You know, I still get a credit card offer once a day probably.

I think the funniest thing, with the political posturing—I'm so over it…I voted for the first and last time for Obama, I'll never vote again… That's all bullshit to me. I don't believe that we have much longer as the American utopia anyways.

"The hole where I was"

Alex Benito

*My conversation with Alex, just like my conversation with Fresno
James, begins coincidentally.*

*Late at night in Kansas City I wander out on my own for some
food. I end up at Mexican restaurant where I splurge on a margarita
and move down a few barstools mid-chips-and-salsa so I can better
see the baseball game on the television. I might be more than a little
eager to shut down and pretend like the world doesn't exist for an hour.*

*Alex, who is bartending, takes note of my shift and asks if I'm a
Yankee fan, because, apparently, they're one of the two teams playing.
I hadn't even noticed, really, I was just tuning out to the rhythm of
the groundouts and the step-offs. Alex says he's from Brooklyn—
Flatbush—then, getting little from me, chats up the couple across
the bar. The guy's doing what I'm trying to do: phase out everything
in favor of the whosey-whatits against the something-somethings.
The woman tells Alex she works in mortgages and, as it turns out, so
did Alex. Until he was laid off.*

*An order comes in and Alex flies to the blender, starting a couple
of pina coladas—his voice, which can boom, matches the strength*

of his athletic build. He's got a hustle in everything he does. I have a hunch that in this former career he might have been what Fresno James referred to as a "baller." Powering up the voice recorder, subtly, I try to get him to come back around to me.

Half an hour later the place has almost cleared out for the night. I catch Alex long enough to give a margarita-filled description of my journey, and ask if he'll tell me about the day he lost his job. He agrees, and I order a coffee at last call.

His mother and father were both born in Colombia. His parents moved to the US around the age of 20, "when my mom was pregnant with me…I was born I guess five days after my mom moved to the US. So I got lucky, became American 'cause I was born in this land…I was the first in my whole family history to be born in the United States."

One of the few other patrons left at the bar—maybe a semi-regular since Alex has joked with him a bit—hears Alex and asks: "Arabian, Cuban, what are you…?" Alex reiterates that he's Colombian and the guy turns back to his beer, a bit wary.

Alex's mom and dad now live in New Jersey. His dad retired from a 40-year career at Ford Motor Company; his mom worked for the IRS for over 30 years.

Alex asks me if I've talked to anyone else who was laid off from the mortgages business. I tell him about Fresno James.

He probably told you a lot of the crap those guys…all the bad loans they did back then, didn't they? I mean, that's how it was when I was brokering mortgages. It was a shady, shady business, man—and I still feel that way to this day.

I lived for a long time in New York. And then I had two kids and had a fiancée and things didn't work out. So my brother told me, "Hey man, why don't you come down to Miami." So I went down there, I got a job overseeing condo communities for a developer. Then I became a mortgage broker.

Total on-the-job training...never went to school or anything like that. And did very well...did very well in Miami, made a lot of money, was well-known around the city. And then I decided to take my business somewhere else, 'cause the amount of clients that I had, the company that I was working for wasn't able to really handle. So I got into...with a bank called CW—, which...everybody knows who CW— is. I worked with them for years. I was one of their top sales reps and became a manager. Back in those days it was high-flying. I was making over $120,000–130,000 a year. Consistently, yeah. We would do...like right now they do $10 million in loans a day—back then we used to do $120, $130 million dollars in loans. We would make a ridiculous commission off that, and that's why everybody was happy in the mortgage business. There were people flipping properties, buying and flipping...it was just a crazy process and it was fun.

I bought a condo in South Beach, had everything I wanted, life was great, driving a new car.

I lived that great life, beautiful women everywhere—you can't get in anywhere unless you're with beautiful women. I went to work every day, I worked out, I was in great shape; back then, man, I was in amazing shape—I did everything I could...

He's clearly still in shape and I point this out.

Yeah but I was way better than I am now. Everything was great. Every day I woke up it was an easy day for me. I mean, we had breakfast at this one spot all the time with a few friends, and then I would go out and work, have a great day at work, come back, beat traffic back on South Beach, get back into my condo. I had a gated community and everybody's car was gorgeous, always parked by this beautiful Lamborghini that I loved just to look at, saying ok, one day I might get to that level, you know?

Yeah, life was great, man. If you make it down there, life is great. Single, doin' real well, and then the bubble burst in 2007. So basically it felt like the rug was taken right under my feet and I fell straight on my face.

I was in the commercial side of the lending, and the residential side was the one that was really hurting the whole company. Once I saw the divisions getting shut down, people resigning, people getting fired, it's just a matter of time before it would affect everybody.

It was just a typical Monday or Tuesday coming into work, shirt and tie, getting ready to rock and roll. Around 8:30 in the morning doors are shut, everything was chained up with locks, couldn't get in, and there wasn't even a guy, or a phone call, somebody telling me, "Hey man, thank you for your tenure for the last ten years..."

Was anybody else outside the building?

There were people. I just remember I just tried to get in, people were like, outside discussing, talking, I was wondering what was going on, I figures somebody got let go, or they closed another division, but after the whole bank closed it was done.

And then we got a phone call later on that day. Talked to somebody and basically told us that, they're gonna mail our last paycheck. It was a gentleman from the corporate offices in California—and basically he told us what happened and said, hey, this is what's gonna happen. We only had certain amount of severance for a couple months that kept your head above water and then that was it.

I just listened. Cause I really needed to hear something really good—please tell me something good, I just tried to listen and listen, and when that didn't come out, I really couldn't say anything. 'Cause what other option—what could I say to him? "Please? Don't do this?" (Laughs.) It wasn't his call, he was just a messenger boy, you know? I just listened and kept my mouth shut and tried to take it in.

I was a little bit in shock. I was just like, wow it's happening now. That feeling comes across your whole body, you know you get that tingling feeling, it's like, damn, I'm jobless, I don't know what I'm gonna do, what's gonna happen, and all that. So I didn't know what to do, I couldn't afford an apartment that I had—that I bought.

I was paying for a $3000 mortgage a month, driving a brand new BMW...I had to basically liquidate everything, all my assets. At least I got some friends from the University of Miami renting out my place, but I'm about $350,000 over my head on that property because of the way it's now appraised. I gotta hold onto that for years now, and it's tough. And basically all my money and credit, all that's wrapped into that one property.

A lot of people in the South Beach properties started either foreclosing or they just weren't paying the association dues for the condominiums, so the condominiums were losing money, developers were losing money. So you go to Miami, you can see half-built condos in downtown Miami with cranes that have been there since 2007 'cause the developers walked away, 'cause they can't built, 'cause no one is gonna buy those properties.

We had to sign a non-compete clause, B— bought our company and basically none of us got hired, maybe there's a few people that we don't know, but the majority of people that I used to work with—we were all out of a job, man. Every single one of us. There was probably—I don't remember, you have to look at the numbers, how many people got laid off at CW—, but it was in the thousands.

Who was the first person you told?

My brother. I called my brother 'cause my brother lived down there. He just told me that he's gonna have my back as long as he could, but you know...

I had a girlfriend, gorgeous girl, she was a model from Germany, she was a beautiful woman, and she left me because I lost my job.

I have two kids, 14 and 11. I was paying child support, so...so it was tough at that time for them, 'cause their mom also was out of a job 'cause of the economy, so we were in dire straits for a couple years. I got behind on child support. My child support was very, very high 'cause I was making great money, so within one year of not paying child support, I was already over $20,000 behind in child support. One year.

Oh man, I thought I was in a ninth abyss of hell. I actually was in my house, outside on my balcony. I was looking at the beach, and then I got a knock on the door, and the guy was like, "OK, we're here to move all your stuff." And I realized then that everything was gonna be taken away from me, like my apartment, I had to give up everything. And then I looked at my kitchen table and I saw plane tickets back to Kansas City, and that's when I just burst down crying seeing all those years that I had to work in Miami to get where I was, to have to come back here and bartend…it's really happening, everything is gone.

The couple across the bar is all that's left and now they're asking Alex for the check. Before they leave the woman tells Alex what bank she works for and hands over her card. She tells him to call or email sometime. Alex stashes the card in the back pocket of his jeans, wipes the sweat from his brow, and comes back over to me, apologizing for the interruption.

I had to come back to Kansas City. Mom and Dad were here, they told me, "Hey, you know, don't worry about paying any rent or anything, go back to college, get a degree." But it sucks 'cause all those years of mortgage industry business, all that experience I got is worthless 'cause I never got a degree, 'cause I was already successful at the age of 21.

Are you going to call that woman who gave you her business card?

I'm so afraid to get back in the mortgage business. I just kinda 86d that world and decided, I'm gonna go into the new world. So those people are not gonna help me in anything, 'cause I don't need clients anymore, I don't need those people. They're not gonna do anything for me…people like that, you can tell. It's just never gonna change.

I'm doing a degree in information systems, it's a computer degree. I've always been savvy with computers and stuff like that, so I'm gonna try to get into UMKC[1]. I got another year and a half. My mom and dad said they're gonna throw this gigantic party when I graduate from college,

---

[1]   University of Missouri, Kansas City

they're gonna invite everybody from South America, from New York and New Jersey, and have this huge shindig. I think it's great that my mom will do that for me, because it's something I needed just for my motivation to get from one place to another.

I'm not gonna be back where I was, but at least it's a stepping stone to get back to where I wanna be in my life. I've already tasted success and I know how to get there, it's just the fact that I had to take about four, five steps back and work my way out of this hole. And I can see light at the end of the tunnel finally, but it's taken eight, nine, ten…(adding in his head)… almost three and a half more years to get back out of the hole where I was.

The Dreamer

"Just don't get any of the blood on me"

Mike Nurmela

Mike is slender and handsome. He says he's always done well in interviews and it's easy to believe him. He is 60 on the button and his shirt is perfectly pressed, his tie perfectly measured, and his thinning hair expertly parted and combed. When he speaks he sounds like a voice channeled by Updike.

He pays attention to details. He's been reading about the history of the area: Lions of the Valley. "It takes you back to Day One here..." he says, looking out the window of the coffee shop where we sit, pointing to modern-day St. Louis just beyond the crowded strip mall parking lot, "...all the Indian tribes, and the French that came up here, the Spanish, and it's a very rich read."

His grandparents were Ellis Island immigrants from "around Odessa. My grandfather supposedly fought the first Russian

*Revolution in 1908, and scooted out of Russia to Poland....Typical
American story, you know, a mish-mash of different ethnicities,
backgrounds, and here we all are."*

*His father worked as a carpenter, and his mother "was a
secretary—a well-educated secretary, but a secretary nonetheless."
He grew up in the Bay Area, "in a very small home my dad had built
in 1951."*

I'm one of those kids that grew up in that era when you had hope
and you had dreams that you could see and touch and reach out for and
get. You knew you were going to get it. It was the middle class dream my
generation dreamed about, and it doesn't exist anymore.

I was the first one in my family to go to college and get out—and
wanted to initially be a teacher, a math teacher. I ended up working in the
lending business, in banks and consumer lending for most of my career.

Twenty-five years in the Bay Area, and then we moved to Portland for
a year and then Seattle for six years with S— Bank. And all the while I'm
doing this...

*He lets his hand float up past his face, like it's on an elevator ride
to the penthouse.*

...making more money and moving up, and then my first wife and
I separated.

I got a new offer from M— department store and they said you can
be director of credit policy for the whole corporation. And they paid me
a lot of money to come here. So another step up, and it came at a time
when I was going to have to support two households, or most of two
households—the kids came to live with me.

So things were looking pretty good for about three years. Then M—
had gone from fourteen divisions...all the way down to eight, and then
it was me or a guy who had been with the company 22 years—my age,
good guy.

Two years...

Mike raises one open hand.

…twenty-two years…

*Mike raises another open hand, bounces them both up and down
as if trying to find some equal measure but, no, none to be found:*

…see you later.

So left that job and one month after my severance package ran out,
I landed another job for $20,000 a year less, so now I'm starting to step
backward.

Five years with that company, and rose back to making the low six
figures, and was offered a job with a much bigger company, and then my pay
was $140 a year, so now I was really feeling good. And then that company
had bad timing. It was one of these companies that was formed with the
idea that if they buy a core company and then start gluing on pieces, they
can find a greater fool—a bigger fool that will buy the whole thing for more
money than what was paid. And this was in the 90s—the dot com boom. So
money was flowing, a lot of times for the wrong reason, but the economy
was very good overall…we had budget surplus. Things were rosy.

And then it crashed in '99…that was the end of that ride.

Then I took a job from $140 down to $90, so again back where I was
twenty years earlier. It was a debt collection company that was losing
about $750,000. The owner let the previous general manager kind of run
things and took his eye off the ball. The owner and I were very close. We
worked together three years. I was his faithful helper, and we turned it
around to where he was making about a million dollars a year, which
transformed the potential value of the company. His goal was to cash out
and retire and take his wife to Florida, play golf. After much back and forth
negotiating, he got his price. And part of that deal was I'm going to be the
Chief Operating Officer. Well, the new owner, I think, just looked at an
opportunity to take on a young guy instead, a 32-year old kid…probably
helped that the guy made about half of what I was making.

So I was called in one morning, and he said, "We're going to let you go." It was such a surprise…I had no idea. He and my boss were sitting in there, they said, "We're going to give you a three month severance package."

That's not a thing you argue. You know, the deal's been done. They've talked about it until they were blue in the face. You just accept it and move on. They'd made their decision, and I was a big boy, and all I could was bite my tongue…

He's still biting his tongue but only for one more moment more before finally coming clean:

Hope you sons of bitches fall over—fall onto the sword. Tomorrow.

He takes a deep breath. Seems like it might have felt good.

Ghandi had a great idea. You know, you expect something from people, you're going to be disappointed, so expect nothing. That way any little thing that's done for you will be a pleasant surprise. Expect nothing. So I didn't really expect anything. It's just disappointing when you find that people talk one way and then, when the chips are down, they run for cover. And it's most people. Looking out for number one… (jabbing his thumb into his chest)…and they're willing to throw anybody under the bus…just don't get any of the blood on me.

Within a day or two I had polished up the resume—it was only three years old at that point—and had initiated some efforts on CareerBuilder, on other search engines, people I knew in the business to get the word out. You want to move as quickly as possible.

I'm 55 at that point, not 50, not 45, and the economy was on the verge of collapse. 2006 was kind of the last good year for the economy, fueled by all this debt. Credit card debt, the mortgage/ATM debt, the illusion that the middle class had money when they really didn't. So finding a job for my compensation level—really any job—was impossible.

I was over a year looking for work, and it really came down to, "Well, we think we can find someone for less money, or just get by without hiring somebody." So, couldn't find a job. I took on selling insurance, so I could do something, and maybe I can do this while I'm waiting to find a good job and keep looking, but it just got worse and worse. So insurance became the business.

You start that career at $0. That's your starting pay: $0. You get commission only. Gradually, you build up to four years in, I will make about half of what I was making at the peak.

My wife, who is at retiring, has to go back to work. She's a nurse. 66-years-old, she's working, and that's aggravating as hell.

No health insurance. I don't have health insurance today.

I went through outplacement three times in my career, got severance programs that included outplacement services, and it got to the point where the third one hired me to work part-time while I did my job search, because they knew my skill at looking for and getting interviews and doing well in interviews. So I knew all these different connections and saw all these people in different venues like me—engineers and teachers and business executives. There is no work for them anymore.

A lot of the jobs are offshore now—good jobs. Twenty years ago, I'll always remember that I went to Disneyland with my kids, and we went into one of these gift shops to try to find something made in America. You turn every damn thing over: made in Indonesia, made in Taiwan, made in China, made in Japan. This was twenty years ago. It's worse now! These container ships; it's just awe-inspiring. Literally thousands of these things on these enormous ships, so they can make this stuff anywhere and sell it everywhere. As long as they pay two dollars an hour versus twenty over here.

Jack Welch—you know that name—former CEO, highly respected businessman and very successful, was quoted at one point several years ago when he was still working: we have considered putting manufacturing on floating factories and literally moving the factory to whatever location we can find the least expensive labor.

We're really essentially doing that right now. These plants can be erected pretty quickly, and you can now build something anywhere and with the shipping costs now and the low labor costs you can sell it everywhere for far less than you could historically do it here. How old are you?

Thirty-three.

In your lifetime, computers have gone from, "Gee, sounds like a good idea," "This really should help productivity, but it's not," to "Man, it really helps productivity now." Everything from automation on the assembly line to cell phones that can tell you where you are and how to get to dinner tonight to these laptops and so on, and you see how people work with them. We carry them 24/7. What we've done is we've sucked every ounce of productivity out of the American worker that we can. You only increase wealth if you increase productivity. That was the Industrial Revolution. We went from an agrarian economy to where now you can make horse carts on an assembly line. It's more efficient. That increased wealth. We can't do that anymore because we've exacted every—we're working 24/7. Take a vacation? What's that?

In 1991, my boss—my boss's boss, who was a senior VP and reported to the CFO—was told when he went to the Arctic Circle—he was one of these adventure guys—"You will take a satellite phone with you. If I need you, you're coming back." This was 1991. And that's the way it is today: You get your emails and your texts. You're not vacationing anymore. And before you go on vacation people work extra hours so that when they're gone, things are caught up, and then when they get back, they're now behind again, so they have to work extra hours. You can't extract an ounce more productivity. There are still things you can do to automate a few more processes and introduce machinery to replace a few more jobs, but we're not going to bring back jobs to the factory floor that built the middle class. You know, the car business. It's amazing to watch if you watch the Discovery Channel or whatever—the how-it's-made channel—do you ever watch that? Did you see a human being on the vast factory floor? Those were the jobs that created the middle class to send me to college.

We're going to lose our home. We've been in the same house 20 years now. We remortgaged the house several times, trying to kick the can down the road. We had a year without pay, so life savings are gone. We sold two cars that we owned. One was a really nice Corvette. We've gone through everything we had. We just fell behind on the house payments.

That business is a lot different than it was before 2008. 2008 and back, if you were three months behind, you were going to lose your home. They would not accept a partial payment. Now we're a year behind, and in the same boat. They've got so many people in foreclosure, they can't really get to everybody, and they really don't want to get to everybody because I think that when they foreclose they will be forced to write down the investment. They're sitting on this monstrosity of past-due home loans. My home has an asset value of $325,000, that's the combined mortgages on the home. In the old days, they could sell that loan and get $325,000; that was the value. Well now, in the current market, that house is worth maybe $225,000. So the bank is out $100,000. In the old days, they would have to write off $100,000 to recognize that loss. You multiply that times how many millions of us are past due on homes in similar situations, they would be literally bankrupt.

Well, the Federal Accounting Standards Board not-so-quietly—but quietly enough for most—two years ago said, "We'll tell the banks they don't have to report these bad loans anymore." 'Cause the rule was at 60 days past due, the banking requirements are that you write down that loan by 75%, and at 90 days past due, you write the loan from a million to zero. The Federal County Standards Board is saying, "No, we can't have this. There's gonna be a mass panic if everybody announces that they have to write down their loans to actual value." You can imagine the panic! Two or three years ago, in 2008, when the stock market collapsed about 50%, a lot of people were pretty panicky, and we had these huge bailouts and so on. Well, the only guys that really got bailed out weren't the consumers; it was the investors that were stupid enough to buy the stuff in the first place.

So they've been given forbearance not to recognize these losses. Plus there's just so many of us. This was a tiny little corner of the bank that handled a few foreclosures a year, and now there's thousands and thousands and thousands of us, so they can't get to all of us, and they don't want to get to all of us.

Having spent a lot of years in the, I called it the "give it away and get it back business"—consumer lending—now I'm getting calls from creditors about past due this-or-that. So, you know, you take that with a big spoonful of humility. A lot of people in that business refer to debtors as turkeys, flakes—how could you get yourself into that situation? "Get your second mortgage and take the equity out of your home." "Take a vacation and pay off your cards." Use those credit cards that were coming by the bucket, bucketloads to your mailbox...huge credit lines.

The bank I use is actually a little bank started by a grocery chain you see here—big grocery chain, family-owned. They got in the banking business several years ago, and the idea was they'll put bank branches inside the grocery store, and then everybody's tried that, and as a former banker we all know it doesn't work. And then they started buying up other banks, and they became a $10 billion dollar, multi-state bank called F— Banks. Well, today, in the local paper, these guys are in huge trouble. And today the Fed put two more directors on the bank's board of directors. It's a prelude to the bank failing. That's my bank, that's where my checking account money is, you know? They have an unbelievably bad problem with commercial loans. It's the unseen problems. Never mind the big banks that have household and commercial loans—just all of these neighborhood banks, these medium and small banks that you see everywhere and they're sitting on this mess of loans where they don't have any clue what things are worth. I mean, what is a property worth that has no tenants? No occupants? What it is worth? They owe half a million dollars or a million dollars on that strip mall. So who's going to buy that? Nobody!

About a month ago, the last attempt to stay in the home was declined. We knew we were going to lose ownership, but we figured we were going to stay in the house. If we give up the house, they would let us lease. We'd become renters. But no, they can't do that because the repairs allegedly exceed $20,000. Like a lot of Midwest homes, we've had settling of the foundation, which is a common problem here. The house isn't in any danger of collapsing. They're just sitting there pushing this mountain of paper. Here comes another stack of folders on their desk for 50 more foreclosures.

So we're now faced with—we'd have to basically rob a bank and have $30,000 to catch up. We don't know where we're gonna go. We wanna have a single-family home, but we may be stuck with an apartment. My wife's son lives 45 minutes east of here. It's a really old 19th century farm home, and it's pretty rough; I don't know if we could live there. And we've got this grandson we're raising. His mother was killed when he was four years old. He's spent his whole life in that house with us. He's 16 years old; he wants to go to school over here, and school starts soon. Spent his whole life with us. He knew that we had problems and we've been pretty open with him about it; we just haven't told him the latest development, that we're pretty sure we're going to have to move, and we don't know where.

I wasn't one of those lucky guys...all I wanted to do when I first went to work was get the brass ring from PG&E, remember them? The electric company. Or a county job, or a government job. That's it. Work 40 years. That's all I ever wanted. I didn't want to necessarily be wealthy, just to have that peace of knowing you've got something in the bank down the road.

Guys like me, more and more of us who have been through these cutbacks and riffs and sales and so on, lost our jobs and been demoted and so on, we don't have pensions. And we've lost our 401Ks trying to make ends meet. So there is no retirement for us. I'll probably work until I'm 70. And I think that's an increasingly common problem for people in addition to the unemployment that they're struggling with, and they find something from Wal-Mart greeter to tire changer...or selling insurance. But none of that pension, no 401K. Now what?

And the myth about the wealthy—if we put them back at the tax rates that they had, we're going to stall the economic recovery—that's baloney. The super rich don't spend a dime on anything we use.

My politics will come out: The very first thing they did when Reagan became president wasn't fix the schools, fix the deficit, fix the roads. It was cut taxes for the rich...and again when Bush II came in, they had control of Congress, the first thing they did was slash tax rates for the wealthy. Can't we just let those tax rates go back to where they were? We're not asking the wealthy to give back one dime. Not one dime! We're just asking them to pay a little bit more like they were, which is nowhere near what they were paying in 1980 before Reagan became president. They weren't unhappy! We have to share the suffering, you know. They're going to become richer no matter what, but when you cut taxes you just make it go faster. What suffering is a multimillionaire doing when instead of making $10 million dollars he makes $9,500,000? That just sounds like a little bit of stupidity to me.

Think about it: A guy has a billion dollars, and he makes 4% on his money, how much is that? It's $40 million dollars that the one billionaire makes. Can you squeeze by on $40 million? That's their income on a lousy 4%, never mind if they make more than four, if they make ten. Just 4%, a heavy CD or U.S. treasury paying 4%. $40 million. So if they make only $38 million—if we ask them to pay a little bit more tax—are they hurting? That's the billionaire. What about the $10 billionaire, or the $20 billionaire? A guy with a hundred million dollars, and there's thousands of those. Making 4%, makes four million dollars a year. What are they doing with that? Just click on Yahoo and type in the Google, "expensive homes," that's what they're doing. Expensive jets, gold-plated jets. Private jet sales are up, yachts are up, mansion sales and values are up, so the wealthy are doing just fine. And they're not putting more than a penny back into the economy. They're paying Jose to come out and mow the lawn.

Money flows to the wealthy through the normal function of capitalism, and all that taxation does is kinda moderate that. They had to just take everything off. You know, take all the restraints off, and now the money's going like a tsunami to the wealthy. The bailouts bailed out the wealthy. B— had to pay an eight and a half billion-dollar fine—not to me—but to the investors. They're getting their money. And the middle class—the working class—is just getting shrunk and shrunk.

I think this mystery to me is why the super wealthy, the people who have—in fact, what's a super wealthy person? One of the popes, Pope John II, not too far back, he said, "I don't understand why anybody needs more than $5 million dollars." Okay, that's a good number. I could squeeze by on that, $5 million in assets, live comfortably. Very few people would have that, let alone ten or $50 or $200 or $10 billion, you know.

You've heard about the admonition that the love of money is the root of all evil, and you've probably met people over your lives and know of people...greed just corrupts them. I think it's what happens to these people. I think it does.

BOOK FOUR

COMMUNITY

Dewitt

Randy Badman

I'm 62. And looking forward to 82, by the way. That's a good thing, to get old. Better than the alternative.

Inside the municipal offices of Dewitt, Nebraska, Randy is sketching the tangle of streets that comprise the village's quaint grid. He marks each spot where he has family: "My grandparents lived over here. My aunt and uncle lived here. My other set of grandparents lived here. My other aunt and uncle lived here. We all lived on the same block right down here..."

Five hundred-seventy-two people live in DeWitt. Randy and his wife, Marge, graduated in the same class at the high school. Their son and daughter have both moved away but come back regularly for visits: his daughter and granddaughter are in for a few days from the Kansas City suburbs. In a few hours the whole clan will head to Main Street for $5.25 cheese steaks, tonight's blue plate special.

Clad in a striped pullover shirt and jeans, Randy is stationed in his usual council meeting chair. He is the chairman. When

I ask if that makes him the mayor he laughs and his face turns
bright red. The placard in front of him confirms only his identity:
"Randy Badman," and never has someone's character so strongly
contradicted his last name.

Technically, it's not necessarily a mayor. The chairman is the one with
the bull's-eye on his back…(laughs)…runs the meetings, basically takes care
of whatever else. My father was also chairman. He was 17 years on the town
board. He tried to get me on earlier than I would, but I had other things…
He said, "Son, you need to get on there sooner or later. You need to give back
something to the town that's given to you." That's how he looked at it.

I lived here basically all my life, except for a year and a half or so I went
out to Denver, Colorado, and worked out there and then came back to the
vice grip plant here after I got out of college. Vice grips, locking pliers—it
started in 1924 here in Dewitt, started by Bill Petersen.

The walls of the village offices are lined with black and white
photos of the vise grip plant through the decades. A copy of the vise
grip patent is displayed near the main entrance to the building.

The plant and the Petersen family, basically, they were this town. They
took turns being on the town board also. They were also chairmen too.
The fact that these streets are paved is because of the plant. The plant
was always here. When you wanted a donation for ball uniforms, you'd go
to the plant. They helped us buy our ambulance. For a small town, we've
got a five-bay ambulance and fire department here. We have two ball
diamonds. We have a swimming pool. They knew they were helping their
employees when they did that because their employees lived here also.

I started here July 16, 1969 in the tool and die shop, doing tool and die
work. I worked on presses, making parts, making tool and die. Everyone
in my family worked there. Both my kids worked there. My mother, my
father; my aunt, my uncle. Both aunts, both uncles, and my grandfather
all worked here. My dad was here for forty-some years; my uncle was there
for forty-some years. My grandfather was there for, I think, about almost

that also. I was there for 36. You just retire out of here, like I said. Do a good day's work. Everybody was close. Everybody knew each other. It was a close-knit family community. At one time, they majority of the employees lived in town, not out of town.

And then in 2001 we had the big company-wide meeting and Alan Peterson said that he had sold the company. I do remember I went home, and I talked to my wife, and we discussed this a long time. I said, "If we're ever going to move out of this place—if we're ever going to move out of DeWitt—now's the time." Because even way back then, when it got sold, we were all very concerned. We tried to put it in the back of our heads, and we worked as hard as we could to do everything that the new company wanted us to do. And by doing that, you kind of forget that this might not be here. We all had it in the back of our mind…but you don't want to think of that, obviously.

We went through all the lean manufacturing things and cut budgets and all this kind of stuff. They always wanted more. Cut the budget, so we cut the budget. Well, that wasn't enough. Next year, we'd have to cut the budget again. And they had laid a few people off. They were hiring more temps than they were permanent, this isn't the only company that's done that—because it's more economical for the company. They don't have to pay benefits. That was kind of a trend here and there, and everybody was a little concerned about it. But you don't think that they're going to take the upper management out.

I go to work at 7:00am, and this was just about eight o'clock. It was January 31, 2005. I can remember the date. Went in, cranked up the computer and the phone rang, and HR wanted to talk to me. I thought, oh, I wonder if something happened on nightshift, and one of the guys or some of the guys did something, you know? Or did somebody get hurt, or this or that. That's what was going through my mind. Going through my mind, being laid off? That was not there.

When I walked in that door, the gal shook my hand. The minute she stuck her hand out I saw nothing but exit papers sitting there, nothing else on the desk, nothing else in the whole room, you know it's not a good sign. That's when I knew.

She had been brought in from down South—from another part of the company—to help basically do what she did. She was doing her job. That's the way it is.

She said, "I'm sorry to meet you under these kind of circumstances." That's probably almost the exact words she used.

They tell you, "Here, this is it, and here's what we're going to do for you, and this is that."

And you say, "Well, is there anything I can do to change this, to keep my job?"

And they said, "No."

So I was escorted back through the factory—that I had been at for 36 years.

They didn't let me go talk to anybody. I remember I got back into the tool room, and I had a guy come up, says, "Hey, I got a problem down here—can you help out?"

I said, "Sorry, Roger, I can't."

And I turned and went out the door, and he stood there with his mouth dropped open. I think they knew then. It doesn't take long for things like that to happen.

I couldn't answer the call on my phone. I couldn't touch my computer. They said, "Call back to HR here at the plant, and we'll schedule a time for you to come back and clear out your desk, your books, all your things." Grabbed my coat and my day timer and I was out the door by 8:30am, escorted by someone else from the office. I think at the time it was one of the bean counters that was up in the office or whatever. It wasn't any easier for him than it was for me, what he had to do. He was just doing what he had to do because he still had a job. Just escorted to the door, and that was it.

You just get this terrible sick feeling, stomachache-type, throw up-type, yeah. You know. You do. It's just a horrible feeling.

My supervisor—my direct supervisor—he went also. I went along with twelve other managers, and it was a money thing is what that one was. It was getting rid of high-end anybody that had been there for a while, obviously was making more, and they got rid of that.

I went home, told my wife. She couldn't believe it either—that it had happened, you know?

I went out and talked to my boss, and we sat around the table and drank some iced tea, and said, "Okay, now, what just happened?"

We went through all the things that you do when you get laid off. We went through anger. We went through depression. And then we went back to anger. You know, you just do. You just run through a cycle through your head, or at least we did. And then it was silent for some times too…neither one of us said a lot for a few minutes, and then we'd come back, and then we'd started worrying about some of the other guys. Talked in general, and then basically probably in circles too.

I called in and went back a week later with one of the HR gals that was there. She let me in. I did it on a Saturday. Rainy Saturday morning, if you want to know more details. (Laughs.) Sad enough, but it has to be raining too. And went in with her and sat there and sorted stuff, and she watched. That went very smoothly because she lives here in town, and she wasn't happy either. It was tough for her even to sit there and watch. It really was. 'Cause she knew all of us that went. I mean, she's friends with all of us. This is a small town: 572 people. You get to know a lot of those 572, and you've lived with them for a long time. It was very difficult for her.

I had a lot of good friends that I had supervised—at one time, I had 39 on three shifts that I took care of, so we had to become close to get the work done. I do remember one of them telling me the next morning they pulled everybody together in the tool room and they said, "You guys here in the tool room, what did Randy do?"

And they said, "Well, he did everything. He ordered, he did this, he took care of the work orders, he did blue prints, did this, did that, scheduling, and…"

"Well, somebody else is going to do it now."

And that was just how it was, and so they assigned it on out for a whole bunch of different people to try to do, and try to take care of.

I had a few phone calls asking a few questions. "How do I do this?"

I was there for 36 years but they had no idea what I did.

Fighting the depression was tough. 'Cause you're depressed, and you say, "I was there for 36 years. What are they doing?" Then you start worrying about other people too. Your friends—what are they going to do? I guess being a manager, that's what went through my head.

October 31, 2008 is when they finally closed the doors. There's a picture over there of the last people that were working there, on that wall right there.

Randy points near the entrance to the meeting room where a large photograph hangs, an aerial shot of hundreds of people gathered in front of the factory.

We got a big lift and went up to take the picture here on the highway.

I personally think when they bought it, they knew it was going to go. They wanted to move it. I really do. 'Cause back then, in 2001, that was the real trend. That's when you could hear this sucking sound in the United States, all these companies going to China and Mexico, wherever. That was the popular thing to do, maybe. I don't know. Or at least everybody thought so. I don't think they're thinking that anymore now, because China's got their problems, and I don't want to get into this political thing. Or we're going to be here a while. (Laughs.) But you know what I mean? Sooner or later, China's going to have to face the same problem we are. They're destroying their country, and it was cheaper to go over there because we have EPA here. Nothing over there. Blow it in the air—nobody cares, you know?

I think the people of China all of a sudden are saying, "Wait a minute. I don't want to work all week for sixty cents." Okay, and so they're saying, "Wait a minute. I would like a little health insurance or something here too. What's the deal here?" See, as China grows—as their economy grows—everything's going to cost more, so they're going to have to pay their workers more too.

We proved that we were within just a couple cents a wrench of what they can make it over there, and they had to spend all that money over there just for a couple cents a wrench. You know how long it was going to take them to recoup? And they had so many troubles over there, and they

would send some people from here—this was after I went—over there to
try to get them to make an assembly line, and to try to get them to do
this—oh, and it was junk.

It's funny about Midwest people, and especially here, around this
area, that worked here. They're dedicated. The last day that they closed
this door, they met quota. They met the quota that they were supposed to
make X amount of wrenches today. They met that. And they were meeting
that, and exceeding exactly what the company told them that they needed,
and they did everything they could to prove to them…'Don't move the
thing! We're fine right here. We can handle it here. We can do it here.' And
I don't know what corporate was thinking. I could tell you what corporate
was thinking, but probably not here. (Laughs.) They weren't. They were
thinking of…I don't know what. Because now they have a product that's
not near as good. I won't buy any vice grips anymore. They have ruined the
vice grip name.

You know, what can I say? Hopefully the American companies are
learning from their mistakes. They wouldn't listen to us when we told
them they were making a huge, huge, huge mistake, and you're not going
to make money over there. But who are we? Who was I? Our guys here,
Director of Operations. Who were we? We weren't anybody.

Corporate's not going to listen. Once somebody with a lot of stripes on
their shoulder makes a decision, they're not going to back off of it. With
big corporations, that's what it is. Does it hurt? Yeah. Sure, am I angry at
them? Of course. You know. But you can't dwell on that. Life's too short for
that. Yeah, it's still tough. I see that thing everyday.

*Randy motions over his shoulder, at the empty plant somewhere
behind him, looming.*

Like I said, I live three blocks from it. I can't come uptown without
going by. Time heals all. Nothing you can do about it. You take a while to
get over all the anger and all the depression, you know, and anger doesn't
do any good, but it's there. If anybody ever tells you it's not there, they're
not telling you the truth. (Laughs.) You get angry.

The town is different, especially after that date. It's quiet. There's no hum from the factory. There's no noise from the presses going up and down. I grew up with that. Being three blocks away, at night, hearing the presses forging, forging. Clunk, clunk, clunk, clunk. Window open, you know, it's a cool evening; you can hear it. That's probably one of the things that everybody talked about. There's no sound. It's gone. It's quiet.

DeWitt had what I call a five-minute rush hour. (Laughs.) And that's when the factory let out. For five minutes, there were cars everywhere in this town. I mean, there was noise, racket, people honking, somebody saying, "Hey, how you doing," whatever, going—zzzzzipppp—up and down the street, people coming over, grabbing whatever they want to grab to go home with, you know, from one of the bars or one of the restaurants here…five-minute rush hour. And after that, it was quiet again.

There's times now in the morning, there's not a car on the street. We don't have a grocery store. A guy tried to get it going, and he lasted about eight or nine months, and he just couldn't swing it.

It's just timing with the economy. Sooner or later, something maybe'll happen. But it's all timing. Life's all timing. Yours, mine, everybody's. Sometimes you have good timing; sometimes you don't. I've had some bad timing since 2005, and I've had some good timing.

I didn't have a thought in my head that I wouldn't retire from here. I figured, "Hey, I can work here as long as I want. I could go at 62. I could go at 60. I could go at 65." A lot of us, we just never thought that we would not retire from here. And we were dedicated, and we did everything we could, and it wasn't good enough for the other company, I guess.

How did it feel entering the job market after 36 years? Had you ever put together a resume?

No. Didn't really have to. But I sure put one together real quick after that. How does it feel after that long a time? I was scared to death. Just plain scared to death. Scared to death of trying to go out and maybe do something different, or a little different. You know, when you do something and you work your way up through a company, you learn as you go, and so you kind of know everything under you, so to speak, basically under the tree that you're climbing up.

It took about nine months for me to get a job, or to find a job. I started at Nebraska Boiler, I believe that was November 28, 2005. I went from making vice grips to being a plant supervisor making boilers. 225,000-pound boilers. They're big. They're huge. I mean, everything is completely different. I was a plant supervisor, and that was handing out work orders, blue prints, things like that.

And then I got laid off in August from there.

About eight o'clock one morning, got a phone call. "Hey, can you come down to Phil's office?" He was the person, the king. I went into his office, and he says, "Follow me, Randy. We need to go over to HR."

I knew instantly. (Snaps.) Just like that. I knew. I just knew. That early in the morning, why would I go into HR if it wasn't…? And it was.

Came in and sat down with the HR director, and he was there, and he said, "Randy, we're sorry to do this to you, but we're going to have to…" You know, "We're downsizing" – they all use "downsizing" or "restructuring," that's a good word too. "Restructuring" is what happened to that one, if I remember right. Same thing. You're laid off. It doesn't make any difference.

I went out and called my wife right away, said, "Well, guess what?"

"Oh no," she said.

I said, "Yep. I got laid off again."

"What?"

And I said, "Yeah, hey, what can I say?"

And she says, "I don't have any words either."

And I said, "Well, I'll be home after a while. I'm going to stick around, clean out my desk and talk to some of the people. I'll give you a call when I'm on my way home." That's what happened on that one.

Then there was a staffing service from Fall City, Nebraska City, and they were looking for somebody at a plant. They wanted to move it, and they talked them into leaving ten people in that plant in Fall City, and they're glad they did. Now they're starting to build it back up. And so that's why there's an opportunity for me to get in there.

And how far is your commute?

Eighty-five miles one way. Probably took me about an hour and 35 minutes. Maybe I should say longer, because that probably means I was speeding. (Laughs.) I don't want to incriminate myself here. (Laughing.)

I'm excited about it...I'm apprehensive also, 'cause this isn't exactly right down my alley, but it's close enough that I can handle it. I have mixed feelings. I've been off for quite a while, doing a lot of stuff for the town, and I'm going to have to be more organized to get everything taken care of and handled.

It'll be a life-changing event for my wife and I. Obviously, it's going to be, because I'm going to be gone early in the morning and getting back in the evenings, if I do come back, and I'll probably wind up staying sometimes, depending on weather, this and that. You know, a snowstorm coming in, it's dark already before I get off of work: I don't know if I want to drive home. So that's going to be...It'll be different.

Empire

On the road to Empire, Nevada, bullet holes pepper the road signs.
This is not important because of any sense of danger. It is important
because this is the middle of nowhere and people have space
to live on their own terms. And sometimes that means taking a
joyride, picking off the signage with open desert all around, jagged
mountains in the distance. Someone shot up the sign telling me I'm
entering the Pyramid Lake Reservation. Someone shot up the sign
telling me I'm leaving the Pyramid Lake Reservation. And someone
shot up the sign informing me that the lane I drive cuts right
through the open range of a horned, cattle-looking animal that I
don't entirely recognize from its black silhouetted figure against the
yellow, triangular backdrop. It resembles some cousin of Minotaur.
The sun streams through the holes where the bullets have tagged
the beast. The sun finds every last space in this part of the country.
The temperature hovers either side of one hundred degrees.

It's a Saturday when Mallery, MJ and I reach Empire. The town
closed last Monday. A chain-link fence encircles the empty homes
and boarded buildings, the motionless factory—all of which are
set about fifty feet off the road. The gate at the main entrance is
locked. Weeds have already infiltrated, rising out of the cracks in

the streets and basketball courts, climbing up the sides of garages and the plastic playground in the middle of the park. All three churches are closed. So is the community pool. The postal code for Empire—89405—has been eliminated.

This was the last company town in the United States, a municipality built for the employees working for one corporation. In this case it was the United States Gypsum Company (USG), which set up a mining operation in 1948, manufacturing drywall. At its height, Empire topped out with a population of 750 in the 1960s. By the time the closure of the plant—and thus the town— was announced in December of 2010, the population had dwindled to 300.

Despite the closure there are four remaining residents when we arrive at sunset.

Tammy Sparks
(pt. 1)

When you're a kid or a teenager, you think it's just the worst thing ever, it's so boring, there's nothing to do—but then again, you walk outside and every kid in your entire school is sitting right there.

When I moved away, I went military, so I've been to New York, lived in DC, Cuba, just all over the place, and I wouldn't trade this little community for that. Ever. Because it's just a feeling of calm and peacefulness. There's just no need to be in a hurry, it's just a really good time.

She greets us with open beers upon arrival. She is the mother of the Sparks family and the Sparks family is all that remains of Empire.

Tammy and her husband, Dana, have one 7-year-old daughter, Sierra. Tammy's second daughter from a previous marriage, 18-year-old Jessica, will be leaving by the end of the year to attend beauty school in Kentucky where her father lives.

Population: 3.

The family currently lives part time in a parked RV just off County Road 441, next to the Empire General Store, which they own—and hope they can keep open. It sits closer to the road than the rest of the town, spared from the chain-link encirclement.

Both Tammy and Dana also work for the military in the Carson City so they drive back and forth on a weekly basis.

They insist on putting us up for the night, providing a room in the small house they're renovating behind the store. Tammy tells us the beers are free for the night but the water will cost us big time in the morning.

When did you know the plant was closing?

They announced the closure in December. It was the beginning of the year before the majority of the plant was laid off. They all ended up having to find new homes, new jobs, new communities, the whole thing. They all left, they all had their houses down there and some of them had grown up and lived together forever, you know, 50, 60 years. My dad worked down there for 10 years. My stepmom, she was there for 43 years, and my mom actually worked down there for, I don't remember, eight years? Something like that.

It was the last company-owned town...so all the people that were here worked for the company. And the sad part was, you know, it's so far from everything, that these people couldn't just move to the apartment across the street. They scattered. A lot of them went to Battle Mountain, to Elko, Eureka, Winnemucca. They did do some job fairs and stuff over here to try and help them...and had quite a good response because they have such a long history of good work ethics up here.

They let them stay in the town until the end of the school year, so even though they weren't working there, they were allowed to live there rent-free till June so that they could go find a place to live. Some of them had to go and get other jobs so they had to leave earlier. A couple of the kids didn't wanna leave. So we had a couple of 'em staying here with us so that they could at least get through the school year before they had to move.

But just last week was the final days. They put gates on the plant and nobody was allowed down there anymore so they had to be 100% out before then. Last week was horrible. It was just somber. These people were just crying, like, "I don't know what to do. I live here because I love it here. And I never thought it would happen, I planned on living my life here, raising my kids here, and I never wanted to leave." A lady came in just bawling because she was mad.

And I'm like, "What is wrong?"

"I need boxes!...I have to pack and I don't wanna do it, I thought something would happen before now, you know?" And she's just hysterical, 'cause they just love it. You just explore the desert a little bit and look at all the beautiful stuff. You got antelope crossings, you got every wildlife there is—right here.

I just feel bad for the people that had to leave their homes. The people that were still living down there, I grew up with their kids who I still get to see, and their grandkids. How many people can say, "I still know the kids I grew up with...I still have friends with the kids I went to kindergarten with"? You can't do that...

Most of the kids that went to the Gerlach high school—Gerlach being seven miles away. They have about 350 people in that town too, that's where the school was and kindergarten through twelfth grade. There was a teacher to child ratio that you'll never find in another school. Most of those students came from Empire. When the plant shut down, all those kids left, so the school shut down too, leaving maybe the possibility of maybe a one-room schoolhouse or whatever, but in turn, it cost all those teachers and all that staff their jobs as well. Bus drivers, cafeteria, janitors, all of 'em—they all lost their jobs too because of this.

Mr. Beaver

Gerlach is a smattering of houses. There is one restaurant; there is one motel. It is made up mostly of retirees. Tammy gave us directions to "teachers row" and we've landed on a gravel road, adjacent the mothballed high school. The road is lined with empty portable homes where most of the teachers once lived.

I knock at the door of Jim Beaver, the science teacher. Apparently he might still be around. A Pomeranian goes wild inside the home, somewhere just the other side of the front window. There's movement behind the curtains and a muffled voice; I can't make out any of the actual words but it sounds vaguely like hold-your-horses-I'll-be-right-there.

Mallery, MJ, and I step away from the door and cluster near the road. Just like the house and the jeep and the wide open desert around us: we bake under the sun. Moments later the screen door slams shut behind Mr. Beaver. He's barreling in our direction—gray hair scrambled by the warm Nevada wind—putting on his glasses. He starts off a little gruff but softens, slowly. We apologize for coming by unannounced and he explains that he's in the middle of packing up: he's only got a few weeks before he must be out of his home. The housing came with the teaching position and the teaching position is gone.

His family is originally from West Virginia, "dates back to 1783
at least as far as I've found." He spent the last eleven years teaching
math and science at the high school in Gerlach. When I ask what
"work" means to him he responds, unflinching: "Work equals force
times distance, you know? Hey, I'm a physics teacher, I'm gonna get
snarky with you."

Basically, just came to school one day and the kids all came to school and said, "the plant's closing." Pretty sudden. That's the first we actually heard about it. USG called the employees together that morning and just told 'em. That was in December, shortly before Christmas break.

We knew that if the plant was gonna close, then there would be pretty serious changes at the school. Actually—that day—the deputy superintendent came out and talked to people and told us, "Well, we don't know what's gonna happen, but we'll keep you apprised."

I know some people decided early on, "Well, this is over." And some of us were kinda holding out, "Well, maybe they'll keep two or three teachers around." I think everybody kinda came to that realization at different points in time. When we sat down and figured out how many kids lived in Empire, we knew we were gonna go down from about 80 kids down to about 10, and it's not fiscally sound to keep the whole school open for that number of kids. It got to the point where it was a done deal and we just had to accept the fact and move on.

It was in May, I guess, that they made a formal announcement of what would happen. They said that "this is what's gonna happen, and we're going to have a two-room schoolhouse with one teacher that will be K–8 and two aides. Actually our secretary is going to be the secretary/ custodian/teacher's aide/groundskeeper and a few other things. And then one of our other aides will be the bus driver/aide/everything else. And if there are any 9–12 grade students, they'll be taking classes online."

Friday of that week, they announced the three people who were gonna stay, and then the rest of us knew we had to move. I wasn't happy about it. I don't think any of us were. We're all out here because we like it here. We came here because this is what we like; where we wanted to be. And we found out we couldn't be here anymore...

At graduation, kids were very emotional, we had a huge turnout for graduation, much bigger than we usually do. Couple hundred people showed up...

And then we had to get down to the business of actually getting ready to go. We were given a deadline of June 17 to be out of our classrooms. I had a lot of stuff built up over that period of time. And so it took a while to get stuff out. My wife helped me a little bit and my neighbor. I finally got everything out on the 15th. Some of it's sitting in my house, and some of it's sitting in one of the classrooms in the elementary school. It's being stored there until I have a place to put it. Those of us that live here have till August 1st to be out *(points at the narrow home behind him)*. As far as I know, everybody that lives here has found a place to live at least, we've all bought houses or whatever, figured out where to live...the rest of us are waiting for openings in Reno.

You have one in Reno?

Not yet. No one does. They have not opened up those positions yet. We got an email week before last that said they expected to have the preliminaries done mid-to-late-week, which was last week. Have not heard anything yet.

I'm originally from Reno...I really don't wanna go back there. I spent plenty of time in big cities when I was in the Navy, I lived in San Diego for about ten years, and Los Angeles, and Honolulu, and I like it out here, it's quiet, it's peaceful...

Jim looks around and waits before he continues: the physics teacher is insisting that I see what he's talking about, that I turn to take in the open desert, the earth's calm buzz extending to the foot of the mountains in the distance, and the solitude therein:

I like that.

Ms. Munson

When we meet Michelle Munson she is vacuuming the empty front room of her home on teachers row. Friends have already helped her move out most of her belongings. A few boxes remain in the bedrooms. On one wall near the kitchen, the word "BELIEVE" is painted on the wall in gold letters. "I used to have a great mirror beneath it," she says. It's not hard to imagine the confident and professional kindergarten teacher looking at herself, preparing for the day, and believing. She is a bright and beautiful 40-year-old, single mother of two children—a 12-year-old son and 6-year-old daughter.

I grew up here. I lived here since I was three. My dad was an electrician for USG and then my mom was the librarian at the school. I went through K-12, graduated.

I taught here for 10 years. I loved teaching. Small community, get to know your friends, your neighbors, all the kids easily.

It was kind of strange cause we were sitting around at Thanksgiving at my grandparents' house, saying, we think something might be happening, maybe a change-up in the management was kind of what we were thinking. We didn't think it would be such a huge "Oh, we're shutting down."

It was after Thanksgiving…just at Christmas. It was sort of like a buzz in the school, and I actually didn't know for a long time what was going on. I had other things happening. And then they said "we have the meeting after school, and it's a mandatory meeting." They brought us all in to talk about it.

You don't ever want to believe it's gonna happen. You think it's gonna happen to other people—back East it happens all the time—but it really hasn't hit this area yet, this community.

What went through your mind?

"It'll be ok," I guess. I'm kind of optimistic. "Everything will be fine, it'll work itself out, it always does, they went through bankruptcy a few years back and it'll turn around, it'll be ok." Denial, I suppose. We all stood around and talked about it for a few minutes and then kind of went home. I think we were still in denial. It didn't really hit me until a day or so later. Pretty emotional.

I'm moving to Reno. I don't have a position yet, but they keep telling us not to worry, we'll have a job, not to worry. It's dragging on and on and on and I wanna know now. I'm that kind of a person. But I just have to know there's either a job there or there's a job somewhere else. I think I'm pretty marketable so I can find a job somewhere.

I'm ok.

I'd rather be in a small school, a small community. But I think you just kinda make the best of your situation, get to know your neighbors, and you can have your own little community there. I'm adaptable I guess.

My son's having a little bit of a hard time of it but he'll be fine. It's just getting used to it, meeting people. I think once he meets a couple of friends he'll be ok. My daughter's kind of excited because there's new opportunities—like, she's gonna go to ballet. She's adaptable and we went and visited her school, it's big and shiny and new and new experiences. She's dying for someone to play with cause her neighbor is gone today, so there's no one…

Doris Tullar

Doris, 51, has always lived in the west, mainly Oregon, Northern California, and Nevada. She likes Gerlach: "I feel like a little kid again—'cause my hometown's just over a mountain somewhere here," pointing out past her front yard where we sit.

Well, for a long time, I was just a fill-in over at the school, and I did custodial work, and I do TA for special needs. And then about two years ago I started being the back-up bus-driver. Then the original bus driver, she and her husband moved back into Fernley. So I was the full-time bus-driver this last year. And still did TA work. Out here you have to know how to do everything. (Laughs.)

I had never drove bus before. It was like, "Oh, you want me to do what?!?" I do remember when I was a kid, every time we would get a substitute driver—oh, the kids on the bus would just give them a terrible time, and I just thought, I would never drive a bus! (Laughs.)

The whole reason why I even started driving bus was the kids—the kids kept bugging me that they wanted me to drive. I had a really good trainer—he had me ride with him a lot at first...I was so scared, so nervous. (Laughs.)

This is understandable considering her short frame. It's easy to imagine Doris being physically overwhelmed by the oversized

steering wheel or the high-set driver's seat. But she learned to
handle it, and fell in love with the job.

I only picked up kids over in Empire. And it took 10 minutes to get them all picked up. It was a real easy route. I enjoyed getting to see them growing up and trying to figure out what they were gonna do with their futures—that's very exciting to me.

Early in the morning, I went over to pick up the kids and they were telling me that they were having a big, very important meeting, and they knew that it was probably gonna be that the town was gonna be closing down...of course news travels fast in our little towns here.

It was just before Christmas. So that was pretty sad there. And everybody just started, you know, trying to figure out what they were going to eventually have to do.

I didn't actually get an official word on my job until the school district had evaluated it all to see what jobs were still needed and which ones weren't. I pretty much knew—as soon as I heard it—that I probably wasn't gonna have a bus-driving job.

It wasn't until the last day of school when it finally hit me: this is it, this isn't gonna be happening anymore. The Transportation Department... they were out here early the next morning, the day after the last day of school, and took every vehicle that had wheels on it back into town... Made me very sad to have to give my keys back...(laughs)...It took a long time for all of us to quit crying...(laughs).

It really upset a lot of families. Not only the ones that had to move, but the ones here in Gerlach, 'cause these people have been friends forever with each other. I was really concerned for the kids, because when I was a kid, we moved around quite a bit, and that's really hard on a kid, you know? A lot of the kids were born out here, and they'd lived out here all their lives. And they're very, very nervous about going to a different school, you know?

I always told the kids that they were the lucky ones because they were getting to move off. I said, "What about us that still have to stay here?" There's not many people here now, not very many kids. My daughter she's gonna be staying at home and doing online classes—so all her friends are gone.

It's not gonna be as—to me—as happy without all the little kids running around, doing things. Kids are important! (Laughs.) Very important, so... It's gonna be lonely and sad.

Everybody's still not believing it's really happening. If they open the school back up again, I hope that they call me back to drive. And there's that chance, there's a lot of things that we're hearing of gold mines opening up and things like that, so maybe it will encourage people to come back.

Gold rush: feels like we've been here before. "We're all in hopes it'll come back eventually," she says. She does not specify what exactly she means by "it" but I can only imagine "it" is everything: the next generation, the opportunity to earn a living, Empire.

Brian Key & Anthony Sherrell

I'm a dredger, I'm a gold-miner. I do that when I'm not working. You can talk to me about my work, my prospecting adventures, my relic hunting—anything.

That's Brian. He's 47 and a long way from home, though he doesn't seem to mind all that much. He defines 'work' in one word: adventurous. "Actually, I think I've been home 30 days in one year," he says. His dad was a teamster, drove trucks; his grandfather was a traveling salesman. Motion is in his bones.

He arrived in Empire hours after Mallery, MJ and I did. We were sitting by the road with the Sparks family, empty bottles crowding our table. I cannot go into too many of the night's details because they are obscured by multiple beers and a strangely-flavored whisky. Tammy Sparks' brother and his girlfriend were there with us, too, visiting with their Chihuahua, Bandit. All the adults were taking turns telling stories. Bandit was interested and freaked out by everything, equally; he had a glow-in-the-dark collar that flashed bright red, lighting up his mug, making everyone laugh. It was somewhere in the jumble of overlapping voices and illuminated bug-eyed faces that Brian emerged out of the black desert and joined the swirl of activity.

Now it's bright morning, early, and we are all hung over to varying degrees—except for Brian who has the air of someone who's been happily awake for hours. We sit in the middle of the Empire General Store, Tammy and her husband Dana are already doing some work on the outside of the building. Sierra, their seven-year old daughter, runs about preparing the "Dolphin Show," which so far involves a Barbie, a small plastic dolphin, a rectangle piece of Tupperware filled with water, and a chair. Eighteen-year-old Jessica is in the corner of the store, her attention craned in the direction of a television mounted high on the wall. Every now and again, someone stops in, from nearby Gerlach, or road-weary travelers crossing 441, looking for gas and provisions.

Brian just happened to be driving through the Nevada desert on his way to visit his daughter in Mission Viejo, California. He was curious to see if there was anyone left in Empire. "I used to deliver explosives to all the mines up here."

He has 30 acres back in his home state of Indiana. He also has a time-share in Maui that seems to be loosely tied to a girlfriend who's no longer around—a story that comes in bits and pieces, interrupted by a number of the females who, upon hearing Brian stopped in for the night, drop by to say hello. He flirts harmlessly and skillfully, letting one woman know that if he doesn't use the time-share by December 1st he'll lose it. He suggests that maybe they should think about it. She says she's ready to go.

Brian's perpetual motion is—without any assistance from his expressive eyes and perfectly combed hair—romantic. He seems to entice everyone with possibilities and opportunities that he spots from far, far away. At one point he suggests—only half-joking, I think—that he collaborate with Mallery, MJ and me on a television show featuring some of the more harrowing jobs he's done. And I think it's safe to say all three of us agree that Brian could, indeed, fetch a princely sum as the latest edition to the effusive real-life-of cable television canon.

Brian's younger cousin, Anthony Sherrill, walks into the store, rubbing the sleep from his eyes. Apparently he showed up last night after I fell prone.

Anthony's hair has not yet been addressed and, like the rest of us, he still needs to wake up. He waves, vaguely, and tracks down coffee behind the deli counter. Brian watches his cousin for a minute, smirking, then goes back to matter of looking for gold:

I actually got gold dredges. I've had the dredge for three years, and I've been researching sites for twelve. They banned it in California, so I sneak in now and do it. I got a four inch triple stage sluice dredge—it's like this giant vacuum cleaner floats on the water and you just put a dive suit on, and it's got a regulator and an air line and a breathing tank and you just go under the water, wear a mask and weight belts and everything, go down 30 feet and vacuum that gravel, and then you hit the bedrock and hit the cracks and the crevices and get up top and go, "Oh! Eureka!" (Laughs.)

And how did you learn to dredge?

Time and talking and research…and thinking I'll strike the mother load, just like a '49er.

Have you had any luck?

Yeah, yeah. Actually, I showed you guys my gold that one day. That little vial. Brought it in…

He looks to Jessica who nods with absent-minded enthusiasm— verifying the approximate size of gold Brian is indicating between his fingers without really taking her eyes off the television in front of her.

I sold a lot of it. It's $1548 an ounce. Forecasted to go up to $2500 an ounce. I got a guy wants me to professionally dredge over in Alaska with a six-inch dredge, wants to do, like, a split the profit down the middle type work. It's pretty interesting. Nugget shooting in Arizona...and New Mexico, most of the areas where the Spaniards was in Arkansas and up the rivers and this and that, I go looking for artifacts. Rifle caches.

What me and my cousin do is we're teamsters.

Anthony has gathered his coffee and takes a seat next to Brian.

Anthony: He got me on.

Anthony grew up in Mooresville, Indiana. His father was a farmer and so was his grandfather. "Mom, she grew a garden and canned everything," he says. "A lot of winters, you're short on money. So you know, we didn't have much to eat on. She'd just go to the cabin, pull out a few cans of corn and green beans. You know, potatoes. Warm 'em up on the stove, and we ate. Never went hungry."

He's 35, and has dabbled in modeling. Like his older cousin, he's handsome. He has a stack of comp cards and an agent in Lexington, Kentucky; he's landed a few print jobs for clothing manufacturers.

They came out west to drive big rigs, hauling massive sections of a pipeline under construction. As soon as they made the drive from Indiana the job was delayed.

Anthony: We had to sit in the mountains and wait for them to fire up. We were sitting up on the lake view area, staying up there for a month and a half.

Did you do any hunting?

Anthony: Chipmunks. Squirrels. I had $1200 when I left Indiana...I was almost out of money. So was he. So we were living on basically nothing.

Brian: His family was making fun of me, that I drug him out there and stranded him, and they were literally making fun of us, laughing. His mom was outraged at me...this outlaw cousin had the good cousin out there stranded. And I said, "Man...we will get jobs. I will get us hooked up one way or another."

You know, this sounds like bullshit, but I've had 47 different truck driving jobs. And that don't include working as a crew member on building warehouses, this and that, and working in a restaurant a couple times, and the jobs in Arizona I got paid in cash working as a heavy equipment operator. The driver is a dime a dozen. Guys work, they get fired. Guys work, they fold. Company goes under. They change hands. It's an ongoing thing. The layoff. Layoff or two checks. Get your two checks or layoff. It's either immediately to another job, or a layoff...I kind of compare it to, like, the fair. Carnies. Travel, pick up, go, set up, work, work, work, pack up, go. Nonstop.

I was in the Marine Corps. Six years. I was a sniper. I learned survivalism. I was a woodsman kind of—and him too (pointing at Anthony) as kids—and it's more of a survival thing...feast or famine. When you're feasting, you save the money. And then when the famine comes because of the layoff, you're pinching pennies, you know? And it's survivalism. Just the same as living off the land when we was up there in the mountains. I told him..(jabbing his cousin, expediting his wake-up)...I was on unemployment. Was very little. But I told him, I said, "Hey." I said, "We can do anything. We can work for this potato place, driving trucks to load potatoes." And we was fixing on doing that! It was like, $10 an hour, but I said, "That's what we can do until we get on the pipeline."

The call to start the pipeline job came, in fact, on their first day hauling potatoes. They got in the car and headed to the pipeline project main base, otherwise known as man camp.

Brian: I think it was a month and three weeks or something, like going on four weeks at the man camp. It was horrendous. Just picture Full Metal Jacket and see the boot camp part of it in the squad bay— that's it. And racks, you know, double bunks. I don't like close quarters like that. I've been to every state in the United States. I've been to Canada and Mexico. I've been to several foreign countries. And to see some of the belligerency and the crap that these idiots do is very appalling to me, you know? And it sends me into an anger state. It takes a special bunch of roughnecks on oil rigs—these guys are wildcatters. Hardcore. You know, you've got ex-Marines, Navy Seals, all kinds of outcasts. On top of that, truck drivers. And traveling like a circus.

There's two different types of work that we do. The train will come in—and it'll bring these 80-foot joints as we call them, or one piece of pipe. They range in size. They can be anywhere from 12-inch to 46-inch pipe, but we was on 42-inch. 80-feet long, 18,000 pounds. Two sticks per truck and sometimes three.

Actually, what picks the pipe up is a giant suction cup. They load it on their trucks on boasters, which is a piece of wood with indentations in 'em. And the pipe lays in them indentations. We strap 'em. Then when we're going up mountains…we have to chain the fronts to keep them from going through the truck, literally through the truck, killing the driver. And then we chain the back to keep them from coming off the back.

We take it wherever the stockpile yard is. They just stockpile it, which is called racking. Then we racked for the helicopters to come in, for them to pick up the severe stuff that we couldn't even get…they're $10,500 an hour to pick the pipe. The pipline has money. It's called the Trans-Alaskan Continental Pipeline…most of it's natural gas.

We done that all winter, I come from Indiana. Went to Winnemucca, and then we went to Leonard Creek, Nevada, which is in the middle of nowhere…I went to Elko…Lakeview, Oregon, Corrine, Utah. All over. All these yards.

Feast or famine. This year's been a little slack. And last year was a little slow. It was just piecework. Go here, go there, this yard, that yard. Just moving like a gypsy.

You see a lot of bad things happen. A lot of friends died. I had one good friend that died of heat stroke in Arizona. Sandbags. Throwing sandbags. Incidents and things happen. Like the guy we was working with turned the truck over.

Anthony grimaces and nods…

And it affects your family. You literally drop what you're doing and go. You don't have no girlfriends. You lose your wives. But you figure I think the highest I made in one day was $700-some dollars.

I wouldn't have any other job in the world, because I thrive off of the change. I cannot stand the same old, same old. If I'm at my house, in two days, I'm going stir crazy. And I'm thinking, "What can I do?" And I start, you know, going…Either wasting a ton of money because I'm bored, or I start thinking of when I can go dredging, doing the mining or something like that. And then I get my phone call…take back off. It takes a special type of individual and special people to put up with it.

Anthony: I've only been doing this right about a year. The first time I come out West is the time he got me on doing pipeline. So not only was it a culture deal, but then I started to work out here. So the only time I come out here wasn't vacation. It was for work. And I just like the West. I really do.

I've had so many jobs. Ship building…I did it for almost eight months. It was different. You get to see how everything's put together, the inner hull and the outer hull. That was in Jeffersonville, Indiana, by the river, next to Louisville, Kentucky.

We were union, you know, and they told us, "Once you get into a bid, you can't unlock it for a year."

I was like, okay, cool. You know, I like what I'm doing.

It was a few months later. There was a break room as you come in. We all went in there, and it was a couple foremen. That's when they told us, "We're taking away third shift. And some people had their bid unlocked and they'll be transferred to lower jobs. Maybe even a layoff." They said it was a time of crisis when they had to take away another shift. And they said they was allowed to do it.

When we got told, people went to the union steward, and the union steward just threw up his hands kind of like, "Well, there's nothing I can do." Kind of like you're on your own. That was the disappointing part.

I was a machine operator, second-class before that happened. I moved to a lower paying job, and it was a welder's helper. I worked a little while. Probably about three, four weeks after that.

Anthony looks to the ceiling, recalling a trail of layoffs.

J— was one of them that downsized...

KP— actually went out of business. They delivered food for BK—. One day I come in...the dispatcher told us, "Well, everyone's getting a big meeting. You need to be there for it." Of course, nobody knew exactly what it was about, nothing like that. Some people had ideas, but we didn't know exactly what it was until we got there. He says, "Guys, we're having to sell our company to another food service agency, and I don't know if they'll keep you guys. We don't know nothing."

I look around the room, you know, and there was probably about 30–35 people. It was pretty quiet, not a lot was said. There were guys crying, you know because how am I going to support my baby now?—and all that.

I was pretty disgusted because I'd been through a couple situations like that before. So it just kind of made me mad. So right in the middle of him explaining what was going on, I just walked out the door. I just walked out the door and said, "To hell with this." I just threw the key over the dispatcher's desk.

It felt kind of good to me. You know, because I just had to show some kind of emotion. I wasn't sad. I was kind of angry, like all these people, and you've got a guy over here trying to support his family, and now he's gonna try and find out how he's gonna do it. It pissed me off.

So where are you heading now?

Anthony: Back to Indiana.

And you got any work on the horizon, or you'll wait and see what comes your way?

Anthony: Just waiting for a phone call. I've been married...

Counting years in his head...

...she'll kill me if I....

...looking increasingly confused....

....about eight, nine years. Eight years. I'm going to try to get my wife and my little one, and we're going to try to get a motor home if everything goes as planned. And just kind of follow the pipeline, just kind of live like that.

Tammy Sparks
(pt. 2)

It's Sunday afternoon, hours after Brian and Anthony have disappeared as quickly as they arrived—heading east and west, respectively. Tammy Sparks catches her breath in the shade outside.

What's the fate of the store? Can you keep it going now that Empire has closed?

We bought the store October of 2010. And they told us in December the plant was shutting down, so I mean, had it two months before they announced the closure of the plant. I don't like to worry before it's time—to me, everything always works out, one way or another it's gonna work out.

The only concern, really, that we have: I get my power and water from the plant. So hopefully something works out where they keep that on so it doesn't shut everybody down.

I live here on the weekends because I still work full time. Really I have two full-time jobs, being military—so I'm just running constantly, I never get a break, it's just chaos all the time. I'm a captain. I'm an ordinance officer, so I'm the company commander for a maintenance company out of Carson City. Actually I have a detachment in Carson City and one in Las Vegas. I have about 167 soldiers that work for me. And of course that's my one weekend a month job, which never works out that way. And then my full-time job, I'm the executive officer for the chief of staff in Carson City, so that keeps me very busy, trying to keep that going.

We come up here—we leave work on Friday afternoon and we have to do the shopping because nobody will deliver out here, so we basically shop for 400 people, is all we do. Usually about six or seven hours worth of shopping. And then we'll drive it out here and load, by the time we're done it's about one o'clock in the morning, so we'll unload all that and then we'll spend the weekend working the store, cleaning up, 'cause there's a lot of remodeling here that needs to be done. And we'll do that.

October to January is really busy. You have all the hunters, you have all the motorcyclists, you just have a lot of campers out here, but mostly hunters—bird and deer and antelope 'cause they're just all over the country out here. And then it slows down really bad, I guess, February through May, it's really slow, but with the summer coming, it picks up a lot.

To do this, you think, oh my god that's so much work—'cause we don't make enough to pull anything out of it right now, I mean, it'll grow, but why would you do that much work for nothing'? It's the feeling of coming over here—you can stand in here, you don't meet a stranger, everybody's friendly, everybody's happy, they're out here because they love it out here. And the second you crest that hill and you just see this town, it's like the whole world just left you. Being out here working I get that. I relieve all the stress from the week before and I'm able to calm myself down.

I just spent a year in Iraq, got back in April. And then of course I'm gone most of July just for travels and meetings and stuff. And then I leave for Afghanistan next year.

You feel ready for that?

I will be. I will be, yeah. It's tough leaving, and then with having the store, too, we've added so much more to our workload. My husband works full time as a teacher, he teaches ROTC in Reno, and so he may have to quit that… 'cause I won't be there to help him anymore. I do all the books and that kind of stuff. He does all the inventory and stuff so it makes it really hard. But we'll be ready.

BOOK FIVE

CORPORATE CITIZENS

"Corporatized"

George Ploghoft

He is 57, and his gray head of hair gets along well with his tan face. If he donned a silk suit he could easily pass for a suave politician. But I get the feeling he doesn't like suits—maybe not even politicians. He prefers t-shirts and shorts; he carries a backpack—not a brief case—as well as his own water bottle and a library copy of Keith Richard's Life.

Originally from Iowa, George followed a girlfriend to Durham in August of 1975. The relationship didn't last but George "fell in love with the trees and the mountains." He stayed and eventually earned an undergraduate degree in psychology from UNC-Chapel Hill.

He defines "work" succinctly as a "four-letter word." He isn't lazy, only insistent that he retain the right to draw a sharp separation between his job and his life.

It's been five months since he became unemployed, and he has only one month of COBRA left: "I don't see much chance of paying for healthcare. I'm basically betting. It's Vegas, and I'm betting that I don't get anything that really needs...you know, if I get cancer or something, guess what? I'm not going to have health insurance,

and they're not gonna treat me, so that'll be it. I just hope that I
continue in pretty good health..."

We meet for lunch in Durham, not far from the university
where he used to work.

Fell into doing laboratory safety work. And then from there started taking classes and learning about environmental health and safety stuff. Setting up management systems so safety becomes part of the job. Some companies actually do that. Most of them just talk about it. So it was pretty frustrating in a lot of ways, because we didn't have any real power. See people doing stuff that they shouldn't be doing...go run and tell their boss who just laughs at you and says, "Well, that's the way we've been doing it for years." It's really kind of a weird field to be in, because most companies don't...They talk about safety, and they don't really...you know, they have all these procedures and policies in place, but do they actually follow them day-to-day on the ground? When it's critical that we get something up and running, what do you think their priority is? Safety? No. It's money. We're losing thousands of dollars an hour not having this rig go. We need to bypass that thing and...forget that alarm—it'll be okay. I mean, this kind of stuff goes on all the time, and then something happens, and they go, "Well, we have all these policies" and then they want to try to blame somebody.

So anyway, that's the safety world in a nutshell.

D—[1] hired me as an Accident Prevention kind of person. I basically worked 40 hours a week, which was fine with me. If you can't get it done in 40 hours a week, either you need another person to help you, or you've got too much of a job, or you're being really inefficient and you're spending your time doing all kinds of stuff that's not really essentially. Forty hours a week is most of your life. Otherwise think about the number of hours that you're awake and sleeping, you know, how much waking hours do you really have? And five days a work, basically your whole day is taken up by going to work.

[1]   A major private university

I was there for four and a half years. June 30th, 2011 was my last day. My boss, who is so good with interpersonal relationships (rolls his eyes), calls me into his office and just says... "Well, I don't know exactly what to say, but your number's up." That's what he said. "Your number's up."

I thought he meant I'm going to be assigned to another bullshit indoor air quality investigation—somebody complaining because the air isn't good, you know—because I did a lot of that. So I just thought, well, my number's up. I'm going to get some stupid assignment that nobody wants. And I said, "Well, what do you mean?"

He said, "Well, your number's up. We're laying you off. You're getting laid off."

At that point, I came close to jumping...

George grinds his teeth, while extending both of his arms in front of him, as if sailing through the air and strangling an imaginary neck all at once.

...like in a TV show or whatever; I know I saw a scene like this one time, where the employee just flies across the desk and just latches onto the guy's neck—you know, that's what I wanted to do.

What stopped you from doing that?

I don't know. Just age. I think I finally got to the point where I can control that. Believe me, I thought about it for a while, while I was sitting there talking to him. Just the way they did it was such bullshit.

They don't even really call it layoff. Of course it's "asset reallocation" because "we need to manage our resources and allocate them into different areas." So D— is very sneaky. I've never seen an article or anything on TV about D— having these layoffs. They're just moving people around. People have lost their jobs, yes, but we aren't going to call that a layoff.

D— has become lately...it has become I guess what I would call corporatized. It's this mentality. And now everything is driven by this bottom line, and you gotta make a certain percentage of profit. Well, we've gotta make 8%. We're only making 6.5%, so let's lay these people off. I see D— is kind of going that way…everything's gotta be run by the quarter. Next quarter has to look like this, so we're gonna do this now. Well, you know, what's the big rush? We're all gonna be nothing, specks of dust pretty soon anyway. Do you really have to worry about "Well, it has to happen this quarter" instead of two or three quarters from now? Is there really that big a rush? Because you're still making money. You're still making a profit. Did you really have to get rid of those people? They espouse the idea that they don't want to be like the corporations. We don't operate like that. Well, now they are starting to operate like that.

I have a friend who works for DW—[1] still does, and he's been somehow saved over the years every time they have this round of layoffs, somehow he's managed to stay there. But he would tell me about back when they were making high profits, they had these little spinoff companies that were only making, like, 14% profit for the year. Well, the goal was 18%. So guess what they do? They sell them off, these companies—these people lose their positions—or they send it to China. Because they're only making 14% profit. Not good enough. "Well, we've gotta please Wall Street. We gotta make Wall Street expectations." Why the fuck do we have to meet Wall Street expectations? Do you not care about the employees? So guess what, you're going to lay people off. You're going to close the facility. You're going to put all these people out of work so that you can please Wall Street? So it's okay for these people to go on unemployment, have to try to find other jobs. You're screwing with people's lives. They're not paying taxes now. You know, how does that help America and this community and these people? Then they all talk ad nauseam about how good corporate partners they are, good corporate citizens they are. Bullshit. How is that being a good citizen?

---

[1] A major chemical company

"Limp along and do it differently"

Teresa Baseler

She's 55 but: "I never act like it. If you saw the PT Cruiser outside with flames on it outside—that's mine. I'm all about the fun. You know, if it doesn't have a rollercoaster…(Laughs.) I go to the beach. Okay, I'm here for a couple hours. Where is the rollercoaster? I've never been to Grand Canyon, because it's like, 'What's there to do?'" (Laughs.) She visits Disneyworld in Orlando every year. I ask about Disneyland in Anaheim. She's a little worried it might be too…quaint. It is quaint, and I assure her this quality is its essential charm but she's not having any of it. "It's all about the rides." Her ginger hair is short and easy, built for the strong winds that come with loops and corkscrews. We meet in a reading room at the Millard Branch of the Omaha Public Library.

Terry has two grown daughters with her husband. He has to keep his job for their health benefits for "another 10 years till Medicare—if it's still around."

When I grew up my dad was a shoe salesman for Bostonian shoes and he was transferred all over the country. Start up new stores, get 'em running, move on. I went to a different school every year. And my dream always was: "I don't want to move anymore."

Someone once asked me, "What do you want to do?"

"I want to get married have a couple of kids have a house that I never move out of and go to work at a company where I can retire." So there's the dream. And thirty-one years later the dream is no more.

I was very lucky to be allowed to grow over the years with the company. I worked at M— for 31 years. So yep, I just kept moving up and moving up and doing very well.

Most of the stuff that I did I was trained on the job. I knew that if my job ever ended I didn't have a college degree. I knew that I wouldn't be able to make the money elsewhere.

I was a senior buyer. I bought all of their furniture, all of their equipment. I traveled around the country for them when they had to open up new facilities and made sure that all the furniture got installed things like that. I had a team of three.

April of 2008 they called us in to a meeting and we were given an organizational chart and told, "We're going to reorganize. We're gonna need to cut back and here's the chart. Here's the hierarchy and the jobs that are going to be available and pretty soon we'll give you the job descriptions so that you can then apply." That same year in February I got my annual appraisal. Rated above average as always throughout my 31 years. Got my $7,000 annual bonus shortly thereafter and then got told 'Well, now everybody has to apply for jobs'.

So we applied and it wasn't until August when we finally got called in one at a time to be told whether we had a job or not. So you just apply and you go through the interview process as if you were off the street. It's an online application and then they send you a personality inventory. You know, pick the ten words that relate to you and then they come up with some little missive about here's what you're all about here's what your personality is like...You don't get to see those results but they get it in the HR Department. The HR person would make recommendations—you know, these are the people we feel that we would like to keep in the company and the manager can choose to interview or not interview. And of course they did it…just as, "Well, we owe you this." All of these canned questions that they would ask. That's kind of how you felt. Like you were going through the motions just to make it look like, "Yeah, we're trying to help you out and keep you here."

I kind of knew there wasn't a job because they weren't giving me assignments and I'm kind of one of these overachievers; I need to be kept busy so I'd go to the boss and he'd say I got nothing right now just go and surf the internet or whatever you want so I knew it was kind of just giving me some time to look elsewhere. There was a severance package involved and I wasn't going to jump ship before I was able to get a hold of that so you just kind of sat there. It was just waiting forever. You just wanted—just drop the hammer. Do it. Tell me I'm here, or I'm not. You know just every day its just anxiety going in: "Do I have a job? Do I not have a job?"

My husband kept telling me "you're safe." Friends kept telling me "there's no way they're going to get rid of you." I'm never one of those people to feel like I'm safe. I'm always "worst case scenario woman" so everybody around me told me there's no way they're going to get rid of you because you're too valuable, you know—too much, you do too much. But you know, I would come back with "no, everyone is replaceable." And we've seen it over the years. You know, they'll figure it out or they'll do it another way or they'll just drop that process and limp along and do it differently.

In my case the whole team was let go. My first assistant was 41 years with the company. My administrative assistant was 25 years with the company and I think what happened was that we were too expensive to keep. After you've been there so long you've got the 401K, you got five weeks of vacation, you get bonuses, you get higher in the salary range.

We were told ahead of time, you know, "Tomorrow will be the day we'll sit everybody down, one by one, and let you know." And so they started calling people and, you know, of course you can't do anything. We all gathered up at the front around my administrative assistant's desk, and just kind of waited for the call on each of our lines. We'd all cleaned our desk out prior to this, you know, just in case.

One person that I had worked with in the past got called down and after she was done she called me on her cell phone says, "I got let go and by the way once they talk to you they move you to another table where there is going to be another gentlemen who is going to talk to you about job search programs. This gentleman has a list in front of him of all the people and I know all the names on the list. Would you like to know if you're staying or going?"

She went down the list and we all knew before we went down to HR because this gentleman had this list in front of him so when I got there I told him you know you might want to put that away. (Laughing.) He was ancient and old he was just surprised that anyone had peeked at it and said anything. It was kind of awkward.

So we knew, we knew before we got down there and once you got down there it was an HR person that you didn't know. My VP, whom I worked with for years prior to even coming to the department, was absent; my manager who I worked with for four or five years was absent. The new supervisor was sitting there with the HR person and had to go through this and tell each of us that we didn't have a job. You know, tough on her, tough on us, you know, to sit through that. They were very stoic, they were very business-like, as if you were off the street and very "I don't know who you…"

They had a piece of paper. OK, I'm going to read it to you right now and you just go through this whole paragraph of blah blah blah and your job is eliminated and you should not say this or that or the other thing and if you want to sign this you can, and if you want to take it home and go to a lawyer you can. Just very, very sterile. You were escorted from the building you know you couldn't come back to your desk and gather anything. And they walked you clear to the parking garage. It was like five minutes 'cause it's a long way from the main building down to the parking garage.

We were walked over to the public lobby in the building across the street. I, of course, called my husband and he was shocked and then I called some friends who worked in that building who came downstairs and we just all kind of gathered in that lobby for a while, just kind of supporting each other and talking about it you know probably for a good

20–30 minutes. There was shock, you know, friends that got left behind, people who I had lunch with every day and friendships with. We just all stood around shocked; some of them crying, some of them just glazed looks, you know. And my husband came down and we went home.

It's how do you handle it at that moment, you know, it's just: put on the public face and fall apart when you get home. So that's what happened. The next day I was a mess. I didn't want to see anybody. I didn't want to talk to my friends who got left behind at the company. You just wanted to sit in a chair and stare.

I was scared even though it's not a hard luck story by any means. They gave me six months severance pay. I knew I had money to fall back on. But it was just still devastating; 31 years of going to the same place. What do you do, you know?

I wasn't surprised that I wasn't kept—maybe just a little bit because of the appraisals I'd had over the years and the good feedback and the great bonuses and my boss would tell me how valuable I was and how great I was. But I think that anyone is replaceable.

I think it goes back to being too expensive to keep because I was in the upper end of the salary range. Although I was wiling to take salary cuts and apply for jobs at lower levels.

And a lot of people were, you know, I'm gonna take my time. I'm not one of those people, you know, I'm just driven, I had to find something, I gotta do something I kept thinking what do I do? Where am I gonna go?

I got a call from a friend who is director of operations at a small, locally-owned camera shop who said, "You know, we need somebody on the front desk. Can you go over?" I felt like such a charity case. I felt like a welfare case or something. I just remember crying and telling him I was scared and I didn't know if I could do it.

And he said, "It's just ringing people up," you know?

I didn't want to do it. Just let me sit here and surf the internet for jobs.

I finally got a job at P— where my daughter had worked. I had applied for a customer service job. I went from making $60,000 a year to $30,000.

This was structured to the point where, you know, you're monitored on your production and your compliance to your schedule. So every morning when you go in, you get on the computer, and it tells you when your break is, when your lunch is. And I remember the first day after training, I had been on a call that went five minutes long, and I thought, well, that's fine. I'm going to break five minutes late...Oh, no. You got dinged for going late, and you got dinged for coming back early. And if you had to go to the restroom...that's an unscheduled break. I didn't need that structure. So I drove myself crazy trying to meet all those matrixes.

I was so scared...everything is automated and although I had programmed computers I think it was just my state of mind at the time I felt like I couldn't learn. I felt like, "Is it that I'm getting old?" I can't do it. I would sit at that kitchen table every morning and cry. I can't go there. I can't do this. I can't get it. I can't. And I was doing fine. I was earning production awards. I was the new gal with the balloon at her desk every day but I'm one of those people. I'm so driven if I can't be the best I don't want to play so I made myself crazy there. You know you doubt yourself...I mean the self-esteem was gone. I quit wearing make up. I let my hair go gray. I gained weight I just felt worthless and I sat there everyday and cried before going to work. I can't do this anymore I can't do this, I can't do this.

I'm one of those people that internalizes it a lot. And like I said, couldn't sleep, blood pressure went up, went to the doctor and he says, "You know, you just have to live simpler. You just have to cut back."

And I said, "I might have to get two jobs."

He said—and this was very sobering—he said, "With your health, two jobs would kill you. You can't do it."

So that's always in the back of my mind, you know?

You just do what you have to do. My husband and I have talked about this. We'll probably always have to work. But yeah, you internalize that, and I think that's why three years later, it still hurts me so bad. I can't let go of that frustration, that bitterness, and that anger...it's strange that it just haunts you for that long. And even now, bringing this up I haven't slept well for the last two nights, just thinking about it.

You know how sometimes it's comforting to go back and re-live some things?—even though it's a tragedy. When my dad died of cancer I spent six weeks sitting by his bedside in hospice. Those were so some of the best times we ever had and it's comforting to revisit some of those scenes in your mind. Not this. This just...hurts. You know? Why we put so much of our self-esteem into our job and you know that's part of who we are. I don't know...Maybe it's because this was my dream all my life and now its gone.

"A certain kind of vulnerability"

Riva Weinstein

We are sitting in Riva's cozy, subterranean kitchen in Stanfordville, New York. This is the room she is currently painting. The new coat is badly needed and the estimate from the professional was too high. "I did the two back rooms, and I'm in the final home stretch." She is petite and youthful, with a calm demeanor.

She has been without a job for over a year. In two days she will be 54. She's had a long career as a writer in advertising—TV commercials and print ads and, "of course, it's a digital world now, so web campaigns and things like that."

I had no idea, really, that anything was coming down the pike, and I was actually really grateful to have a job, and feeling very lucky that I had one.

I was in my office, and it was around three o'clock in the afternoon, I think, and I got a phone call from the person who was the creative manager, and we had a really nice relationship but really didn't have a lot to do with each other on a daily basis other than saying hello, so it was odd for her to call me. When she asked me to come into her office, I remember my heart just racing, because I knew something wasn't right. And as I walked into her office, I kind of boisterously sprung into the room saying, "What are you, going to fire me?" (Laughs.) And, sure enough, she was sitting there with my boss, and they were very apologetically responding to me, and saying, "Well, it's not firing, exactly. It's not really that..." I had been a real asset to the team, and it was very unfortunate. They made a big deal of the fact that they were letting me go that week because, if they did, I would get this ARRA benefit. The government was subsidizing your healthcare, which obviously made a huge difference over the course of a year. So I guess they were trying to do the right thing.

I was leaving on vacation for three days. In the status meeting that morning, I happened to mention that I was going to be leaving the next day for, like, three days. I just reminded them that I wouldn't be there. So I realized in retrospect, after being called in at three o'clock in the afternoon to the office, that I had sent them into a tizzy, because they were probably planning on letting me go on Friday, which is the day that all good people get let go. They had to pull it together on Tuesday, in a matter of hours, so I'm sure there was a lot of running around.

I do remember them sort of whisking me downstairs to this exit interview where someone I had never met before outlined all the details of the noncompete and confidentiality, and all these other things, and I remember sitting there and saying to them, "Do we really need to go over this right now? Like, could you give me the papers and let me sit with it, and I'll get back to you when I get back from this little vacation that you've ruined for me?" (Laughs.) But of course, no, it had to be all signed right then and there. You basically can't leave the building without having signed everything.

I remember, aside from the fact that I didn't know this man and had never met him before, he was trying very hard to be very compassionate, but it felt so unauthentic. It felt so packaged. And, you know, in retrospect, whether it was or not—I don't know. Obviously, this was his job so there was a certain amount of rehearsal to it. I guess, maybe you want a sweet little old grandmother to tell you all these details. (Laughs.) I don't know...

I went back up to my office, and I really didn't know what to do with myself. You know, people give you a hug. What can they say? They're just thinking, "Oh god, not me," you know? And then of course, slowly, a couple of people wandered in, and the guy who I considered to have gotten me the job was just so sweet, and said, "You're a great writer. It has nothing to do with you." Gave me a big bear hug, and then joked about, "Do you want the bottle of wine?" I had bought him a really nice bottle of wine when I got the job. He said, "Do you want the wine back?" Which was great. I mean, you need a moment of levity. You need a moment like that.

I guess a lot of people would storm out, but that's just not me. I was sort of hell-bent on collecting all my stuff and using that time to process it. I guess I needed to process it. I didn't know what to do with myself. I kept packing the stuff up. Finally, the creative manager came in and said, "I think you should go home." (Laughing.) You know, she was really nice. And I was really worried about that, I guess, because you certainly see how people get locked down, shut out quickly....

She stops to gather herself.

I think I was just...I'm sure I was just depressed. I remember feeling quiet, quieter than normal. It chokes me up now to think about it. Even a year later, it still hurts. It's like, you know, it does. I think it's really human.

One of the interesting things about the whole process for me is that of course it creates a certain kind of vulnerability. I think anybody who gets fired experiences that. I knew that fighting it was not really going to help any. I went through being laid off once before, and spent a number of years sort of fighting it, sort of bull in a china shop. So I think it opened up for me this understanding that there was something to be said for being vulnerable and open, and I think it's also has a little bit to do with age. Obviously, we hopefully get a little wiser. But there was a certain kind of vulnerability, and it's helped me to learn how to ask for help a little bit more.

I had seen so many people throughout the course of the year or two before also losing their jobs, and people getting really desperate in a way that was really striking to me, and sort of calling out for help to get jobs and stuff like that, and I guess something in me clicked too, that there's nothing wrong with that. That that's actually what you have to do. I mean, sometimes you have to be a little desperate for people to pay attention. And I'm definitely a very independent person, and I'm always, like, I take care of myself and stuff like that, and maybe this is age too, is just realizing that it doesn't always serve me. When you take care of yourself really well, nobody really offers to help you either, because they just figure you've got it all down pat, and you don't need any help. So it's even more important to ask for it—because nobody realizes that you need it. And I think that's certainly been true of me.

One of the things that happened in the course of having been laid off, or fired, or whatever you want to call it: A lot of stuff comes up, and one day I was sitting on the porch, and I remember I was blogging that I had more time on my hands—that I was not working, I was living. And I was sitting on the porch, and I open the mail, and you know these silly social security statements you get of how much money you've paid in and how much money you'll get and all this other stuff? It really struck me because my now-husband, then-partner and I had been together for 20-plus years, and it suddenly occurred to me, in this moment of vulnerability, that actually, we wouldn't be benefitting from one another's social security payments, despite the fact that we were probably common law, husband and wife, whatever. And so that created this other "ah-ha" moment in this vulnerability of realizing that we could actually take better care of each other as we got older if we were married, because there was no reason for us to be married until then. We didn't have kids. There was no sort of upside to it. And that little "ah-ha" moment started this conversation that we had for…I don't know if it was weeks or months, but we went back and forth, because over the years, one of us would want to; the other wouldn't. It was always back and forth but it was not a big deal, and it really started this conversation. At the end of the day, we ended up getting married and having a beautiful wedding in Hawaii.

I've been out of work about a little over a year now, and it's kind of gone up and down. Obviously. I mean, that's life too, right? I look for work every week to varying degrees of intensity but I've also explored what it feels like to not be working. Sometimes panic strikes. I have to say, the last two weeks, for some reason, I've felt really panic-stricken. But it's interesting, 'cause it's almost like I get more panicked when I actually have interviews. Like, I had an interview last week. And somehow that process puts me in this really stressed-out situation more than not working.

Out there, interviewing, it's really odd. You know, it's odd to be interviewed by twenty-somethings...I've now had two situations where I've been in interviews where the person I've interviewed with has literally thrown my resume across the table, in like, a very off-handed...Like, I don't even know what they were thinking, it's not a very respectful way to treat someone, no matter what their age. And yet that's kind of the environment you go into. In this time period, it's such a buyer's market that I think when you're out there interviewing, people feel perfectly okay with treating you any way they'd like, and I have to tell you: They're not very nice. It's really amazing. They're not courteous. And it's kind of shocking, really.

"A little post-it in your head"

Duncan Foster

He was born in Bristol, England and grew up for several years in Toronto, Canada, before moving to Burbank, California when he was eleven. Duncan, now 59, has moved about an hour south and lives with his wife in Orange Country.

His mother was from Edinburgh; his dad was an atomic engineer from London. "My dad was a good guy. He's dead. A year ago. It happened just after I got unemployed. A tough year. But you know, you get through it. You keep slogging away."

A tenor in his church choir, he speaks with a smooth, confident voice.

I was building edit bays and broadcast facilities. And for about ten years I did that successfully. Changed companies about three times, always looking for better opportunities, larger companies, better access to more equipment. What happened then was that the Avid came out—the Avid was the first computer-based editing system—and basically, my expertise with all these complicated devices, working on timing and code and master control and editing sequences and everything else—all that information became obsolete overnight. I looked at that, and I went, "Well, time to move on." So I had to remake myself. I went into AV design, which was just emerging. Projectors were coming out with the JVC huge projector, things like that.

All the way up until recently, anytime I made a job transition, inherently, they were most always by my instigation. I would work five to seven years, depending on the company. And then I'd leave on a Friday, start on a Monday at a new company. That's always been the transition.

I had been working in Burbank at a company called A—. After I was there for two years, they moved to Santa Clarita. My house is in Fountain Valley. So now I go driving from Fountain Valley to Magic Mountain everyday. So four hours a day of travel. Holy shit. But I was making a lot of money. And I was running the division, and I loved what I was doing, so I made the sacrifice.

A— had integrated all the Apple stores globally. And so we had done about $70 million dollars of installations all over the world. Basically all the wiring in an Apple store, all the screens, the LCDs, all the backbone, all the IT, and all the control. We would go in, rig it, wire it, put it together, hold their hands, get through the first day, have the line of people coming in and make sure everything was working. And it was intense work, but it was lucrative, and it was well done. We did projects for Disney—all big projects. They were competitive to bid, but we won. We had worked on a project rebuilding the Mark Taper Forum in downtown Los Angeles. We'd already wired the Hollywood Bowl two years before that.

Then the owner started looking at other projects we were doing, where the money was out one year, two years. They were big projects, million dollar projects. And they looked at their bankers that were getting tighter and tighter with funding our projects, and they got very nervous. They made a decision to eliminate my division completely. Here we were, so successful, and they eliminated the division, because they were afraid of the recession. They looked at what the bankers were doing with the tightening of the funds, they looked at all the scare stuff on the radio, and they freaked. They just freaked out.

I had actually been out—it's very interesting—I was in the hospital. I had gone in for gastric bypass surgery, because I had come down with diabetes. And so my doctor said—this is a year and six, seven months ago—and he said, "Okay, here's the deal. You've got Diabetes II. In five years, I'm going to start cutting things off: legs, whatever." He said, "Take the surgery. It will be gone."

And I said, "I don't like surgery."

He said, "I don't care if you like it or not. This will really solve the problem."

I have this surgery. I'm out for a week, and I come back in. The first day I'm back from surgery—and I'm not supposed to be back for two weeks—my boss says, "Don't come back. Just take two weeks off."

And I said, "I know I'm not well, but I want to come back. I've gotta keep things moving."

And he said, "We need to talk."

And I walk into the controller and sat down with him, and I said, "Well, what's going on?"

He said, "Well, I got some bad news. The partners have decided to close the division. And my job is to keep what you built alive long enough to make a controlled exit, and we'll finish these projects and then leave." Basically, he just said, "We're going to have to let you go. I'm giving you two weeks notice. I want to pay all the bills that we owe you. We owe you a $40,000 backlog from last year. We'll pay that." And he paid off all the monies that he owed me, and then I was gone. Two weeks notice. Two weeks after seven years and $50 million dollars…

You know what happens to you when you get those words, is you get very still. You get very, very still. You're cold, and you're numb. Because it's your life. You've got a wife. You've got children in college. You've got a boat. You've got your house. You've got your mortgage. You've got your bills. And your bills just kind of trickle-down like a little Post-It in your head, you know? You're just kind of seeing all that stuff, and you're thinking,

"Okay. How much money do I have in the bank? How long can I last?" You go into survival mode.

Car's full of all my junk and everything, my office, my life for the last seven years. And I looked at the buildings, and I just said, 'I won't be back. This is it,' you know? And I called my wife, and I said, "Hon, we've got a problem."

She said, "What?"

I said, "They just let me go."

She said, "What?"

I said, "Yeah."

She said, "But this is your first day back from surgery. How could they let you go? I mean, you're not even supposed to be there."

I said, "Their decision is to let me go now."

And of course, I'm not well, because I just had bypass surgery, and you know, even with a week—I mean, I had been on heavy drugs for four of those days, and I was in a lot of pain.

I said, "Okay. I've got a two hour drive to get home on a Thursday afternoon." I said, "I really gotta focus. I can't afford a car accident, even though I'm numb."

I drove all the way home. And I saw my wife, and we just sat at the living room and kind of stared at each other. I said, "I can't believe that they're doing this."

My wife said, "You know, you'll get a job," and "You've never been out of work." So I wasn't really worried. I figured I'm a professional. I'm highly credentialed. I have an incredible resume. Of course I'll have work.

Well then, I started the process. The next day, I started putting a resume together, because I hadn't had a resume in seven years. I had to put it all together. I knew some guy that was a headhunter in my boat club, and he volunteered to give me his resume writing services, and so we worked through about nine iterations to get it up to a professional level.

I started calling all of the companies that I would normally have worked for in the past. Contacted all of the people that I knew in the industry, which was a lot of people, and nobody was hiring. Nobody was hiring at all. Five companies that I had worked for in the past, three of them were no longer in existence. They had all folded in the last year because of the recession. Folded.

Now I'm used to leaving a job on a Friday and starting on a Monday. I'm out of my element now. And not only that, but because I was vice-president, I was extremely well-paid, so I'm now looking at trying to find something comparable to that. Making a quarter of a million dollars was not doable. I can't even get any sales positions, because I'm overqualified. So it was horrible. More and more people in my position were being laid off. All the middle managers are getting killed because they were heavily leveraged in pay, and you could immediately make a gain by eliminating them and keeping the soldiers working somehow.

And for six months I was out of work, without anything. I mean, I had unemployment, but I didn't have any opportunity to get a job. And I was interviewing all the time, and talking to people all the time, but everyone's saying, "You're a great guy. You've got this great reputation, but we're not hiring. In fact, we can't even figure out how to get the doors open right now."

People went into panic mode, and so if you thought you might lose a job, people were dropping their pricing, so from a standard margin of maybe 22%, it was now folding down to about 11%. Just to try to keep you going. Standard business was starting to dry up. Corporations stopped investing. They stopped building rooms. They stopped building videoconferencing. All of their projects went on hold.

Ignorance got me through it, because every day, I figured I'd have a job. And every day, I didn't, but I figured the next day I would have a job. I spent a lot of time at home doing home projects, getting things done, and I spent a lot of time studying the marketplace, trying to figure out an angle that would work. You know, someplace to really go. Secret to success is being value added, and if you're value added, it means you have something somebody else doesn't have. So you have to understand what the market is and what you can bring to the table. So, that all being said, I think not knowing I was going to be out that long is the only thing that sustained me. If I had known I was going to be out for six months, I would've freaked.

I finally took a position with another company called E—. They did the sound for the Super Bowl. The last project I won for them before I left was Pepperdine University, which was a $1.7 million dollar contract that I closed on my own. And we went in and we built that, and as soon as we finished that, I was gone. That was the end. Out of the blue.

I got called in, and he said, "You know, I've got bad news."

I said, "What?"

He said, "We're going to let you go."

And I said, "What? I did a million-seven!"

"We've morphed and we're part of this financial crunch, and my decision is to trim the newest employees—and that's you."

And I said, "Okay. I understand." You can do it with less. Make them work harder.

The guy said, "I hope you don't hate me for this." 'Cause, you know, I know the guy real well, and we were friends.

And I said, "Well, I'm not exactly pleased. I've done good work for you."

"We want to just fall back to where we know we're going to be okay until the recession's over, and then we'll see what we can do."

That's what they did.

I asked for four weeks, which he never gave me. He gave me two. And he said he would pay me commission for six months, which was fine.

I was shocked, because I didn't see that at all. And, you know, after a million-seven, you would think you were comfortable. And I knew that there was a lot of business that I was working on, but I felt I had made some good inroads. It wasn't right at the point that I wanted, but it was not zero.

I called my wife, I said, "One year later, babe, we're back where we started."

I'd already been through it once, so when this happened again, you're still numb. Because I had never actually been terminated ever in my life. I've never had that "we have bad news" talk. Here I am, within twelve months, getting it twice. And in one case, I'm managing a $10 million dollar department, and in another case, I'm managing about $1.7 in sales. So I'm trying to figure out what the hell's going on.

You understand, I'm used to every time I change jobs, I got hiring bonuses. Three to five thousand dollar hiring bonus. I was always moving up to get better and better pay. I would get guarantees for what I was doing, whatever. In the last year, no hiring bonuses, no guarantees. They bring you in at whatever they can get—usually the lowest they can get—and everybody's worrying about the bottom line. Everything's the bottom line right now.

Part of me goes, "Well, it's a fricking world recession, and you're in the middle of it, and you're just part of the carnage. You're sales-driven. I really had to talk to myself to continually reassure myself that it wasn't me. Because it makes you think, what did I do? I screwed up. How did I screw up? You start analyzing it. And then you go around in circles and you can't really nail anything, because you really didn't screw up.

So, very hard on my ego. You know, a lot of what you think you are—I mean I bought a 36-foot yacht. Beautiful boat. It's only three years old, brand new. I can be really strung out at work, and just tense, and I'll go, and I'll spend five minutes sitting on that boat, and I'm going, "Oh yeah. This is why I do this shit."

Got a beautiful home that was up to a million dollars at one point, now down. And, you know, three thousand square feet, and I remodeled it three times. Three kids, now almost through college. Two are in college. And one through a Master's program. And you're feeling pretty successful, and all of a sudden, you realize that you're zero. You don't have a job. You don't have any cash flow.

My wife works as a teacher, and so I have her income still, but her income is actually being pulled down, because they were pulling work from her too. She teaches math at Garden Grove high school. She was getting about five unpaid days a year. So she was seeing her income coming down very slightly, maybe $5,000 less a year. My income was coming down $145,000 a year. I was making about $250,000. You know, because between us, we were doing $350,000 a year. You do a million dollars in three years, right? So it's significant.

So I started cutting back on my bills. I got rid of my personal gym. I got rid of my personal trainer. I got rid of my cable. I didn't buy a new car.

I started paying off my car and just making sure the engine was running. I got rid of every little thing I could in overhead to trim our finances right down. And you're trying to figure out where you can dismantle your life to bring it down to about half of what it should be. And that's a painful process, you know? Very painful process.

There was an advertisement in the paper, a little cartoon on the wall, and it said, "Hiring: Those Who Are Unemployed Need Not Apply."

There is now a stigma. If you're out for more than six months, it's because you are incompetent. It's because there's something wrong with you. You're spoiled goods. And that's kind of where it's getting. Some of these people that I've talked to—I've had other sales people who have worked for me also that have been out of work for over 12, 13, 14 months—they could not get even interviews, because they said, "You've been out too long. Obviously, there's something very wrong with you; no one's hiring you." And you've got the stigma. When you're unemployed for a long period of time, psychologically, you're damaged. Your ego is way down. Your self-worth is way down. Your confidence is way down.

There's so many people who are desperate to contact people for sales that you can't even get to people anymore on the phone. They're not answering their phones. And you can't get to people with emails. They're not answering their emails. So how do you get to the clients? Because there's such a feeding frenzy of people trying to get hold of anyone to get business, that the people who have business are putting up walls. Huge walls. And it's really a disaster. Unless you have a personal relationship with that person and can break through the wall, how do you get though to them. They've got a huge 18-foot wall and a moat between me and them. We have grappling hooks. We have helicopters. But this is getting really insane. I mean, there's such a negative energy there that you have to overcome before you can even get to say, "Hi. I have a solution for you. Do you want to hear it?" So it's tough. It's a tough game.

Work is what you do in the day that defines who you think you are. You know, my minister would say, "That's bullshit. You are what God thinks you are." But really? You are what you think you are, and what you think you are is what you do with the 80% of the workweek. It's not your wife. It's not your children. It's not your things, your toys. It's what you do. That's who you are. And when they take that away from you—they being whatever—then you're nothing. You really are nothing at that point. Even though you still have a wonderful wife who loves you and adoring children who love you and parents who love you and friends who love you. Somehow, it never touches that hole...your own value and work are tarnished in a big way. A lot of people I know are on medications, antidepressants, Valium, drugs, whatever it is to dull it. Drink a lot.

The weirdest thing that happened was I left the church. After my second layoff. We were at rehearsal, making some comment about what we were doing in the tenor section or something, and I suddenly realized that I needed to get away from the church.

And I said, "You know what? I need to go find something new." Just like that, after 15 years. I've given it all my money. I've given it all my time. But I need to leave and start over again. I found that I wasn't getting fed. Music wasn't feeding me enough. And I need to get away, and I've got to get away from church, and I've got to get away from everything, and I need to find myself. Because there's so much angst. So much angst. Not that I was angry at the church. I just needed something totally new, totally absorbing, to keep me on an even keel while I dealt with this job stuff.

I look at my years, and I'm not a young chicken anymore. And you keep thinking, in your mind, "I thought it was going to be easier when you got older." I thought it would be easier when you're not in your acquiring mode: You're not buying houses, you're not buying boats, you're not putting kids in college. You're cutting down on the other side. And I don't see it getting easier. You're working and scrapping just like you did when you were in your 20s. And I'm glad I lost all the weight, and I got more aggressive, and, you know, tailored my clothes and did all the things I had to do to get back to where I needed to be to get more aggressive, because that's what we have to be. There's no gliding anymore, if there ever was.

"Lift and load"

Steven Hay

We're sitting on the back deck of his home in Spencertown, New York, perched on a hill. The Catskill Mountains are in the distance. Though urbanization seems galaxies away, Albany is, in fact, only 35 miles north. Steven's father, who bought TV time for advertisers, came to the area in 1979 and "built his log home two lots over. I helped after my famous tour with the teamsters delivering the wrong truck to Baltimore."

Steven is 54 and engaging—asking as many questions as he answers—and articulate. His mouth hides behind his bushy, graying mustache. His brain seems to move fast, gobbling up information and giving it in fluid rotation.

He has a been unemployed for over a year, and his benefits are set to run out at the end of the month. In preparation, he's made a change: "There's no local industry that needs my talents that I've been able to find yet, so that's why I'm going into real estate. That's my new job. I have my first client, possibly. They have not signed yet. I made the presentation to them to list their house, and they should be getting back to me."

The chair where Steven sits is positioned in the one spot at his home where he can get cell reception—but only rarely. "I get no cell phone reception on most every day. So that makes it difficult for my real estate business, but I'm trying."

It's 8:30 in the morning; we have an hour to talk before Steven has to leave for the park across from St. Peter's Church. "Today I'm going out to introduce myself to the community. They have a 'Summer in Spencertown' day, and we're going to put out a table, have a drawing for a wreath,[1] give out my business card, speak with the people, and say what I'm doing. Maybe they'll like me, and they'll consider me as their real estate agent." He seems to be a man that, calm and determined and capable, will, one way or another, make it work.

My father whispered to me—the way that the person in *The Graduate* said "plastics"—My father said "computers," 'cause I had taken a lot of computer courses, and I was always interested in them. So I started by taking a computer course.

I looked for a job and joined M—. In the old days, M— was "Mother Met," and they were wonderful. They took care of you. They understood when you had sickness or illness in the family, and as long as you did your job, you were taken care of for life. But after M— became a public company, roughly 2006, things began changing, and suddenly they were leaner and meaner, reporting to stockholders, and they started expanding consultants in their business units, and they decided that our unit would be a good candidate. I did I.D. administration for the Windows NT, Lotus Notes, Main Frame access.

M— decided that it would be really nice, after eleven and a half years, to unload my pension and my healthcare. They wouldn't have to worry about that anymore, and so we were now contractors for S—. We had to go through a drug test, and we had to be interviewed and say why we'd make a good S— employee. And then what they did they call a "lift and load." A lift and load means that you have the same person, the same

---

[1]   His wife, Eileen, specializes in assembling wreaths out of dried flowers and leaves.

computer, the same desk, the same office space, and in our case, the same line managers. Everything else is the same except now you're working for S—. S— didn't have a pension; they only offered the 401K.

I found myself after a year, being approached by my manager, 10:00am in the morning, and he came up to my desk, said, "Steve, you have to come with me now."

I said, "Okay, Dan," and I knew right away what it was 'cause other people had been let go earlier, six months before that, and they said it wasn't going to happen, they were done with staff reductions, but it turned out that this was not the case.

My manager was rushing me to get out the door, and he said, "We have to meet off-site. We have to meet off-site." So I grabbed my lunch, and I went off-site.

When I went to the Holiday Inn Express, I found they had rented a conference room, and Dan was there, his regional manager was there, and someone from HR at S—was there, and they told me that I was being let go. Not due to any performance issues, but simply that they no longer needed me.

We're sitting there in this Holiday Inn Express, and first thing they do is they tell me about COBRA, and all the different things I can do, benefits I have. Then they said that if I signed a nondisclosure agreement, I would get a nondisclosure payment.

So I said to them, "I think the reason that you're letting all the people go is because you're worried about age. You want younger people working for you." I said, "The three people that had been let go before were also older people in the group, and I'm the next oldest."

I didn't know at the time, but two other people had also been let go after me. They're rushing me through this exit interview, and I found out later that they had rented the conference room at the Holiday Inn Express for a certain length of time, and they wanted to get all the exit interviews done without paying extra time.

Rest of the day, I ate my lunch at the picnic area near the hot dog stand in the office park, and I waited for my manager to empty out my desk. She brought all my personal stuff out to my car on a trolley. It was very upsetting to get the boxes and boxes of your stuff. I guess it was annoying for my manager to have to pack it…(laughing)…but they couldn't let me back in to do it.

And then I came back to my wife at about one o'clock, and I said, "Guess what?"

And she said, "You been let go."

And I said, "Yes." I said, "Now we have to decide what we do next."

I went through the whole unemployment process. It turned out that I looked for a job—I put out about 100 resumes, I would estimate—and I had four interviews. Just had the fifth one, and I may have one more, and that will be it. What you know and what you do, your job may not exist anymore. Your job may not be available. A lot of companies may be off-shoring your job.

I'm now living in my parents' house. My parents passed away in 2005. My wife and I married in 2002, moved into a townhouse in East Greenbush, and then we had to sell it to move back here. It's very large for us, my parents liked to entertain. My wife, my daughter and I, there's just the three of us, and we're wondering how long we can hold onto this house with the expenses of real estate in New York and property tax and how much we have saved for retirement. And in 11 years, my daughter will go off to college, and we have to pay for that, and that big chunk of cash coming out at that time—$37,000 each year, I'm guessing now—that part won't go towards our retirement. And who knows, with medical care now. My parents lived to 79 and 81, if we could live to 97 or 88, will we have enough money to last that long, or will we be in the county home? Nursing home. We have no way of knowing. So it's an anxious time.

Human Resources

"I thought that was a positive thing"

Dominick Brocato

He is 58 and has lived in Kansas City all his life. His shirt is pressed and tucked. His hair is definitely not gray, nor do I think Dominick would allow it to become so. He carries a notepad encased in a leather pouch. His appearance is immaculate and I can confirm it is not easy to remain so well turned out in the July humidity that grips this city, wringing composure from those who are exposed to it.

Both my grandparents came from Italy. Palermo. My dad was a mechanic. It was very much a Ward and June Cleaver kind of environment. My mom stayed home all day, and she cooked, and she came home and wore the aprons. My mom died when I was 15 and it was devastating for me to go through that. My dad had no idea what to do at that point, how to run a family…I had a sister that was five, a brother that was seven, then I had an older brother that was 16.

I immediately took charge of the family and started doing all the things that needed to be done to keep the family together. My mom kind of trained me and taught me some of those kinds of things. And I think that just kind of carried on, and I always wanted to be a protector, and I think that's why I was always successful in the roles that I was in, because people trusted me. I've been in human resources for many years, and one of the things about human resources is that you're always there for other people, and you're always trying to help their lives and help them to see things in a different manner, and I guess I've always been good from that standpoint. I didn't want people to be scared. I wanted to create an environment where you look forward to going into work, and you don't feel pressured and you don't feel scared or intimidated—that, to me, is my responsibility.

For the last 20 years, I've worked for D— Systems. They recruited me two different times into the company. Both times were to help change the culture. They had gone through a lot of reorganizing back in 1987. They had a lot of turnover at the time when I joined the company. They finally decided after going through five different managers over a six-year period that maybe they needed to bring someone in that had people experience, and more people skills. And my background had been in human resources, so they took a chance and brought me in. Luckily, I was successful. The turnover within the first year had dropped approximately 20%. They approached me and asked if I'd be interested in being the employee relations manager for the entire operation. And so I did that.

After being in that role for about six months, the division was pulling away from D— to be a standalone entity, and they had asked would I be interested in coming and running that operation.

That lasted for about a year and a half. They had a different philosophy as to how they managed people, and because of their philosophy of empowering associates to do what's best for themselves—and if they did what's best for themselves, that was best for the company. Sounds good. But it didn't necessarily work. Associates were taking, like, 30 days of sick time a year and so forth. So at that point, in 2000, my old boss called me

and said, "You've got to come back and help put all this back together."
And so that's what I did.

And we totally changed the company around. A lot of the things we
were doing were kind of cutting edge, and it was exciting, it was fun,
making a difference, changing the culture, and putting things in place
that the company had not had before, and, you know, we were going in
the right direction, doing all of the right things.

In 2009, our existing Chief Operating Officer had made the decision he
was going to retire at the end of the year, so a new Chief Operating Officer
was brought in. He had different views towards how things should be run.
We knew that in the operation that he came from, which was in Boston, he
had had 12 layoffs in the last six years. So every six months, he had layoffs.
But we felt confident, because our President had said we were never going
to have a layoff. And we very much believed in what he had told us.

This particular Chief Operating Officer then, in that first year, wanted to
have a layoff around Thanksgiving time, and the President and exiting Chief
Operating Officer said, "No, we're not going to do that. That's not how we're
structured." The Chief Operating Officer who was retiring left in December,
and at the first of the year the new Chief Operating Officer went to the
Board of Directors, and he convinced them that the company needed to go
through this reorganizing and restructuring. And even though the President
fought it, my understanding is he was told to give it up, that they believed
in what the new Operating Officer stood for, and so that's what happened.

It was kept quiet somewhat, but I could tell that something was
changing. I knew something was going on.

Besides having all of the responsibilities for organizational
effectiveness and development, I had responsibility for quality assurance.
We were developing and putting in place a lot of different programs in
order to make it easier for a person off the street when it came to quality
checking the work. We were also speaking with some outside companies
as to what it was that they were doing. All of sudden, when it got to the
point where we were going to actually have these meetings with outside
companies, I was not invited. And again, I was in charge of that particular
department.

So, you know, at first I tried to tell myself, 'Okay, it's the high-level vice presidents that kind of want to talk through this,' but then, deep down, I really knew that that was not the case, that they were not including me in these meetings because I was not going to be around. So for those few weeks, I still had to manage myself. I had responsibility again for 1,000 associates within the operation. I still had my day-to-day responsibilities. And it was hard to keep, sometimes, that professionalism, and act like everything was okay when I knew, deep down, I was not going to be around.

The main person that brought me into the operation was moved to another division within the company. He respected me and believed in what I was doing, and that's why he brought me into the operation, but he was moved to another entity of the company and became President of that operation, and that's kind of when things started changing in my life, in my role.

The company then sent a letter out, probably about three weeks prior to the layoffs, saying that the company was going through a reorganizing and so forth, so, you know, at that point quite a few of us felt that we were part of that list again. You can tell, the way you're communicated with and the lack of the communication. So it wasn't a total shock from the standpoint that I knew something was happening.

It was hard through the holidays to know this stuff; I didn't say anything to my family, because I didn't want them to be worried about it—but yet, deep down, it was hard to be happy knowing that everything you had done for an operation, and all the people that really looked up to you and respected you and trusted you—which is another reason why I was brought into this role—all of a sudden, I was going to be out of the picture. I would say that probably during that November time period until it actually happened in February were some of the harder times in my life.

My actual date was February 4th of 2010. It was a Thursday. I still remember it very well. They had started on that Monday, and they had said that if you survived until Friday, that you were safe with this first round of layoffs. And so I got my call at 9:30am to come into a conference room, which is how they were doing it...

It was low-key. You know, they obviously just said, "Because of restructuring, your position now has been eliminated." They did it in a very effective manner, I have to say. It was very pleasant. I felt that I was very professional in the process, because again, I suspected that it was going to happen, and at that point, why be negative and why act in an unsatisfactory manner. I had heard that in some situations police had to be called and that sort of thing, and I would never do that, nor did I want my reputation to end that way with the company.

I still have the utmost respect for the company and for the President of our company. The new Chief Operating Officer, he doesn't know me. He doesn't know who I am. All he knows is a name and tenure and what I was making, and I'm guessing those were the reasons that decisions were being made.

The managers, you know, had a scripted process to go through—then there was a representative from an outplacement firm that you spoke with immediately. We were going to move into another conference room then to talk. It was occupied, and so she said, "Do you have a discomfort with us just going down to the deli and talking?"

And so I said, "No, that's fine."

On one hand, I'm thinking, what if people come up to me? And that did happen; a couple of people realized what was happening. One person was crying, and I thought, okay, I don't need this. So we finished our conversation as quickly as we could, and then she said, "We'll talk again on Monday when you come into the office."

I just kind of walked out the door, went to my car, and it was just, you know…it's kind of a surreal feeling of "this is really finally happening." The place I thought I was going to retire and never have to worry about—it's all changing.

D— was not the highest paying company in Kansas City; there were a lot more companies that were higher paying—but the one way I always sold good people coming into the company was that we were secure, that we've never had a layoff, and all of those types of things, which now I somewhat feel guilty I was saying all those things. Since February of 2010, there's probably been around 800 of us that have been let go.

I kept hinting to my wife that something is probably happening, but her being the type that worries about everything, I was just kind of very subtle with it. And she honestly did not know until the day I came home at 10:30 in the morning with the box that, you know...I said, "Hey, I'm starting outplacement on Monday, and we're going to work through this." I was positive.

She was just quiet because you know, my last son was graduating from college. I put three kids through college. We were finally thinking, "Finally, now, we're going to be able to live and travel and do stuff just for us," and I know she was sad thinking through that, realizing we finally got to this point and now this happens, so...I still think of that too, and still wonder why things happened the way they did, and obviously, you know, we always hear "there is a reason" and so you just kind of tell yourself, "Okay, it's gonna happen. I don't know when, but it's going to happen, and I'm going to understand why this happened at this time in my life." That's about all you can do.

I was anxious, and I was ready to get started and begin my new career, and so I started outplacement on Monday. They gave you a choice. They said you could wait 30 to 45 days to get your head straight and to do whatever you needed to be done, and at that point, I was very anxious to get the ball rolling. And I felt that I had enough skills that it was going to be fairly quick for me to find another position. I knew that now was time to start a new beginning, and I still try to have that feeling. But it's hard after 17 months to keep realizing that maybe something will never happen.

Done all of the things: I've been part of job clubs. I went back to school. I got an advanced certificate in employment law. I mean, I've done all the things that they say you're supposed to do when you're unemployed to show that you're not losing your skills and that sort of thing, but for whatever reason, it's not making a difference for me yet. And I'll say "yet" hoping that it's around the corner, but it's hard to keep staying positive when those things happen.

In the outplacement meetings that I went to, you have classes on how to present yourself, your appearance, how not to look old and keeping up with the times, and I felt like I've always done that. I'm thinking I'm doing everything that I'm told to do, that I'm trained to do, but yet, for whatever reason, it's not happening. And you still keep looking back at yourself, thinking, "Am I saying something wrong? Am I saying too much?" You keep trying to psychoanalyze everything to the point where you can drive yourself nuts.

I would say between April and August I probably had 45 to 50 different meetings that I would just initiate on my own, asking someone, "Can we just go have coffee, or just go to lunch?" So they'd get to know me and hopefully, if they remembered, they'd say, "Hey, Dominick, I met with him. He may be someone you want to talk to…"

I spent a lot of money doing that. The majority of people where I would say, "Can we just go to coffee?" I didn't get a lot of response. If I'd say, "Hey, let's go to lunch; I'll buy lunch," I got more takers. And that was okay, if I thought it was going to work to my benefit. Sometimes I would say, "You pick the place." I did that a few times, and after a $40 lunch I realized this isn't going to happen anymore. This is not fair. I guess I was really shocked that people would allow me to go ahead and pay knowing they're working and they're with a company, but again, I made the offer, and I was willing to do that. And I'd always try to end every meeting saying, "How can I help you?" And quite a few would take me up on that. So I mean, I always tried to leave it from that standpoint, followed-up with a thank you note, wrote out personal thank you notes, sent cards, had cards made with my name on the front. So I did all those things that I don't think the average person does.

I would say, from an Internet standpoint, I have filled out and put in resumes for about 380 to 390 positions. Of that, I would say I have heard back from maybe 20 people, which again, that's why they tell you in outplacement, "Don't waste your time on the boards." But after a while, you feel like that's the only thing you have left to do. You kind of run out of people that you could keep asking to go to lunch or go to coffee.

Interview-wise, I would say I've gone on maybe 40 interviews over the last 17 months. A lot of the times that I'm aware of I've gotten close and gotten in the top three candidates. But for whatever reason, have lost out. And like I say, sometimes you can find out just because, you know, I've been in the area for a long time. I've been part of a lot of human resource organizations within Kansas City. I have a lot of contacts, which I think shocks people, saying, "If anybody's got contacts, you do, so why isn't it working?" And then you start getting paranoid and self-conscious about that, thinking what is wrong? Why isn't this working? I've always been a dedicated, ethical employee. Always had positive reviews. My reviews over the last nine years with the company, I was ranked a 4 on a scale of 1 to 5, so I always had good performance.

I've always been in the role of helping others, so, you know, why can't you help yourself? I've always been in control. I'm the only one of my brothers and sisters that went to college, you know. They would always tease me about being the big shot and so forth, 'cause I wear suits to work...I've always been in roles where I had an office, and that sort of stuff. So I always feel like I have to work everything out internally, just like when my mom died, I had to work that out. Again, back then, you didn't go to counselors, nor could we afford to do that, but me and my brothers and sisters, we needed that. Why would someone that has four kids die at 36? We needed to work through that. And I don't think we ever honestly did, so I haven't...I read a lot of books, self-help and that sort of thing. You just try to figure out, there must have been a reason. Just like when someone dies, there must have been a reason...

I've run into people, I've run into guys that are selling shoes at Dillard's and so forth, and just thinking, "That can't happen to me. That's never going to happen to me." And now I'm realizing, with some of these guys that have been unemployed now for two years, that I'm getting close to that date. And how is this happening? How is this happening when I've been in such control?

I learned, obviously, now, after 17 months, that it has not necessarily easy to secure another position, and I think a lot of it had to do with my tenure with the company. In my mind, I thought that was a positive thing. I've learned that now, with the way the market is, that that's not a positive thing. I've learned in some meetings I've been in that companies are asking that recruiters and headhunters not even present them people that are 50 or older. They are not interested in people that have been unemployed for six months or longer, because they feel something must be wrong with them, that they have not been able to secure a job in that time period, which again is so disappointing to me to even hear those words, and then they also have made requirements that if someone has been in their job for 15 or more years, they're not interested in seeing them either, because they feel that they're set in their ways, and they haven't updated or learned new skills, so they would rather now have the individual that moves every two to three to five years. They feel that they are more valuable to them. So again, a lot of the things that we were brought up with—a lot of the ethical things that we thought were going to make us successful and that we did to show our dedication to a company—now is used against us. And obviously all those three things—being with the company for more than five years, being over 50, and being unemployed for more than six months—I have all three things against me, and as time goes on, I'm getting more concerned as to what's going to happen, and am I ever going to be able to secure another position.

I question now, going forward, what types of things need to be put in place to protect people, as myself, that are 50 or older. I wonder if something should be put in place, and I don't know if that would ever happen, that people who are 50 or older can't be let go from a job unless there is criteria or performance issues that should cause them to be let go.

I've continued to try, obviously, to secure a position, have even interviewed for positions making 50% less than what I was making before. But again, you're not given the opportunity because people are feeling—employers are feeling—well, you're just taking that until you find something else.

We're having a new Trader Joe's coming in, and when I found out that you have benefits even if you're a part-time employee, I thought, "Okay. Let me try this." Of course, I did. I called, and they said, "Well, you're at the bottom of 800, so we'll call you as soon as we go through the other 799 above you." I thought, "Wow." I don't know what those next steps are going to be, and like I say, for someone who has always been in control and educated and so forth, you never imagine that these times are happening. But they are.

For the last two months, I've…I don't want to say I've given up, but I've just kind of taken a break from all the stuff that I've done before, thinking I need to regroup. I need to get my head straight. I need to clear everything out. And so that's what I've done for the last two months, but yet every day you feel guilty: I should be doing this. I should be calling. But then you get to the point where you run out of people to call. That's kind of where I'm at right now.

We both have old cars. I've cut my cable and those sort of things. Obviously with the air conditioning and so forth, you kind of change the thermostat. This was the first new house that we lived in—we bought and built three and a half years ago. Next month the other house that we left would've been paid off. So of course, you constantly think of that stuff. And obviously I wouldn't have to then be pulling out of my 401K to make house payments and those sort of things, but we've done all of those things, which is making me sick because I always emphasize to new people coming into the company how critical it is to participate in 401K and all of those things. But, you know, at this point, in order to survive, I'm having to live off that and pay the penalties.

I have friends that keep telling me that I should try to apply for food stamps and so forth. I may get to that point, but right now…I can't force myself to do that yet and I don't know why. There's just something about it. Even going to unemployment. It was very difficult for me. I remember the first time I went. I had come from a networking meeting, and I was dressed business casual, and this one woman saw me, and she immediately came up to me, and she goes, "What are you doing here?"

And I said, "Well, it's my first day of…I have to fill out my continuation of benefits," or whatever.

And she goes, "Let me help you do that." She goes, "Because I see you don't fit in here."

I had a gold pen, and it was just gold—it wasn't real gold—and she goes, "Put that away." She goes, "You just use pencils here."

If you've ever had to go to an unemployment office…I'm self-conscious when I go. I don't even know what you do to get food stamps and that sort of thing—but I'm really hoping I don't have to get to that point.

The other negatives that I'm finding, at this point too, has to do with benefits. Obviously, the company provides you with COBRA for 18 months. Luckily, President Obama had put in place a subsidy, and so we were just paying 35% of the amount, and the companies were paying 65%, and again, that was a fabulous benefit to be put in place.

That's effective for only 15 months out of the 18 months. So starting in May, my benefits went from $333 a month to $1,000 a month. I never thought I was going to have to be concerned about that, because I was very much convinced that I was going to have a job by then.

I have been going through trying to find insurance, and I've hired two different brokers. I have been denied insurance coverage by every major company within Kansas City, because I had a pre-existing condition, and it was a pre-existing condition that started back in 2007, so the five years has not expired at this point. And companies will not insure me. And that's devastating. I've always been fairly healthy until I had this one issue. Now I'm realizing that possibly starting in August, I will not have medical coverage. And for someone that's always been in control, always tried to do the right things, always paid to have coverage and do the things that are appropriate, now we're in this position of not even being able to be protected. Now again, in 2014, that's all going to change because of the laws that are going to go into place—and hopefully still will go into place, even if things change at the top—but I'm not sure what I'm going to do.

I've even talked to the one doctor that I go to and said, "Okay, so starting in August, if I can't pay, how is that going to affect my still coming here to see you?" This was a conversation we had two weeks ago.

He was very silent. He didn't answer me.

You know, Truman Medical out here is where indigents go that have no insurance, or street people, whatever. And I said, "So, do I just need to start going there?"

And he goes, "Well, I'm sure they'll provide very good care for you."

I was totally taken aback by him answering me that way. He said, "We all want to get paid."

I'm going to have to now make some type of decision, and I'm not exactly sure what that is. I would venture to guess that there's probably a lot of us that are 50 or older that have some type of pre-existing thing that has happened that is now not going to be covered, nor are you able to get insurance for. You feel like you're just totally out-of-control, and you don't know how to get that control back.

I always used to tease my wife, because all she ever wanted to do was watch *Leave It to Beaver* and the *Andy Griffith Show*, and I'd say "Why is it that that's all you ever want to watch? There's so many things on TV."

And she said, "Life was so simple, and you didn't have to worry about everything that we have to worry about today." And she said, "I just want to pretend I'm back in that time again." And after she said it, I finally realized what she really meant. When you watch some of those shows, life was just easy. Kids could walk the streets, and it's amazing how different life is now compared to how things were back then, and obviously we didn't go through all of the things with employment and the economy...I mean, I'm sure there were some of those issues, but not to the degree that it is today. Will we ever get back that? It makes you wonder. That's one of the things that I've tried to emphasize when I do interview, is that we need to get back to the basics, and I think a lot of companies have gotten so far away from living the basics and really caring about the day-to-day and how people feel about coming to work.

"My profession is people"
Roni Chambers

She speaks often of pursuing balance and seems to have success finding it: she's a career corporate professional who references Lynrd Skynrd lyrics and bares a tattoo on her arm. She is a vibrant 55, a mother and a grandmother, and her smile makes frequent and infectious appearances.

I was born in D.C., and I spent most of my life in Florida. I worked down there and closed down a theme park. We laid off 900 people in Florida, Polk County. That was actually my first taste of this unemployment world. I got a pink slip but happened to make it through.

How's that? Why would they give you a pink slip and then let you make it through?

I made myself completely indispensable to the park president. I did the payroll when the place was closing down. I set up job fairs. I interacted with potential new employers, set up interviews, did things like that to try to get 900 people employed. I transitioned quickly into a place where he needed help. I was the sole breadwinner in my home, and I had three children to feed. When you have that burden, you find a way to make it work. So that's what I did. I became indispensable.

There was one position open. It was a trademark analyst position. I had no idea what a trademark analyst was. I didn't know what a trademark was. I have a horticulture degree. So I went to the Orlando Public Library, and I researched trademarks and copyrights, and I went on that interview, and I sold myself to that attorney, and he bought it...(smiles proudly)... and I became a copyright analyst.

I did that until AB— offered me a trademark job. And I came to St. Louis in 1991 with my three children in my station wagon taped together with duct tape to take a job here, which was the best thing I ever did.

In 2000 I took the position in Human Resources as an HR generalist. And it was great. I'm all about people—my profession is people. Our business model was about loyalty, and loyalty from the employee to the consumer, and all of the people in-between. During my very long, wonderful career at AB—, we didn't lay people off. We were a long-term career employer. And so that was an unfamiliar thing for us as people professionals at AB— until that awful day in November of 2008 when the merger deal closed, which was a takeover—that wasn't a merger.

At some level, it was intuitive that something was going to have to happen. I mean, there were $78 billion dollars in debt as a result of that merger. Takeover. So if you were astute—if you were paying attention, if you were at a certain level in the organization—then you knew what was going to happen. And it became apparent very fast that it was going to be a very different company. I mean, their business model was different from our business model.

We had 1,000 plus sales people all across the country. I found myself in a situation where it was going to be my responsibility to lead a team that was going to layoff those people. So, you know, there's a lot of backroom stuff that goes into that. The planning process is large. You bring everybody to the table: compensation and all of the backroom HR people, comp and employee assistance programs and security and payroll, and all of those people have to come to the table to make sure that the package is airtight. So we worked for quite a while doing that.

There was always lots of conversation. Lots of rumors. But you had to be pretty intuitive and astute to know that the planning was going on. It was very private, very confidential. And it had to be. I mean, for legal reasons, it had to be. To protect the company from what was going to happen. And as a people professional, I prided myself in making sure that those decisions were being made for the right reasons. There were certainly opportunities to eliminate people that one might not get along with, but we didn't go there....we made sure that we made the decisions correctly. It was a business.

What was it like keeping that private?

It was awful. It was awful. I can tell you that I cried for months. Yeah, it was really hard, emotionally and physically. I became a different person. It affects you. And not in a good way. Not at all. I had to work very hard to stay balanced. When you live in that world, you have to make sure that you surround yourself with really positive things. I mean, I watched the Hallmark Channel, because it's good. It feels good. It's like washing the sludge off of you at the end of the day. I had to take a shower. That's how bad it was.

We set out in five cities to bring people to the table to separate them from our company. There was an HR person and businessperson at the table. So the businessperson delivered the workforce reduction, the "for business reasons" conversation, and then the HR person pulled out the package and went through it and made sure that the person understood all of the elements of what was gonna happen. I didn't let them go back to their desks. I took their belongings that they brought to the table, and I walked them to the door. And I said, "Anything left at your desk, we'll send to you."

There were security guards at every single one of those layoffs. And if they weren't sitting publicly in the hallway, they were on the other side of the cubicle so that if there was ever an instance where I felt that I was in danger, that security guard was there.

In one day I probably separated—across the country, between myself and the rest of my team—a couple hundred people. And they were people that I had worked with for 20 years.

It's not just about that person. It's about everything that is part of them. So it's about children and spouses and mortgages and groceries in the pantry. It's more for me than just shaking someone's hand, taking the keys to their car, and their computer and their cell phone. It's about all that other stuff. And that was hard. That was tragic.

In St. Louis I worked with an amazing vice-president who, in the way business works, you would think would come to the table and deliver the message from a business perspective and not be touched by it. Most aren't. But this man, he was amazing. He didn't take the heart piece out of it like most businesses would. And I'll never forget him for that, because he allowed it to be the right way. He allowed it to be real. He allowed all of those people to cry, and he cried with them. And that was important to me.

We did fly a certain level of people here into St. Louis. I sat across the table from one gentleman who had been with AB— for his entire working career. He hadn't been paying attention, didn't really know why he was coming in. We didn't tell him why he was coming in.

To sit across the table from a man who's 45 or 50 and end a relationship that completely defines them—defines them as a man, defines them in their church, in their community, in their town—and to end that and watch that man cry will be with me forever. And it's really a shame that as human beings we allow that to happen. That was my biggest lesson in all of this. That changed me. I had to take his computer and his phone and his car keys and put him back on a plane, where he would have to take a cab home to tell his family that he didn't have a job anymore.

For 18 years, I hired people and helped develop them through leadership classes and spent some of my time mentoring employees and their managers through difficult communication problems and performance issues...to go on developing for 18 years then spend two years dismantling that and separating all of those people from what they came to call their family, that was hard.

Roni stops for a moment. I tell her that the horticulture degree she mentioned came to my mind—the image of nurturing a plant forever and ever and ever, and then being told to rip it up. She nods, steadies, and continues:

It was inevitable that once that business piece of it is gone, then the overhead has to go too. I was 55. I was expensive. And I'd been there a long time, 20 plus years. And so it was intuitive that if anybody was going to need to go, it was going to need to be…me.

I knew it was coming. And so I thought I was ready. In fact, there are some very young, bright HR professionals that have children that they still need to raise. And so I wanted it to be me, so they could stay and feed their kids. And I don't mean that in any martyr-y kind of way. My kids are all grown and gone, and they have their own children, and my weddings are paid for, and my college educations are paid for.

It became clear in probably late 2009 that the human resource department would be in the next batch. So I started to get ready to do that, prepare for that. Emotionally.

On March 15th my boss came and sat down at my desk and he had his little white packet.

"This is it, Roni."

And of course, I knew what that little white packet was, because I had delivered hundreds of them. There was no reason to go through it. It was what we did. It was what we'd been doing since the end of 2008. There wasn't much else done. It was "cut people." From the time of the takeover until the time I left, we'd been downsizing.

I had prepared, to the extent that I didn't have seven boxes to take out with me. I had one little box. It was awkward. To walk out of a place that you've been going to for so many years, to say goodbye… when I walked out—like that man that I described earlier—my identity was that too. I didn't know it until I got on the other side of the bricks and mortar at 1 AB— Place. But it became quickly apparent to me… and I reference it as the bricks and mortar because it is tangible. It's a building. It was my home. I mean, I remember at 35 being this young, naïve girl coming from this beach state where I had this great job in the sun to this. I had never been in a ten-story building, or even a nine-story building. (Laughing.) I'm telling you, I walked up to the door that very first day. It was September 1st, 1991. I had my little briefcase in my hand, and it was empty. (Laughs.) And my purse. And I walked up to the front doors of that building, and I looked up, and I thought, "How in the hell did I get here?" I couldn't believe it. And 20 years later, I come out of that building with a box, and I couldn't believe it. Although I knew, I couldn't believe it. So what do you say? You just go. You just go.

I went home and told my kids. And one of them was living at my house with his wife and new baby between selling a house and buying a house. You know, we opened the wine bottles and spent the evening talking about our blessings. There were no tears that night. I was very happy in the beginning. The first three days, I felt free.

And then the emotional part hit, and it was big. I cried a lot. I slept a lot. I drank a lot. And I ate a lot. I didn't talk to too many people. I didn't go out in public. I didn't interact with anybody. I worked in my yard. I broke all my nails. I was in the dirt. It was sort of a nurturing thing that was going on: I couldn't help people anymore, so I was sort of working in my yard. And it was like my whole life changed. And it's hard to even put words to what happens to you, how you feel.

In my severance package, AB— gave me an outplacement opportunity. I wasn't ready to engage in that right away, but it had a time limit. I was getting close to the end of that time limit so I needed to engage that service. So 60 days in, I called this outplacement company, and I thought I'd healed myself to the point where I could go sit and talk to somebody, which, in fact, was really way too soon. That didn't work for me. It was very medicinal. It was like going to the doctor's office. And it just wasn't good. It was actually a waste of money for AB— to buy that for me. I sat in that office and cried. Again, remember: I was prepared, and I'm still crying 60 days later!

I had great skills. I was a respected part of the senior leadership team at AB—. I was a director. And believe me, you don't get to director's level at AB—as a woman—very easily. So, you know, I've done my work.

And I thought I knew what I was walking into. But I will tell you: What I learned out here is that this is a whole different world. The last time I looked for a job was, like, in 1985, and everybody in those days had recruiting offices, and you went into a recruiting office and you filled out your application, and I don't even think I had a resume. You just filled out an application and, you know, you connected with a recruiter, and he liked you, or she liked you, and there was a job board, and "Oh, this job looks good for you," and you get interviewed and you get hired. And I thought I could do that. But that's not what this world is like anymore. There are no more recruiting offices. There are no people like that. It's all done on job boards—Monster and CareerBuilders and all those places. But there's no physical touch there. So you can't sell yourself. You have to do it on a piece of paper, and they all look the same.

Part of the work that I had to do emotionally was I had to figure out who I was. And that doesn't come easy at 55, when you've spent 20 plus years in one building. So I had a lot of peeling back the layers to try to figure out who it was that I was. And you can't successfully get involved in a job search until you've done that. So there's a lot of work that somebody has to do to even be ready to look for a job in a complicated job search market. Because it's not about going in the front door anymore. It's about going in the back door.

I wanted to blow this city. I needed to be someplace outdoors. So in March of this year, I sold my house, and I moved to the country. And I bought 10 acres and a barn and a pond and horses…a garden. I'm thinking, "Gosh, I can grow my food."

I'm 55. Ten acres? Horses? Tractors? What the hell am I doing? But I had to do it. I'd never had a horse in my life, but every time I was around a horse, it touched my soul. When you're forced to make decisions, you make them. When you aren't forced, you don't. So when we aren't put in difficult situations, life goes on. It passes us by. And part of that life-changing thing for me when I walked out of 1 AB— Place was I needed to learn how to live it every single day, with risk every day. It's never safe. It should never be safe. It should never be complacent and comfortable. And so shame on us for getting there. We miss it. We sleep through it.

As tragic as I make it sound—because it was at the time—it has become, along with having my children, one of the most important events in my life. Because it changed my life forever, and in a positive way. Hard. Still not making any money. This is all volunteer.

She motions to the empty room behind her. We're sitting on a small stage in front of approximately 300 chairs, in a downtown building owned by the Catholic church. Roni is the executive director of The GO! Network, which has been given most of the floor of this building to run the non-profit charged with helping the unemployed community in St. Louis.

I found this place quite by accident. I came, and I never left. And I never left because GO! Network—in addition to all of the tangible stuff— the skill building for the 40 to 60 year old that needs to learn how to write a resume and do an elevator speech and get in front of a team of people that are doing behavioral interviews—in addition to all of that, we're about hope and encouragement. That's really what this is about. This is about a community coming together and supporting each other to become retooled for redeployment in the community.

I talk to people about it all the time: this is about recreating yourself, and in the space in which we look for jobs. So you have to recognize— you have to know—first of all, you gotta know who you are. And you gotta be going after the right jobs, because having been on the other side of that desk and looking at a stack of 200 resumes, I can tell you: They're not looking at the stack of 200 resumes. If there's a connection, that goes to the top. They're doing word searches. So if there's a keyword, and you've got it in your resume—and I will tell you, there are even people out here in this job world who put a keyword in there that doesn't have anything to do with their resume, and they make it white. They don't black ink it. They white ink it, so you can't see it. But it gets picked up in the word search, and you end up in the stack, but you really have no business being in the stack. This is desperation. This is "How do I get in the stack?" "How do I take myself from 200 to five?"

I'm in this age bracket where, I mean, we're all 40 to 60. And it's about relevance. It's our responsibility to make ourselves relevant. If it means dye your hair, you dye your hair. You have to be responsible for making those decisions. And unfortunately, at 55 or 57 or 48, sometimes you're just not...you can't get there. And I'm worried about those people, because I'm not sure they'll get employed. And that's the scary part. Not everybody can make that transition, and as a country, that scares the hell out of me.

If I go back and look at sort of the landscape of St. Louis in the last 20 years, Ford's gone, and Chrysler's gone, and Union Pacific's gone, and Southwestern Bell is gone, and AB— is almost gone, and hundreds of people have been put on the street. And their jobs are never coming back. So they have to find something else to do. And that's what we try to do here. My work is about nurture. That's the definition of work for me: nurture. People think that because all of these job openings are in places that are technology-driven—all in cyberspace—that it's a high-tech job search. It's really a high-touch job search. And it's high-touch through the relationships that you make in all those coffee shops, in all those volunteer opportunities, in your churches and your schools and all the things that you do when you put on your suit and you go out into the world with no place to go.

High-Touch

"I'm one of these numbers in there"

Dawn Eilers-Dunn

Dawn, 54, is counting on her fingers all of the people on her suburban block in Irvine, California, who are unemployed: "on our short little street, there's been many of us that have been affected…you don't have to go far to find people that have been affected by this."

She's marred with two kids, 17 and 20. She was born in Southern California and graduated from the UCLA. Aside from a short stint in New Jersey, she's always been a west coaster. She knows this sunshine well enough to stare into it without sunglasses.

Dawn built a successful career in Human Resources, chiefly defined by 22 years working for a national bank. She did her personal banking with the bank that laid her off. When she deposited her severance check they held it for seven days. For seven days they held the check they, themselves, had written.

When she talks about her job she still catches herself using "we": "We generally are a little more hands-on. We? My god. Holy crap, where'd that come from?"

I think we kind of knew that a date was coming up, and we knew we were expecting something. We had somewhat heard through the grapevine that they were going to maybe take one person from our department.

I didn't get a phone call. It's this email just to me...I mean, here's the email to me:

From: ▮▮▮▮, Irene
Sent: Monday, November 10, 2008 9:54 AM
To: Eilers-Dunn, Dawn
Subject: Position Elimination Letter and Release

<<Dawn Eilers-Dunn.pdf>>

There is no, "Hi Dawn, this is Irene. We finally got the information." There is not even an intro on it. All it has is this attachment:

▮▮▮▮▮▮▮▮▮▮▮& CO.

POSITION ELIMINATION OVERVIEW 11/10/2008

Dawn Eilers-Dunn 578951
Job Title: EEO/Dispute Res Cnsltnt-Sr
Most Recent Hire Date: 01/30/1987
Termination Date: 01/08/2009

As a result of integrating our businesses and determining our current staffing needs, your position will be eliminated and your employment at ▮▮▮▮▮▮▮▮▮ a division of ▮▮▮▮▮▮▮ Bank, N.A. (collectively with all its affiliates, subsidiaries and parent, the "Firm"), is scheduled to end on the Termination Date above. This Notice Letter is intended to provide you with answers to your immediate questions about your position elimination and summarizes the severance pay and related benefits and services for which you may be eligible. More information is available on the Severance-Related Resources site on ▮▮▮▮.net.

EXHIBIT A
DATASHEET

The following information is provided to employees of ▮▮▮▮▮▮▮▮ Bank, N.A. or its affiliates and subsidiaries (the "Firm") who have been selected to enter into a Release Agreement ("Agreement") with Firm in connection with the reduction in force at ▮▮▮ Von Karman Ave, Irvine, CA 92614 during the notification period effective 11/10/2008 through the Termination Date of 01/08/2009 (the RIF):

1. The decisional unit is the group from which the Firm chose which persons would or would not be part of the RIF and offered an Agreement in connection with the Employee Relations - Waugh.

2. The class, unit or group of individuals eligible to receive the consideration under the Agreement are all persons in the decisional unit who were selected for the RIF and offered a Release Agreement. Individuals were selected based upon business needs.

3. To obtain the consideration set forth in the Agreement, an eligible employee must sign and return an Agreement provided by the Firm no earlier than 60 days before Termination Date (11/10/2008) and no later than 15 days prior to Termination Date (12/25/2008). Once the signed Agreement is returned to Firm, the employee has seven (7) days to revoke the Agreement.

4. The job titles and ages of persons in the decisional unit and information as to whether each such employee has been selected for separation in connection with the RIF are listed below.

I'm one of these numbers in there:

Age Distribution Report

ER Consulting
Current 1/8/2009

Age	Selection Decision	Number of Employees		Salary Grade	Job Title
32	To Be Released	1	(1)	L10	Employee Relations Analyst
33	To Be Released	1	(1)	L08	Employee Relations Cnsltnt-Sr
35	Retained	1	(1)	L08	EEO/Dispute Res Cnsltnt-Sr
	To Be Released	1	(1)	L09	Employee Relations Consultant
38	To Be Released	2	(2)	L08	Employee Relations Cnsltnt-Sr
39	To Be Released	1	(1)	L08	Employee Relations Cnsltnt-Sr
40	To Be Released	2	(1)	L08	Employee Relations Cnsltnt-Sr
			(1)	L09	Employee Relations Consultant
43	To Be Released	2	(1)	L07	Regl Mgr-Employee Relations
			(1)	L08	Employee Relations Cnsltnt-Sr
44	To Be Released	2	(1)	L07	Regl Mgr-Employee Relations
			(1)	L08	Employee Relations Cnsltnt-Sr
45	To Be Released	3	(2)	L08	Employee Relations Cnsltnt-Sr
			(1)	L09	Employee Relations Consultant
46	To Be Released	1	(1)	L08	EEO/Dispute Res Cnsltnt-Sr
47	To Be Released	3	(3)	L08	Employee Relations Cnsltnt-Sr
48	To Be Released	3	(1)	L07	Regl Mgr-Employee Relations
			(2)	L08	Employee Relations Cnsltnt-Sr
49	To Be Released	1	(1)	L11	Admin Assistant
51	To Be Released	5	(1)	L07	Regl Mgr-Employee Relations
			(2)	L08	EEO/Dispute Res Cnsltnt-Sr
			(2)	L08	Employee Relations Cnsltnt-Sr
52	To Be Released	4	(1)	L07	Regl Mgr-Employee Relations
			(2)	L08	Employee Relations Cnsltnt-Sr
			(1)	L11	Admin Assistant
54	To Be Released	1	(1)	L08	Employee Relations Cnsltnt-Sr
56	To Be Released	1	(1)	L08	Employee Relations Cnsltnt-Sr
57	To Be Released	3	(3)	L08	Employee Relations Cnsltnt-Sr
58	To Be Released	1	(1)	L08	Employee Relations Cnsltnt-Sr
59	To Be Released	2	(1)	L07	Regl Mgr-Employee Relations
			(1)	L08	Employee Relations Cnsltnt-Sr
60	To Be Released	1	(1)	L08	EEO/Dispute Res Cnsltnt-Sr
61	To Be Released	3	(3)	L08	Employee Relations Cnsltnt-Sr
70	To Be Released	1	(1)	L08	Employee Relations Cnsltnt-Sr

That's about as personal as it got. Let me just say this: I was leaving a job of 22 years of service, and everything happened by email. That's what kind of struck me...there was nothing personal about it.

I would go into court for the company and fight for them. I represented the company with discrimination claims and employee complaints—stuff like that. So very much wore the corporate hat. And covered their ass. I covered their ass big-time. You just have this, this like "I am the company"-type attitude. Even though there's always a part of you that kind of protects yourself. One of my jobs at one point was to write for the company communications, and, you know, schmooze: the corporate mission statement, that crap. And massaging it, how to make a horrible issue sound great. It took me a long time to learn how to write that way, because I'm more blunt. How can you possibly make this sound like your almost happy that you're health premiums went up 50%? You know, that's hard to do. It took me a long time to learn how to write that way. And I'm sorry to say that I got better at it, but that doesn't mean I felt good about it.

So what did you do the day you got the email?

I think I called my peers. I remember feeling kind of shaky.

I had to wrap up all my work. I think part of it is that there was my one peer who was going to remain, and whatever I didn't finish was going to go to her, and I…I thought I wouldn't want to be the guy left behind. The guy left behind is going to die.

The company was very decentralized, so I worked with probably five people here in Irvine, and my boss was in Chatsworth, which is 75 miles away, and corporate at the time was up in Seattle. But I worked in a department with about five peers. Everybody's all over the country. So everybody, we all communicated via email or phone calls. I printed out some emails, just of people saying goodbye:

Thank you for all of your hard work and dedication. You made such a good team
and I appreciated all that you did. Your work was always noticed by peers and
managers. All I heard was constant praise about each of you and deservingly so.

Please keep in touch and feel free to call me for anything work-related too.
Here is my personal info.

I am sending this message before my access stops. I only had the opportunity to
meet many of you in person a few times but feel I know everyone well as a result
of our many conference calls. I have been fortunate to work with the finest
ER/HR professionals in my career here at ███. I wish you all THE BEST.

Regards,
Ken

Although I expressed my sentiments during our December all-up call, I just want
to take this one last opportunity to say what a privilege it has been to work
with such an incredible team of HR professionals over the last (almost) 4 years.
It has truly been the best job I've had so far and I will miss ███ and all of
you terribly. However, I'm comforted by the fact that not only are you all very
talented professionally, you are also good, caring, hard-working people that any
company would be lucky to have on their team. I'm certain you will all find
opportunities that although unknown at this point, (and if you're feeling what
I'm feeling right now a little scared of the unknown!) they will have their own
unique gifts of new challenges and new relationships. I always say that the
best part of any work experience are the lifelong relationships we build with
special people....so thank you for all the memories and what I know will be
long-lasting relationships. This is not a goodbye, but an au revior, as I know
I'll see or speak with all of you again in the future.

Please feel free to reach out to me if I can help in any way with your job
search. Take care and best of luck!!!!

With Love.....M

I just recall my last day. I was completely by myself. There was no goodbye party. There was no nothing. I was responsible for packing up all my stuff. You know, I could've dumped files if I wanted to, but I didn't. My last day, I was, you know, in my office by myself with boxes, and I remember having to do the old—literally, the old—schlepping out your stuff. Putting stuff on a rolling chair and rolling it out the door. That was a bummer, because you...I gotta admit, it was a very lonely kind of...22 years, and there's nobody there. I walked out and...I hugged the security guard. And that was it. I was just like, "Wow. Okay. 22 years."

"Cancer: so happy it's not me"

Renee Zimmerman

I was a very senior paralegal in real estate finance. I was making a pretty decent salary. So it was a very big fall from grace, to say the least.

The first time I talked to Renee we met in New York City, near the office where she is currently doing a bit of contracted work. We sat at a small bar in a nice restaurant in Hell's Kitchen. The bar was probably a bit too small for Renee. Many bars might be too small for Renee. She is petit, yes, but she's also feisty and her personality does not reconfigure to any room. Every time she walks through the door she is, to her credit, unabashedly herself.

We've now reconvened in her small home in Union Beach, New Jersey—just a short walk from the ocean. She hasn't been in the place long but she's already put a lot of work into it. Renee is a youthful 50 with her hair tightly pulled back, and her ex-boyfriend—the "he" referenced throughout her account—is in the backyard, trying to set

up a giant lawn canopy for the summer. Every now and then they
yell back and forth at each other, neither hearing the other clearly.

I had called him up—he was an old boyfriend of mine. I had this foolish dream—for many, many years, I had believed that I had had a true love in my life. And it was him. I looked on Google—he was easy to find, he had that fake business and storefront—and I left a message. And he called me an hour later. And so we got together. And he pursued the hell out of me. Showing up at Prospect Park at seven o'clock in the morning and hanging around and just showing up and showing up and sucked me in.

So here I am, that morning. 4:30 in the morning, and I don't like getting up before the birds. And I'm getting up because he wants to go skiing. I was going for him, because I don't care about skiing. We pull into Hunter Mountain, the crack of freaking dawn. Sun is just coming up, and my phone rings. And it's a knee-jerk. Your phone rings. You have it. You answer it. I pick up the phone. I answer it.

"Hi Renee." Carrie takes the lead: "As you know, Renee, we've been looking into the paralegal staff, and we've not been busy," and da da da, and, you know, "We have to downsize. Unfortunately..."—and you can hear the chuckle in the back of her throat—"...we have to let you go...and don't come back into the office. We'll send you your things." And that's it. You're not getting paid...if you want a severance, we'll throw you two weeks pay like you're a dog...

So I'm in the parking lot, and of course, now I'm thinking, "F you."

When this happens my face turns white. He knows that this is like... "What happened? What did they say?" Because of course now, everybody gets curious, because it's the curiosity factor, which I really hate. "What did they say?" What the hell does it matter? I just got basically thrown out the door!

I had packed wine and food and I opened it in the car right after the call. Oh yeah, nine o'clock. Open that bottle. I never really had any shame about drinking early anyway, but oh, this time, it was open that sucker right now.

It caught me off-guard. And I never expected a phone call. Not on my day off. And so the whole of it: All the blood goes out of your face.

Your heart's beating in your stomach. Fear it was a new feeling to me, unfortunately. I know this ugly feeling.

It's sooner than I wanted it. And I choke. I needed another couple months, because I needed my house to be two years old. I needed a little more money in the bank. I needed just a little more distance. I'm trying to be calm. Later, I cry. I do cry later. Overwhelmed. I don't really cry out of boo-hoo sadness. I cry out of frustration. I do, like, emotional eruptions. Frustration. Anger. 'Cause I do anger so well. And the only person you hurt is yourself. Nobody else feels your anger. I do wish they could.

I went in to go to the bathroom, because immediately I had a bowel...I could feel my body was just reacting. When I come out, I don't know what to do with myself. And so I think we went across the street to get breakfast, because I wasn't going into the lodge. I was so miserable. I was just thinking, get home and just start getting organized. I'm thinking, I've got this brand new duplex that I now have to get rid of. Because this is an enormous chunk of change—$3,000 a month—an interest-only loan. And it's gonna suck through my savings in a heartbeat, because I'm getting $400 a week, and I'm going to have to pay taxes on it.

The drive home is longer than ever. It's over three hours of just stuck in the car time. And I'm really trying to focus on what I need to do next. Open bottle in the car. I drank it all the way home. I didn't care. Kill me now.

Then the phone calls start from people from the office. "Oh, we heard," and you're fun gossip. You're fodder for the day. And I know that. So it's...I don't even want to call it a double-edged sword. It's a one-edged sword, 'cause it's just coming right for your throat, 'cause everybody's happy it's not them. Cancer: so happy it's not me. And by all means, poo poo for you, so sad, but I'm so glad it's not me. And, "Oh, we heard this," and "Did you do that?" and "How do you feel?" Because you want to hear me crying. You want to hear me broken. And I'm not doing that. I'm not doing that.

I just jump into get-rid-of-this-house mode. Start taking photos and really start focusing on that. But I'm never thinking, for a second, that it's gonna take that long for me to jump back into the job market. Resumes, you know, I've got everything up-to-date, ready to go.

I'm thinking I'm going to get this house on the market and everything's going to be fine. I knew I would sell it. I never expected the market to fall out and continue to fall out, because it had already been two years in the process, from 2007 to 2009, had already been so much going down that how much further could this possibly go? And of course, as you see, we're still going. And it's not going to end anytime soon.

Thank god a contract was signed but it went through every dime I ever had. My buffer zone was gone. And any dollar I made on the house was gone with it.

Whatever it's going to take…I'm just going to plug through. Went back to school and got an appraisal degree. Went to school one night. And my boyfriend moved all his stuff out. While I was at school. So I came home to a note that said: "I don't want to live with you anymore."

Okay.

The years leading up to this, I was financially in a much better position. He didn't pay for nothing. He got wined and dined like a company on a daily basis, while he's going through his divorce.

You can only give away your self-esteem. No one can take it from you. You have to give it away. And I wasn't willing to give it away. You can take my job. You can take my position. You can't take the person that I have built from the ashes. You can't. I won't give that to you. That's not for sale.

I really thought I was prepared. And I thought, maybe six months. And I had no idea how. A few years ago, you felt that you had a value. That you were a value added to that position. That's over. You are just a dog, a clog in the wheel, and just go. It's that environment.

And the bleed factor: We will take you in as a temp. We will make you work many, many hours without pay, because you have to. And you can't complain about it or even so much as look like it bothers you.

Now I'm just grabbing at straws. I can't even get a $15 dollar flipping-a-burger job. I'll take a job. I'll let them throw whatever they want to throw at me, 'cause I have to take it if I want to survive. There's nothing to look for. And I can't just go bartend, or go do something…Because they don't even exist. There is no under the table anymore. So I'm getting my $400 dollars a week, and I'm cleaning, and I'm cooking, and you know, I'm working.

Nobody really has a clue what it feels like to just have nothing and no one to count on but yourself. And you're a disease. If people have you around, they might catch it. So you're not invited to things, because you're Debbie Downer. You're not fun to be around, because everybody wants to complain about their jobs.

I have fallen so many times and never, ever got the option to just lay there. Because nobody's coming...Nobody's coming to rescue you. There's no knight in shining armor. There's no fantasy. Good luck and have at it. I can't count on a job. I can't count on my loved ones. I can't count on a marriage. I learned so early to count on nothing. It changes everything about you.

I realized this morning, like a wounded animal, people do not want to help you. They want you dead. Like a wounded dog. No other dog is coming to do anything good. They're not coming to lick your wound. No, no, no. They're coming to bite you, 'cause you're down. And if anything I found during that entire time, every person, every thing in my life went full-blown attack. Nothing became better. If you weren't ready to help yourself, there was nobody there ready to help you. It was just not optional.

I think it's kind of survival of the fittest.

"He could look like he's about to cry, you don't know"

John Bauman

He is the consummate salesman, gregarious and energetic—he always seems to be hopping just a bit, even when sitting. His wife, a successful accountant with an MBA, was invited to interview for her current job after John infiltrated a conversation he overheard in the locker room of his gym: "I walked over to them and introduced myself and said I've got a great person that would work for what you guys are talking about. Hey you never know, those are the places where the conversations are happening—the joke about the golf course: I mean, if you're out there hearing the conversations, you're out there."

John, 32, grew up in Cleveland in a middle class family. His parents put him and his two siblings through college. "My mom makes the joke, don't expect anything when she's dead, 'cause she gave it to me for college. And she's like, that piece of paper is gonna get you farther than the forty grand I give you when I die. And I think that's huge, I really do, that piece of paper opened up way more doors for me than what that cash is gonna get me down the road. That's gonna make the cash in my opinion."

He and his wife have a nine-month-old daughter. John would like to provide for her the same opportunity and pay for college. "I feel like there's enough stress out there when you're trying to figure out who you are as a person when you're getting out of college. To take some of that out of the equation so they can figure out what they want to do, I mean, that's big for me. I'd like to be able to provide that."

He graduated from the University of Dayton in 2001 and went into medical sales.

He was laid off in the summer of 2009.

I was with the K—divisions for almost five years. K— manufactures everything from surgical packs to products that you're going to use on wounds to catheters—you name it, they manufacture it. What our job is, is to go out to either hospitals, long term care facilities, home health facilities, talk to the people that are purchasing these products, and get them to use yours versus the other seven manufacturers that are calling on them for the same exact products.

I had some success all five years. There was never a year where my numbers or quality of work was ever a concern. If you do well for them and you make them a lot of money, they end up rewarding you with trips and nice commission checks. I had a great living coming in for my wife and myself.

In the sales world, all of us live in our cars, all day long, or in our home offices. We are constantly on the phone with each other. When you get into the medical world…you're kind of out on your own island. So you have to be in communication with other reps in other cities like it's an office. It kind of keeps you going. So the conversations are always on the phone with each other and you're all, "What's going on out there? What's the new product coming out?" That happens multiple times throughout the week.

As soon as you find out a conference call is coming from the sales force, doesn't matter if it's a basic conference call about changing of insurance or a new product coming out, there's multiple conversations going on until that conference call happens. So I'm on the phone all morning, going, "Alright what'd you hear?" 'Cause some have their ear to more people at corporate and they kind of get more of the buzz. So of course you're calling the people who have the relationships with the people at corporate.

You find out very quickly that it's something going on with the structure of the organization. You think it's like the head guys, you always think it's gonna be middle management—in our industry, they'll move around the guys that are two pay grades above you, they're the ones that get moved on to another position way before the sales rep. The sales reps are the guys that are the foot soldiers, that are out there, they need you talking to the people that are purchasing from you. So you never think it's gonna be the reps. Maybe that's naive. But you feel like you're the one a little bit further away from it. So that morning, when you start hearing that it's about the structure of the organization, you don't think it has anything to do with you, like, eh, maybe it's your boss, you know, that kind of scenario.

Well, then you find out on that phone call, it hits—and you're hearing the VP of sales telling you, "It's everybody. We're not just looking at middle management, we're not looking at management—we're looking at the whole division." They were lettin' us know that we were all going to be losing our jobs.

I was in a parking lot of a gas station sitting there in the air conditioning because it was like the beginning of the summer. I was sitting in the car listening to it on speakerphone with a dropped look on my face going, you gotta be kidding me—right now? Like, this is not how I expected this conversation to go. It just…It's like a dagger to you. You know, you're just like, what am I gonna do? Holy crap, this is big.

They open it up for brief discussion, questions. But at the time it was so quiet on the other end. And at a lot of times it's quiet because most people mute their phones because we're in cars, we're on highways, people are ordering coffees. The guy who doesn't mute his phone with his dog barking, you're kind of "M-f-ing!" to yourself because you're like, "Put your phone on mute, I don't wanna hear your dog or your washing machine." (Laughs.) So it's real quiet anyways, but normally when they open it up there's always the same people that are very question oriented and wanna pipe in and ask a question, and I think there weren't as many questions as normal. You don't know what questions you wanna ask, because it's all kinda just like someone just punched you in the face.

I don't think the anger sets within those first 20 minutes that you find out that you're losing your job—it's shock. I think it's a little surreal when it all happens, 'cause you're not expecting it. You're hoping to hear more of positives at the end of the conversation and when they're not there, you get off with all these questions you wanted to ask that you didn't ask, and you're on the phone calling your manager, calling other reps, and trying to figure out—did this really just happen?

And so as soon as that conference call gets off, it's a buzz again of conversations with, "Is there any opportunity?" "Can I move to a different division?" You're scrambling. I think it's like that with any position, but when you don't have the ability to have a conversation one-on-one and see your face, it's almost more difficult. I enjoy sales because I have a conversation in front of my customer, and I can read their reactions, and it's a lot of body language—if you're leaning forward and talking to me, I know you're interested and engaged. If you're back and kind of drifting off, I know you can give two—whatevers—about what I'm saying. It's a lot of body language. When you get a conference call and you just hear that you're cutting the division and "we're not sure what's gonna happen here and more to come next week"—you can't read that guy's facial expressions, I mean, he could look like he's about to cry, you don't know. So for me, hearing it over the phone, it hurts a little more, because it's not in front of you.

We make a pretty good living in the medical industry, and all of us have decent size mortgages…and to anyone that has a mortgage, I mean, it's clenching to your stomach to find out you have to call your wife and say, "I've got two months to figure out how I'm gonna, you know, move on and carry this nut that you pay out every month in your life."

The first person I called was another rep on the team. I think I wanted to talk it out a little, and make sure that I was understanding what was about to happen a little better. And then I talked to my manager right after that, cause I'm sure the six of us were calling him at the same time, so I knew there wasn't a chance I was getting him on the phone right away. I had multiple conversations before I even called my wife, because I dunno…it was definitely more of a sensitive phone call to me. I've never been let go of a job, and I think that ticked me off even more 'cause I was a good earner for the company. I thought they would take care of the guys that have year after year done well for them, even though there are guys that have been there 20 years. That part, I felt like I was getting fired, you know, versus dissolving.

I think I needed more time to take it in. It was a harder conversation with my wife…so that call was a little worse for me. I have a very good support system; my wife is completely behind me in my jobs and my career as a sales rep. She was less worried than I was. I think I took it more personally like wait a minute, you know, I put in some good sweat here for the company. That ticked me off more. So that—and nerves—got me way more than my wife.

Now that it's happened once, I think in the back of my head I'm like, "Eh, I'm expendable, just like anybody else." It stings. So I think I've built a little bit of a callus from it.

It went up all the way to the top dog in my division, who I still don't think has a position. You know you see all these people on LinkedIn and you kinda see where they're at. I've talked to the guy who actually sells my products—I keep in contact with him, he's a friend of mine—so he sells twice the amount of products that he sold before when I was carrying half his bag. And so now he's just spread more thin. So he's like, I don't call and I don't talk to any of these customers under a certain dollar amount because it's not worth my time. So to me, I think they're selling themselves short with having such a big bag for one rep to carry; you end up being more of a distributor, you know a little about a lot versus being an expert on your products and being able to have a good conversation about them.

BOOK SIX

PUBLIC DOMAIN

Parks & Recreation

"The little tiny voice that talks to women"

Sue Whetten

We've met in Fort Collins, Colorado, a part of the country where people tend to give driving directions oriented by the mountains. "Out here people don't talk about left or right" but everyone carries awareness of the Rockies' jagged peaks to the west—the only serious interruption to the open sky all around.

Sue has learned to live with rattlesnakes in her garden and in her driveway. "Babies are way worse...baby rattlers can't control their venom, and so when they bite you they send it all in."

She grew up in Ohio, the granddaughter of Polish and Italian immigrants. Since her layoff at the Botanical Gardens in Cheyenne, Wyoming—45 miles north—she's landed a part time job at a the Fort Collins nursery. She's also keeping the books for a small

venture her husband has just entered with a friend named Snake.
They make various models of aluminum bicycle trailers. "We
bought Cycletote in December with Snake. It's really just Snake and
my husband, and I'm just here for the show." (Laughs.)

Naturally I grill Sue on the biblical and poetic implications
of entering into business with someone named Snake. She assures
me he's not only trustworthy but vital to the operation's success:
"Snake does all of the building. My husband's specialty is he's a
material scientist. So it's dealing with issues of…can we convert
this aluminum to a lighter weight aluminum? Then the rods too—
do we need as many as we have? Do they need to be exactly the way
they are? It's not a question of necessarily making more profit. We'd
love to be able to sell them for less."

We sit in the warehouse where all of the aluminum mixology
takes place. Sue, 55, beams with pride and hope in the space. She
sits on a work stool, relaxed, legs crossed, arms dangling over her
top knee.

She originally earned a degree in psychology but never
really used it; instead she roamed various retail gigs before
becoming a full time mom. She raised two sons, worked through
an unexpected end to her first marriage, and went back to school
for a horticulture degree. She wanted to get her hands dirty again.

When I was a little kid, I used to swap my brother mowing the lawn
for washing the dishes. So getting my hands dirty: always. Doing it for
money…boy, I don't think I ever really thought it was possible.

I had done my internship at the Cheyenne Botanic Gardens, and they
finally got money to hire another person so they offered me a full-time
position. It's about an hour drive from here. It was the best job in the
entire world. I will never in my whole life have…Well, maybe I will. If I'm
lucky, this will be it.

She lifts her open hands to the workshop where we sit.

But I don't think I'll ever have a job as great as it was. The nice thing was that I knew it was a great job. I can remember a couple of different occasions where I would thank my boss for having hired me. (Laughs.) I was a horticulturist, so I played with plants, got to pick plants, grow plants, take care of plants, got very good at killing bugs. (Laughs.)

We were city employees, and so we did other things for the city. I got to design city parks, I got to work on different city projects—we planted all of the annuals that are throughout the city, so there were lots of crews going out, doing that all the time. My boss, Shane, also encouraged me to write, so I wrote for some magazines, both national and regional. I gave talks to women's groups; I gave talks to four-year olds.

In Cheyenne, they have a zero tolerance for any kind of acting up in school. And so probably about once a week, I'd have a 13-year old, usually a 13-year old boy, who had gotten into some trouble, and he would spend eight hours with us working off his court-appointed time. And those days were great fun, because the kids were kind of treated like an adult. Most kids were eager; they would come back to me and they would say, "What next? What next?" I'm not a classroom teacher, but I'm a natural teacher. I teach all the time.

I also worked a good chunk of every day with volunteers, most of whom were seniors, and that was just, you know, a whole huge group of friends, who, hey, thought I was kind of cool because I knew stuff! (Laughs.) Maybe I'm wrong, but it felt like the average age of our volunteer was over 70. I'd say the oldest ones—and some of the best—were in their upper 80s. The last one that I worked with, he passed away on my watch, but he was 93 when he died, and he was still volunteering for us.

When the budget got tight—when everybody's budget got tight—they started talking about massive city layoffs, and we knew it was a possibility. I always knew I was vulnerable. I didn't believe it. I really didn't get it.

The city didn't have the money—especially the city of Cheyenne, because it has state buildings downtown that don't pay the same kinds of taxes; in fact, I don't think they pay taxes. And so there's a lot of expenses in Cheyenne that don't exist in the rest of the state. And the state had been giving the city a certain amount of money every year, and that money was cut, and so that's where they had to take, I think it was three million dollars out of the budget.

The state's great, you know, there's a lot of mineral, oil stuff in Wyoming. My understanding is that the state is fine. I suspect, it's sort of like what I told my ex-husband, at one point: "You know, you're gonna wake up one morning and realize you didn't have to do this." I think it's sort of the same thing for Wyoming…the state has the money.

I think we knew the day the announcement was going to be made, and we had gone to city council meetings where we asked for them to let us all take pay cuts and work one less day, and that kind of stuff, rather than lay somebody off, or somebodies. 'Cause it wasn't just parks. It happened throughout the entire city. And they said no. They kind of felt that, you know, it was better to make the cut and let just a few people suffer rather than have everybody suffer. I don't know what I think about that. (Laughs.)

Shane, my boss, always said that a botanic garden the size of the Cheyenne Botanic Gardens has 17 employees everywhere else in the country. We had seven. After they built the children's garden, it was seven and three-quarters. But still, it was not many people at all to run the gardens. And so we were hoping they would spare us.

It was probably the day before…I said something about, "Well, I can do this next week, if I still have a job," and my boss kind of jerked just a little. And I thought, oh, he thinks I'm going. If he's a good boss and he knows, he shouldn't tell me. He probably really knew at that point.

I think it was a Wednesday. It was March 30th. He walked into the office…shortly after nine and he said, "Sue, we have to talk." And he closed the door behind him.

And I said, "Oh, this isn't good."

And he said, "Well, we have to go downtown, and you have to turn in your keys and sign paperwork and all that stuff. And they're going to lock you out of your computer." And so the first thing I did is I transferred all my files to one of the other folks' computers, because I was afraid if it didn't get turned back on, there was stuff they needed.

It was painful. Because not only did I lose my job, but they ended up one person short. Actually, they ended up a person-and-a-half short, because their secretary—our secretary—ended up being the secretary for both the botanic gardens and for the forestry department, so she was back and forth.

I like these people. I understand they had to do what they had to do. And I also understood they probably had a pretty crappy day by the time it was over, so I wasn't out to make it any worse. It wasn't my boss's idea. It wasn't anybody that I worked with or interacted with. It was sort of like that thing out there in the universe had done this to me.

Went downtown. Cheyenne's tiny. It's a little tiny cute town; it's adorable. Went downtown, signed my release papers, had to turn in all my keys. Couldn't drive the truck back, you know. Shane had to go with me, 'cause they wouldn't let me drive their truck, and as an employee, you're not supposed to drive around in your own vehicle on the job, so I couldn't drive my car downtown; we had to take a city vehicle downtown.

Came back and collected my stuff, cried with some of my volunteers, and left...Came back to Fort Collins almost right away. I was like, I have to get out of this city, you know? I went to the store. I brought this really bright pink, beautiful blouse. (Laughs.) I went home and...I have a fantastic garden. From a distance. (Laughs.) It's really weedy, but it's a great garden. And so I took a picture of myself waving from the upstairs window. It's a long-distance shot. It shows the whole garden. It shows a mountain range behind me. You can see Wyoming. I live near the dams, so you can see the dams in the distance. And I just took a picture waving to the volunteers, and wrote them a letter that basically said, don't worry about me. I'm doing good. I missed them. They were the best part.

I still don't have a lot of friends in Fort Collins. Most of our going out in the evening and stuff was in Cheyenne, it wasn't here. So not only did I lose my job. I lost 90% of my social circle. And then I came back down here, and it was like, "Um, okay."

I tell people that it's nice not to have to make the commute anymore. That's bullshit. The commute was really not hard. If you ever make the drive between Fort Collins and Wyoming—and Cheyenne—it's quiet. Unless it's windy and there's trucks on their side, it's quiet. It's a fairly easy drive. It's almost straight. You can pretty much not turn the wheel the entire time. You pass antelope. You pass buffalo. You pass horses. That's your whole ride. You pass eagles. So it was kind of a nice...Getting up at 5:30 and out the door by 6:30 was a little hard, but...I'm a morning person, so it wasn't horrendous. I really didn't mind the commute, and if I started making it again, I wouldn't mind it at all.

I'm a country music fan; it's one of the perks of living in Colorado. But I took the Wyoming station off my radio, 'cause it was too painful to listen to it. Although occasionally my pickup truck still has it, so...

I re-worked my resume. I tried to figure out what to do next. I am 55 now. I was 54 then. And I started thinking, "You know, I'm getting kind of old to pull weeds."

My husband has a good job, great benefits. I was fine. My kids are grown. Their college is paid for. There was never any financial worry, except for the little tiny voice that talks to women who have ever been divorced in their life that says, "I don't have my own security."

How did you manage that little voice?

You know, it's a good question. For starters, I am in a great relationship. We've been together for coming up on 14 years. And so that's...It's easy when you know that you're pretty secure, and the likelihood of "it" happening is pretty remote. But still, once you've gone through it once— and I didn't think it would happen that first time, kind of caught me by surprise. So I liked the fact that if everything went wrong...with the job in Cheyenne, I knew that, gosh, if everything went sour again, I'm okay. I could at least pay the bills. You know? I could make it 'til retirement age. I guess I just have to know that it's not going to happen. It's not going to happen. But there is, there was that little voice. There is a vulnerability that never completely goes away.

City Hall

"Using the resources wisely"
Christine Myrick & Granketha Major

It was Granketha who emailed me, said she'd be willing to tell me her story. When I pressed my luck and asked if she'd do so on camera she balked at first but, eventually, once she'd succeeded at roping in her friend Christine, agreed.

They meet us in our hotel room, which is located in middle of neglected office park sprawl in North Kansas City. This afternoon I met the hotel owner downstairs. He's a New Yorker, trying to give the place a face-lift to attract budget business travelers, though I wonder if such travelers exist in this area—there are a lot of available spaces in the surrounding office buildings.

Both women are a little camera shy at first. Christine—who mostly goes by Chris—asks if MJ and I will be photo-shopping their images, demurely suggesting that they need help improving their appearance. I assure her they'll be looking just fine on their own and Granketha, who has dark black skin, tells me she just wants to make sure we know what we're doing with the lighting. She tells of a funny re-occurring situation in her life, in which someone is photocopying her I.D. and she catches a glimpse of the second-generation picture made up mostly of white eyes and teeth: "Okay nobody can tell who is that. You need to lighten up the toner on that!"

They both have a good sense of humor and they display it openly, alongside open hurt.

Chris, 59, grew up in California, the granddaughter of Norwegian and German immigrants. Her father was an aeronautical engineer and her mother was mostly a homemaker. "I'm old enough that my parents went through the Depression."

She has a bachelor's degree in public administration from Kansas University. Her hair is spiky blonde and she displays a singular blend of strength and vulnerability. She is a proud mother and several years removed from her 29-year marriage with a business professor.

Granketha's family is mostly in Louisiana. Her dad was in the air force and opened his own dental office with the money from his military career. Her mom was a teacher and bus driver. "We didn't have an extravagant life at all," she says. "But he loved his job. He loved it. My dad's mother, you know, she lived most of her life on welfare, and my dad's dad, he would send money, but he wasn't in the house. So my dad wanted to make sure that we were family."

Granketha—I love typing her name almost as much as I like saying it—is a splice of her father's name (Grant) and her grandmother's name (Etha). "They fought for three days, so the nurse named me," she says. "And my dad hated my name. He told me that it would be a problem when I tried to go get a job because, he said, 'They already know walking through the doors what color you are.'"

I respond with something overly diplomatic, suggesting this might not be the case but Chris cuts me off at the pass, backing up Granketha's claim with a steady nod before proving that such first impressions can be misleading: "I used to work at a prosecutor's office. This guy's name was Roosevelt Jones and the joke was… (smiles and rolls her eyes)…we know who this is. Come to find out Roosevelt Jones was a 68-year old white man." This makes us all laugh and then we start coming up with stories of people who we thought we had pegged until we actual met them—from Granny's recent encounter with a certain Tyrone to MJ's ex-girlfriend, Jamal.

Despite the fact that Granketha doesn't have any children, let alone grandchildren, she is commonly known as Granny. "I've been called Granny since I was in the third grade—second grade actually."

Granny, 41, originally came to Kansas City in 1999 for a yearlong internship in the City Manager's office. She ended up working in the city's revenue division with Chris. There is no easy way to describe the rapport between them. They are both exceptionally blunt and considerate—with the world but especially with each other. Together they laugh and cry without reservation.

Chris: We worked in City Hall.

Granny: I handled all of the paperwork. I also oversaw the front desk administrative staff. And I handled a couple of special projects. It was just so many things. Chris was a manager.

Chris: Yeah, I actually stayed home and raised my children for 12 years, and then I went back to school, and I got a paralegal degree, and I worked as a paralegal for seven years, and I really enjoyed it. But I realized that I was very bossy, and I needed to be the manager. I started working for the city in '96, and I was pretty much the golden child. You know, I did very well there. I had about seven supervisors who worked for me. Moneywise, I was well rewarded.

Granny: Moneywise, it was never that easy. I always had a second job. Sometimes third. And one time, I even had four. So it was always a struggle to get paid compensation-wise. I came to Kansas City after I completed my Master's degree program, but I never was able to realize the financial aspect to go with it. So it was always difficult for me.

Chris: And that's because you were in an administrative assistant. It's just a job classification. It doesn't really define what she does. Just like my job, I was a senior analyst. That didn't really describe what I did, because I was really a manager. And you're not gonna really make the money there unless you can break into the actual management part of it. And that's the hardest thing to do, I think. And I was extremely fortunate that when I got there in 1996, they had actually hired me to project manage. So I did that, and it really went really well, and I was really happy with it.

Granny: I didn't like her.

Chris: You didn't like me?

Granny: No. Because she would make me want to punch her in her face. (Both women laugh.) She was…Ooh, goodness. She was bossy.

Chris: I was nice though. But I had a job to do, you know?

Granny: She doesn't have a quiet thought in her head.

Chris: And I would tell you I don't have a hidden agenda. This is who I am. If I have a problem with you, or if there's an issue or whatever, I'm going to come and talk to you honestly about it.

Granny: I like that. I value honesty above all things. And the fact that I know where she's coming from, I know she's not going to lie to me. And when you have that kind of honesty, I value that above everything. And I have to give it to her. She was honest with me.

We would've still been there if they had not laid us off. And then it was the way they did it. They passed an ordinance to do it.

Chris: Kind of sneaky under the table…what they did was they passed an ordinance so they could strategically RIF[1] people. That meant that you could be targeted by whoever didn't like you.

Granny: A popularity contest…these things don't happen formally. They happen in the elevator. They happen on the stairwell. They happen informally.

---

[1]   Reduction in Forces

Chris: We were left in a very vulnerable position with our management leaving, changing. We had like a perfect storm happen. We lost our division manager, and that was the job that I thought I would be able to get. But then we also lost our department director. And it allowed a lot of bad things to happen. It completely changed the dynamics of the division and the department, and it became a pretty terrible place after that really.

We both knew someone who had gotten hold of the list. So we knew it was going to happen.

Granny: There was a list. And this list was made in December of the year before.

Chris: So we knew it. The list changed a little bit but basically stayed the same.

(Pointing at Granny:) She didn't believe me when I told her she was on the list. I knew about the list, and she's the only person that I told. I knew it was confidential, and I swore her to secrecy, but I told her.

Granny: And then we couldn't tell anybody. Being around your coworkers all day long, knowing, looking in their faces, and then, you know, hearing all the chatter. It's like you're in one of those movies and you don't hear anything going on but the world is going on around you. It was hell.

Chris: It was horrible.

Granny: It was hell, because we would see each other—and she would come to my desk—and I'm like, "Chris, don't come to my desk. Don't tell me." Because she would say, "Yes, this is going to happen." Again, it's...I'm holding out. I'm going to be the good Christian. I'm holding out.

Chris: I had been relegated. They were kind of isolating people that were going to be going, so you knew what was going on. I used to have a big office, almost as big as this room, and I ended up in a little cubicle. But the woman on the other side of the cubicle from me, I knew she was going to be RIF'd. I just felt horrible about it—I knew and I couldn't tell her. And she was really devastated. She'd been there, what, 23 years or something?

I am thankful that they did mine on Thursday, because they did the bulk of the people on Friday, and they had the cops there and everything.

I was sitting at my desk all day because I knew they were going to be doing it...and I don't know what your faith is or anything, but I sat there and prayed all day long to give me the strength to not cry. 'Cause I did not want to cry, though I might now…

Chris tries to collect herself and fails, but continues talking all the same. Through the tears, she blurts out the rest:

Chris: So they took us in a room. They said your job's been eliminated.

Granny: She went before I did. It happened for me April 3rd. That's a Friday. And they brought us into the room, and then they…just said, "Okay, we can't use you." And there was nothing to say otherwise. "You can't come back for a year, and you have to sign off on the severance" and all that. In that same office, they got rid of what—five or six of us?

Chris: More than that…We were all told separately. Well, there was another person in the room. You always do things in twos. If you're manager and you're giving bad news or whatever, you're going to be in twos. So mine was another division manager and my acting director. They walked me back to my desk…

Granny: You got to go back to your desk. We couldn't do anything. We were escorted out right then and there. They barely let me get my purse. I had to leave everything. I couldn't touch anything. You didn't get police, did you?

Chris: No.

I'm curious to know about that escort. Did you have any dialogue with the security people who were walking with you? Or did it happen in silence?

Granny: It was like a tomb. It was like a tomb. And then I had to make an appointment to come back and get my stuff.

Chris: I was only able to go back to my desk to get my purse, but I said, "You really think that I didn't think that you were going to do this to me?" I said, "My stuff's already gone." And they just looked at me, like, shocked. I was taking my stuff home every night in a backpack or whatever, so that when that day came…

Granny: I think that I thought, oh, at the last minute, God was just going to save me.

Chris: Well, I hoped that too, but I still prepared for it. It was very demeaning, because they stand over you. I can remember turning and looking to her and just saying, "You know this is wrong, that I'm not the person you should be doing this to." And then the two of them escorted me into the elevator and down to the first floor and out the door.

Granny: The press was outside the building, and they were like, "Can you talk to us?" They knew. In fact, it was pretty well known, because when I called to get unemployment.

Chris: Oh yeah, they knew right away.

Granny: Because they had been keeping up with it. I'm like, why my little job got cut? I mean, I made no money. They were not going to save anything from me. And so you're like, "Well did I do that bad of a job?" You know, you question yourself. I did all of the right things. How could this happen?

Chris: Honestly, you have this feeling of "Really? Me versus that person?" You know, it's like, "Okay, I could work circles around those people, and it's going to be me?" They actually took the job that I used to do, and they farmed it out to three people, and made three full-time positions that the only thing that they do...And I did it as one person. And I'm like, "Really?" It's a very embittering experience. Very much so.

And I mean, I was the highest paid person in my division, so it wasn't like I'd ever been considered to have done a bad job. Obviously, I wouldn't have been rewarded as I was. I mean, my salary increased $50,000 in 13 years.

Granny: After everything passed, I was very angry for the first year. Very, very angry. My mom was my base. We talk so often, you know, her support is what I need. I had told her what Chris told me before, so it was a countdown to see whether they were going to really do it. And so I told her they did it. And she said, "Come home. You can come home. You're okay." I'm the oldest child, so I'm bossy. And so when I'm emotionally distraught, it's hard for her to take it. You know, she lets me calm down and then she says, "You're going to be okay." And I said, "I'm going to be okay." But it hurt. It hurt to the core. I was very angry for a while.

I think even with all of this, about six months before all of this happened, I read a book called *Nickel and Dimed...Bait and Switch,* and then *Nickel and Dimed.* I don't know how to say the author's last name. But it helped me. It helped me, and I thank God that he kind of put that book in my face, because it kind of helped me see that it wasn't me. That these things are in cycles. It kind of prepared me mentally, and so I found myself having to comfort other people.

Chris: About two weeks after I got RIF'd my mother got sick. I packed my two greyhounds in my little car, and off we drove to California. And I went out to take care of her, and she died.

Chris begins weeping. Granny comforts her and begins speaking to give her more time:

Granny: We did all the right things. We went to school. We worked hard. We tried to be efficient, but that wasn't respected. And now I see people every day that aren't working, and it's just like, what do we do? I told somebody, if I had the body for it, I'd go get a boob job or something and go to my next interview naked. (Chris laughs hysterically.) It would help me get at least an interview!

Chris: The problem is you can't get to an interview. That's a problem. I never in my life had a problem getting into an interview and getting the job. Pretty much: I interviewed, I got the job. But this is a whole different ball game. If I try for a lower-level job, I'm overqualified. There's so many people out there for one job that you have to be exactly what they're looking for. And the job descriptions are written very narrow. And they can find those people, because there's millions of us out there.

Granny: And then I hate the fact that you take the time and do the cover letter so that it won't be a generic cover letter. You take the time—even try to address a person in particular, all the things that they tell you, you take a whole day and a half to get this cover letter perfect, and they take two minutes and send you a two line "I'm sorry..." Or they don't send you anything at all. You feel like a prostitute going for these jobs. Hire me because I'm the best…I can turn tricks for $20. You feel like a prostitute trying to get these people to look at you. What do you have to do?

You know, I think one of the things that got to me, because I'm a black person. Sorry, I'm just going to bring race into it. But white people are now having to live the life that I've had to live. (Laughs.)

Chris: It's true. It's very true.

Granny: And so now we're all in the same boat, and we can start from a proper base.

And that's another thing, listening to the media at the time, nobody was saying anything about the huge job loss. They just overlook it. We're struggling, and they're trying to sell us stuff on television. It took them a whole two years to even recognize the job loss, and that's another thing that made me very angry. You don't speak for me. You don't know. You're in this Ivory Tower. Even our city council. I told our mayor: "It'll be a cold day in hell before I ever vote for you again."

And now I'm over 40, so I'm not young. I'm having to talk about why you're not working for so many years, or what are your skills. If you don't use it, you lose it. Having to worry about keeping current, making sure you're not obsolete.

Chris: After I'd been unemployed just about a year, I hired a company to help me rewrite my resumes and to do all of this stuff. I paid $3500 for it. And in a regular job market, it would've worked. It would've been great. But in this job market? I didn't throw my money away, because I still do have good cover letters and a good functional resume. But it hasn't gotten me a job. And networking? You know, I worked on these big projects. I had tons of people that I networked with. Some of them have lost their jobs, and their companies have been bought out, and they're miserable too.

Granny: Who are these people that you need to network with? And they say, well, we have a job fair. You go to the job fair, and they don't really have the jobs there. They're just like, "We'll just take your resume." You know, are you serious? Do you think we're crazy? Either you're going to hire people, or you're not. And I think that I've gotten disillusioned with a lot of the job fairs. They don't really have anything there. I don't know, just networking with people, you have to find the right people to network with. And that's not always obvious.

I volunteered at a hospital. I was thinking about going back to school. And I volunteered at the hospital from January to September, and they said, "Well, we'll try to hire you." I thought, okay. It wasn't ideal. It was horrible. I tried so hard to stick with it, but when you have 25 different trainers, that's not a good situation. So they let me go in February. And I'm like, oh gosh, how do I explain this one on my resume? And it really cut into what I had in unemployment. So it's just very frustrating.

Chris: Yeah, and I did work for the IRS, and that was a horrible job. That was the most difficult job that I've ever done for, like, $14 an hour.

At the end, they're like, "We'll see you next year!"

I'm like, oh no. No, you're not going to see me next year. Now I'm like, "Yeah, you probably are going to see me next year." (Laughs.)…When I hit about two years and, you know, you see this stuff on 60 Minutes and you hear the pundits and there's a lot of talk right now saying that people 40 and above will never work again.

Granny: See, she buys that. I don't buy that.

Chris: Well, I don't buy it for you. I buy it for me. Because I'm older, I have kind of given up. I have to apply for jobs, and so I can't completely give up. But in my heart, I've given up.

Granny: You know, I don't see it that way. I've always been the type of person to use my faith and to let God lead me to where I need to be.

I think I'm beginning to see that maybe I shouldn't be working for somebody else. My dad was a dentist. I thought he was the craziest person, because he took all the risk. Now I'm changing. Now I think it's everybody's duty to do things for themselves, especially when I think about how the state is trying to keep everybody down and from being free.

Chris: Don't get into her crazy politics.

Granny: My problem is it's in the government's best interest to keep growing itself. When I see these different pundits, "Oh, the city will shut down. The government will shut down." Heck yeah! Shut down. Because half of those people don't need to be there in the first place. If you reconstructed the work, you wouldn't need all of those people there.

Chris: I do believe after being in the public sector for 16 years that you could probably get rid of 50% of the people. Now I believe in a good work ethic, you know. That's not conservative, or...

Granny: That's smaller government, Chris.

Chris: No, it's not about smaller government. That's good public administration. It's about being more efficient, and it's about using the resources wisely, which is not done.

Granny: That's conservative.

Chris: Don't label me.

The back-and-forth hits a crescendo and both women cackle.

Chris: And I don't want to be at this point. I mean, I want to go back into public service. It's what I went to school to do. That's what I want. I don't see it happening.

Granny casts a suspicious eye on Chris, who responds quickly:

Chris: I'm still a bureaucrat. I still believe in it.

Granny: And we talk. We talk about that all the time. We're gonna make a conservative out of her.

Chris: She's going to take a liberal California Democrat and try to make her a conservative. It's not gonna happen. I think she's nuts. You should see what she puts on Facebook. I'm like, "Oh my gosh. This is so crazy." I want my pension. So I want the city to stay solvent. Because I want them paying me for many, many, many years.

Granny: I wanted to get everything that I could possibly get: applying for food stamps until unemployment would kick in, going to the full employment council to see if there are any programs that I could get involved with. Just not being helpless. Getting out there and hitting the pavement to know that this is not going to beat me. That's one of the reasons why I participate in a lot of political and community things, to just keep my mind going. I'm not obsolete. I can do. Just give me the chance. And I drag her with me.

Chris: And I've done some volunteering, still doing some volunteering. And I go to the gym every day. That's my salvation. My structure is to get up and go to the gym every day. I set my alarm, and I get up at the same time. So that I don't fall out of that practice. But it's been getting more difficult. Once I hit two years, it was like, wow, this really sucks.

Granny: That's the big thing. It took me a very long time to get used to waking up and not going any place. I don't like that. I like to have a purpose. Not having a purpose is very hard for me. People ask, "What do you do?" I don't know what I do. I don't know what I want to be when I grow up. You hear people say, especially with the unemployment debate and whether they should continue, "Well, they'll never get off of it if you don't stop it." And I'm like, do you think I like this? Do you think I like having to jump through hoops to get money? I don't. I really, really don't.

Chris: Me neither.

Granny: I would much rather not have you to oversee what I can do or not do, and having to report in…but I need it. And I'm gonna go for it. And then before I even got the unemployment, I had food stamps. Big mistake. The next year they asked for the money back. "Oh, we miscalculated."

Did you have to give some back?

Granny: As long as I owe them, they'll never be broke. (Smiles.) What am I going to give them?

Chris: You can't squeeze blood out of a turnip…Honestly, you know, just within the last couple of weeks, I've pretty much had an epiphany that I will never work again as I did. When you've been two years unemployed, that's a huge problem. With my age…

Granny: I kept saying, I said, "This is a new world."

Chris: Now I have a survival plan. My survival plan is cash in my last 401K here in a couple weeks. I can live until the end of the year on that. I can file a new unemployment claim, because I worked for the IRS for four months. I can do that in October, then I'm going to go back to the IRS in January, and then I'll go back on unemployment, and then I can start collecting my pension from the city in December 1st, 2012. And it's just survival, you know? It's frustrating to have worked so hard and done all the education and all that and you can't do anything. It's incredibly frustrating. I could've never imagined myself in this situation. Ever. Not in my wildest imagination. And I don't think it's going to end.

Granny: I'm from Louisiana. I still have family there. And they tell me, "What you have to do is come home." Well, I don't want to stay in my mother's house, especially having no job and taking all of my stuff and my dog and everything to her house. That's not fair to her. I'm an adult, and I need to deal with this like an adult.

Chris: Nobody ever gave me anything. I worked my way. I was married with three kids, going to school, going to grad school, working 50, 60 hours, and I worked to where I was successful. And to have the rug just pulled out from under you is horrible. It's horrible.

And then you lose your health insurance, and you have all those other things that you just completely take for granted when you're working. You know, the preventative care and all those things that you just took for granted. All of a sudden you don't have that anymore.

I recently went to Truman Medical Center, which is a teaching hospital—it's for indigent care. I was able to qualify for a discount. The problem is I can't get an appointment. I'm supposed to see a dermatologist about some basal cell carcinomas going on, and I can't get an appointment. And so I guess they'll see me when they see me. I don't know.

Granny: I haven't signed up, but I will. Right now, I've been footing the vitamins and…

Chris: It's just survival. Now it's just survival. I've been very thankful this whole time that I've been able to pay my bills. I still have a roof over my head, and I have food. But I've had to borrow money from my daughter to make it through. And it's just survival. I was making a really good salary, so I was just buying whatever I wanted to, whatever food I wanted to. Now I shop at the Dollar General. And that's okay, but it is definitely a lifestyle change. And there's no room to spend money on anything else. You just pay the minimum you can on your bills, and I do that just to stay current. This was a time when I was hoping to have all of my debt paid off so that I could take retirement early. Obviously that's not going to happen.

Granny: You decide, okay, what things are important? Do you keep your Internet? Do you keep your cable? Do you have a landline? I thank God that I paid off my car.

Chris: Yeah, my car is eight years old. I'll never be able to buy another car, because there's no wiggle room in $320 a week, which is what we get for unemployment. That's it.

Granny: So you have to juggle, and you have to see, okay, how am I going to pay this? And honestly, how I've made it is I've lost two important people in my life that left something for me, and that's how I'm able to do what I can do. I would much rather have the people back.

Her voice becomes rickety and suddenly tears roll down her round cheeks.

Granny: I lost my 98-year old aunt and my 90-year old uncle, and I'm happy they left me things, you know? And then when I got the money, I had to pay taxes. I had to pay half of the money in taxes.

I haven't been able to go home in two years. That's kind of hard. I stay in a crappy apartment because I can afford it. And just having really no pride whatsoever in saying what you will and will not do.

Chris: Well, and I have a grandson, and I can't go see him, because he lives in Washington state, so that's been really hard.

Chris's face sets, and both women are quiet for a moment.

Chris: I'm still angry. I am. I'm bitter. I don't want to be. But I am. It's kind of hard sometimes, because I go to the gym with the same people I used to work with. You know, I love my gym, and I wasn't going to change just because I didn't work there anymore. But sometimes it's hard to see them, you know? Some days, some weeks, months I have no problem at all. And then sometimes it will just hit me. It's like, I don't want to look at those people. I don't want to see them at all.

Granny: Yeah. I think it's more of a mental thing, like, "Dang, we need to be working." And we'd love to. We would love to be working. Working is a good thing.

Chris: Working, doing anything really.

Granny: And a place to be every day. Getting up...You have to contribute some way. You know, you don't just rely on others. You better be working. The idea of work and what you do is very strong in me. You have to have something to define you, and this right here is not defining me. And so it's important for me to have something to do to say I've contributed in some way.

Chris: And for me it wasn't a job. It was my career. It's no more. It's gone. As I grew up and then I became a professional, that defined me. Just like it used to be a male-dominated thing that that defined the male. Now it defined me, and when I didn't have it anymore, it was like, who am I? What do I do now?

Granny: They tell you all of these things, "Well, you just hang in there," and you want to punch them in the face. You're like, are you serious?

Chris: I'm tired of people, "Oh, it'll work out. It'll work out." It's been two years and four months, and it's not working out. People who have jobs say that. Don't tell me that, because you know what? I don't believe it. I used to believe it. I don't believe it anymore. I mean, it's gonna work out some way. But it's not gonna work out the way that I want. I'm just waiting for how it's going to be resolved to be revealed to me as I go along. It's a very hopeless feeling.

Social Services

"The ceiling shouldn't be talking to people"

Kelly Graham-MacDonald

She grew up mostly in Florida, first in Ft. Lauderdale then the central part of the state in "a teeny tiny town with one stoplight and ten churches." Her parents divorced when she was young. "They loved each other, but they should not have lived together. Alcoholism is not a fun thing to grow up with." Her mom raised her—and held many jobs over the years, including that of truck driver. Her grandmother could "shoot a squirrel between the eyes at ten feet away with a shotgun. So I had some strong women in my family."

Kelly is now 41 and married. She and her husband have lived in the same Indianapolis apartment for 14 years.

She is probably overweight but has recently become more healthy, losing 70 pounds with changes in her eating habits: "First

*of all, we couldn't really afford to go out to eat all the time, and
secondly, I can actually taste the chemicals in things now."*

*She recalls how she ate when she was working in social services:
"I would, like, stop at a fast food place and cram something into
my mouth on the way to my next person's place. And, like, most fast
food doesn't even taste good to me anymore…If you cook at home
a lot, or you don't buy things that are pre-processed and stuff, you
can tell the difference."*

*She has a B.A. in psychology and sings in the Indianapolis
Women's Chorus.*

*Like others who were deeply invested in their work, she
unknowingly slips back and forth between the past and present tense,
and always when hitting on matters of possession or identity: I have/I
had, we are/we were, and various other complications. And no matter
her tense, she does not stray from the memorable refrain: "my people."*

One of the things that made things really difficult for me, since I got
laid off and had a hard time finding a job, is that I'd been working since I
was 15. In Florida, my mom had to sign something saying that it was okay
for me to work that young, and I had to do it on the condition that I would
keep my grades up and everything. I worked full-time with two or three
jobs at a time. I saved up all my money with my first job and bought my
school clothes for the next year, because my mom was a single mom, and
I felt so good being able to help out.

I was at my last job for 14 years. I worked with people with disabilities.
I was a QMRP[1], and in the state of Indiana, you have to have so many years
of experience, plus a B.A., to have that title and to be able to write people's
programs to help them with their lives. And I loved what I did.

The program that we had was the semi-independent living program.
It was called SILP, and it doesn't even exist anymore in the state of Indiana.
It was for the highest-functioning people with mental retardation. The
goal was for them to have the best lives that they could have, where they

---

[1]   Qualified Mental Retardation Professional

were as independent as possible, and had the least amount of paid health. So obviously that's not a money-making thing, but it was the pinnacle of what they wanted services to be for people...they wanted people to have the best life that they possibly could have.

We were a for-profit company, R—, named for the man who founded the company in Wisconsin. And he cared about people with disabilities; it's why he founded the company. And then his sons owned it. The company got bought by M—. They're in about 38 states, I think.

We saw more and more that not only did people not understand what we did—even our direct bosses—but they didn't really care. They're like, "Well, you're not making a profit."

I'm like, "We've never made a profit. It's not what we're in the business to do, this tiny part of our company"—because we had group homes that made lots of money, because you already own the property, you have people there, you know. That's why they were squeezing more and more people into apartments: say you have three people in a place instead of one. That one person has their allotted amount of money that the state's going to pay, and the government—the federal government—is going to pay to have their services provided for them. Well, if you have three people, then you have one staff person for all three people. You're tripling your money. The push was really to get them in apartments with two or three people. And my people—I had people who lived on their own. I had one lady who was divorced and had lived on her own for 16 years. It would be like telling a 50-some year old person that, "Yes, you've been independent your whole life, but sorry: You have to have a roommate, or two or three."

I have a person who had his own apartment for 12 years, and now he's in an apartment with two other people. They're nice people, but it's not the same freedom.

I would be unhappy. If I had to have those kinds of services and live in a group home, I would be the worst client anybody had ever seen, 'cause somebody telling me it's time to get up...I have to eat at a certain time? I can't have a snack because I didn't make my bed? (She laughs incredulously.) If my bed's made right now, it's 'cause my husband made it! I don't necessarily always make my own bed, you know?

So that's why people will act out sometimes. If they have so many rules, they might just say, "No way, I'm not getting on the van," because that's the only power they feel like they have in their life. And I always tried to make whatever we did fun. Like, even if it was going to an appointment, or I had to pick one of my people up and take him home, I'd put on some music that they liked, and at stoplights, I'd be dancing. And they'd be like, "Oh Kelly, what are you doing?" Or they'd laugh and dance along with me, you know, depending on the person.

If you're making things fun, that's a much better way to enjoy learning. I was able to teach one of my people how to write checks. Because of his eyesight, he couldn't see them, so we got checks that were big enough so he could see, and he can write all his own checks now. It took years, but it was really neat to be able to see differences you made in somebody's life.

I loved my people. I felt like I got eight amicable divorces when I got laid off. I still have a few of them that call me and ask how I'm doing and tell me about their lives and things, because for a lot of them, I was the person that they saw the most. Some of them may have seen their families two or three times a year, and I was in their home at least twice a week.

I worked probably 60 hours a week. We were on call. Two of us were on call a month at a time. So we might get a call in the middle of the night. It was salaried, so it was just whatever anybody needed. The people that I worked with all had mental retardation of some type. The IQ level has to be below 70, and can range down to 30. If you think about IQ levels for quote-unquote "normal" people—I don't like that term, "normal," because who am I to say who's normal or not?—but for the average person, someone with, like, a C-level grade average kind of thing, it's probably around 100.

About half of my people also had mental illness issues but they were able to independently take their medicine. I would make sure that it was picked up once a month but they could fill their pill boxes and take it on time and everything. I would know just by the tone of somebody's voice if they hadn't taken it. If somebody with schizophrenia was saying that the people next door were kind of out to get them, I'd be like, "How's your medicine going?" and "When's your next appointment?" "Maybe I should call the doctor."

I was able to set them up with community assistance, where they didn't need paid help to do things. Like, one of my people still has a friend that takes him grocery shopping once a month. They go out to dinner, and then they go grocery shopping. Because it's not that he can't pick out his own things, he just has arm crutches because of his cerebral palsy, so he cannot physically bring in all the groceries. It's just the hauling them around that he needs assistance with. But if you don't know somebody, you're not going to necessarily know to do those things for the person.

There were two people in our program. One person plus myself. We had sixteen to twenty clients, depending on the time, because people could actually graduate out of our program, where they didn't need paid help anymore. One day—it made my day—I went to stop by one of my people's places. It wasn't a set time, but I needed to drop something off for her. And she was vacuuming, and I could hear her cackling over the vacuum cleaner, laughing out loud, going, "Kelly is going to be so proud of me." I did not knock on the door. I let that moment just be there, you know. I thought, "How cool is that, she's motivating herself while she's doing something she knows she needs to do," even though she hated to vacuum the house. (Laughs.)

I saw a show on TV where they were making these people's workplace hostile. And this one man was saying that he came to work one day, and he didn't have a desk, and all his stuff was in boxes, and he was told he had to work next to the copy machine. He felt embarrassed, carrying the boxes to the new workstation—because nobody had told him that his desk was going to be gone or anything. And I realized that they were doing the same thing, making my workplace hostile, and they wanted us to quit. Nobody told us that they were going to rearrange the office, and we should get our personal things or pack up our desks or anything. I was there on a Friday. I came back on a Monday, and we had no cube, no desks, no nothing.

So I just went in, and I had a fit.

And I'm like, "Where's our stuff? What do you mean we don't have a desk?"

"Well, you can work in the conference room if nobody's going to be in there using it."

I'm like, "You have got to be kidding me! This is ridiculous." I started crying because I was very upset. I felt like they just didn't understand at all what it was we did for a living.

Three times…there were big layoffs and then everybody at the office would have to re-interview for their own jobs, which was really fun. Not demoralizing at all. (She rolls her eyes.)

I remember just feeling nauseous the whole time. My co-worker was really worried. She didn't have a B.A. She just had her high school education, but she had done this kind of work for so many years that they kind of grandfathered her in. She was really afraid that she wasn't going to make it, because they had changed her position title at one point. They changed it to Program Director, and at that level you needed to have a degree.

I was told January 14th, 2009. On the phone, by the way. The woman who was like two bosses up from my boss called me. I was driving. I had left one of my people's house, and I was on my way to the other. I pulled over the car.

They just said that they weren't gonna have the SILP program anymore. We were one of the last ones in the state to have it.

I was like, "Well, what's going to happen to my people?" Right that minute that was what I was asking. And then there's that "What's going to happen to me?" thing too. I'm thinking in my head, how am I going to pay any bills? What are we going to do?

She said, "By Friday, you'll need to have said all of your goodbyes and everything."

I'm like, "What?!? What do you mean? How am I going to tell all my people?"

I had to call Jackie, the other person that was in my team. I called her first, because I was making sure that she knew what was happening. And then I called my husband. I told him that they weren't going to have our program anymore, and he was going to have to go beat somebody up, because he wanted to protect his Kelly, 'cause they made his Kelly cry. (Laughing.)

This was a Wednesday, and so it would take me the whole week to be able to see all my people, because I had people from Noblesville to McCordsville and all in-between. They weren't centrally located or anything for my convenience. It was where they wanted to live. I had two weeks—I had to fight for it—to say my goodbyes. They were all very difficult. Most of them cried. I mean, it was just very hard. And I tried not to cry and to be positive. I said they were going to be in good hands, and I was going to tell everybody exactly what they need in their lives, and I never, in any way, made it sound like I had been let go.

People with disabilities, a lot of their self-esteem is what they get reflected back to them. I made sure that all my people knew that I still cared about them, and it had nothing to do with them. I tried to make sure that they knew that they'd still get the best care possible, because why would I set them up to fail after I had been with most of them for 10 years? Why would I destroy their lives in any way, shape or form? I cared about my people.

One of my people had severe depression for a while, and he takes medication, and he was like, "Well, I'm just going to kill myself if you're not going to be here." And I had to stay with him so he could calm down. That was really hard. One person was like, "This is ridiculous. I'm going to write letters. I'm going to call them."

I was yelled at because people were calling the office. They got mad at me that people were calling. Like I was turning them against the company or something.

They called and said that I need to make sure that I tell my people that they are not to call, and I need to stop poisoning them against the company.

I'm like, "No. I would never do anything like that," you know? And so I'm already devastated, because I've heard that I'm losing my job, and then I'm getting calls like this. I had to pull over off the side of the road, because I was so shaky about the conversation, you know? And I'm like, "I just would never do anything like that."

One of the things that you're never supposed to tamper with is people's right to use the phone and communicate, and I'm getting yelled at that my people, unbeknownst to me, are calling and being upset that I'm not going to be there anymore. I'm like, first of all, "Shouldn't you be proud that they have the ability to call the people that they need to call when they need to call them?"

I didn't ask anyone to call. These people love me. I am good at what I do for a living. I would spend the time with my people doing what they needed one-on-one, face-to-face. They were wonderful. They still are wonderful.

We had our own little niche, and it's just gone now. Unfortunately, nobody in Indiana has those types of services. The waiting list in Indiana for programs like ours is about 10 years, and it has been since I started. It's getting longer, because they're cutting back on how much people are getting paid to provide services. There's programs out there now where you don't have to have staff in someone's home if they need 24 hour care. You can have cameras in their home. That's legal in the state of Indiana: to have cameras in people's homes. And somebody at an off-site place watches, like, eight people's places' cameras. It's like being under surveillance. If you have schizophrenia, first of all, that's a really bad idea, if you already think people might be watching you. And then secondly, talk about invasion of privacy! They're not allowed in our state to have the cameras in people's bedrooms, so there's an issue with people escaping out their bedroom windows if they're supposed to be under 24-hour surveillance. They go to their room and then they run away. I cried because this girl said that she was so excited, because there weren't cameras in her bedroom. So she would close the door and dance in her bedroom. You should be able to dance in your own apartment wherever you want to, whenever you want to—it's your place!—not afraid that cameras are going to be looking at you, so you can't dance freely in your own place. If you want to dance around naked in your own place, you should be able to do that too.

And there can even be speakers in people's homes, so if they need reminders about taking your medication, the sky can go, "It's time to take your medicine." To me, that's just absolutely horrifying. The ceiling shouldn't be talking to people with mental illness issues anyway! It just seems soulless to me. It really does.

Just unfathomable. But there's companies here that do it now. It's much cheaper than paying the same amount of staff people that would be in eight homes.

Most of my people had jobs. One of my people was independent of federal funding, because he didn't need social security to get by, because he worked full-time. And he still needed my help; he had issues with needing help with bills and things. But he could go and get a job. I don't know about today, you know, if he were to get fired or laid off. I don't know that he could go and find another job, if I'm having this much trouble finding one.

The severance, it was going to be two months for 14 years of work. It's not very much. They tried to short me about a week and a half of pay, and I called, because one check should have been a full check, and it wasn't, and I had to call Minnesota to get it straightened out. They wouldn't even let our local HR people deal with it. I had to talk to an HR supervisor, and that took a few weeks.

I tried to stay positive. It was really hard at first. I moped around a lot for a while. I tried to pretend to other people outside that I wasn't.

I grew up with some food issues that were passed down. I came by them naturally. My mom would stress eat. Like, she would go in the bathroom and eat things, which is not a normal thing to do. And I ate quite a bit when I was off, and weighed more than I ever had in my life.

Between my husband and me, I'm the one who made more money, because I was in management. Luckily my husband has had his job steadily since I got laid off so we have insurance. He keeps looking at the want ads, you know: how long is it going to be that he'll have a job?

I got to the point where I was interviewing way outside of my field of expertise. I was putting in applications at all the movie theaters around. I like people. I like movies. I can sell tickets. I don't care. You know what I mean?

I got a part-time job offer, teaching at I— Community College, but I'm a little nervous, because on the new hire paperwork, it says that there's going to be credit check, and I have terrible credit. I mean, we had no money. We were barely scraping by. We had to go to food pantries. I tried to figure out what in the world we were going to do financially. We ended up having to file for bankruptcy, so I'm still afraid about whether I'm actually going to get to keep that new part-time job. There was no question of that in the interview, about your credit. And so as soon as I saw that on the new hire packet, I made sure to email my new—hopefully future—boss and say, "I want to be upfront with you right away...we had had some rocky times, and I hope that that doesn't affect their decision to hire me." But that's kind of scary, that being laid off for two years can affect whether you can ever get another job or not. If I get a job, my credit will be better, because I'll have money to pay for things.

One of the nice things is I've seen my husband a lot more than since I've been laid off, because we hardly ever saw each other. He works a 3–11 shift, and he works every other weekend as well, and he just has Fridays off, so if I was leaving at eight o'clock in the morning, there were some days we wouldn't even see each other.

We've never had any children, and we've been going to a fertility specialist, but it doesn't look like it's going to work out, 'cause that's pretty expensive too. And adopting's expensive, so I don't know. I'm dealing with all kinds of disappointments. I try to stay positive, but it's hard.

In October of last year, we actually couldn't pay our rent, and we had to go to the Trustee's Office and get some help. In Indianapolis, we have different townships, and the Trustee Office can provide assistance for rent or electric, and you have to like, bring all of your receipts. We brought this folder of everything. You just kind of bring them your life and show how much money you have coming in, and how much money you have going out, and they see if they can help with the difference. And because we went through the Trustee's Office, they hooked us up with Thanksgiving assistance too. They told me where to be at a certain time, and Kroger supermarket had semi trucks out there, and they were just giving people bags with, like, hams and cereal and stuff. You know, it was really humbling.

They have a neat program there where you can go and do volunteer work to kind of make up the difference for the money that they're putting out for you, and I liked where they sent me, so I just went ahead and worked full-time there, doing volunteer work at the Martin Luther King Community Center, and that was kind of cool, just to be helping people. I felt like a productive member of society again.

Emergency Services

"You don't ever want to see a helmet on the floor"

Ciri Castro, Pete Peres & Damon Truitt

I'm sitting in the fire department union hall in Camden, New Jersey. It took me some time to get here.

I began a few weeks ago, stalking Engine 9 between Westfield Avenue and Federal Street, less than two miles from City Hall. The first time I approached the station no one was there. I returned the next day and still no answer—but this time there was a truck in the garage. I waited a minute or two, watching the drugs and money changing hands across the street in the parking lot next to check cashing spot. When I rang the bell once more, Ciri Castro appeared suddenly at the door of the station. He had just returned from a call, short of breath and sweating through his shirt. The truck behind him was still dripping water from a thousand spots and just beyond it there was a charred helmet. Ciri, looking both fatigued and wired, somehow had the patience and energy to sit and talk with me. Camden, the second most violent city in the US, is his hometown. There have been deep cuts to the police and fire departments, testing the city's capacity to respond to emergencies. Ciri kept his job— clearly—and maybe even picked up a few more since the layoffs.

He is 36 years old and his sweat beads against his shaven head. He looks to be about 98% muscle. His father emigrated from Puerto Rico so he could go to college, become a professional, raise a family. "American Dream, the whole thing...I guess we got here too late." I asked Ciri if he could put me in touch with firefighters who'd been laid off. He pulled out his cell phone and told me to start writing down names and numbers.

After several weeks and several phones calls, I'm in the Union Hall with Ciri, Damon Truitt, and Pete Peres. There's a rainy Wednesday outside the windows of the room where we sit. The union only recently acquired this place and they're still moving in, painting, patching up. In fact nothing's really been put in place other than scattered chairs and a couple of rectangular tables—and a trophy, of course, from the annual football game against the New York Fire Department. The only ornament unboxed, it projects sacredness.

The layoffs in the Camden fire and police departments happened in January of 2011. In the following months, the city brought some of the firemen back through federal grants and reallocated tax revenue. Pete has been rehired; Damon has not. "We were sworn in again," Pete says, "and honestly, they were trying to make it another media event, you know, swearing us in. 'Oh, bring your family.' I don't think anybody brought their family. And we had to do all of our paperwork again. We were new hires—that's what it was."

Like Ciri, Pete's family is from Puerto Rico. He's stocky and keeps his Verizon baseball cap pushed back so he can rub his forehead. In addition to working for the fire department, Pete keeps a second job installing cable. At 45 he's heavily involved in the Camden community. He took his Little League team to play baseball on the lawn of the White House. He has a son at Rutgers and a daughter at Brown. "I've got an Ivy Leaguer studying psychology and hopefully she'll gets her PhD. 'Cause then she'll set her own path. She is a product of Camden's charter schools. But she'd have made it anywhere."

Damon is 37 and maybe somehow even more muscular than Ciri. He has shiny silver shirt and dark, calm eyes. He watches everything closely and doesn't say as much as the others; his interjections are always more terse—and more loaded, too. His wife had been a police officer with the city but also lost her job. They received their termination letters a week a part.

Born and raised in Camden, Damon survived a public school system that, in yesterday's newspaper, unveiled the ICE-T[1] program, which will pay 70 high schoolers $100 to attend the first three weeks of class. He and Pete both shake their heads when I ask for thoughts on the program.

"I think Camden can infamously be known as a place that takes care of kids that can play sports but don't have a lick of education," says Pete. "I do baseball and all that and I get the kids that come from outside this country— Dominican Republic, Puerto Rico, you know, even Mexico—and that's all they're thinking: they want to play baseball. That's gonna be their key to get out. And they have no idea."

There are many abandoned and burned buildings throughout the city—an arsonist has been busy this summer. Ciri suggests that I see North Camden for myself—the neighborhood he calls "zombieland," the neighborhood where he takes his daughter to school—but warns that I'll probably get pulled over by a cop because I'm white and, generally speaking, white people only go to zombieland to pay for drugs and sex. Of course the warning assumes that there are cops on patrol in the area.

Damon: January 18th, we had to turn our gear in. 67 guys…

---

[1]   "I Can End Truancy"

Pete: You're talking about a third. A third of us were gone. And we're like, guys with 10, 12 years. And police officers I heard as much as 12 to 15 years were laid off. Then you lay off 180 police officers.

You know, it was a somber moment. We felt like this was a new day as a group. We're united by our brotherhood and sisterhood when we graduate the academy. You know, we have our class. Now we have a new class. It's the class that got laid off.

We wanted to be united in our act to turn in our gear, and we had a big march down Market Street with all the firefighters that were going to be laid off. The police officers, what they did—and his wife was there (motioning to Damon)—they put their boots down to show solidarity amongst those police officers. And when we got to the headquarters at the fire department, we made a line, and we laid our helmets down.

Damon: I can honestly say that January 18th was probably one of the saddest days. I haven't seen that many grown men and women cry—probably only at a funeral. That's how sad it was that day.

Ciri: When you have an individual that's killed in the line of duty, they lay their helmet on the individual's casket, you know, out of respect. They killed our morale. They took our guys away from us. And they killed it. That's what it meant to me. Seeing the helmets on that floor. You don't ever want to see a helmet on the floor, because that means something's wrong. It hurt.

Pete: After we all turned in our equipment, it was just like, to go home to what? We've committed ourselves to public safety, to be firemen, to risk our lives, to save lives, and yet here's what we get.

It really changed my perception on what the politicians represent. We begged and pleaded with our council members: don't vote for it. Don't support the layoff. Send a message. I would've loved—even if it would've just been one council member—to just say, "No. I can't vote to lay these people off." Not one of them did.

When a firefighter or a policeman dies in the line of duty, all the politicians are right there, you know? But in this case, no one. We had families with children. Damon, his wife…they have children, their house. They were living right here in Camden. It was like, you guys are laid off and that's it. You know, we're blaming the union. The union didn't do enough. They didn't give back enough.

Now mind you, we have to pay more into the pension that I'm paying into because the government borrowed money from my pension and never paid it back. Now how's that fair? That money came from money that I earned, you know?

Damon: New Jersey owes the pension system millions of dollars. Millions. And won't repay it. I mean, that's straight gangsterness to me. I just think they're all mobsters, really. For real. Gangsters. You hear about Christie, this guy, he's been on more vacations his first six months in office than I've been my whole life. 'Cause they do nothing for the poor, and it is all for the rich. Like, the middle class…It's like, they're going after teachers, firefighters and police officers. All these people are public safety, and you got teachers who are for the kids—you need teachers. If they keep messing with the public safety, little kids are not going to want to be cops and firefighters anymore. It's not even going to be worth it. Honestly. If they keep taking their benefits and salaries, they might as well go work behind a desk somewhere.

Pete: Become a politician.

Damon: Or become a politician, yeah.

Pete: The mayor came up on the forefront here and said that the unions did not want to give any concessions, and that basically tied her hands in doing all this. They have the senior citizens buying it too. Like, everything that the senior citizens have to pay, it's all our fault. It's the police and fireman's fault.

Damon: Yeah, the perception of the firefighter is that he sleeps all day.

Pete: We come in the morning. We have responsibilities. We have chores. We have to go over every piece of equipment including the fire truck and the fire apparatus. Make sure that it's operational. Any little thing that's out, we have to write a report and coordinate with our captain. Then there's training. We encourage those who aspire to be captains and chiefs to study. Read. But in the meantime, yeah, I do have to rest my body because I don't know if I'm gonna be in a major fire.

Now it's like, the politicians don't have my back, the community somewhat is turned against us in the sense that politicians were able to get the citizens to perceive that "Oh, they're just overpaid. They're causing your taxes to go up." You know, we're the cause of the property tax. How is that fair? And I know because I'm in the community. I understand people's perceptions. And I said, "When did becoming a fireman and a policeman make us the bad guys?"

Damon: The thing that really gets me is it's not like it's a regular job, you know. You know, firemen, you're away from your family for a whole day, a whole 24 hours. And then you never know whether I'm going to come home, whether he's going to make it home or not. Anything can happen, you know? You inhale all types of chemicals throughout your career, and you never know. After you retire…you might not even be able to enjoy it. People made a lot of sacrifices to become firemen and police. You know, cops get shot at. My wife had a pretty decent job. She was a manager. She left all that to become a cop. She was actually studying law enforcement. So she was almost finished with college, finishing her Associate's to become a parole officer. Once she became a cop, she had goals on being a detective. And in six months, she had no job.

Ciri: Now you're putting more strain on guys, 'cause now you have less rest in between. This job is mentally, physically and emotionally stressful. Shouldn't my life have some worth? I mean, I'm doing what I do because I love to do it. Why can't I be compensated for it? If I'm gone, who's gonna take care of my family?

Damon: I'm actually angry as we speak now. It's rough. It's been seven months now, just been trying to survive as best as we can. It's really rough. I'm just totally angry at the city. I have no faith in the politicians. They're coming at the public sector—they think we make all this money, and we don't really work, and we live in these big houses. No. Me and my family, we just want to live comfortable. My wife was only making, like, $32,000. Our combined salary wasn't even $90,000. And then you read about politicians, people in Christie's camp, they're making $180,000 easy. So it's just ridiculous to me.

My kids' birthday was just Saturday. They're in school. They don't know really what's going on. As long as we got a roof over our head, food on the table, they're not concerned. My oldest daughter, she knows we're out of work, but she don't really say anything about it.

Pete: I was born and raised here. Went to school here. I still own my house in Camden. I volunteer my time with our Little League baseball. I made the sacrifice because it was in my heart to serve the city. It's disheartening to go through what we went through in the academy to get this job. People that left great paying jobs, like his wife was a manager, making decent money. To take a pay cut. To become a police officer in this city. It's a prideful thing to be. "Hey, I'm a police officer. I'm gonna do this, and I'll make the sacrifice." And this is how you repay me?

Ciri: I am one of the trainers in the academy. I helped out with the last two classes to get brought in. It's like teaching kids…. They're crawling, and I'm teaching them how to take steps. Some of them dreamed of being firemen. To see them leaving…I took it real personal, because these guys are like my little brothers. Some of them loved being—this is all they had.

Pete: Out of the 31 firefighters, 15 came back on money that the mayor had gotten through the South Jersey Port. Supposedly South Jersey Port owes Camden tax money, something like that, and they were able to draw up some money to get some people back. Then they had the SAFER[1] Grant, which was through FEMA. Sixteen of us got back on that. There's a seniority order. The chief had to work with the civil service to make sure they had the right guys coming back.

Ciri: It was getting really heated, you know? It came to a point where, you know, it was police officers and firefighters. Then it trickled down to where it became senior guys and junior guys. And sometimes it takes some of us to just step up and be like, look, it's not about you. It's not about me. It's about these people out here, man. (He swung his finger in circles, as if tracing all of Camden.)

Pete: And I'm praying he (looking to Damon) gets back.

Damon: Hopefully something comes through. I actually just came from filling out an application this morning. It's a basic driving job. I think it's medical transportation or something like that.

I have a couple little hustles that I do. I clean carpets. I also cook. My uncle's actually opening a restaurant right down the street. I think it's

[1]   Staffing for Adequate Fire & Emergency Response

going to be open by the end of the month, so I'm going to be helping out cooking with him. I gotta keep busy.

Ciri: And Damon's a hell of a pancake maker, let me tell you. He makes some of the best pancakes. This guy, he can cook. Just don't call him Johnny Cakes. He don't like that. (Laughs.)

Pete: They downsized this city so much, there's only one battalion chief for the entire city of 80,000, you know? One emergency is what we're prepared to handle. Things are happening because of that, you know. Fires, people getting hurt, crime. At one point finally the chief admitted that the crime rate had gone up. In my trip to Capitol Hill to see Nancy Pelosi, she said to me, "Who in their right mind lays off that many people in the most violent city in the nation?" Camden had been the most violent city for the last three years—until last year, it dropped down to number two.

When you start messing with public safety and individuals that have to deal with the work, that's destruction coming, man.

A firefighter out of Engine 10 was responding to a dwelling fire in the Fairview section of Camden. Their responding ladder company that was there is now closed. So they had ladder companies responding from further away.

Damon: Coordinated attack.

Pete: Anybody who knows firefighter tactics and operations, you have a coordinated attack between the ladder company and the engine company to coordinate ventilation so there's no flashover. That engine company's there by themselves. They're waiting for that ladder company. In the process of them doing what they had to do—no coordinated attack—flashover. A firefighter burns his face. And that was it. One of our brothers got hurt.

That happened over the weekend. That very Monday, we were picketing City Hall, letting the public know—look at what's happening here.

There was an arsonist in the city. I don't know if you guys heard about this. In the last two months, there was a series of fires in Camden. Major fires and major property that was a certain type of construction that was very hard to fight. The one I was on was a 12-alarm fire. It was out there all day and night. Had companies coming from all over. Now, could that fire have been prevented had we had all companies in place that day? Only God knows, I believe that, but a good point is that Engine 8 was permanently closed, which was close to where that 12-alarmer happened. Maybe if Engine 8 had gotten there, we could've prevented the mass destruction that happened that day.

I know that everyone's hopeful that we will get everybody back. We need that. We're so understaffed, you know. We really would like to keep fighting until we get back to our original 12 companies, the chiefs that were in place. It was a sense of comfort for us to do our job knowing that there was manpower there. Now, in the back of my mind, I'm hesitant. Because if I go down, that manpower that's supposed to be there to save my life isn't there, or isn't going to be there right away. And this is something you try to reiterate over and over to these politicians, but I really feel as though they have a sense of "who are these guys who don't do nothing," you know?

Ciri: They say, "You guys take your time. Don't rush to the job if you're getting hurt." I'm sorry, but this is what I'm trained to do and what I love to do. I love to help people. And if somebody's stuck in a burning building, I'll be damned if you're going to tell me to slow down. I'm gonna get there, it's what I was put on this Earth to do…my calling.

We're talking about having two guys per truck. There is no way you can adequately staff a truck with two people. You can't. I'm driving. You have an officer. What are we going to do? Now he's supposed to run with the hose by himself? He can't. That really killed morale right there. And it just started like a domino effect. We have to work twice as hard, but we do what we do. And I'm going to work with what I have, even if it's less. I did five and a half years in the military. It's nothing to me. I've been given scraps—and made coal to shine like a diamond later on. (Smiles.)

Pete: We're going to keep fighting. I picketed City Hall. And the politicians didn't like that. They didn't like the up in your face. You try to be professional, because I don't want to get arrested. But we pressured the mayor. I supported the mayor before she got elected. And now it's just like, they're careful with me. Which is okay. I have no problem with that. I stood up for something I believed in…

The last city council meeting I went to was where they voted to allow them to research this regionalization for the police force.[1] Everyone who spoke that day, 60 or so people—majority weren't even police officers and firefighters—said, "We don't want this regionalization county police department." You would have to eliminate half the police force and start all over. Not one resident said, "Yeah, support this. We want this." Not one. And the council still voted to do it. So where are they getting their feedback from? I thought the council in particular was supposed to represent the people, you know? Why waste my time here and wait three or four hours just to speak? And then you have two minutes, "Oh, you're done." Some of them won't even look up at you. Sometimes I feel like saying, "Can you pay attention to what I'm saying instead of writing and reading or whatever you're doing?"

I really feel like going to the council's a waste a time, because I think they have their mind set on what they're gonna do. I was upset. I even said, my words to them was, "You know, I come here as my last faith in you, because I really am losing faith." So I don't know. I think that will be my last council meeting for a while.

It's funny how the perception is we are all in this together. The governor, the mayor, they say are all in this together. Well then, take a hit. Take a sacrifice. Our mayor wanted to increase her staff's salary...

Damon: By 10%.

Pete: The governor was quoted—I saw the interview—someone asked him, "Why don't you take a pay cut?"

And he says, "That's apples and oranges."

I said, "Is it?"

Our governor's a piece of work, could've solved a lot of issues if he had just taxed the millionaires, the tax that Corzine wanted to implement had he won. But this guy, I guess, sold his soul to those people in the sense of elect me and I won't tax you. Money rules the world. I honestly believe that. The mentality of the rich is, "I earned it. I'm blessed. You're not. You didn't earn it. You're weak. You deserve to be where you're at, and I deserve

---

[1] "Regionalization" of the police force would give the state of New Jersey authority over a local law enforcement unit that Camden would have to, in effect, share with other municipalities.

to be where I'm at, and I don't need to do anything to help you." It's that mentality, you know—it's a scary mentality.

Ciri: We're trying to do the best that we can as a union. We do fundraisers.

Pete: We have a separate account for the laid off guys to try to get some money in their hands to help them out. Obviously, there's no way we as a union could give a firefighter a full income. But we're trying. Most of us are trying to do the right thing. Morale is terrible, it's just terrible. And all the damage that's been done here, I don't know if it's repairable. Maybe if we can restore the entire fire department to what it was, and maybe also replace these elected officials that haven't necessarily represented us. And it's our fault too, because we have to get out and vote. And that's the thing. Camden is taken for granted because they feel like any politician can come in here and do what they want. They say, "Camden? They don't vote." The Mayor can win an election here with 2,000 votes in a city of 80,000. How does that make sense?

Ciri: My kids love what I do. My nieces and nephews love to say that their uncle's a firefighter. My dad's a firefighter. That right alone is enough of a drive for me, you know? My kids are the world to me. I have two nephews that in the beginning it was a little rough for my brother, you know. He made a couple bad judgments, and I helped raise his kids as well. And I have a nine-year old daughter. That's my heart. That's my drive. If it wasn't for that little girl, who knows where I would be. She's the one that made me change a lot of things in my life.

Now I just found out this year she's not mine. She's nine years old. You know, it hurt. But she may not be mine, DNA-wise, but she's mine. You ask her who she looks like, she'll point right at me. When I look at her, I see things that I am, how I am. She's always quick to help. She's always quick to jump up and do something for somebody. And I notice that that's her watching me, because she's always spent a lot of time with me.

My kids are fine. You know, not doing as good as we were before, but love's free. We could be in a box floating down the water, as long as they're with me, they're happy.

Damon: I've been in the city of Camden my entire life. I mean, you know the city of Camden is one of the most dangerous cities. It's not that hard to go get in trouble. I got the job when I was 32 years old. 32 years, no trouble. I finally catch a break, get a career. Firefighter. Doing pretty good for myself and my family. You know, we're living comfortable. All that gone. Now what I was making, I'm probably getting half of that. Every time I turn around, my bank account is overdrawn. I mean, I'm to here—(raising his hand to his forehead)—with New Jersey and this city. If I had an opportunity, I would leave, I would fly. I think what they've done is turned a career into just a job.

Pete: Just a job.

Damon: It used to be a career. When you're a fireman or a cop and you get that call, you don't hesitate. You don't think about nothing. You go. And that's what happens. On 9/11, they went. And they made the ultimate sacrifice.

Pete: It's disheartening to not feel…you know, after 9/11, police and firemen were the be-all glory of this nation. Now we just don't feel that honor anymore. You know? We just don't. We don't feel honored anymore.

After we finish up at the Union Hall, Ciri takes Tasha and me to see a couple of the areas where they've put out some of the big fires. The site of the 12-alarmer wiped out nearly a block and is covered with flyers from the EPA noting they've been around and everybody else should stay away. I stare at the jagged piles of broken bricks and the rain begins to pick up. Ciri has to get back to the station. Before he leaves, he tells us to call him if we're still around for dinner—he'd like us to join his family.

BOOK SEVEN

FRINGE

"This is my latest"

Kaitlin & May

Reno is a city awash in eponymous tattoos and shuttered casino buildings: there is a lot of pride in this town, and emptiness too. Amid the bold and limping are May and Kaitlin, whose stories say something about the edges, and also something about the center.

Kaitlin has black hair and pale skin. She's the outgoing one, the one who spotted us the moment we walked into the place and pulled us over. Her face mostly defaults to a smile, and she can probably start—and sustain—a conversation with anyone. At 22 she's studying English and Women's Studies at the University of Nevada at Reno (UNR). She can't decide whether to commit to a Women's Studies major. It'd mean more classes—and more challenging classes. It would mean more work. But she seems to want it.

May's a bit older, 26 and fidgety. Her eyes wander and I can't tell if it's because she's nervous to talk to us or if she's coming down from something—or both. She has an uncontrollable energy beneath her haze. Her hair is blonde and her eyes prefer the floor.

Kaitlin and May are roommates; they met on Craig's List. They sit at a table with Mallery, MJ and me, drinks all around. The walls, floor and ceiling throb with music; Guns 'N Roses gives way to The Murder City Devils. Lights flash here and there but the club is mostly dark.

May just graduated from UNR with a degree in psychology. She had a job at the school in a computer lab. Since the beginning of 2009, the university has cut more than 600 budgeted positions. May was laid off a month ago. She knew her job was temporary but it ended sooner than expected. She begins on a sarcastic note:

May: It actually was an accounting error is how they explained to me. (Rolls her eyes.) The budget cuts did not allow the money that the department needed. So they let me go in June even though I was supposed to work through the summer.

They had to send me an email and I knew what the email was about but of course they wanted to tell me in person. It was about eleven in the morning. I knew what was going on but it wasn't official until they told me in person. And they took about a half an hour to tell me what I already knew.

What'd they tell you?

May: We're closing for the summer as of June. And this was the day before June 1st. I just said I'll be using you for a reference and thank you for telling me in person. I hope I get paid for this meeting. (Laughs.) I'll be putting it on my time sheet. (More laughing.)

Who was the first person you told?

May: My parents. I told them they fired me early.

What'd they say?

May: Well, that sucks.

I ask May what her parents did—or do—for a living. She doesn't want to say. I ask what her grandparents did for a living. She doesn't want to say. She's done talking about her family.

What's your ideal job?

May: Just teaching and working with kids, maybe. Educational psychology—or education.

Moments later her name is called over the loud speaker and May puts down her drink. She walks across the room and disappears behind a curtain. After a stark silence between blaring songs, "Silence of the Setting Sun" by Amber Asylum comes over the sound system and May emerges onto a small stage under a disco ball.

I stare at Mallery and MJ, trying to avoid all else. Then it feels weird not to look. So I turn to the stage. That's not right—so I whip back to MJ and Mallery. They look equally unsettled and we all speed up on the drinks, the only safe place to anchor our attention.

Kaitlin openly stares at May on stage. She grimaces, just a bit, and breaks into commentary:

Kaitlin: For the record I did make her into a stripper. I made four of my university friends into strippers. This is my latest.

Kaitlin eyes May's movements, studying with a distinct focus.

Kaitlin: She's still learning so don't judge…

Kaitlin is Kaitlin's real name because Kaitlin is proud to be a stripper. May is not May's real name. May has been at this a month and looks rigid on stage. MJ and Mallery look rigid. I feel rigid. It's too early on a Friday night; there's a spattering of patrons and they

are all otherwise occupied. May does not steal away any attention.
Kaitlin continues to track her:

Kaitlin: I just said to her, "You know, you could make good money. And the economy is shit." She doesn't have a job. We can't pay for this apartment. I'm like, "Dude, there's a job at the strip club." You know, embrace your fucking goddess, empower yourself and listen to music and make money.

One of my friends, Lisa, she strips full time with me. It pays for her school—straight A's, neuroscience. So it really works with her. Another girl totally failed. It was horrible. She was shy. You can't be shy and do this. She just did it once. It just doesn't work for some girls, you know.

I like to break it down to the hour. I was making fifty dollars an hour last night, you know. So I remind myself of that and I'm like, "Okay, I'm doing the right thing." You know? It pays off, it pays off.

I think waiting tables is degrading—you want to talk about that? The way people treat you. And it pays less. Why would I subject myself to that? No. I want to be a stripper. I want to strip. I love music. I love to be sexual and express myself. You know what's funny? I feel much more comfortable naked on stage, in front of a bunch of people, than I do at a coffee shop. Or just giving a presentation in my class. This (nodding toward the stage) has made it to where I can approach professors, I can, like, talk. I'm better at public speaking.

But I still get nervous fully-clothed in front of a class—I'm, like, naked up there!

My top's off: I'm unphased.

Kaitlin likes to read, these days it's all about feminism: Full Frontal
Feminism, Who Stole Feminism. She blogs about stripping, having
sex, menstruating, dating. She's written openly—and speaks
openly—about having an abortion. Her ideal job is "making my
living as a writer." She has a sex column; she's trying to start a
student magazine.

Her mom knows she strips.

Kaitlin: Basically I told her "I'm 22 two now I'm gonna start stripping full time. If I make a hundred dollars a night, I should be able to start paying for school so…

I don't get any help, I pay for everything.

And my hair's falling out and I cry but it's okay. It's not that bad. I think you just really have to embrace it, you know, you got to own it.

She gets up to check with the DJ.

Mallery, MJ and I polish off our drinks, no words.

Kaitlin rushes back over with orders for us to sit in the chairs nearest the stage. We get up and file toward the front, a sudden posse; the spare crowd stares at our awkward crossing. We take our seats and there is no leg room whatsoever: our knees smash against the stage, which rises even with our eyeballs.

Kaitlin comes out to the opening notes of Muse's "Supermassive Black Hole."

Considering the height of the stage, and our proximity to it, we have to look up at a serious angle to see Kaitlin's face. She slinks down onto the floor under the lights. When she looks at us, her smile is a bit more nervous than it was back at the shadowed table. I'm smiling too—also nervous-looking, I'm sure. I peek at Mallery whose mouth is as twitchy as mine. Also her eyes are bulging from their sockets.

Kaitlin crawls to the edge of the stage and puts Mallery's head between her breasts. She backs up and smiles at all three of us. She confesses she's nervous to dance in front of us after talking to us.

I think we all might have preferred to continue with conversation instead.

But work called, and now Kaitlin twists around and spreads her legs in front of MJ and me. We both see a small white string sticking out from her underwear. My eyes swing over to MJ in time to see the color run from his paralyzed face. Mallery soon turns to stone and now we've all spotted it. Kaitlin continues across the floor, slinking and twisting and opening herself in various ways.

Moments pass, or maybe years, and finally another woman who works at the club approaches the stage with a dollar folded neatly into a fan, which she uses to shield her brief conversation with Kaitlin. And suddenly all expression leaves Kaitlin's face—or every expression befalls it, I can't tell which. She closes her eyes, sitting on her knees, probably seeking escape, only to return with open eyes moments later. She swings away from us, toward the back of the stage.

She spends a moment alone, mostly outside the perimeter of circling disco ball light, still slightly swaying to the pulsing notes. Within a few moments she pivots back toward us with a smile that is all at once destroyed and resolute on repair. She continues dancing, throwing in jokes, reassembling her dignity. She moves until the end. The song fades out and we clap wildly.

"Got the t-shirt to prove it"

Scott Cooksley

Scott, 46, comes from a home twice broken: "my parents married, had me, six months later, got divorced, and remarried when I was 4–5, and then divorced when I was 13." His mother died four years ago; he was her caretaker for over a decade: "She was a diabetic for 51 years. Hard core."

An only child, Scott has lost touch with most of his extended family. "We kind of separated out, my mom's side of the family kind of got disjointed." He anticipates some might find him on Facebook now that's he recently joined—it's only been a few weeks, and he's a little wary of the thing altogether, as he tends to measure closely how many people he lets into his life: "A lot of people know me—but I have very small groups, I can count on one hand close friends. But that's just my choice."

He's had a few marriages; the most recent ended in 2006. He keeps in touch with two grown children who both live in different states.

We are sitting in Scott's office at the St. Vincent's Food Pantry in Reno, Nevada. He keeps his thick glasses pushed into their proper place, despite a broken temple, and his gray goatee is closely trimmed. The charity he works for has been around for over seventy years. Scott is currently the manager of distribution. It's June and he's planning for Thanksgiving: "I'm already collecting turkeys for our holiday distribution. I actually put in my order for this year, an order for 400 turkeys—the week before I even gave stuff out last year."

When I started here two and a half years ago, we were doing about 5,000 to 6,000 people a month. Last month, we did just under 27,000. This month, on a slow month, we're gonna do about 25,000 to 26,000. We only have two paid staff work here. I have a core group of about 40 volunteers, so it's a very volunteer-driven program. Six days a week we do this.

It's pretty basic: we give a monthly supplemental box. Anywhere from families of one through six. We also do what we call dailies, which are bags. Today it has Starbucks instant coffee in it, they have fruit, box juices, crackers, cookies—whatever we get.

Working people, people that lose their jobs...one of the first things you lose, or you give up, is the food—it's the easiest, "Oh, I only need... I can skip a meal." You start with that, you skip a meal.

Two years ago, we distributed 1.1 million pounds of food. Last year was just over 2 million. This year's gonna be about 2.4. Next year, I'm actually trying to get us set up so we will distribute 3.5 million pounds of food. Our community is about 420,000 people, to put it in perspective, that's our last census. When we're done with this month, this is the fiscal year, that's one way we count, we will have fed almost 254,000 people. So almost half the county came through.

Most of these people that we get are not homeless—that's kind of a stereotype, people usually think, oh, they're homeless. I would say less than ten percent of my clientele is homeless. A lot of people don't want their friends or family to know that they're getting this kind of help. Most people, I find, once they get the courage to ask for help, they're past that point, they should have had it three or four months before. The majority of people don't wanna be there—they try to get out of it. They're caught in a rut, they don't know how to break the cycle.

I was there.

Couple years ago, that was me standing out there, looking for food. I've been with these people—been there, done that, got the t-shirt to prove it. I'm not proud of it, it almost darn right—excuse me, I'm gonna swear—damn right about killed me. Literally.

I worked for E—[1] for five years. I was a restaurant manager, I was making really good money, I had a lot of perks, most of them were unsaid perks, but you get perks being a restaurant. It was a great company—I have no hard feelings with the E— family, they were great. They're wacky, it's like a soap opera, you got four brothers and a sister, they're in their 50s now, or pushing 60. They're great. Grandkids are in there. I thought they could have made other cuts, and not necessarily personnel cuts, to save the money. But from my point of view, that's past, I don't care, I can look past it. Again, I cut that part of my life out and I'm done with it, and I'm moving on. That's something that I had to do.

About three to four months before, I had a feeling that they were gonna do this, that they were gonna cut. Not my first rodeo so I, I mean, I've been around, I can see it.

I would say, back in November, I had a feeling that was what was going to happen. I was laid off in February, February 28 I believe it was.

Then the day before they cut us, I got a phone call late in the afternoon, saying, I need to have you come down at 4:30. As soon as I got that phone call—and I got it from our food and beverage director—I knew what it was about. Oh, they're gonna go ahead and cut me, Ok.

Go in there, and they go into this conference room, food and beverage director's right here, HR director sitting right there—who I was friends with, and still to this day I really like him, good guy—and they tell me, "Well, they're eliminating your position."

---

[1] Large casino

And I said, "Ok, no hard feelings."

I wasn't shocked, I really wasn't, I wasn't mad. I was hurt, of course, you know, I'm not gonna be stupid or deny that. I was hurt. I was the easy target. I had set it up so my guys could work without me, I had it set up really well. Which is what you're supposed to do, as a manager, department manager—the operations still should go even while you're not there, it should go smooth so you can go do whatever you need to do.

So that was my day. That evening I went out to dinner, met a friend of mine, he was working in a casino. The next week I talked with friends, kind of relaxed, didn't really do much of anything 'cause now I didn't have a routine. I was living in a weekly motel when I left—when I was fired. I had lost my mom, I had lost her eight months before. I moved from Reno over to Sparks, neighboring cities like Minneapolis-St. Paul. And I was living at a weekly there, and then I started running out of money. I had friends I was mooching off to try and get rent. They were helping me, I would get rent, but sometimes I had to use it to get some medical stuff.

Twelve years ago I had a heart attack. I actually had five heart attacks in an eight-month period. I was 34. It killed me. I was gone for eleven minutes—ten, eleven minutes. You basically come back from the dead, cause that's what you are—I'm not trying to be dramatic about it. All your energy in all your cells has been drained out of you, cause all your hormones go out, all your adrenaline. They say it can take anywhere from twelve to eighteen months...to get them back into what would be full strength. And it took me a month just to be able to go up and down a flight of stairs.

I went through cancer. I've gone through four bouts of cancer in the last three years—just finished up my fourth. I've had skin cancer, had liver cancer, had lymphomic Hodgkins, and then I had another form of Hodgkins. So I've had some hard times. I wasn't working, didn't have an income, people were hounding me 'cause I owed, and all that. Basically I was shutting down. I was over in the park over at Sparks off of McCarran, sleeping under trees. I did that off and on for about five months. I've eaten out of the garbage cans, given up my medical stuff, lost all my stuff and had to start from scratch. Know that. Know what it's like to go for a week or two or three or four without taking a shower, days without brushing my teeth and maybe just using my finger to kinda...

Scott smashes his index finger up against his clenched smile, scrubbing back and forth.

...maybe get some of the gunk out of my teeth. I know what that's like—it ain't fun.

I wasn't getting income, living with my friends, depending on them. Hey, I need a pair of shoes, and just hopefully they'll notice, maybe they'll buy me some...those kind of things, you know, it's embarrassing. Just some basic needs—can I get some mouthwash? You go to pick up mouthwash at the store, you go shopping with your friends that you're living with, they get their stuff—can I get a bottle of mouthwash too? Can I get some soap?

We give out hygiene kits—hygiene kits are huge. You start losing your self esteem, your self worth and all those things if you can't keep yourself—even combing your hair, brushing your teeth, wear a little deodorant—whatever it might be—cleaning your glasses, having glasses that work right. I got all excited when I would get, let's say, a bottle of mouthwash. You hoard it—and then you start hoarding things 'cause you didn't have them for so long. So when you get that first paycheck and you actually get money and you wanna go buy—you wanna buy food 'cause maybe you've been without food; you buy all this food but then you don't know what to do with it, and you don't wanna eat it, you just wanna sit and look at it, and "Oh, I don't wanna use it 'cause I may not...if I use it now, I won't have it tomorrow." That's kind of the mentality. It's definitely changed my perception, the different things I've gone through in the last four years. And a lot of it basically started from losing my job. Not saying that the other stuff wouldn't have happened to me, but that was a key moment in my life, when I lost that job, because I didn't have the stability, I didn't have a routine, I didn't have a circle of friends or companions or acquaintance—I lost that. Let alone the money issue. I lost a lot there. Self respect. Self esteem, whatever you wanna call it, I lost that. So then how do you go back to rebuild that?

I had some really good friends…one night I called them…and three or four of my friends got together with their trucks 'cause I still had some stuff. Moved me into my friend's house. I was there for about a year and a half. That's when I started volunteering here—it was two years this past April. I was volunteering here for almost eleven months then I was asked to take a part-time position. We hit it off, and they liked what I was doing with the food pantry and kind of liked what I was doing for the community. Slowly getting my life together, I was still living with my friends, I was finally getting a paycheck, $200 every two weeks—but when you have nothing, that's a lot. And this last September, I moved out into a weekly motel, which is just down the street here, I moved from my friends'. I needed to get on my own and I did that. And this past February, I moved into my own apartment for the first time in I don't know how long. It was a great feeling to pay that first month's rent. It sounds funny, especially at my age, but those things mean a lot.

Generally speaking, from my own experience and what I see with these people that have lost their jobs, they give up their own personal food to make sure the other members of their family can survive, they give up their own medical so they give it to their family. You might be a diabetic, well, I don't need those shots. You do those kind of things. We see a lot of that with people, you see multi-families, multiple households, joining households. Maybe one car, there are two or three families sharing it.

My job here is to identify some of those people, especially families, to get them on the right track. To get them to agencies that help, that I can help maybe get them to move up and get out of their cars, get into the monthlies, maybe out of the monthlies and into regular apartments, get them financial aid, get them food aid, whatever medical they might need for them and their families. Their pets—'cause pets are important too. When somebody's homeless, pets are the last thing that they give up. They will stay homeless if they can't have the pet. They share their food with their pet, even though it may not be good for their pet nor them. I see it every day. I've been here two and a half years…so I understand, it's not a quick fix for people. And I think the community, the society, needs to understand that.

We're the service arm of the Reno diocese of Catholic charities. A lot of people assume if you work for a Catholic organization you're Catholic. But I'm not Catholic. I'm not gonna bag somebody 'cause maybe that's their faith or they don't have an identity to any kind of faith. That's OK too cause that's their thing. It's like saying somebody you can't approve of because of their living arrangements. Or their social arrangements. Who cares? If they're happy and they're not actually hurting anybody, I don't care. I could really care less, 'cause you know, you come into this world with nothing; you basically leave this world with nothing—and what you do in between, you really have a lot of choices.

A lot of these people used to be what would be considered the middle class, which in my own personal opinion, we don't have in America anymore. I don't think we have a middle class. I think it's been gone for about seven or eight years. Whose fault is that? It's ours as a society. Here's the big problem in this country with the way we look at/deal with unemployment, and deal with people that need services and stuff: most those people, it's not by choice. But now with the government assistance programs, that are supposed to be assisting, they're being paid—or told— not to work. And I think that's the problem. They should stop extensions and take that money and put it into jobs programs, put it into job training programs, education programs so people can get their GEDs, so people can get daycare so they can go to classes so they can go look for work. You got a lot of single parent families—not just moms, but dads, that have kids. They're not being given an opportunity to do this.

My grandparents went through the depression, and they had the jobs programs, that's when all the social programs started putting people to work. Maybe all they were doing is giving people a room and food, but gosh darn, they were working, at least they felt better about themselves. Why can't they do that here? They talk about it. Why can't that money be used?—it'll help self-esteem. It'll probably help cut down on criminal activity. Abuse: mental, physical, spousal, child. Cut down on suicides. Cut down on mental health issues. If people could be working and doing something, to prove themselves, to stabilize themselves, to get food—it all starts with the work. You have to have four walls and a roof, you gotta have food—but you need to be working. These people that are retired, they don't just sit around and do nothing. I have a lot of volunteers—the average age of my volunteers is probably close to 60. They're working even though they're volunteering—I'm not paying them. In a lot of respects, I'm benefitting from them, they're talking about their experiences and things like that. When you're not working you're not part of that. That's a big thing to me. It's not just to get an income, it's to get the self-worth, the self-esteem, to feel good about yourself, to build your friends up, to get in working relationships, to get into all that. You have to have that.

"Step-by-Step"

Tout Tou Bounthapanya

Her father was a military man. In 1975, when the communist movement gained control of Laos after decades of civil war, he was on the wrong side of the triumphant Pathet Lao and was sent to a work camp. As a teenager, Tout Tou crossed the Mekong River and escaped to Thailand with her younger brother. She describes many pinpoint details—such as climbing out of the water, hungry and disoriented—while skipping countless others that she does not, or cannot express.

After four refugee camps, "We came over here, we didn't know what to do, but thank God the American government help us…like you know how my dad say, 'I want you to have freedom.'"

She now lives and works in Fresno, California, helping immigrants get jobs. Many, like Tout Tou, arrive under refugee status. In this environment the pursuit of employment takes places in a whirl of confusion and isolation. Depression seems built into the experience. Tout Tou has confronted suicide and attempted suicide throughout the communities where she lives and works.

*And she's overcome her own self-destructive thoughts: "I was going
to hang myself, and one time I bring out this long knife that I was
going to slice my stomach." She smiles a lot and she holds back tears
often. She has long black hair and engaging, kind eyes.*

*The funding for the non-profit program that pays Tout Tou's
salary will expire at the end of the summer. She does not know if
she will have her job past September. It's easy to see how she excels
at what she does, helping people grasp information outside of their
usual parameters. When we first spoke on the phone and I was the
white guy struggling to make sure I understood her unfamiliar
name, she made it easy: "Tout Tou. Like, not one-one or three-three.
But two-two.' She speaks an individualized and excellent brand of
English that makes her unconventionally communicative.*

Right now I'm working here at FIRM[1]. The mission statement is
sharing Christ's love to build community of hope with new American.
And I've been working with FIRM, like, over eight years. I started as a
volunteer about 15 years ago, and I work right now as a job developer
in the Job First Employment program. And the Job First Employment
program is to help the refugees that live here five years and under.

They say, "Yeah, we need help. We need jobs. Any job," you know? Any
job. They say they are healthy they want to work anything, as long, you
know, however it take.

And it is not that easy to get the job, because the clients we have, most
of them are limited in English and don't have high school diplomas. But
yes, they do get jobs, mostly production jobs, and then if the job requires a
lot of English and education, then there's no opportunity for that, because
it can take a long time to learn.

And I also help clients with their paperwork. I connect with the
employer and ask them if there's opportunity for them to open for the
people that speak limited English to work, or if there's available positions.
And if they do, then I will call them and then pick up applications for the

---

[1]   Fresno International Refugee Ministry

clients, and then help clients fill out applications, and then also help clients translate about what it means. And so before you get the job, you have to know what the job requires. You have to know what the employer requires.

I have to do it step-by-step until the clients get the jobs. When you fill out application with me, when I help you do step-by-step, it doesn't mean that you get job guarantee. It's still up to the employer to pick who they want, but at least you give yourself opportunity to go out, to look for job and do the best you can. And then yes, one of these days, you will meet that goal, you will be the person working and supporting your family without worry so much about what kind of job you can have. But I mean, it's not as easy as I can talk, but I always give hope. Because I have hope.

And some of them don't have cars. Sometime we travel more than three, four towns. They don't have driver's license yet. They're still learning. Want to get driver's license to be independent, you know? They have to ask relatives or cousins to drop them off. Or some friend. But sometimes friend and cousin and relative are at work, and they can't get it.

You know, when you come to the new country, you have to adjust to new language, new environment, learn new culture. Everything is really stressful, and we need help. It's like we need one another. And yes many people become successful and become independent, like many people out there. It's not easy, I know that because I used to be like that.

I remember when I first came to the U.S., I was already 16 years old. I don't have any...I don't know any English. And I learned how to ride the bus, and I got lost so many times, and I cried. Because I don't know how to get home. And if I call my house and say "Can you pick me up? I'm over here."

Say, "What's the name of the street?"

I don't know. I don't know how to read. How do you spell it? I say, "Let me see." Do I know how to spell?...Do I know A, B, C?

I used to be like that, and it took me over 20 years to understand...I mean, the first four, five years, of course I learned something—but still need to learn. Learn, learn, learn, learn. It's really challenging to learn to pass each step. Once when they're past that, it makes life easier. I know that it's not easy. When I was first looking for jobs, there's so many people. There's like 20, 30 people. There's only one available position. I feel like, "Okay, I'm not as good as others." Sometimes I say that. You know when you want to be normal like other people? But it's not normal. It's like you feel discouraged sometimes, and you feel bad and depressed.

When they get a job they think it's permanent. It's not becoming permanent like what they think, even though they try their best. Because some employers say, "It's slow, and so we have to cut off hours." But it's not them either. We don't blame. It's the economy. Think about yourself and your family, and think about your life. Like, life is important as long as you stay alive. Like, when I escaped from Laos, I didn't think I was going to be alive. I think I was going to die already so many times that I pass out. But thank God. God still give me life, and I'm still alive, and I'm still breathing right now and talking to you. And I just talked to them like, "Please don't feel sorry if you don't get a job."

I also help like social services, because at FIRM, we have many different programs. Like, for example, we have...the vocational ESL[1]. Also we have the English and citizenship class. If you are a refugee and you want to become a citizen, you need to learn, right, so you know what a good citizen needs to be, and you need to learn about the test. So they would come in the morning, like, Monday through Friday. They start from, like, nine o'clock until 11:30a.m., or sometimes 8:30a.m. until 11:15a.m. They all learn English, and then they will learn how to become a citizen, and they will apply for the test.

Education is important. Some of us don't have the education yet, but a lot of us do. And we try to teach each other to become successful in the job market. Like right nowadays the job market is so low and so many people lost jobs, and like my clients, some of them wife lose job. Some of them husband lose job. Some of them both lose jobs. And some of them just get cut hours.

I also, myself, is a victim. When the economy slow down started in 2008, I get cut 50%, and my husband get cut 50%. I used to lose hope. I used to. But thank God, now I have hope. I have hope in that one day I will be with the Lord and have no more pain, and whatever pain right now,

---

[1]   English as a Second Language

I thank God. I will not blame anyone and I don't blame anybody, but I don't know what to do. The best thing I can do for all of us, my family, my friends, my co-workers, my employer is pray. I pray. I pray every day as long as I can, because I know that everybody's important...

She stops for a moment then continues through a rush of tears:

Sometimes I'm thinking that I'm not a good worker, that I cannot get jobs for the people. I see all these things that happening around the world, I don't know tomorrow. What's going to happen tomorrow? I don't know. I may go to sleep tonight and don't wake up, and so I say, "Okay, God. Thank you for today." And so I just do the best I can. (Continues talking through tears:) And I'm praying for all of the people that lost jobs, and the people that kill themselves or kill their spouse or kill their children or hang themselves or whatever they do just because so stressful about the economy. But now I have so many tears of joy. And sometimes I have tears of sadness...Thank God for the tear.

Luis Gonzales

I meet Luis outside the unemployment office on Mt. Ephraim Avenue in Camden, New Jersey. He agrees to walk with me across the parking lot to Popeye's Chicken so I can hear his story. At the table he opens a large envelope and takes out a tidy stack of papers—copies of his resume, unemployment paperwork, and letters from the unemployment office.

Originally from Puerto Rico, Luis is 44. He came to the US in time to complete his last year of high school, graduating in 1986 from Camden High.

Luis has a strong understanding of English but has always had a somewhat tenuous relationship to language altogether: "I never talked until six years old." He shrugs as though confounding himself a bit. "I can't pronounce that letter R." This still remains true for Luis, the letter seldom fully forms inside his mouth, but he works patiently and diligently to get as close as he can each time. He is a patient speaker, something I envy as someone who gallops past most words, injudiciously prioritizing speed over precision.

He was laid off most recently in 2009. He and his wife have been married for seven years; they live with her son from a previously relationship.

I work third shift. 11:00p.m. to 7:00a.m. Lumberton. So far like maybe between here and down there, maybe about a half hour drive or 25 minutes. Big company.

I live in Camden. Not really bad. You know, when you pick good side but bad side, everybody…a lot of people be on the corner and stuff like that, you know, fighting about this, about that. That's why Camden be the second on murder in the United States.

I've lived in Camden almost 25 years. Twenty-five years ago, people listened with respect. Right now, people have no respect. You notice in the daddy or father, mother, the grandson, like that.

I've been working about fifteen years. I started in '96. You know, back and forth, between layoffs and stuff like that.

They've done other layoffs in the past?

Yeah. Yes. In 2008, he let me go, layoff. He called me back. He said, "You want to go back to work?"

I said, "Why not?" Better going to work, because more distress is on the house. I see on the news people watching TV all day long, people mentally depressed more. I saw people die from staying in their house, you know what I mean? Watching TV all day or watching games, stuff like that. I saw people die like that.

Where did you work?

This company makes labels for all the shampoo. All the stickers are the same. We make all the labeling. On the outside label. We make all the colors. Making ink. Color. Color matching.

Where did you learn to do that, or how did you learn?

Well, I go step-by-step. When I was starting, I do a power wash, cleaning up. Another supervisor, he asked me, "Do you want to learn any more stuff?"

I said, "Why not?" Now step-by-step, I say, "Okay. Let's go start."

He showed me how you formulate formula. You have to do everything by 100% color, you know what I mean? You have to make it all the color together. Some color is more weaker. Some color hard. I'm using my hands all the time. Depend what compound make the color. Before we need like manual...not anymore now. We have a machine now. You put in the percentage what color was supposed to be there. The paste color—put it in the machine. The computer we start like in 2000, I think, or 2001. Mixing a lot of ink.

So when did they lay you off?

February 10th of this year. I think it was Tuesday or something like that. I don't know. Well, the day before, on the 9th, people talking layoff. People rumoring, talking layoff. Next day, on the 10th, about five o'clock, Supervisor come. "Luis, I'm sorry, you got laid off." Well, he tried keeping me in there, but he said, "No, it's not you." My supervisor, he said it's slow. That's it. Really slow. Shut about three or four machines down. We have about 23 or 24 press on the company.

I said, "Okay. It's no nothing," you know? What do you want me to do, you know what I mean? I can't do nothing. Signed out. That's it. I left. I finished my hour, you know what I mean? Unlike some people. Some people left right away, go home.

I was depressed, you know what I mean? When I trade my car, I saw that the old one is paid and full, and this one, whatever I got now, it's not paid in full yet. I owe—balance is $8,000 now. It's a lot. Really hard. My wife: "I told you don't trade this car." I said, "Too late." It's really hard.

I don't complain about the company because it got good benefits, 401K, stuff like that. 401K, when I got laid off, I had to take all the money off, because I had to make a payment and stuff on my car, stuff like that. After that, no more money for 401K.

So are you looking for other jobs?

Oh, yeah.

Have you had interviews?

Right now I'm filling out this application. This is Board of Education for school. Doing like a janitor cleaner or landscaping job. So I'm trying to fill out this one.

Right now, I don't have anything. I have to wait to see if we have another unemployment extension. But right now I have nothing. Zero. I don't want to keep extension. I want to go to work, you know what I mean? It's better. I want to keep it working, because when you're working, you know, you're not in distress.

So what will you do if you don't get the extension?

I will have to find a job somewhere. I'm not being on the street, you know what I mean? I'm not a person like that. I have to find another job somewhere. No matter how hard it is. I have to go get the job.

My mom lives in Puerto Rico. My father lives in the United States. He lives in Phoenix. He retired. He worked in Puerto Rico at a construction company. My mom and my father separated. Separated about 25 years. I think that's why the whole family…everybody separated. There's no more communication between me and my brother, my sister, my other sister, stuff like that. I'll be close with my brother. We have communication. A lot of families are breaking down because separated…

My English is not really perfect, you know what I mean? I try my best, you know. Right now, at my house, we speak Spanish. My wife, she speaks English, but she not good. Well, she's lived in the United States for 10 years, but you know what I mean, she's scared of talking English. She thinks about the people making laugh or something like that. She's afraid about that.

I'm married, but I don't have a kid. She got two kids. Her daughter, she left from Puerto Rico last month. I have a stepson, he's almost 20 years old, but…he looks like eight years old. That's a problem right there.

He drinking medicine all the time. We have to keep it like that, because when he's angry sometimes, when he got attitude or upset, you can't say nothing to him.

My wife, right now, she don't work none. But she would try to get social security, because she's got a lot of stress about the kid. Because he needs special aid. Right now, she got a lot of depressed. She don't want to do nothing. I have help her sometime. She's saying, "Leave me alone" because she don't feel good. She said, "What happened? How did you lose your job?", you know what I mean?

She wants to go back to Puerto Rico because, you know, she missing her daughter and grandkid too. She said, "No, I don't want to be here no more."

I said, "Why not? You live in the United States for about 10 years." Better life here, you know what I mean? Plus you can't get SSI in Puerto Rico, you don't got that. All the social security—she's not going to make money for her son like that. You don't have anything down there. Why would you want to go back to Puerto Rico? You don't have anything. You can't depend on your family. One week or two week, after that no help you out. You're making by yourself everything. Sometimes you're better keeping friends better. No family. No depend for family there. I don't know what she'll do when she goes down there. She go be finding another boyfriend or whatever, you know what I mean? We still married. You know, but something's wrong.

"I feel like I'm ready to clean up the world"

PARC

The Pioneer Adult Rehabilitation Center (PARC) in Clearfield, Utah, is a sprawling complex of office space and factory floors. Situated in a business park in this sleepy suburb 30 miles north of Salt Lake City, it is a non-profit organization that seeks, and in some cases provides, jobs for those with extenuating circumstances, chiefly— though not exclusively—those with mental conditions: autism, Down's syndrome, developmentally delayed adults. It also works with people who have a range of adverse physical conditions— anything from diabetes to bilateral hearing and visual impairment.

The ideal model is placing an individual in a local business, providing on-the-job support until it's no longer needed, then peeling back and taking on the next person waiting to be helped.

In its onsite warehouses, PARC brings in contract work for individuals who require a more closely supervised environment.

Discrete tasks are accomplished in different workshops within the complex, and each space has its own buzz of conversation between focused workers. In one room janitorial uniforms are laundered, next door scrap metal is sorted for the military, and, in the space beyond that, cardboard boxes are assembled.

PARC also provides contracted services at commercial and government sites throughout the area. Seventy-five percent of the individuals employed through those contracts have a documented disability.

One major contract was for custodial cleaning throughout three hundred buildings on Hill Air Force Base in the nearby town of Layton. Because of federal budget cuts, the contract was reduced twice in two years. In 2010, 33 people were laid off, followed by 43 in 2011—over 40% of the 176 that were originally employed on the base.

Dusty A. Nance

He is 33, slender and unshaven. During conversation, his eyes wander but his attention doesn't. His t-shirt and jeans are covered with paint stains, mostly dingy white. His grandmother, who has kindly driven him up to the PARC center, waits outside in her sedan.

Dusty is the third generation in his family to work at Hill Air Force Base. His grandfather was an airplane mechanic; his father is retired military man. Dusty began working there after high school.

He has a big set of headphones around his neck. "I listen to Marilyn Manson, goth. All kinds of stuff...I like to ride my bike. Get on the bike trails, and all kinds of stuff." He is the only person I've talked with who made a point to openly declare his party affiliation: "I'm strictly Republican. It's the way I'm going to live my life."

When he speaks his syntax feels either raw and disordered, or directly inherited from various sources in his life.

He's excited about two early Republican candidates: Herman Cain—"Herman Cain wants change in the world"— and Michelle Bachmann. "She's a woman who wants change too. She wants to work hard for it and clean up this mess we're in."

I was working at the base in janitorial. Just like bathrooms, vacuuming. And then the layoff come, and like, then, what do you do? It's like, you just deal with it.

Did you like the job?
Yeah, I did.

How did you find out about the layoff?
I just got a call that you're laid off. I'm like, "Okay."

Were you at home when they called you?
Yeah.

And who called you?
One of the bosses here.

So how did you react to that?
It's pretty devastating when you get a layoff call. I just learned to deal with it. Can't do much about it.

And how long ago was that?
The 31st of May. Middle of the week. Probably ten o'clock.

So what did you do after you got that call?
We's went through a meeting. An hour and a half. Some people walked out. Some people stayed. It's like, some can't deal with it. They were pretty upset. People were frustrated, or they were aggravated. There wasn't right mind frame. They were just frustrated. Pent-up anger and all kinds of things. It's like, what's going to go on? How am I going to pay my bills? The bill people don't understand you just got laid off. Like they won't work with you and all kinds of things. It's like, you just deal with it as much as you can.

When they said, "We're doing a layoff," did they tell you why?
They didn't have all of the bits and pieces together yet. I guess it had to happen. They were running short on money.

And have they explained it to you since then?
Not really.

So you stayed for the whole meeting, and then what did you do after the meeting?
We got our information, and we figured it out from there.

And you went back home?
Back home. Just got my Xbox, started playing Blackhawks.

Are you a big video game fan?
Not too big. My friend, he's a bigger fan than I am.

So is it his Xbox?
I have one. He has one.

So I guess that was sort of a good way to put it out of your mind for a little bit. Play a game and just think about something else.
Yeah, because frustrations don't help. The stock market crashing up and down. You know, everything else going wrong. That's probably what happened. 'Cause the stock markets control everything.

What was your favorite thing about your job at the base?
Just getting out of the house every day.

Who do you live with?
My grandparents.

And where's your mom?

She lives in a group home now. She would run off, and she drank a lot. But she knew the choices she was making. I try to go see her. I get busy most of the time.

Do you have friends that are having a hard time too?

Quite a few. Yeah. We help each other out. It's like, just stay positive. Then the health insurance won't pick me up, because my mood swings and all them problems. We picked up COBRA, and that's a pain in the butt.

It's expensive too, huh?

Yeah. They say Obamacare ain't gonna kick in til 2014.

So you're really waiting on that, huh?

I'm not too enthused about it.

Why not?

Because it's not in the right direction.

So what do you think would be the right direction?

Get some better healthcare things and cut down not so much on the heavy premiums. This government saying we got plenty of jobs, I don't believe that either. Obama says we got plenty of jobs, and I don't see 'em.

Are you able to get health care from the government?

If I get my disability, yes. I'll have that in November. You have to wait five months, and then it kicks in. I get $991 a month.

And will that be enough to pay for what you need?

Yeah. It will.

Do you get regular care? Do you see doctors regularly?
Yeah.

Do you have good doctors?
Mm-hmm.

Do you get along well with your grandparents? Do you like living with them?
Yeah. It's different. But it works out for me. It's a better environment for me.

My dad lives in Lincoln. He's retired military. My dad went to the Iraq war, come home with Parkinson's. 'Cause the government said there's no chemical weapons. He come back in '94, and he's already shaking like a leaf. And that's pretty much how it happened. They tell my dad there's no chemical weapons, and that's a bold liar right there.

Now he gets $2,000 a month out of the government.

I visit with him. It's like, thank god my dad did serve this country not being an illegitimate, saying we don't need these wars. That drives me crazy.

He knew he was going to come home sick, and nothing he could do about it. He was a tank driver. Like I say, I'm glad my dad served his country. I'm proud of my dad.

My dream job was to be a DI, Drill Instructor. But that didn't happen because of my disability, so I just took whatever job that I could get. It's just hard and everything. This economy, the way it's running down. It's like, "Wow."

How long had you been working on the base?
16 years.

That's a long time. Did it feel like a big change?
Quite a bit. When you got bills to pay, like, "Wow."

So what are you doing to make that happen?

I just go around Syracuse, see what needs to be done. Painting, doing lawn work. Just little odds and ends. Sitting down all day long drives me nuts. I like being out in yards all day long. I know a lot of people in Syracuse. Syracuse, Utah. It gets confused with Syracuse, New York. (Laughs.)

I was painting a deck for a neighbor. She just had surgery, and she didn't have a ramp to get home. It was like a pale white. It took me two hours yesterday and an hour today. I put four or five coats on. I was doing it yesterday in 93 degree weather. These are ruined, totally...

He tugs at his t-shirt, looking down at it.

I would've loved to have been a drill instructor. You wake these kids up. You send these kids to war. They don't know what's left or right. Yeah, you have to tear 'em down. As the Marine Corps says, "We tear them down and build them back up."

What do you think that does for a person?

It shows them this world's not as safe as they think it is.

His last words before leaving: "If you don't vote, the government can get corrupt and run amok...Get out and vote this next time."

Brenda Jackson Scott

We sit in a small conference room in the PARC office building. Brenda, 52, has arrived exactly on time for our 9:00 am appointment. There is a sobriety in her demeanor. If she isn't interlocking her hands she's crossing her arms—always clutching something. She has curly black hair and once in a great while she lets her face explode with a terrific smile that never completely shakes a trace of sorrow.

I was born and raised here at the Hill Air Force Base. My dad was in the service. We did all of our recreation activities out on the base when we were coming up. We lived actually in Ogden, but we went to the movies, bowling and dances and stuff at the Hill Air Force Base during our teen years and so forth.

My mom worked three jobs after my dad had left, and so me and my sister, we had to clean. We had to do everything. We had to iron…we did laundry—we didn't have a washing machine. We did have one, and it broke down, and so we had to carry the baskets to the Laundromat. We were just little, bony kids. I don't know how we lifted those baskets, but we did. And we would draw our mother's bathwater. We'd iron her clothes, lay them out on the bed. My mom just passed away this last time that I was working for PARC.

I was a custodian for buildings 847 and 120. And I enjoyed it. The people were very nice. The 847 is where they do a lot of trailers, put the tires on, and they fix a lot of government vehicles. And 120 is the headquarters for the base, and they have a lot of generals and colonels up there and important people. I enjoyed it. I really enjoy the people in both the buildings. They were very nice to me.

On Monday, Wednesdays and Fridays I did the restrooms. Then Tuesdays and Thursdays, I would go around and vacuum the offices. I had to do the break rooms also. A lot of times I would wipe things down. And I kept the kitchen area clean. I would sweep and mop there. And then we had extra days during the month so we would deep clean.

I became a supervisor. And that lasted for a while. And then I quit, and then I came back as a custodian. And I didn't pursue to be a supervisor anymore. I just like working on my own mostly. Mm-hmm. I really enjoyed it. Well, I'm a cleaning person, so. (Laughs.) I like to move around. I don't like to be sitting down at all.

They called us to one of the checkout points where we could walk in and clock out. And they told a group of us, "You know, there's possibly going to be a layoff," and they didn't know exactly who's getting laid off, and they would let us know in, like, 30 days.

It was a little devastating though…I should say a lot. For me and my coworkers. It was rough because we were all hoping that it wasn't going to be us, me. You know… "I hope I get to stay," we all kept saying.

And the thirtieth day came, and they let us know. It was Wednesday. It was the last day. We were at lunch, and they started calling people from the lunch table at the restaurant, and I was like, "Wow. How do they do that?" We're at lunch, you know?

They called the first guy, Mike, and he went. And we were all, like, "This is it."

Lunch was over. I don't even think I got to the second part of the building and the phone rang, and it was the supervisor: "You need to come down to the office."

I said, "Am I getting laid off?"

And he said, "We can't tell you anything. Just come to the office."

So I knew it was...I put my things away and went down.

They were calling us in four or five at a time, and they had someone there with the packets and all. And they were trying to be consoling.

He said to me that he was so sorry about the layoff, and that he really appreciated my hard work and, you know, it was devastating to him also.

I just said, "Obviously not. I didn't do a good job." I was being mean. I was so hurt. I was being mean, because I was angry and hurt. When it came, it was kind of, you know, unbelievable, but it happened. All the way up to the end, we just had hope that we could...everybody at the table that we ate lunch with got laid off except one person, and so that was really devastating. A lot of people were hurt and crying that day. Me too.

I was devastated. I cried a couple of days, and then just got more depressed, actually, and then there was nothing for me to do. I started cleaning my house over and over. There was nothing dirty, so...(Laughs.)

I decided to start doing something with myself, because sitting around wasn't doing me any good, because I'm used to moving around, so my body started getting stiff, and I didn't even walk and get up out of the bed. I took sick because I didn't have anything to do, and I was just sitting around, and my whole body started to ache me.

I've been married almost 11 years, and it's not working. I was staying at home, and I didn't like what I was seeing at home during the day while I would be at work, so it stressed me out. It made me even more sicker.

I decided to get divorced. You know, I had been wanting to get out of it and finally I just decided I was leaving. It's time to make changes. I've been trying so hard to kind of hold it together, but it's not working out, and it's making me ill. I think there was just a lot of built-up stress between knowing I was going to get laid off and knowing that I needed to get out of my marriage. I went through a lot of things. More than the average person would go through in life, I should say.

And so I moved. I went on my vacation, and I did not return home. I just went to my sister's. She had been asking me to come, and I had the opportunity. So I went. I'm just glad that she and her husband saw that I need help. And I do. And so I'm just grateful. She helped me with my kids a lot. She's just been there for me. We've always been tight because we're just a year and a day apart, so she's a good girl.

I went and got me a storage and so I'm in the process of moving my things. I decided that I needed to try to get my life back on track, you know. I decided I need to step up my game and do better for me, because that's all I have is me. And you know, I have three kids. I need to try to live for them. And so that's why I decided I needed to get out of this relationship and hopefully continue to work and be prosperous in life. That's my goal.

My daughter's 23, and she's a hard worker. She works for a restaurant. She was working two jobs at one time, and it was a little much on her. She's a good girl. She's pretty responsible. She's got her own place, and she works hard. She's on time and everything. She's got pretty good work ethics. I think she got that from me, so I'm proud of that. And my son, Sean, lives in Chicago with his dad, and he's here over the summer. He's a mess. Teenager. And so it's a little rough. He's trying to find a job because he needs school clothes. He comes, you know, we buy him school clothes and stuff and then he goes home. Well, this year, I'm not employed and my sister's not employed, and my daughter is the only one employed and we all chipped in to help send for him. So we don't know what we're going to do about the school clothes yet, but we're hoping he gets a job. Hopefully we'll get him responsible, because he doesn't show any signs of being responsible at 16. (Laughs.) He wants to drive, so I told him he needs to start showing me more responsibility. He wants to lay around all day, and then he wants you to jump up and just take him driving. You know, you've gotta show me something first. Show me that you are responsible, that you're more mature before you get behind the wheel.

Then I have a nine-year old son, Zane. He and Sean were taken away from me…Sean went with his dad, and Zane was adopted. But the people that adopted him still let me see him every month, and so sometimes I get to see him twice a month, or whatever, you know. They're pretty lenient. And so that's a good thing…we had him last weekend.

I miss my job. I haven't got over not being able to come to work, you know, get up and go see my friends, you know, or meet the people in the building. We've been very supportive through each other, to each other,

I should say. People had given me their numbers. And then some of us don't have any phones anymore, so, you know…

I just miss it all. It was a lot to do. It was enough to keep me busy all day, every day, so you get used to it. You get into a routine of things, and then it just seems like it's just a natural thing to do. Right now I'm just struggling trying to find something to keep me busy every day all day. I started walking. It helped to change my diet. Been eating a lot different, because I'm not…I guess I don't need all that fat stuff I was eating to keep me going through the day, so…I feel a lot better though, actually. I've lost a few pounds. (Laughs.) I feel a lot healthier. I feel like I'm ready to clean up the world.

I have my little bomb out there. It's a Buick Regal. It gave me a little trouble, but I'm trying to get through it. Hopefully keep it running. I can keep looking for a job. Now I'm just going out looking from day to day the best I can, you know. I still want my job back. That would be the ultimate, you know, the best thing to happen right now. If they find that contract and we could get our jobs back, it would be so sweet. You know, there's nothing like a job with benefits. I think that's what hurt us all the most.

I've been pursuing other things. I'm thinking about opening my own business, you know, because I love to clean. It relaxes my mind and all, and so I enjoy it. Before I started with PARC, I was cleaning for a few of my mother's older friends, and you know, they're older people, and they need company and they want you to do different things, sometimes they want you to cook for them, so…You know, I'm a good cook. I do all kinds of cooking, for real. I like Mexican food, Chinese food, Soul food, Italian food. I eat all kinds of food. So I love to cook and clean, and that's just who I am, so I figured why not try to start something on my own. If I don't get my job back.

There's nothing like doing the work that you enjoy.

"4'11", I ain't never scared"

Vondretta Jameson

My dad was never really a part of our life. My mom worked, and my dad is a crackhead. You know, me and my brothers, we got the same mom and dad, but my mom held it down. You know, we was on welfare. We never missed a meal. We always had Christmas and birthdays, and she never talked crazy about my dad to us until we got grown. She didn't want us to grow up and have that anger or that bitterness or none of that on our heart for him. She wanted us to learn this on our own far as what kind of man he is. You know what I mean? She never said, "Well, your daddy just a sorry ass nigger." Never done. She just: "What you need?" And she always made a will out of a way, even if we had to eat a Miracle Whip sandwich. So we just survived.

What do your brothers do?
Nothing. Sell drugs. Nothing. Nothing.

Her family is from Dayton, Ohio. She has her aunt's name because her aunt couldn't have children of her own. "My grandmother said she didn't have a name for her daughter. So when she was in labor in the hospital, she was laying beside a French lady and the lady gave her Vondretta. I said, 'You could've named me Tasha, Ebony, Tammy, Tamika…'" She laughs, shaking her head. "I guess my name's supposed to be French."

Vondretta's mother worked in a GM factory, as did her grandfather. "He worked at GM all his life. My grandmother didn't have to work. She had seven kids, and she had to sit down and watch the kids. You know, back in them days, the mother didn't work. She just whooped ass and cooked food and cleaned the house."

Vondretta, 35, has worked as a STNA[1] since 1999. "Basically I've been doing like uniclerk work, receptionist work, working in nursing homes, things in that nature. So that's all I know is medical work."

Mallery and I talk to her inside an empty office at Nancy's Place, a women's shelter at the corner of Long Street and Sixth Street in Columbus, Ohio. Vondretta walks in with a newspaper under her arm, folded open to the employment classifieds. Her collared shirt is yellow, her shorts are plaid, and she shares a vibrancy with the bright colors she wears.

This is Vondretta's second time in a shelter. The first time was after she was evicted from her apartment. "I couldn't afford to pay the rent. And they didn't even try to work with me, like, you know, I had more than half. I probably was like, $40, $60 bucks short, whatever. And they just weren't going for it."

Nancy's Place is able to give thirty days of room and board to each resident. Vondretta has a bed for two more weeks.

I was doing home care, and it was like the older lady…I was doing five hours a day, then she…Well, she had three slipped discs in her back. Three, four, and five. So they was prescribing her 120—no, 180 Percocets. She will literally take two Percocets and be ready to go for a drive, and I told them that's very dangerous.

---

[1]   State Tested Nursing Assistant

(Imitating older woman:) "I'm not high. I'm not high."

"Oh, yes you are high. You very high. You higher than me when I'm smoking weed. So guess what? You don't need to be driving with me, and you're 76 years old, and you took two Percocets."

She's old. Then she driving all up on the curb.

I told them: "Y'all get in the car with her, and y'all drive with her, because I'm going home with my two kids."

It's like, "Well either you can take the job or you can leave it."

I said, "You gonna talk like that, I'll leave it." Because my health is more important than this little $8 an hour.

I went to Dayton in 2010, found me a job for a pain clinic. I was a receptionist. We had to be at work at nine. We worked from, like, anywhere between nine to seven, nine to eight. If a good day, nine to five. And we never seen no good days. Probably once. Well, Fridays was half-days.

How long were you doing that job?

About a year.

The people that owned the pain center, they were chiropractors. They call it a pill mill because the doctor was giving out 380 methadones and stuff like that, just killing them right on off. So the state passed that law, and everything changed. The laws passed something stating that it had to be a pain doctor to run the pain center. So what they did was instead of them selling 51% on the clinic, they sold the whole clinic. They didn't tell nobody what was going on until we seen this new man come in and clean house. He asked 'em which ones, like, should he keep, but he end up not keeping nobody. He brought all his own staff, and he got rid of everybody…as of June of this year…it was a Monday. I know that. I ain't forget that day. Matter of fact, it was June 20th.

It was morning, around 10:30am, 11:00am. He comes in. He let 'em know, let everybody know, "Well, today will be your last day. " I think that his staff was more professional. 'Cause the people who owned it at first didn't know what they was doing. They didn't even have a list of all the patients that came here. You know, everything was just so out of whack.

What could we say? You gotta take it and run with it. That day, we worked the whole day out. We worked the whole day out, but we was told not to come back, you know what I mean?

Tell me what the next few days were like for you.

I smoke a whole lot of weed. That's what I do. Drunk a whole lot of Budweiser.

I'm just being honest. That's what I do. I'm a very blunt person, and that's just it. I do smoke marijuana. But crack, cocaine, heroin, hard drugs? No. I like the fact that people still think I'm 22. (Laughs.)

I was more discouraged than angry. I mean, 'cause that was like a movement, you know what I'm saying? From one day you getting a check every two weeks to you don't know where you're gonna get some money from. You get out here, and the economy is so jacked up. But I was on the phone taking care of my business, because that's the income. Y'all fire me for no apparent reason, you feel me? So everybody filed unemployment. I got mine. I don't know if they got theirs.

I sat for a minute in Dayton, Ohio, contemplating what I'm gonna do. I realized all the temp services down there kept saying, "We have no work. We have no work. We have no work." You know? So I put my car in my mother's garage, and my friend from down here picked me up. I just got in Columbus on July the 6th. Couple weeks. And I've been surviving ever since. It's been survival mode. Gotta survive…get me a new start…I'm in a shelter right now. But I'm lookin' on the brighter side.

I got two cousins down here. I wouldn't go stay with them. I'd rather be here. Gotta be in at eight o'clock, get up at six in the morning. That's what's gonna make you get up and go look for something. You can't sit around all day and expect for someone to give you a handout, because it's not gonna happen. I don't care how much you pray to God, you still gotta get up and move. So if he give you breath to move, you might as well just get on up and find you something to do. Instead of just sitting around feeling sorry for yourself all day. You know, this is just a pit stop for me. It's not nothing permanent for me because I know I expect better of myself, you know what I mean?

You get three meals and a cot, somewhere for us to sleep and be comfortable, where we don't gotta worry about we gonna get raped or anything like that. We cattycorner from a man's shelter...you got rapists, pedophiles, all kind of things across the street. You gotta be at work at seven, you walk out of here at 5:30a.m., catch the bus, you don't know which one of the men is waiting in that parking lot for you. 'Cause he seen you get up every morning consistently...you walk to the bus stop, you don't know. I think that's more scarier for me than anything. 'Cause they can choke you out and kill you on accident. Just choking you the wrong way."

My room is very clean. I know what I do. I come in, I take a shower, I lay down, charge my phone, talk to my kids already. I'm glad we got curfew at eight. I don't want to worry about, "Damn, I got 30 minutes to get there, and if I ain't there by 8:05p.m., they're gonna take my bed." No. Seven o'clock is my limit outside. Hot days like today...five o'clock is my limit today. After dinner, I'm coming back in, go to the back, smoke a couple cigarettes, drink a couple Pepsis, and that's the end of my day. I'm done. I'm going to bed. Six o'clock comes quick. 6:00am.

She stops for a few moments to unveil a smile:

Now I probably don't get up at 6:00a.m. when they say, "Get up." They probably gotta do another sweep and come back around at 6:45a.m. (Laughs.) Then I get up. Like, okay. I'm ready. Let me go brush my teeth, get my clothes on. You never know what kind of phone call you gonna get. You put an application in, and you then forgot about it. Here you go. You jumpin' again.

I'm working part-time. It's called Triad Home Health Services. I go home to home and just make sure they cook breakfast, clean up. You know, just little stuff. I do, like, between four and five hours a day there, get paid weekly. I ain't trying to do too much, because I get unemployment, and so once...I mean, if they gonna give me eight hours a day, yes, I will stop my unemployment. But I don't want to stop and then, two weeks later, y'all tell me, "I don't have no work for you." That's crazy.

Some of the girls, they sit around and feel sorry for themselves. You're dealing with different attitudes. You're dealing with dope heads. You're dealing with pill heads. You just dealing with women in general...It's a whole new ballgame in the shelter. I don't want to put my energy into that energy, because it ain't worth it. You know, it's up to you on how you gonna move and how you gonna get up out of here. It's up to you.

With this economy, the homeless is getting younger and younger and younger. And it's amazing, you know what I mean? When I was 21, 22, I didn't think about no shelter. I didn't think to sit along a gate all day every day. Don't do nothing. Sitting on the corner. They getting younger and younger and younger. They ain't getting older. They getting younger. I couldn't imagine my kids out in the street sleeping all night, sleeping with different men, men lined up to get a blowjob. You see all kind of crazy stuff out here. You see used condoms. Just all kind of stuff. Girls got HIV still having unprotected sex with the guys out here. I just be amazed. Girls bring their little babies down here and sit in the sun all day. It's 95 degrees outside. You don't think your baby cooking? Like an egg! They worried about that next hit. You know, and they gonna look up ten years later and they gonna be still standing there on Sixth Street wondering what happened to time. What happened to time is you was worried 'bout some dope! You know what I mean? To each his own. If that's what floats your boat, I'm gonna let your boat float, but that ain't what float my boat.

I never imagined that till I got here. It's amazing what you learn in a shelter. You learn a lot. I just be amazed, like, and how old are you? You know, I'm 35. You know what I mean? I have been places and done things. Y'all still babies. 18, 19. Out there taking pills, smoking weed with crack. It's amazing. You can't blame all that on the economy. Y'all too young to blame that on the economy. Y'all don't got no records. Y'all probably just don't want to be obedient by y'all parents. Well, y'all can just get out there, get a job, go to school. What's wrong with that? Your parents probably was some dope heads, so they just fall in their foot tracks. That's how I put it. I mean, 'cause these are really some babies out here. If y'all look along this gate right here...

She points in the direction of the chain-linked fence just outside the building.

...y'all will be amazed at what y'all see. Literally. And it goes down at nighttime. You gotta go inside Greyhound to be safe, 'cause there's really some crazy monsters out here. If I had to sleep on the toilet and put my foot up in the air where they can't see me, that's what I would've did. But I know I was safe. I don't want nobody to come in there do nothing to me.

Me being at the shelter, this is something I have to do for me to get back on my feet. I mean, I don't want you to just give it to me, because I want to appreciate what I got. And that's what's gonna happen. I'm gonna appreciate it more because I did it on my own and I knew how hard it was to get out here and get it.

You know, my kids are 18 and 16. They're big girls, you know what I mean? My youngest is with her dad, and my oldest got her own place. My 18-year old, she's at St. Clair Community College. She's taking up business management. My 16-year old, Honor Roll student. They bright kids. You know, I called them before I called anybody. You know what I mean, they know every step of the way, Mama gonna call, or I don't call them, they gonna call me.

"Mama, can you send $50?"

"Yeah, I can send $50."

We talk every single day. They call me at nine o'clock.

"Well Mom, is you in the shelter?"

"Yes, I'm here. Gotta be here at eight o'clock."

"Okay, I'm just calling to make sure you safe."

"Okay, I'm safe."

You know what I mean? Long as I feel like I got my kids on the right track, they don't have to struggle with me, you know what I mean? 'Cause I'm gonna be strong and make sure I pull through this, to make sure they all right, you feel what I'm saying? You know, 'cause my oldest, she got off-track there for a minute. So I put her in Job Corps, and she knew I wasn't going to play with her. It's either you gonna finish, or you gonna get emancipated, and you gonna take care of yourself. So she finished, and now she's taken up business management. She works. No kids. So I just think I was on the right track with my girls. That's the best blessing I got though. 'Cause I don't have to worry what my kids gonna eat, where my kids laying their head at, why my kids in the street, you know what I mean? Because you know, little girls, it's easy to intimidate. You know, smoke some weed, or do some drugs, or anything in that nature. I got the type of kids, they love to go to school. I want them to have things that I didn't have far as I want them to be in college. I want them not to have kids until they can have money where they don't have to end up in a situation like right here. Because most women don't have nowhere to put their kids where they're safe or where somebody gonna make sure they eat or take a bath, got clean clothes on, brush their teeth. You know, my kids...I'm blessed enough to have that.

I have always been the type of kid to get what I want. You know what I mean? Not just a handout, you know what I mean? 'Cause if they see me, like, well, she gonna keep a job—first and foremost—she gonna keep a job. She gonna keep her car fixed. And she gonna keep her kids together. You know what I mean, I might have a job, go to work, come home, and I'm gonna sit at my table and make sure I cook dinner. And I'm gonna make sure I eat, and I'm gonna make sure I feel good by the end of the night. But you still have to be motivated because some people get a job, and two weeks later, they quit. What you quitting for? Where your income gonna come in at? You wanna work for a check?...It's gonna be gone in two minutes. I can spend that on a purse. Wham. All the money gone. What's the purpose of that?

Long as I stay humble and pray. You know, I haven't been in church since I've been down here. That's not a good thing. I'm the type, I was raised in church. I go to church every Sunday in Dayton, Ohio. You know, if I went to the bar last night and came in at three this morning, I'm gonna get up at eight, because church service starts at nine. I'll probably miss Sunday school, but I'm gonna be there at nine o'clock praising God, you hear me?

You know, but I got so much going through my mind, and it's like, I can't stay focused. You know what I mean, when you gotta stay focused, and I'm focused on the important things, but my mind is always drifting off somewhere else too at the same time. That's not a good thing for me. During the day, my adrenaline's pumping. It's pumping, I'm moving. I'm going. I'm on buses. I don't care if it's all the way out West, I'm gonna get there. Take me all day, I'm a start at seven in the morning, so I'll be back by seven.

I'm in survival mode. You know, I'm blessed enough to have someone to watch over my kids, you know, while I'm doing what I gotta do, take care of my business. I'm not gonna play with it, you know what I mean? But in the same token, it's hard. It's very hard. I mean, I'm blessed enough to where I can go buy me a sandwich, where I don't have to stand on the corner and ask for money or nothing like that, or I don't have to prostitute myself out or nothing like that. I'm blessed enough to have money. Get me some soda if I get thirsty. Go to a library, chill out for a minute. You know, but I'm still on my grind far as finding work, finding somewhere to live, you know what I mean?

We gonna start this tomorrow—Saturday some apartment complexes is open. I'm tired of giving them $25 dollars. 25, 25, 25, 25. The 25s keep adding up, and you keep telling me no. So that's like a little discouragement, right there. 25, 25, 25, 25. Them a lot of 25s. Them 25s is adding up to be hundreds. It's harder for me, because I have a felony. It's 14 years old, you know what I'm saying? They think that everybody is criminals and crooks or whatever. But it's old. You know what I mean.

I cashed a $10,000 check. I did that in '97. I was young. I was peer pressured into the situation. You know, "We can go to Atlanta. We'll have a ball. We can do this…" Yeah, we did all that, but I didn't know that 911 was coming to pick me up. Didn't know that. If I knew that, I wouldn't have…

Some of the girls went to jail. Marysville. I call it Mary's house. But some of the girls went to Marysville and did a couple years or whatever, while I did five years papers. You know, they felt like I got off like a fat cat. But y'all record, y'all been out in the store stealing. Stealing ain't my thing. 'Cause I think that the walls and everything talk. They gonna tell somebody I'm doing something. But y'all record is worse than mine. This is the first thing that's on my record, and that's what the judge looked at.

And it's been 14 years. You know, and they charged me with grand theft. I paid most of it. I just owe $680 now. I was on probation for five years…and I was paying like, $250, $300 dollars a month on it. I still kept paying $100, $200, $100, $200…I don't want this on my record. So I'm gonna pay the $680.

I feel like after six, seven years and you ain't got in no more trouble, you should be able to get a job. You should be able to feed your family without having to go out here and do illegal things. That's why so many people in the world is doing illegal things, because society don't give you a chance. I mean, they give you a chance, but you really gotta be out there on your grind. You gotta be out there, you know, making things work. So that's the state of mind I'm in. You know, you can't just sit around and think somebody gonna give you something, because ain't nobody gonna give you nothing.

Every job I go to, I'm upfront about my felony. I mean, either you're gonna take me, or you're not. But don't please have me sit right here and fill out all this paperwork and then you tell me no. I'm gonna tell you before you give me this paperwork. Don't tell me you can work with me, and then I put everything down, and you can't work with me. That's what's gonna piss me off. But I still gotta watch my tongue. Keep it moving. So that's just my goal, you know what I mean. You just can't be hotheaded and think you gonna get somewhere. You can't be hotheaded. Even though you want to be. You ready to take somebody's face off, but you can't be mad because they told you no. They told you no. They're gonna tell the next person no, probably. (Laughs.)

I guess it all depends on how strong you are. I mean, if you ain't strong, you not going to make it. That's all to the situation. I mean, you gotta be strong out here. You know what I mean? You can't let one "no" stop you. No, no, no. Give me a million no's, and I'm gonna keep on it. God gonna walk me on a path where I'm gonna get something that's gonna say yes, yes, yes. You know what I mean? And that's not gonna be no, no. I got a lot of no's. You know, sometimes I get discouraged. I want to cry. Like, "Man, Lord, I don't know what's going on." And then all of a sudden, a couple of days later, I'm just getting yes, yes, yes, yes. You can't just stop because you got 15,000 no's, and no yeses in the middle there. You can't stop right there. You gotta stay humble and keep it moving.

All these black men: "We black. We men. We dope dealers. They're not going to do anything for us." Yes they are! Stop selling dope and quit getting all these dope charges, and you'll be able to get somewhere. So I mean, I don't know. It's all about a survival thing out here. Either you gonna survive or you ain't. That's it. That's all. So I just feel like I'm with the survivors.

Right now I'm going through a case of assault and domestic violence. I was in an abusive relationship. He beat me. He stabbed me right here. And the doctor told me if he went an inch down this way…(pointing to her gut)…he would've hit my main artery, and I would've been dead. So that's a blessing right there by itself. You know, He kept me here for a reason. I ain't gonna be the one that crawls. I ain't doing all that. I might take a slap or two, but guess what? I'm gonna come back. You know, I fight back. 4'11", I ain't never scared. My brothers taught me very well how to fight back. They taught me very, very well. So what I did is I popped him with a pot of grease. And his head popped wide open. He had to get staples in his head. When I popped him upside his head with that pot, I really didn't know that I hit him that hard that it would really pop his head open like that. I really didn't mean to hit him on the top of his head like that but, you know, in the same token, I'm kind of glad. I feel sorry for it, but I'm glad. These days, women gotta fight back. If I have to, I will put you in your grave, 'cause you ain't gonna keep hitting on me. I ain't your punching bag. I don't care about your mama. I see my mama get beat up all her life. I ain't your mama.

I try to tell my kids, "You don't let no man. You leave him. You don't let no man hit you." It's not worth it. So my youngest, it got to the point where she said, "Mom, what would happen if I stab him?"

You know, it took me by surprise. I'm like, "If you stab him?"

She said, "What if I stab him and he just died?"

I said, "Baby, I'd have to take that charge. I couldn't even see you doing a day in jail." So that right there woke me up, like it's time to go. 'Cause baby girl ready to pick up a butcher knife and take him up out of here.

They ready to hit him with hammers and anything they could pick up that's heavy. Just knock his head straight on off. That's why I had to get out.

That was in 2009. I'm going through the case now. Because they caught me at the park drinking, you know? I was at the park, had a can of beer. Police rolled down on us, threw the 50, which is run my background check, had a warrant, went to jail, now go back to court August the 12th. Here. So hopefully they'll throw it out, because I caught that case in 2009, and now it's 2011. You know what I mean? So hopefully everything go right for me.

I know there's something out there for me. There's something greater for you on the other side, but you just gonna have to get there to get it. You gonna have to strive to get it. You don't stop at one stop and think somebody gonna give it to you. You know what I mean, it don't work like that. So you gotta keep going, no matter how low it get. Non-stop right there. It's always gonna be a brighter side to the other side that you on. Feel what I'm saying?

This shelter, man, it'll take the breath up out of you. It'll take your soul away from you if you let it. If you weak-minded and you feel like God put you here for a reason and this is who you are, and you fall in that trap... Some young ladies fall in that trap, like, "God put me here for a reason. Evidently, he want...." No, no, no, no, no he did not. He didn't put me here for that. He put me here to see how strong I am. I ain't gonna let you tell me no other way. No. He put me here to see how strong I am. I'm gonna show you. I'm strong.

BOOK EIGHT

FAMILY

"The perspective that he could see"

Dirk

Dirk—a marathon runner and devout Christian—is a man of discipline. After becoming unemployed in 2010 at the age of 37, he started job seminars at his church in the Kansas City suburb of Olathe. He arranged motivational lectures and practical workshops: helping others helped him. He is the son of educators in a family that goes back several generations in this part of the country.

He was only unemployed for a five month period, which he consistently refers to as "the transitional period." He's still settling in at a new job—sales for a precast concrete company, which happens to lease office space down the hall from where he worked before said transitional period began. He asks me not to use his last name. After his perspective is published he's worried someone might "Google me…and they will see a bunch of stuff about me being laid off and unemployed."

We sit in his new office; Dirk is at his new desk. The walls and cabinet surfaces behind him are covered with images of his

*family—his wife of 15 years and three daughters—everything from
a Batman & Robin Halloween to a gingerbread house Christmas.*

We've heard on the news with the economic downturn a statistic of unemployment that's been right at around 10%, and in my case—in my industry, the architecture engineering and construction industry—it's closer to 30%, or even higher. So I knew it was a long road ahead. My wife and I just took this seemingly impossible situation and just gave it to the Lord and said, "We're going to trust you. You've always met our daily needs."

Well, I found out on August 2nd, 2010 that my then-company was restructuring, and that their Kansas City sales office was closing. My boss called me—he showed up and I wasn't at the office, so he called me and I was just a few blocks away. He said, "Hey, I'm at your office. I need to talk to you." So I actually called my wife on my way to the office, and I said, "Well, I've gotten an unannounced visit from my boss, and I think this is it."

There was a little bit of a pattern there by the time it got to me. I was the top sales performer for the company, so I was actually the last one to go. I was the last regional office to close.

That conversation that day in my office was pretty by the book. I think with it being a real structured and regimented process, I'm sure there's some lawyer training for doing that. There's certain things you say. There's certain things you don't....

He sat in my office. He's a close friend of mine. We worked together closely and got to know one another. We'd been over to one another's houses. I still consider him a close personal friend. It was a difficult conversation for both of us. And something very peculiar—I noticed he was kind of stumbling over his words a little bit, and this is a really well-spoken guy. And he kept looking over my left shoulder, just off to his right, and I thought, "Well, this is a tough conversation. He's probably just thinking or getting his bearings." And he left the office and I of course called my wife, and then I just kind of sat here in stunned shock.

She was really amazing throughout this process. I mean, I just can't say enough about how supportive she was, and we just...Yeah, I mean...

He stops for a moment, silent, hands tightly clasped.

...You saw it coming, but it hit you out of nowhere. And I did something that I've never done before. I thought, "Well, he seemed so uncomfortable. What's it like to sit in my office?" And I got up, and I walked around, and I sat in the guest chair where he was sitting when he was talking to me. And I looked. I wanted to see the perspective that he could see. And I looked over where my left shoulder would have been, and here's pictures of my wife and my three daughters. And I thought, "Oh, gosh." I mean, obviously I was having a little bit of a worse day than he was, but I actually felt a little bad for the guy. We talk about these corporate executives being these heartless, soulless shrews that just see numbers on paper, but I don't think that's the case. I mean, there's a human element there, and you know, I think those folks have their breaking point, and I think I saw that. I feel fortunate that that has always been at least one step above my pay scale, to actually do the laying off. I've never had to actually do that before. And I feel fortunate.

I began a new routine of just basically going out every day and making a full-time job out of looking for a job. And you know, a lot of things surprised me. It surprised me how much it had changed since the last time I'd been out looking, which was six years earlier. I mean, I didn't have a LinkedIn account or anything like that.

My wife told me, "You've gotta be the hardest working unemployed person on the planet." And I would get up, get ready practically every day, and make basically a full-time job out of looking for my next opportunity. And I knew I had a lot to offer. I mean, I had done $44 million worth of sales volume in six years. So I wanted to take my time. My father's always told me, "You don't have to make very many moves in a career if you make good ones," and I had made a couple good ones, and I planned for my next one to be a good one.

I stayed positive. You know, I'm an optimistic person. But this was a tough thing to go through. If there was a low point: I remember there was one company that had, according to the senior recruiter, 500 applications they went through. They interviewed about 30 of us on the phone. They flew into town, saw six of us in person, and then got it down to three.

And I had kind of made up my own mind. I had set myself a deadline. I wanted to have this figured out by the time my severance package ended. And I found out the day my severance package ended that I didn't get that job that I had been in the process for well over two months, so that was probably the low point. And I just felt like God's timing is not always ours, our own, and if I wanted his very best will for my life—not just his permissible will, what he'd think would be okay, but his perfect will—I was going to have to wait.

You know, we're people of faith. I don't mean to be overly heavy-handed about my faith, but it was just such a pivotal part of my experience. I'm not really telling my story if I don't interject that. We just really, you know, just relied on the Lord during that season. And I've gotta tell you a couple of things. One, I remember, it was a couple of days later. With my kids, we sat down and we told them what was going on. They were young enough that they really didn't understand, and we didn't go out of our way to really explain the gravity of the situation.

They knew my schedule was a little different. I mean, the company came, and I had a company car that they came and got. So the younger ones knew daddy has a different car now. The younger two were not nearly as aware but my oldest, my seven-year old, she gets an allowance, and she really had a pretty good grasp of it. She understood a job's how you get money. Money's how you pay for things. This is kind of a big deal. And I remember we were having dinner, and we pray before every meal. That's kind of how we roll in my family. And she was concluding her little prayer and said, "God, please help my daddy to find a job." And my wife and I opened our eyes, and we look at one another, and we both…That was the first time that both of us got a little choked up, at that moment.

I would not throw out the cliché "I got laid off and it's the greatest thing that ever happened to me," because it wasn't, but I would not be honest if I didn't say there were definitely some surprising positives to come out of that. I mean, you accidentally end up spending more time with your kids.

We were financially pretty fiscally conservative people. We had saved. We were ready for something like this. We might've been more prepared than some. But at the same time, we were a one-income family, so from the other standpoint, we maybe had less of a safety net. Not knowing how long this was going to be, we slammed on the brakes and went on a full financial spending freeze, and you realize how little you can live on. And it was just astonishing. That was a huge lesson that we took with us going forward.

You know, the first thing to go is the lattes. We paid for our fixed expenses. We paid our house payment. We bought gas. We bought a few groceries, although my wife's one of those extreme couponers, so sometimes the grocery store pays her. (Laughs.) You don't want to get behind her in the checkout line, believe me.

And then the other thing—just to be really candid—I mean, I've always gotten a charge out of doing things for other people. I mean, that's my comfort zone. And one of the things that the Lord really taught me through this experience was that I needed to humble myself, and put myself in a position where I'd be willing to receive a gift when somebody wanted to meet a tangible need in my life. And that was probably the toughest lesson for me. My 16-year old niece loaned me her car. Talk about humbling.

You realize how ingrained in our society what you do for a living is in terms of being connected with you, because you walk out, you meet somebody, the first thing they ask you is "What do you do?" So there's definitely some coming to grips with that.

Bride & Business
Partner

"Never even kissed him"

Candice

Moments before Candice walks into the coffee shop, the sky opens up and a burst of hail pummels the city. It's strong and vanishes quickly, leaving everything outside more bruised than wet in the immediate aftermath.

She appears suddenly, short of breath, apologizing for being late. She has a bright white smile that pops against her tan skin. She is 29, born and raised in Salt Lake City. Her grandfather was a fireman at the Tooele Army Depot about 40 miles away, to the south of the Great Salt Lake. Her father works for the Utah's Department of Alcoholic Beverage Control.

By her own description/admission, Candice drinks "a lot." She once contemplated selling her eggs to cover her living expenses but in the end decided against it: "I don't know if they'd even let me, I drink too much." She laughs after saying this, and it's a laugh that quickly becomes familiar because she keeps running back to it. I resist asking if she was raised Mormon, just to spite the most obvious question.

She slouches in her chair, comfortably chewing gum, but still very much at attention, bouncing her crossed leg, ready to go.

It was September 2008. I had some weird circumstances, because I tore my ACL ligament and decided to get it reconstructed and I was managing a bar-lounge-outlet at the Canyons and so I decided to get surgery, with the idea that my job was going to be there when I got done. So I called my manager and said, "Hey, look, I'm feeling healthy, I can walk, you know—can I come in and talk about my schedule?"

And he's like, "Yeah, you should come in." I went and he was like, "Oh, actually, we've just dissolved that position entirely." So after being without income for two months, I found myself with no job and...I lived in Park City at the time and that place was hard to get jobs anyways.

Did they tell you why they dissolved the position?

Nope. They had just made a transition to a different owner. I really had no—it came out of nowhere. I really wanted to stay within the management side of everything and so I asked them if there were any other opportunities anywhere and they just said, "No, we're just completely scaling back right now...you know, sorry."

I was so mad that I just got out of there. I get really upset, you know, and I was just like, "If that's the deal, that's the deal." I'm not going to argue...or, you know. I'll take the unemployment benefits.

And so you had a meeting, you were angry, you walked out, and what did you do with the rest of your day?

I drank. (Laughs.) You know, after that, I started drinking a lot. I wouldn't say that I'm an alcoholic, but I certainly drink a lot more than I ever have.

And how do you feel about that?
I've gained weight. I don't do stupid things or black out or, you know, but I'm gaining weight. I don't work out as much. Doesn't make me feel very good. (Laughs.) I lost everything I had, I almost had to move back in with my parents, and so I was paying about $375 a month for health insurance. I had to sell my car and get roommates—I was living by myself at the time and…I actually…did some other pretty crazy stuff to make some money at the time—nothing, you know, bad—but just like things I never thought I would do. Or need to.

Like what?
(Laughs.) Um…I better not say. Yeah, I better not say. I got involved in some business deals that just kind of happened to fall in my lap, that saved me from moving back in with my parents. Uh, probably not legal, but…I feel good about what I did; it's not a bad thing.

And you feel good because…?
I was able to help somebody else out, and it helped me out, so it was kind of a win-win situation.

Candice contemplates revealing more, I contemplate asking for more. In a sudden beat she shifts to other things:

I kind of had a weird summer, that summer right before I got laid off, I tore my ACL, broke up with my boyfriend of five and a half years…and so, it was like, all these spiraling events, which led to the job loss and it just like all fell apart. (Laughs.) I had some issues with my knee surgery. I had nerve damage due to the anesthesia. So—I'm just starting to feel better. It's what?—now, almost three years later? And I'm just finally getting to a point where I don't feel terrible all the time.

I'm working now, just bartending, just trying to make money. So I basically have had health insurance for three and a half weeks now. And I've seen quite a few doctors, and a dentist, and I'm probably going to lose it in two weeks. You're required to work 25 hours a week but in the summer time it's just not possible to work 25 hours a week. So—going back to having no health insurance and having pre-existing conditions and...I don't think health insurance is in my future until I find a full-time career job.

After getting laid off I decided to go back to school. Bachelors in Communications. I have two classes to go and I'm done. I wanna get done with school. I dunno, it seems like even a Bachelors degree anymore doesn't really mean much, so...Do I incur more debt and get my master's degree and maybe find a job with a, you know, an ambiguous degree in communications? Or do I just continue bartending and beat the hell out of myself?

I don't wanna work night shifts anymore, you know, I'm tired, I'm old. (Laughs.)

I remind her that she's 29 years old. She laughs some more.

Bartending gets tiring...standing on your feet all day. You know, I'm not a construction worker...that work's really hard, but...schmoozing old men gets old. (Laughs.)

Last year my boyfriend and I considered moving to California, looked into places, got fairly serious about it, he had a couple job interviews and—we just looked at rent, and there was just no way, no way we could do it. It still might be in our cards but...

I've basically been looking for work since I got laid off. I don't stop looking.

Have there been serious leads? Close calls? Good interviews?
Um...No.

How many resumes have you sent out?

Well, Monday alone, I spent a full workday writing cover letters, sending out resumes, I probably sent out about ten. So that's one day in the last two years. So at least a hundred. And who knows when you fill those out online. Where does it go? Does anyone really even get it? Is it just like the digital nowheresville? So, I've been trying to network a lot lately, that's why I've done two internships, I'm calling everyone I know, I finally figured out that that's your only chance to get a job.

After all this, man, I don't *wanna* work. I'm bummed—I'm bummed about working. You know, I always had such a great attitude about it and now—if feels like nobody cares about you, as a worker. (Laughs.) You know?

So, if not working, what do you want to do?

I dunno...

If you could do anything to fill your days, what would you be doing?

I've been telling my boyfriend maybe I should start havin' babies. (Laughs.) I don't think that's a good reason to start having kids. (Laughs.)

I tell her I have a hunch that might be another version of work. We talk about other important things—her health, friends who'd also been laid off—but I'm having trouble concentrating because I'm stuck on her secret. What was illicit enough to make her want to keep it confidential and at the same time positive enough to make her smile honestly when she said it made her "feel good"? I don't want to go on half-listening so I double-back, asking if she might take a fake name in exchange for her story. That's why her name isn't really Candice. As with most of the conversation, she cut right to the chase:

So...working in Park City, you're friends with a lot of people from around the globe and—I ended up getting married for money. So I'm still married. Almost done, thank god, um but, you know, it worked out, it really did, it worked out for him—he's a great person, I've known him for quite a few years, and this type of thing happens very often in Park City. Very often.

How much time between the layoff and the marriage?
So it was September 15th. We got married December 15th. Fairly fast. I hadn't had any income so I was already like running on fumes. And so, yeah.

Did you ever actually live with the guy?
No. Never even kissed him. (Laughs.) We'd see each other occasionally; we used to work together a little bit. It was just kind of off and on. We were never like calling each other up and hanging out, but certainly good acquaintances. Yeah, so I've been paid enough money to pay off most of my debt.

Can I ask how much money he paid you to marry him?
Sure, I mean the base pay was $7,000 and then basically the last two years I've got all of our tax money back, which has been about another $3,000. So I would say around ten grand.

He's from Peru, very smart guy, is trying to do his best here, you know, it's not that he doesn't wanna go through all the hoops to become a citizen. I've never even really looked into what that takes, but he asked me, and I trust him, and so I did it. We're pretty inland. It's a lot safer. The guidelines aren't as strict. I certainly wouldn't have done it in California.

And so when he asked you that, did it catch you off guard?
Oh, absolutely. (Laughs.) You know, I was at the bar, you know I'm on my crutches and, or, I think I had a knee cast on. And he just said, you know, "I have something to talk to you about, can we have lunch tomorrow?" And we did, and he told me, and I was like, "You know, I just don't know about this, you're gonna have to give me some time." And he bugged me for probably a week or so, maybe two weeks, and I finally said yes.

We have credit cards, car loans, I'm on his lease, nearly anything that you could hold together. I have two phones. I don't carry the one with me, and I text and we stay in touch with that phone.

Yeah. So, I mean, I could be caught, and I worry about it, but it's not that likely. It was a risk I was willing to take because the person I married is very smart and obviously he doesn't want to get caught either. And we hired an attorney so he's helped us the whole way. He was recommended to us by someone else who had used him and so…I feel pretty legit.

When we went into the interview, the lawyer was talking to the interviewer about their gardens, they were talking about growing tomatoes, and asked us like four questions. I'm like sweating, like ahhh I hope I remember all this stuff, and they asked what his birthday was, what our address is, show me your checkbook…

We've just sent our final paperwork and are sending for his green card. As soon as that happens we'll probably wait another month or two and sign for a divorce. I guess.

It's scary. It was really scary. I mean, even now I'm not divorced yet. And I'm scared. They could come and take me to jail at any time. But I didn't wanna move in with my parents, you know? Twenty-eight years old and…yeah. My health bills—even though I had health insurance, you know, going to see a physical therapist three times a week, a doctor once a week—those co-pays really add up, and then three different MRIs and you know, I'm still paying it off.

Mama & Classmate

"I wrote the vision"

Sandra

She is 59, a mother and grandmother many times over. She asks my age then laughs because I'm only a year older than her "baby."

Mallery and I met her yesterday, outside the Fresno mall that houses the local Workforce offices. She was a bit suspicious of us— understandably, considering we are strangers who approached her cold outside a mall and asked for the story of the day she lost her job. She told us if we came back the next day she might be able to talk to us so we've done just that. Today she's still suspicious but our return seems to have reassured her in part.

She still doesn't want to tell me her last name. I tell her that if there's anything she says that she doesn't want me to include on the record she can let me know and I'll omit it. She squints at me sort of strange, asking why she would tell me something if she didn't

want it to be shared. She has a point. She grips her purse tightly and
wears thick glasses.

We sit on a wood bench just inside the entrance to the mall; we
only have 45 minutes before her appointment at the Workforce office.

My husband is a jack-of-all-trades. When we came from Southern California, up here, they wouldn't give him a job, 'cause he's black. 'Cause we moved in an all white area. We didn't know. We just moved to Madera, California. So what he did, he got me, him, and all the kids, and we had this lawnmower that kind of goes by itself. We done cut yards. We did that for six months to survive. And people's neighbors watchin', they come and said, "These folks are cutting yards, and they be happy in Madera."

We was out there in the hot sun, boy, my God, I felt like I would fall off in the dead heat, but we had to survive. We had four kids. They were young, so, you know, we had to put them through school. And so when nobody was gonna give them a job, we said, "People like their yard done, 'cause they don't wanna be out there and do it." So we did. That's how we made it. All my children, I have four of them, they was not allowed to date 'til I got a diploma in my hand. I got four: two boys, two girls. They weren't allowed to be outside. We had a big pole light on the corner of my house. If they didn't come in before that light came on, they got their butt whooped. Just straight like that. My oldest boy, Ronnie, is 46, 'cause I had my children young. And so my kids, they know. One of my children when they turn 14, my husband made them go down to City Hall, and made them get a job. All my children started working when they was 14 years old. And before they was 14, my husband took them out there, made them cut his yard, 'cause he's teaching them the value of a job.

Finally this man said, "We gonna build a Wal-Mart here in Madera." He said, "What can you do?" So my husband's been a tile man down in Southern California. He said, "I do anything you want me to do." He said, "If I don't know how to do it, I'll go on YouTube and find out how." So what happened—when they finished building a Wal-Mart in Madera—they made him supervisor over the floor. So we did janitorial nights. And he worked at Wal-Mart during the day. And that's how I paid my way through school. Doing yard and janitorial. 'Cause I went back to Madera High School, 38 years old and got my diploma. Because I didn't want a GED[1]. You can do it. I mean, I had all the kids, young teenagers, bust them upside the head they're so smart aleck…I was called 'mama' after that. I sat in the class with them and so I could get the diploma. And I had my cap, my gown, and we all marched and got our little diplomas.

I'm a home nurse, and I get with patients individually. The family I worked for had a son is eight years old. I've given him CPR, 'cause he almost died a couple of times. I take care of him from head to toe. I clean him. I bathed him. I'd keep his hair done. Suction him. I'd take his G-tube out, replace it. Oil him down. Feed him. He was like one of my kids. The mama didn't have to do nothing. When nighttime came, all she had to do was put him in the bed, because I give him his bath; I give him his pajamas. Everything. All she did was put him in the bed. When he needed oxygen, I gave it to him. I was there. I gave him total care. All she had to do was look at him and call him by his name. That's all she did. And because I did everything, she could tell him, "Come here." He won't come. But all I ever said, "Get you right over here." He'd come. That shows you how long and how close I was in that family. You see what I'm saying?

She had another baby, which I helped her raise from birth up till the baby's two years old. I was like his grandma, or what you wanna call it, like that. Two kids wouldn't go to the grandma. They didn't know the woman. She hadn't been out here for four years. That's one thing she got angry at me when she first come—because she seen how the kids was running to me. Wouldn't let her hold them. She wouldn't hug 'em. They don't know her.

And she kept saying, "What? You trying to take my place?"

And I said, "I got 11 grandkids. Why would I want to take your place? I just wanna do my job." I said, "These are babies." If you take care of a child—I don't care what color you are—that kid gonna come to you. They gonna come to you. You showin' this child love, that child gonna come to you. 'Cause it's kids. These are kids. 'Cause I'm black, they Spanish and Hawaiian—all these kids are looking for is love. I've been around these

---

[1] A series of tests that certify completion of high school level academics for someone who does not have a high school diploma.

kids years. Total care. You don't expect that kid to want to come to me? Come on, now. So, like I say, that was my situation.

And the way I got laid off, the lady that I had been taking care of her son for so many years…here's what she did: I came to work, like I normally do. Me and her left, took the little boy for a doctor visit. Come back home. 'Bout one o'clock, her and her mother's supposed to go somewhere. They didn't tell me where. When they come back, then she tell me, 'cause my shift was almost over. I'm doing my everything, daily stuff I do, and she comes and says, "Will you sit down a minute?"

I said, "Okay," but I didn't sit down.

I ain't thinking that, you know, they gonna leave.

"Sandra, we just want to tell you that I'm going back to Florida next week."

And I just looked at her, and I said, "How long you been planning this?"

"Oh, we've been talking about it for about a month."

I said, "You excluded me in the program?"

"Well, I'm sorry."

I said, "Sorry ain't paying my bills, baby. You could've told me ahead of time so I could prepare myself." I said, "Look, let me go sit down for a minute." And I really sat down then, and I just started counting back from 100. I had to get to one, because I got really ticked off. I tried. I did my best. So she didn't have to do any of that work. I was three years. He was five when I met him. So yeah, I was mad. I was mad.

But you know something? I really feel like this happened for a reason, because I'm finding out how strong I am, in one aspect, and how weak I am in another. Because, now, I could've act a fool when she said what she said to me. I could've lost my temper, 'cause I'm quick-tempered, okay? So I really think this was a reason. Because it's not what happens to you. It's how you handle it once it does. And 'bout five years ago, someone would've done me like that, you would call the police on me. I would act a fool. Because you knew—you knew what you were going to do; you could've told me. You look at my face every day. I've been at your house three years now. You knew what you had planned. You knew. Y'all had already planned it. Tell me what's going on. Hey, we're no kids. No. We're grown folk. But to be sneaky and dirty? No. Could've told me. You lookin' at my face every day. So, like I said, five years ago, she'd have been calling the police on me, because I would've kicked her ass, excuse my French. I'd have whooped her and her mom up in that house.

I finished my shift. Because what choice I have? I couldn't walk off the job, so that was it.

When I went home, I was…..ooohhhhhh….

Sandra makes a grunting sound—peeved, to say the least.

And then I just said, "Okay, God. You know what this is all about." I gave it to him. (She glances up at the sky.) I know he hears me when I pray. There's no doubt in my mind.

I was really shocked. I was ticked off. I felt betrayed. On the weekends, when this child would have a medical problem, she'd call me. And I'd get up out of my bed and go and take care of that child. Off-duty. This sort of thing.

I mean, I had so many mixed emotions, I didn't even want to go to work the next day. I was hot. But I needed the money, so I went the next day. I didn't have much to say. Did my job, worked through my whole shift. And the whole time, they tried to be nice to me. I'm like, "You can't be nice to me. You jacked me up. You betrayed me. You stabbed me in the back. You did me wrong. So don't try to play with me now."

It was cold for me. You know, this happened on a Tuesday. By Friday, they both said they were sorry. Sorry ain't paying my bills.

Next week they were gone. Her and her mama had called Florida. They've got a lot of relatives. They got an apartment ready, everything. Called, paid for the U-Haul to come and get their stuff, everything. In one week, I was out of a job.

And I've been looking for a job ever since. It's about two and a half months.

Without a job, you can't go nowhere in life. You can't. Whatever job you do, you have—do it in excellence, so that when everybody else quit, your boss ain't gonna let you go, because you have good things for his place. So all my kids got jobs.

Work shows your character. Because without work, you can't do nothing. 'Sides, how you gonna say you want something, and you don't work for it? If you don't work for it, it ain't gonna mean nothing to you when you get it. Because it was too easy. You gotta work.

And, you know, you would think a nurse should get a job everywhere, but you can't. Because I'm an LPN[1], not an RN[2]. RNs are in demand. LPNs are not.

Well, here's the thing: They've been trying to cut us out for the longest, because medical assistants, they teach them a lot of things that they teach us. So they could pay that medical assistant eight dollars an hour. They gotta pay us $21. You feel me? So if they can pay them little, what they need us for? So that's why I went back to college. This is my second year to become an RN, 'cause RNs are in demand.

When I went to high school I paid for it myself. I worked as a janitor. My husband helped me. And I did it like that. I worked at night, and I went to school during the day. And now for college I'm getting a loan. 'Cause I'm too old to try to pay for all this stuff working as a janitor. I'm almost 60 years old. I ain't trying to push no mops. Not me. But like I say, that's pretty much it. Right now, like I say, I'm in college. I'm going here...

She points back over her shoulder to the Workforce office.

...to workshops, 'cause it's been almost, what? Ten, twelve years since I try to go get a resume. Talking about going out and looking for a job—I ain't done that in years. Time brings on the change.

Let me tell you something: I'm getting mine. When I plant that seed, that's what I want. I wrote it on the wall. So like the word of God say: Write the vision. Hon, I wrote the vision, and I'm on my way.

---

[1] Licensed Practical Nurse
[2] Registered Nurse

Daughter & Caregiver

"64 doses"

Amy De La Roza

Amy was born in Virginia. One grandfather was a sharecropper; the other was a baker who ended up with baker's lung. "You get flour coated in the lung and it starts growing tumors, and it fills the lungs up and you can't breathe."

She and her husband—for whom she provided haircuts in exchange for dinners early in their courtship—met at work. "I was his secretary...he didn't even know I was there initially but he heard me laughing over the partition, and he says, I gotta meet that girl." Indeed she has a distinct and affecting laugh; it surfaces frequently, always after a quickly drawn breath, which is momentarily held, then released in a rush. She has a frank sense of humor. Describing a situation at the school where she had her most recent job: "I have parents sit down with me to talk about their three-year-old in a conference, and the first question was, 'What should I do to prepare them for their SATs?' And I looked at them and said, 'Let's make sure he knows where the bathroom is, because if he doesn't, they will not let him take the SAT.'"

I offered to meet anywhere that was convenient, near her current home in Anaheim, California. We talk over a couple of large sodas in the McDonalds inside a Wal-Mart off the 5 Freeway. She comes here sometimes with her grandkids: "I have a three-year-old granddaughter and I have a brand-new grandson, born March 29th."

Amy has a frightening amount of energy for someone her age— she's 60. She seems at least ten years younger that she is; maybe because her hair isn't gray, or because she moves around a lot in her chair, or because she speaks so fast, like a teenager who's just been introduced to coffee.

My husband and I called ourselves the layoff twins. In the time that we were married, in 36 years, between the two of us, we experienced 35 layoffs.

Part of the problem was that he was in a dying profession. He was an office supplies repair technician, and when it all went electronic with computers and stuff, because he was over 50, they didn't train him. This age discrimination thing has been around a long time. And it's all illegal and all that crap but they do it anyway and you can't prove a damn thing. You're toast. It used to make me mad but not anymore. It's not worth it.

I was eighteen years younger than my husband, that was part of the problem. He was all done and but I still had to work. He had this very heavy regimen because he had this serious stroke, which left him like a five-year-old. On top of that he had congestive heart failure, and on top of that he had heavy diabetes, and was very prone to infection, and because the neuropathy had set in, he would cut his legs and not know…he was a bleeder. And my daughter had left home, and it's not fair to be constantly calling her to come take care of daddy, it's not her responsibility. So I said, we're gonna go to assisted living—the only thing that makes sense. You'll have a group of activities, you can participate, you can sit and sleep. If you get up and walk away, they'll come see if you're bleeding…(Laughs.)

So we did. And my parents moved into the Alzheimer's unit in this particular assisted living center at the same time. My mother—who they thought had Alzheimer's but it turned out to be a circulatory dementia—she was having problems. I was able to keep an eye on them and keep an eye on my husband.

I got an offer from a Christian school, just out of the blue, hadn't applied or anything, but I knew somebody who knew somebody—it was one of those things. I went over there and taught and did extremely well, beautiful references, all that good stuff. And then they said, you know, because you can handle anything from infant up through the eighth grade, we wanna put you on as a floater, and take you out of the classroom. Right now, we're growing, it's going nuts and everything. And I said, "Well OK, but I really prefer to have my own class when it settles down for you again, but you know, I'll be the team player, I'll do that." So I did. And then in the middle of all this, the bottom fell out for everybody.

The timing was a surprise. I had noticed the attendance dropping, because as a floater, I have to go in and count my kids and I knew attendance was down, and I knew people had pulled their kids from school. But they had scheduled me all the way till February, even scheduling me in for special vacationing teachers and stuff, so I thought I was good till spring.

I walked in actually to turn in my lesson plan for the week and she said, "Oh, just sit down." And handed me an envelope and said, "That's your final check, and we're going to have to let you go today." And she told me about the low enrollment and everything and apologized and said, "There's also a recommendation in there for you, if there's anything else I can do for you, you give me a call." She said, "I just don't even know where we're going, I've never seen the attendance do this." She said, "We may even close, I don't know."

After she said that we teared up, women tend to just cry. And so we did. She looked at me and, "So what are you gonna do?" she said.

I said, "I don't have any idea, I really don't know, but I'll figure it out."

I know she laid off two-thirds of her staff that day.

Because I was floating, I had all my things in my car and so I didn't really have anything I had to collect. I walked out the door...

I drove home. I had told my whole family. They all kind of knew. All three of them—mom, dad, husband—they had to go to the VA[1] for stuff and so I just loaded them up in the car and we went to the VA hospital and spent the rest of the day up there.

That came to an end in January of 2008. I got these three old people, and they were going through money like there was no tomorrow because they had special needs, and I sat there, and I said, by the time I pay somebody to come in and help them, that's what I make. And so I just decided I would stay home to get them settled in, let the economy get a little better, 'cause initially nobody knew it was this bad, you know?...So I stayed home and about six weeks into that, my husband, all of a sudden, lost his kidneys, overnight, like that. I mean we knew they were gonna go, but...like that?

He was supposed to have a surgery to get a fistula[2] in and he was supposed to do all this stuff but we hadn't done any of it 'cause they told us, "Oh you got about six months." But then when he collapsed on the floor and was all gray I knew there was something wrong so we called the paramedics. The doctor said, "His kidney can't function at all."

And I said, "What do you mean, where's my six months?"

And he said, "Oh no no, he's got to have dialysis now..." Blah blah blah...

So they had an emergency surgery and go in through his neck for the first set of dialysis, they cleaned him up and then put a port in his chest, and then we had this surgery and that had to heal for six months 'cause the diabetic heals very slowly...It was a mess, and trying to get the insurance company to move was like hell on earth. Actually it wasn't the insurance company so much as it was the HMO provider—can't find a hospital bill, can't find this...

He ended up getting another 15 months. With him having to go to dialysis three times a week, he couldn't drive himself because he wasn't capable, because of the cognitive issues, there was no point in me going

[1] Veterans Affairs

[2] Surgically created passageway in the body.

to work, 'cause it would cost me more to get him transported than to do it myself. So I did that at the same time as taking care of my mom and my dad.

So my days would start at five in the morning to get him up, showered, dressed, down to dialysis by seven, then back, get my mother up, showered, dressed, to breakfast, and then my dad's stuff ready. And my mother was blind, very hard of hearing, took her false teeth out one day and said, "They're not going back in." And I mean, short of a crowbar they weren't. She just wouldn't let you put them in. What're you gonna do? The shape of her mouth had changed as she was going through her illness, and they no longer fit. So they would be pinching. And we didn't know that. When we finally had that explained to us, she wouldn't sit in the dental chair. There's really nothing you can do about it. (Laughs.) So then I had to start pureeing her food, and feeding her special, she couldn't swallow her pills…

I ended up doing haircuts and manicures and pedicures and wound care and…I really should have my LVN[1] just because I've earned it the hard way, not because I've gone to school, but I mean I learned how to do all this jazz because my husband had open wounds on his legs they had to stay wrapped. Sometimes they could walk and sometimes they couldn't—both of them—so I had two wheelchairs going, my dad losing his vision, losing his hearing, whole left side upper quadrant paralyzed. So he had issues where he needed help, you know, he can't button his pants, he can't take the top off the bottle, he doesn't have but one hand, so anything that needed two hands was mine. And so it didn't make any sense for me to look for work, it really didn't. And we finally got to the point where we had enough income coming in, 'cause all three of them were vets, and they all three qualified for home care.

Your mom, your dad and your husband?

Yeah, all three. Vets in their own right. So we had enough income, we could pay the bills…we could take care of their little special needs, 'cause of course my mother was in diapers and I mean, just, lots of expensive things. And we did that, and the medications—I added it up

---

[1] Licensed Vocational Nurse

one day, 'cause I had everything written down—I was doing 64 doses of medication a day, counting over-the-counter and prescriptions and shots and everything. And I said, my goodness, no wonder I can't keep it straight. Way too hard to keep 64 doses a day straight, and some of them were repeats, and those are very confusing, 'cause you remember doing it earlier, but when earlier did I do it?—was it yesterday or was it today? So I just had, I had this big checklist, and everybody got checked off, and then I had to do blood pressure, and I had to do weight—my husband was on a call-in thing where I had to send it all in over the computer and then the nurse would call back and chat with him, and because he was super super critical.

My husband ended up having a another stroke—and it was enough of a stroke that they couldn't give him the heart medication anymore because his heart was also damaged and he lost his blood pressure, couldn't do dialysis. So he died at home—we put him in a hospice and he actually died that night. He was 77 when he died. And he had a gigantic stroke, which was just a gift from God, because this man was a terrible patient and he didn't get better as time went by, and I couldn't take care of him anymore. He was heavier than I was, he'd get out of bed, fall down, I couldn't get him back up, would have to call paramedics, they were calling me names 'cause "this is the fourth call today" and you know I get all that—but what do they want me to do? Do you want me to leave him on the floor? That's my choice. He got through his death, we buried him in the end of April of 2010, the very next day, I took my dad to the doctor cause he'd been having prostrate troubles for a couple years, and they say, oh now he's got cancer of the bladder.

The next day?
The next day. The day after that, my mother has a heavy fever, I'd never seen it before. And I take her in, they take her to the hospital, and she's got a systemic infection, likely not going to survive.
Ok.

Then I come down with bronchitis. And at this point—still don't know my name 'cause I lost my husband of 36 years—I said, "Really? Don't you really think I've got enough here?" (Laughs.)

I'm thinking you should change your name to Job.

(Laughs.) My pastor called me Job for the longest time.

So we get done with all of this, and I'm going, OK. We kind of have covered that curve: got my dad through bladder surgery and got my mother home from the hospital, everything seems fine. But then we go to the doctor for my mom's post-op and he does a urinalysis and says, "She's got MRSA[1]."

I said, "You've got to be kidding me."

And he said, "No she got it in the hospital, probably."

I said, "Well why isn't she sicker?"

He said, "The bladder…it's common. It will stay like that and Monday it'll explode like a bomb, and she'll be dead in minutes."

I said, "Oh my God, what do I do?"

And he said, "Put her in hospice. What else you gonna do?"

Well of course my mother didn't want to go to a facility and my dad didn't want her to go, so we kept her at home, so then we're into the diapers and the rolling and the whole ten yards, and the hallucinations and…it's so…I fed my mother that morphine because she needed it. She was so…She would have been so afraid of everything without it. And I just kept pouring it to her, as much as they let me give her, because she was hurting, developed tremendous bed sores, we had these huge open sores, and I said, I don't care, I'm going to give her whatever she wants.

She passed away in August. So then my dad couldn't stand to be in the apartment, and I wasn't real fond of being there anymore either, so the week after she passed we packed up her things and moved out of there, which is how I ended up in Anaheim—'cause that's where my dad used to live with mom. He went back to the same apartment complex

[1] bacterial infection

that they lived in for eighteen years. And we're still there but we're going to have to move. He can't live there anymore because of his disabilities getting worse and worse at this point, but that's fine. I'm just getting to the point...I really don't even question any of it anymore, I just go, ok, well now we're gonna do this. But anyway, I decided I would really like to go back to work—it would help me deal with losing my husband, who, even though he was like a five-years-old, was a delightful five-year-old, and still my very best friend in the whole world.

And my father and I...I won't say we won't get along, but we got along better before my mother died. He's become very crotchety, very whiney, very dependent—was not any of those things before she died. And his whole health picture went south like fifty points. And I really think some of that's starting to come back now, 'cause he's starting to deal with the grief. But I'm still trying to deal with my own grief, and he's coming, dumping all his grief on me. And I'm going...I really want to work. I mean, I really want to work.

How do you dump your grief?
I spend a lot of time praying. I have wonderful pastors, poor Steve and Rob get emails at three in the morning. I mean, not that they get them then, but they've just been very patient and they have truly walked me through this, they have been fabulous because it was just hell on earth, it really was, it was just terrible. And then the other thing is, when my mom and my husband died, we lost 50% of our revenue in the family. Actually we lost almost two-thirds of it, but my dad had a pretty good retirement independent of the VA benefits.

I can't afford medical insurance for myself and what insurance I can afford, they don't pay crap—so why have it? I spent everything I had to keep my husband alive as long as I did because in insurance we hit the donut holes and there were things they wouldn't pay for. I just cashed in my 401K and I kept him alive. And I knew I was doing it, it was a conscious decision, and if I had to do it again I'd do it again. But I really thought I would go back to work and with no one but me to take care of, no problem. Because when I last was working, I was making $50–60,000 a year. I'm a very simple person, I don't need lots of goo-ga stuff. I'd be fine. Work another 10 years, be fine—because I'm healthy, and I really don't look my age. The problem is, when they find out when you graduated from high school, they figure it out. (Laughs.) And they all make you write that down, but I got interviews out the gazoo and nobody would hire me. And finally I went to a headhunter, one of the ones where you pay them, and I said, "I want you to represent me."

She said, "You have excellent credentials, you test well, your skills are fantastic, wonderful experience, wonderful references—but I would not represent you."

I said, "Why not?"

She said, "Because you were born in 1950 and we can't change that, and I won't get you a job, and I won't get any money." And she said, "And you can quit looking, it isn't gonna happen, Sweetie—not in this economy." She said, "If you're already working and you're 55 plus and you're doing ok, they keep you, but if you lose it at that point, you don't go back."

How did that hit you, how did you respond to that?
I was angry. I've worked hard all my life, never done anything to deserve any of this. The VA is actually paying me as a destitute widow. I'm not proud of that, but it is money coming in. He would want me to use it. And I can have that until the day I die if I don't marry or make five cents—literally five cents, I mean, I can't make a dime. It's a benefit that's available to me 'cause he served during the war. He served during the Koran War, in the Navy. My mom and dad were World War II. She was Navy and he was Marine. Which is another reason my dad's whole personality change is just blowing my mind because the Marine doesn't do that, doesn't do any of the things he does. But that's my issue, I have to deal with that. And I am, little bit at a time. I'm learning to keep my mouth shut and not talk. (Laughs.) Unless it's really important. You kinda choose your battles. I'm like, "Is this gonna be important next week?" (Shakes her head:) "We're not gonna fight about it." I do everything for him except the bathroom—thank

god he can still do those...I can see it coming. And that's alright, I've been through it with two other people, I can do it again.

When my father dies, I'll probably go live with my daughter and her husband. I've been invited to. And I'll either do that, or, if I could find it, I would go to the mission field as a volunteer and just scrub toilets or whatever in an orphanage, I wouldn't care. I would do that. What have I got to lose? Nobody else wants me...(laughs)...so you might as well find something worthwhile to do.

I should be doing other things because I've become very unproductive because I can just sit at home. I can always put it off till tomorrow. Oh am I good at putting it off till tomorrow. I have to work with myself to get out of my chair and do things, and I don't know how much of that is the grief factor. I'm still dealing with the fact that I lost my mom, 'cause when I lost her I was still dealing with the fact that I lost my husband. And it's kinda like, I don't know how much of this is that I got lazybutt, or dealing with the emotions...

I find that not working, I've kind of lost purpose, because no one's gonna make me do the next thing. For a long time I felt like I don't have any value, and sometimes there are still days when I still feel like that. But mostly I've gotten to the point, it's not that I don't have any value, it's just that I haven't met anybody that needs what I have. And someday I will meet somebody who needs what I have, whether it's to work, or to be a close friend—I've had a hard time finding friends because when you're a caregiver like I am, you lose your friends, cause you don't have time to go to the movies and to dinner and to drop everything and go.

My husband was a wonderful guy in a lot of ways, but he was very Victorian, and so the affection was very couched, and he wasn't one to say, "Gee you did a really great job of this..." I didn't get a lot of that from him; I got all that at work. So now I don't get it anywhere. (Laughs.)

I think particularly in this country, if you are a competitive employee and all of a sudden you lose your job, you kind of lose who you are. And it takes some time to get to the bottom of who you are, and I think somebody who probably isn't a Christian would probably have a much harder time, because I get a lot of my value from just that Jesus thinks I'm important; I'm a child of the king, you know? And I can say that. And if you can't say that, then you really gotta feel worthless when all this happens to you.

It has made the things that were super important not really important anymore. My credit's in shambles because I gave it all up to keep my husband alive, and that would have just totally destroyed me 10 years ago—and I don't care, really, I don't care. (Laughs.) I can't own anything anyway. I don't even own the car I drive, it belongs to my dad, 'cause I can't have it, if I did I lose my benefit...so I don't own anything, and when you don't own anything, you don't care what they do without your credit. (Laughs.) There is some weird freedom with it. You begin to value other things. It's more important to me that my grandchildren have a smile on their face than that I can impress somebody in an office environment. It's more important to me that my dad goes to the doctor and all the notes are in order and everything's right and I know I've done a good job and the doctor tells me, "Wow, you did a great job with him," than it is for somebody to say in an interview, "Yeah, we're gonna hire you." The things that you can do become more important. You really get a lot more joy out of them than when you did a lot of things well but didn't really have time to concentrate fully on any of them. In a way, it's better, and certainly, I'm better off than people who have to go in every day and wonder if they've got a job. I don't. The only way I get fired is if he dies, and if he dies, he dies, and then I have to figure something else out, and if it's the rescue mission, who cares? They got bathrooms too, I'm sure I can clean them. I'm really good at bathrooms since I've been taking care of all these sick people. (Laughs.) Really good at bathrooms. You just kind of deal with it. But you don't deal with it till you accept it. There's a real tough trail to accepting it, but once you get there there's a tremendous freedom.

Wife & Terminator

"You don't want me here anymore"

Deborah Troutman & Paul Murphey

They are unconventional, individually and as a couple, because of imaginative choices and steadfast independence—two things often romanticized but rarely demonstrated.

Deb is 54, Paul, 58. They sit side by side on their couch; both relaxed, both in crisp white tops and glasses. They've been together for seven years. Paul has his sleeves rolled up. He is the son of a college professor, "so there was always an assumption that college would be part of the deal for me." He has a soft voice and is a patient speaker, deliberate with all that he says and it pays off: he expresses engaging thoughts clearly. He grew up in a house with art

*and music; he played the French horn and guitar. He is someone
who explores disparate curiosities: in college he bounced from the
theater department to business school before finally pursuing a
career as an architect. And now, at 58, he is still considering new
options, still allowing himself to be led by curiosity.*

Deb grew up in rather different circumstances: "We had some
velvet paintings." She looks to her husband who doesn't give her the
laugh. "My mom and dad were blue-collar type workers. I was the
first one to go to college. In most of my extended family, there wasn't
a sense that that was important. When I went back to college in
my thirties, my mother said, 'Why would you want to do that? You
could do payroll somewhere.' It just never occurred to her. We didn't
have a book in my house growing up. No one read. We had a TV.
We didn't have any music. There was just no cultural opportunity.
My family watched roller derby and drank beer out of a can. It's a
very different upbringing than my life has been."

Deb shares qualities with Roni Chambers in St. Louis and
Dominick Brocato in Kansas City: she is a human resources
professional who demonstrates the qualities required for that type
of work through her hospitality, an acute sense of boundaries, and
the attention with which she listens and speaks. She also has a dry,
ironic sense of humor.

Paul and Deb have both been married previously. She has two
grown sons: "The 29-year old has two children, ages seven and
three, and he is getting married in August. And I'm thrilled. They
are the most amazing parents. I would have loved to have been that
kind of parent. So just a lot of pride about that."

Paul is "maybe too embarrassed to lay out all the details about
my previous marriages. I'm very happy to be in this one."

"I decided not to take his name because three other wives did
it," Deb adds without anything even approaching a smile.

"Actually, only one. The other two kept their names. Smart girls
after all."

Across a few moments of silence, Deb and Paul share smirks that reveal they are—in their own peculiar way and somewhere deep down—laughing together.

"One of the things that fascinated me about Paul was he had done this travel, and he had this career in Los Angeles and was well-read and would go to nice restaurants that would intimidate me, and it's been a whole different experience. And I now have a lot of books. And we talk about architecture, and we talk about all kinds of things. So most of my education has probably happened after college."

"It's nice to have somebody to share with," Paul says. "So, you know, we both get something out of it." He smiles at his wife.

We are in their orderly St. Louis condo. They've set out an assortment of cheeses and fruit and crackers and bread. They offer us fresh-brewed herbal iced-tea.

Deb and Paul worked for the same company on two separate occasions: when they first met in St. Louis and again a few years later in Southern California. It did not end well either time.

Deb: We've been married a little over two years. It was interesting, because we were planning a wedding—a very sustainable, environmental wedding, and we were growing little succulents for people that were going to be at the wedding—and then found out that I had to have some major surgery, and I decided immediately, "Well, I just want to get married." And on Sunday, I got on the Internet, and I filled out an application—a marriage license application—set up an appointment for Thursday at 3:45pm at the courthouse, and we went down and got married.

I went out Monday, and a friend of mine said, "Buy this dress," and I bought that dress, and I made a little bouquet of flowers in the car on the way down there, and we stayed one night in a hotel and came back home.

Paul: Some of the flowers from the bouquet came from shrubs in the parking lot of a shopping center up the road from our house.

Deb: Alright, I stole some.

Paul: They've grown back...

We can't remember what our anniversary is either. I think it was March 27th.

Deb: 29th…I don't know, it was a very fast deal.

Paul: In 2004, I decided to move back here. There's a teacher that I had who was extremely influential in the way I developed who turned 90, and I wanted to spend some time with him before…you know, while he was still around. So that's what got me back here. And I ended up just consulting as an architect with three or four firms. One of them was Deb's firm. And a friend of a friend gave her my resume.

Deb: This friend at the firm said, "Leslie tried to set me up with this guy, Paul, but he's, like, in his fifties, and he's a sober alcoholic, and he was married three times."

And I'm like, "Wow! Somebody that doesn't want commitment and can be my designated driver. I gotta meet this guy!" (Laughs.) So I called him for an interview, and thought, "Well, let's see where this goes," and so we hired him as a consultant, so it really wasn't that I was dating an employee.

Paul: Well, we had met on a professional basis to begin with, so…I mean, that's all we knew about each other to start with, and we discovered that we liked each other as people. And my view of it is that it was just really intimate and fun to see the other person in both modes and get along in both modes.

And we had some basic rules. We wouldn't take work problems home with us unless it was something we could really make some progress on. We were sharing management of the office a little bit—I was hiring and taking care of staff and things, and that's your area also. So it was a team effort, I guess. Somehow, we were working toward the same goal.

Deb: I think we had a lot of professional respect for each other, and really learned that, when we work together, I couldn't do architecture, and he couldn't do human resources. And as soon as he realized that, everything was fine. And so, you know, I am so serious about, if I'm hired to do a job, I'm hired to do a job, and if I couldn't work with Paul, then I shouldn't be doing that job. Because no matter what the circumstances are, I have a business commitment.

Paul: We loved working together, by the way. It was just a lot of fun.

Deb: Yeah, it was great. Paul was hired to do a specific project. The idea was when that was up, that would be the end. Well, other things came up. They decided to send him to Phoenix to help with a project there. But at some point, he was coming into the office saying, "What am I doing here?"

So I talked to the principal, and I said, "David, there's no work for Paul, is there?"

And he said, "No."

And I said, "Why don't you let him go?"

And he said, "Well, he's talented. He's a good guy and everything."

I said, "Well, I'll just do it." I mean, it's just not the right thing, to keep dragging him along. It's not good for the business, and it's not good for him.

I had to let him go.

We got together for dinner one night, and I said, "Paul, they don't have any more work for you, so I need your badge and key...But we can still have dinner, so..."

Paul: I can still stay at your place. (He smiles.)

Deb: Right. Right, right, right. So that worked out...

I continued in that role, very successful. What my specialty has become is start-up human resources companies that have never had somebody there and take everything that they've got going and evaluate it and design some systems and processes and things like that. So I stayed there, and Paul worked at a few different consulting firms. He was very fortunate: he's very good at what he does.

Paul: So I got an offer to make a little bit of money in Newport Beach—

Deb: A lot of money—

Paul: —And that's what got us back there till the economy did what it did. I started working there for this new job in March of 2007, and you were there by June, I guess.

Deb: My brother lives in Southern California; I'd been there quite a bit. And I said, "My kids are gone. Oh, yeah. Definitely. Let's jump on it and just go." Didn't even hesitate. So when we got there, things—within a year, a year and a half—things really started to change as far as economically and our ability to keep jobs. And it just really took a toll on us over a period of four years.

When we moved to California, I did not have a job. I had some money available from the sale of my condo that I could use to live on, and I found a job...I was hired to do a combination of some business development, marketing, and human resources for the company Paul was at.

Paul was on leave for his hip replacement. And the conversation began at work with the CFO that Paul was not going to be brought back. And I was in this dilemma, because the agreement that we had is personal life is personal life, business is business...so I would go to work and have these discussions about how this was going to transpire with Paul leaving, and how we're going to deal with any severance or anything like that, and I would go home and be able to say nothing...Paul started to suspect something was going on...and at the very end, I bowed out and said, "This is just such a big conflict of interest for me. I can't do this." And shortly after that, I actually was courted by another company and was able to leave at the same time he left. So I actually backed out of that termination.

It was very stressful, and at that point, I realized even though we enjoyed working together, I could never do it again. We really had professional commitments, and it was a terrible struggle. It just was very difficult, and I know even at the end, he said, "Well, because of my age and my disability, don't I have a case?"

And I said, "Well, you can look at the EEO[1] website. That's where you would find out about discrimination. I can't coach you on that." And so, you know...I just held it together through the end.

Paul: I had been out for about two weeks at that point, and I had just gotten to the point where I could...I think had gone into the office a day or two before with a cane to just say hello, and on that visit, we scheduled a meeting, the boss and I. I went in, we sat down in the conference room, and it took about 10 minutes before I understood what was being said, and I tried very hard to get a clear statement. I ended up having to call the CFO in Detroit to make sure I understood what was going on. I mean, it is

[1]   Equal Employment Opportunity Commission

humiliating to get laid off. It took me several months to stop being angry about it. I mean, I was really angry. Looking back on it, I'm not quite sure why. But at the time it was extremely painful.

I was fortunate that it happened fairly early in the current cycle, because I did get severance. If it were happening today, it would be, "See you later." So that helped out a little bit. I've always been more happy giving my money to credit card companies than saving or investing. But I had a little bit of a 401K from the previous, eight-year job, and lived on that for a while.

Deb: I went to another employer. They found me. It was a great company—they had about 60 people. It was an environmental company, which is my passion. And they were engineers, and they were doing wonderful work. And I started in October of 2008, and by January, they realized that they had some serious financial trouble, and they brought a very heavy-duty CFO person in to look at everything and realized that they were in more trouble than they really had ever thought. And so layoffs began. And we started with 10 people, and then it was another five, and this continued on, and they really were trying to making it work. Fabulous company. Wonderful people. And so it continued, and I thought, well, my job's pretty secure—because when business picks up, you need a human resource person to build the staff back up. Plus, during that time, morale becomes so low, everybody is frightened for their job, and everybody is doing double the work. So it seemed like the most critical time to have a human resource person.

One day, my boss, who was fantastic said, "Let's go outside and take a walk." And I knew she was going to tell me that the assistant was let go. And she did. And then we continued the walk, and she said, "Well, Deb, we really can't keep you on in this position. We didn't have a human resource person before. You were the first one. We're going to absorb that, and we need to let you go."

I said, "Joanne, I work 45 hours a week. Who's going to do that work?"

And she said, "Well, a lot of it just won't be done."

And I said, "Who's going to be there when people want to come talk?" That's really my biggest concern, because I spent a lot of time doing employee relations. And people come in, and they talk to me about all kinds of things. They talk to me about their families. They talk to me because they can't get along with their boss. They don't know what they're doing in the job. Whatever. And that was the biggest concern: "Who's going to talk to those people?"

And she said, "Well, their bosses will."

"That's why I'm there: because they're not going to talk to their boss!" And I said, "What are you going to do when you have to hire people back?"

And she said, "Well, we'll do what we did before. Somebody will take over. One of the managers will find applicants and…"

I just thought, "How can you do that?" And I really tried to talk to her about part-time, what about consulting? Is there anything I can do to make the transition even easier? And there wasn't. They just couldn't afford it.

That was the first time in my life I had ever been let go from a position. During my career, I had this discussion with many people that we needed to lay you off. They did something really bad, you know: absenteeism, or they violated policy, or did some damage, and we need to let you go. And it was never the case that it was okay for me to do that. I always felt horrible. So many times, when people are laid off or they're discharged, I walk them to their desk and watch what they pack up. And I have boxes in my office already, because I know it's going to happen, and I walk them over there, and it feels horrible, because they know you knew days ago, and pack up their things and, at times, depending on the situation, walk them out to their car, put their things in their car. Somebody said to me, "You must be used to this by now." And I said, "The day I get used to this, I'm in the wrong job." Because these are people's lives. They came to work with their lunch that day, and they're going home to tell their family they have no work. They have no income now. And I take that very seriously. I've never had anyone storm out. Never in my career had anyone bring a lawsuit. When I would be in a room with a manager and the person walks in, they know right away. People start instant messaging each other: "So-and-so just came out of the office, and they're crying. This is the time." And it just spreads like wildfire. Everybody realizes they're vulnerable.

It's interesting, because the people who stay feel so bad. They're sort of the survivors, you know, and they wonder why they weren't chosen. But most places, employees get to be like family. You're there more hours a day in your waking hours than you're anywhere. This is your family. They know what's going on with their kids. I've let someone go, and their wife had a baby the next day. Somebody couldn't close on their home because they had no job at the time. And so the people left behind just feel terrible.

Sometimes people walk in and say, "You're letting me go, aren't you?" It just takes you back. When that happened to me, I realized I was one of those people. I called Paul on the phone, and I said, "I have no job. I don't know what I'm going to do."

Went home, and you're just kind of in shock, even though you know you didn't do anything wrong. You just can't even believe it, that you don't have anywhere to go the next day. And you don't know how you're going to get any money. You know these bills are coming up, and you have no income.

It's so hard when people are laid off or fired—discharged for any reason—regardless, to move onto that next step. Right away, you have to be able to pick yourself up and say, "I'm going to file for unemployment" and try to get through a system that is unbelievably bureaucratic and difficult. And even though I'd done benefits for years, I started reading the paperwork and thought, "Oh my gosh, what am I going to get here?" As soon as you're on the other side, it's a completely different thing. And in the end, up to this day, I realized it's really made me understand human resources better, and what people actually feel when they're let go. It was just very painful. You're immobile for a while. You don't even start to look for a job. You just sit there every day going, "I don't have a job. Nobody might ever hire me. I don't even know how to look for a job. I don't have a resume." You have nothing. You're in no way prepared for it. And nobody can tell you in advance that that's going to be the way it is.

Every phrase is wrong. For a human being hearing it, any phrase is wrong. There's downsize, laid off, terminated, discharged, let go, we need to separate employment, we need to part ways. There is no way to say it that anyone can hear anything but, "You don't want me here anymore."

Paul: That's pretty much what I felt too. You're not good enough anymore, is what it comes down to. You're just not good enough.

Deb: Yeah. What you've done isn't...We'll just do it without you.

Paul: At least with you...(looking at his wife)...you, being a professional with those skills, you know what to say and how to be clear. I couldn't get my boss to come out with it. It was this kind of dancing around the thing, so it's good that you could be clear with people.

Deb: I think it's so important how you treat them in that very moment that it happens. Usually, I would coach managers, because it's their responsibility, really, to tell the person. But I'm there to kick them under the table if they say something, especially something like, "I know just how you feel," or "This really hurts us as well." You do not know how I feel. And I just can't believe when people say that. I want to jump across the table and wring their neck and say, "What were you thinking?" It's like a parent saying, "This hurts me more than it hurts you." It doesn't, you know? There's no way that is going to make it okay. And, you know, I think the best thing you do is you treat somebody with dignity, regardless of what they've done. And let them leave with integrity. Let them say goodbye to people if you can. Call them afterwards, ask how they are. There's been a few people I've contacted back and said, "Let me help you with your resume."

Did anybody call you to see how you were?

Deb: No.

Paul: I think it really is hard for most people on both sides, and it's tough to get it and to receive it. It's just hard. So I can understand the motivation for wanting to do it with some distance in it, but it's not the right way.

Deb: Yeah, it's interesting, you know, even not being happy at a job. To lose a job even though you're not happy is still just a real kick. If you stop to think about it...

If you had a choice, you probably wouldn't stay there, but because they made that decision, totally different thing.

Paul: By the time everything was going to hell in California generally with architecture and construction, I was really tired of it. Again, needed another sabbatical. So I had no idea what to do. I knew I didn't want to do that anymore, so I tested myself. Personality test: Meyers-Briggs, and whatever other stuff. And discovered I wasn't cut out to be an architect. So I went to Orange Coast College, and I thought, I have a rational mind; I'll try some computer classes. I can make some money doing that. I hated it. In fact, I just stopped going to one of the classes. The only 'F' I've earned in my life. But horticulture I liked. So here we are. I don't know what I'm going to do with it. It's kind of...So far, it's been tough to convince people that I'm serious about this and I can do the work, but it'll happen. St. Louis is a community of a kind that Southern California is not, so I think it's just a matter of time.

I'm wondering if you guys have had any significant lifestyle changes?

Deb: I'd say yes.

Paul: And I'd probably say no.

Deb: Apparently his life hasn't changed.

Paul: The circumstances change.

Deb: You're used to living with less.

Paul: I'm used to bouncing around. I went to Singapore in 1983, expecting to be there for two weeks...I ended up staying for a year with the two bags I arrived with, and talked my way into a job with the friend of a friend. Somehow, I've always gotten what I needed when I really had to have it.

Deb: I think there have been significant changes. We don't go out to eat. We never go to a store for fear of buying something.

Paul: But I've lost eight inches around my waist, so, you know, okay. Having been heavy all my life, I'll take that.

Deb: Yeah, that's a good thing. We started really watching what we eat. We eat very little meat. We eat healthier. We eat a lot of fresh food.

Paul: By the way, I should say that I'm extremely fortunate that I can have this "everything will be fine" attitude. I don't have children. I owe some money to some faceless companies, but my needs are fairly to the point. I doubt that I would feel this way if I had a family and a crisis to deal with. So for what it's worth, I try to appreciate how good I have it in spite of the job situation.

Deb: I've been one of the primary breadwinners.

Paul: She has supported me for two years is what she's trying to say.

Deb: Right. And even before, as my kids were growing up, that's what I did. So the fear of not having money is I think very different than Paul's, because I don't have a sense of who will provide it if I don't. I have to. And I might not be taking care of my kids anymore, but the sense of responsibility and obligation to find a way to bring money in is really important.

I think the biggest and most difficult thing is that, at this point, every bit of retirement money is gone. We've had to live on all of the retirement money. Neither one of us has health insurance at this point.

Paul: Again, I'm used to that. She's not.

Deb: I've never, ever been without health insurance. And the interesting thing is, in California, when you're unemployed, you collect unemployment, and that's all taxable. And when you withdraw your 401K, that's taxable—and there's a penalty. And it throws you over into another tax bracket, because you needed to take this money out, even if you didn't spend it all. You had to take it to prepare. When you're most vulnerable and you're taking it out, that's when you get hit. I was doing consulting work, and when you do that, you don't have anyone paying the 7.65% of your social security, so you pay both. So 13.3% on that, plus the penalty, plus the tax, plus tax on unemployment, and the next thing you know... Now we're paying the IRS for taxes on money we don't even have. We have debt now on money that we had to take out of our own retirement funds. And it's frightening. We're in our mid-to-late fifties, and the realization that there isn't going to be any retirement. I'm glad Paul's in school and pursuing this, because we'll work for the rest of our lives.

Paul: Which is not a bad thing, anyway. If it's work that you enjoy, why not.

Deb: That's true.

Paul: I show someone my resume now, it's got full-time student and horticulture services consultant or whatever I called it, and then some high-powered architecture jobs. And there's not a lot there to go on in a real world sense. So I'm looking forward to getting a regular job, so that I can have that as an option. It's a weird way to break into a new field. Years ago, I would've thought that was the wrong direction. But not anymore.

I just recently stopped worrying too much about what possibilities are suitable, and if we're done tonight in time, I'll take my Trader Joe's application over a couple blocks away from here. I never thought I would see that as a viable option for myself, but we have gotten to a point where I just need to make a little money somehow.

There's literally a limit to the resources we have available at the moment, which is two or three months. So something will shake loose in that time. I'm reasonably certain. It always has.

I can't really explain what happened. I know literally what took place, but I don't know and don't quite care how I ended up where I am today. I know what I'm doing now is something I love, and I want to keep doing it. And that's nice, you know. Growing food is a good thing to do for people. I get a kick out of anything that grows. It's the sort of magic that got me. The connection to the universe, if you will. It all sounds really silly, really sappy, but that's what it is for me.

Very hard to find that as an architect. There was always a little bit of disappointment for me in that you're in this noble profession that is theoretically capable of taking care of all sorts of problems, with huge numbers of people...but it's not like the dirt and the seed and the water.

I'm even looking forward to it all dying, because that's part of the process. There's a life-sustaining quality to it that I appreciate, and I respect. To me, it's very real life, because sometimes, you have to be tough and pull the damn thing and throw it away, even though it's a perfectly good plant. Other times, you have to be very kind and gentle and coax things along. If it weren't for you (looking at his wife), I'd probably just be out in the garden from now on and forever just weeding plants.

Deb: Yeah.

Paul: But you're worth coming out for, of course.

Deb: Thank you. Because I'm not going to crawl around there. I might be one of those you pull and throw away. (Smiles wryly.)

Paul (Smiling back, equally wryly): No sign of that.

Deb: Good. We thought about, "Well, why don't we get one of those five dollar, ten dollar booths at a produce market?"—a farmer's market. And, you know, we're growing basil and tomatoes. Maybe we can go down there and make a little money. But part of that also is passing it onto people who would enjoy having it.

Paul: I'll try growing herbs or something that restaurants can use. I'm not sure that's where it will end up, but for now, that's what I do, and I like it. We'll see where it leads. I'm not at all bothered by the idea that I don't know what I'm doing. I enjoy the process, and the getting from here to there.

Deb: I'm working contract on a part-time basis. It's going to end at the end of July, in two weeks, and I'm really frightened. I don't know what's out there.

I have applied for jobs, and there were hundreds applying for jobs. There's very few companies that feel like they need human resources. I spoke with a recruiter. Last week, I sent out an email to every contact that I have—and I have a lot—saying, "In two weeks, I don't have a job. I know you don't know of anything right now, but can you think of anything I can do?"

My resume says HR consultant since 2009. Every time I get a resume, I know what that means. It means you can't find a job. All the employers look at, and it's like, "What are these gaps?" And I know since 2007, that these people have worked six months, one year, two years here, done consulting. That's the way it goes. It doesn't mean they're at the bottom of the barrel, you know? And there's so many people that say, "Well, they always get rid of deadwood first." And I hope that's not true in my case. There's still plenty of people out there that think that's so unacceptable. And they know what horticulture consulting is and what HR consulting is.

I'm not as much of a believer in that you do the right things, the right things come along. Because I feel like that's happened. I've done the right things, and it's been one thing after another out of my control that has gotten me to this point.

You know, at this point, it's going to be maybe finding retail or doing housecleaning. We were driving last night and said, "Oh, Westway Cleaners is hiring. Maybe we should go in there." And it's like, the thought of working...And I mean, it's not that that's not an important job, or somebody shouldn't be doing that job, it's just having had this career and, you know, a Master's degree and this great income and all this security, it's like, "Wow. Working part-time in a dry cleaners. This is where we are right now." Something. Something to bring money in. Because as Paul said, we have just a few months left.

Paul: I read recently that New York State passed a law that prohibits employment ads from stating that they will not hire people who are unemployed, currently, because that's become part of the deal. If you don't have a job, you're not considered hirable, which is a little bit backwards, I think, at this point.

Deb: For me, there is a frustration and a disappointment that the people that have the power to make some differences cannot talk to each other. And the things that we are so impacted by just seem like they're not going to get to it. They are not going to figure it out. And the people that have the money are holding things up, in my mind. There's such denial that people are in the situation they're in. I thought people without insurance were in the bottom ⅓rd of the income bracket. We've made a lot of money. We've contributed a lot. And we don't have anything.

Paul: The scale of the disconnect at the moment is bigger than any of us realize, and the decisions that are being made are so completely foreign to what real life is about. I think our basic views of what the government ought to be and how people fit into it haven't shifted significantly, but the confidence that there is a system that we can depend on is gone. And it's pretty much every man for himself. And that doesn't speak well of our collective future, if you ask me. Sooner or later, we need each other. Being human carries that with it.

Providers

"She was carrying us"
Erik Hill

Erik Hill, 37, lives in Tacoma, Washington, not far from where he grew up in the apple-rich Yakima Valley. His father was a career military officer-cum-schoolteacher, the first in the family to graduate from college. Erik's grandparents emigrated from Finland. One grandfather built houses; the other helped build the Soo Locks on the Saint Mary's River in Michigan. As for the earlier generations: "I like to say we were some sort of Viking kings." Erik mixes gentle with burly and is endlessly adaptable. He'll find friends in any room, regardless of whether it's packed with Republicans or Democrats. I have seen this on many occasions, as Erik is one of the few unemployed that I talked to for this book to whom I am not a stranger. We first met in 1995, when we had both just arrived in New York City, ready to get eaten alive. He was one of the first to welcome me, even though the surroundings were as unknown to him as they were to me.

He has been back on the west coast for over a decade now, and most recently he worked in sales for a carpet and tile cleaning company that handled commercial and residential accounts. He spent his days satisfying current clients while doggedly pursuing new ones. An average week started with twenty to thirty calls, talking to current clients, future clients, clients that the company hadn't worked with in a while. He sent letters, he sent emails, he went door-to-door on cold visits, handing out business cards, asking receptionists how this particular office or that particular office addressed its carpeting cleaning needs.

His goal was to have 10 "real" meetings a day. "That doesn't count stopping in and visiting people but actually having a business meeting talking about something, you know, where we're going to sell something. Just stopping by with some doughnuts didn't really count."

I was laid off two years ago. The thing is when it comes to a lot of sales positions, especially for a small to mid-size company, if you don't see it coming you're not paying attention.

There were two sales folks…working in commercial sales, working on going out to meet as many people as possible. We were getting little hints that something might be coming up. We had to take a test for our sales aptitude at one point. It was an online test and I think my boss was using it as a way to decide who he was going to let go. So we took the sales test and the other person was let go.

A few months went by…I remember talking to the bookkeeper and I asked the question about when my vacation benefits kicked in. And we both realized I had about a week and a half to go before that would kick in…If I didn't finish my year they'd no longer have to pay me vacation… The next day a meeting was scheduled for Friday with the boss.

I spent that morning—instead of going out on sales calls—just sitting and cleaning out my desk, cleaning out my computer, cleaning out any kind of things I was working on that didn't belong to them.

What did you clean off of your computer?

Well, sometimes you've got excess files, duplicates, things you don't need. I didn't delete anything that belonged to them. But you know there might have been things like I was talking to this potential new person, you know, maybe I had a sales plan about what I was going to do the next three or four months, what my goals were, who I was going to reach out to. And that didn't belong to them. So I deleted it. I packed my briefcase, everything that belonged to me that was personal. I went into the meeting and waited for them to do it.

It's hard to remember exactly how the meeting went. I think I blocked a lot of it out. I can't remember the exact words to be honest with you because at one point I just saw him talking. I wasn't even listening anymore. I was just waiting for the 'Thank you. Goodbye.'

We talked about those cost-cutting measures; he had to save money... He was just straight up about how money wasn't coming in...where his cash flow was at...Money wasn't coming in.

I understand when you're running a small to mid-size company sitting up at night, the day before you have to pay everybody, it's got to be a daunting task. And when sales aren't coming in for whatever reason—you know, whether someone is slacking off or they're just not getting the sales—it's just not happening...so I understand why he did it. How he did it was a little bit of a bummer...There was no severance, no vacation pay, just see ya.

I think that's what really affected me, thinking maybe you're looking too much at the numbers and the metrics and the excel spreadsheet and forgetting the fact that that little number you see on column A, row seven is an actual person with a wife, with a kid, with a car payment, with a mortgage, and is actually from your country, from your neighborhood, and is a viable person in the community.

I said, "I'm going to leave early." And he said, "Good." And that was the last thing I heard from him.

When people get laid off or they leave, one day you're sitting with all these people, you're all friends, you're all getting along. Everything is fantastic…The next day you're dead to them. For whatever reason, whether they're uncomfortable or they're scared they are going to lose their own job, whatever happens there it's a whole different dynamic. It's like you've got this scarlet letter. They don't want to catch the disease of being laid off.

The thing that was a little distressful about getting laid off…my wife was two months pregnant. And we kept it to ourselves. You know, when you first get pregnant you worry about anything can happen so you keep it to yourself for about eight weeks or so. So I come home to my pregnant wife and let her know I was laid off.

She's got a great job, lovely friends, benefits and the whole thing. And she's going to work. And so I said I'm not going to play around. I'm going to find some new jobs because I hate this not working. In the meantime, I'm going to take a little of the money we've saved up and I'm going to change the flooring in the bathroom.

I ripped up the old linoleum. You know, it's this fixer-upper we bought a few years back. And I found all this pressboard underneath the linoleum. It was as if someone took an old stereo cabinet apart and used that for the flooring. So I go, "That's wrong…' and I kept tearing it up, kept tearing it up, kept tearing away at it. And I found there was a little bit of leakage underneath the bathtub. Long story short: take a grenade, throw it in your bathroom and close the door. I had this thing ripped out to the studs. Everything was gone. The walls, the ceiling, the flooring was ripped out–you could see the dirt. We had to go in and re-pipe everything, had to re-floor everything, had to put the walls back up, had to put tile back on, new bathtub, new toilet. It just kept getting worse and worse.

I had a friend, really knowledgeable, he's a contractor and really knows how to do things the right way. And I said to myself that's the most important thing: it has to be done right…So he would come by in the mornings and say, "This is what you need to take care of today." And I'm like, okay, for the next three weeks I have $250. So I'll buy what I can for $250 and do the work myself…make sure all the piping is right, make sure it's all up to code. Every day, that was my job.

This was in June of 2009. And we got everything fixed and completed in December. The baby was due in January. We had a toilet but we had to go to shower at the Y. So every morning I got up with my wife and we'd go to the Y and walk around and get exercise for the baby that's coming and we'd take showers at the Y. And I have to give her a lot of credit because I don't think I could have done that. Not in that situation.

It got to be about September, October. My parents were going to come out to meet the baby. They were going to come out around December, you know, come hang out until the baby comes. And finally I said I can't do it. I'm not going to make it by myself. My parents, I called them up and they flew out early. And they actually helped out financially to make sure we did everything correctly.

It all hit at once, and the same time I'm trying to find ways to bring income in. And I'm not getting hired. You walk into certain situations where there's like 300 people applying for one position. So I decided to go into business for myself and decided to go into real estate. Took my test online and got into that business as well. So at the same time I'm trying to bring in money and fix the bathroom.

When we bought this house it was like, you qualify for $650,000.

Erik breaks out into a sarcastic sales pitch voice:

"It's going to be amazing!"

We looked at what we qualified for and how much we could actually afford if all hell broke loose. And we went for a much lower cost house. Just because we wanted to make sure we could keep our house. And of course we bought at the height of the market so we're all competing for this small little fixer-upper. But the idea was that you buy the small fixer-upper and...in a matter of months the value is going to go up.

Again, he breaks out into a sarcastic sales pitch voice:

"The valuation is going to be incredible!"

So we hoped to go in there, valuation goes up, refi, and take an extra $50,000, $60,000–because the house had already gone up $100,000 in one year. Figured we'd wait six months, one year, then go and deck this house out the way we wanted to. That didn't happen. So here we are with that situation going on and I get laid off. We had the joy of the baby coming but this is our first child so we didn't know what to expect, we didn't know what was going to happen.

There were a lot of nights and weeks where I just laid awake…I think you find yourself in a little bit of denial. The enormity of everything happening at once gets so heavy that it gets to the point where you just say, okay. I mean I got to the point where I said all I have right now is I've got the next eight hours of this day. And I'll just do the best I can with this time. Because if I really sit back and think about what's happening, if you do that helicopter perspective, I'm probably going to run away. With my wife. But you know, it was a lot to carry. And I think it was even more so for my wife because she was carrying a baby, carrying us. And she had to work right up until the baby came…the best-laid plans didn't really happen. What you do is you learn to deal with where you're at in that situation. And you go, okay, this is where I am at this moment, these are the cards I have and I'll play the best I can with my ability. And if it doesn't work out we'll reshuffle and try something different.

There's a lot of money we still have to figure out, pay back…I have an amazing group of friends. Talented, kind, generous—the whole bit. Couldn't ask for a better group of friends. And you get invited to do all these wonderful things. We're going to Cabo, you know. We're doing this, we're going out for drinks, you know, blah, blah, blah. There comes a point in time where you go: do I go out? Or do I buy groceries? Well obviously you buy groceries. But what it turned into was you can't really tell people, "I can't do this."

"Well why can't you do this?"

"Well, I just can't afford it right now—that's where I'm at right now."

"No, no, no, come out, we'll buy."

That's not the way I wanted to live, that's not the way I wanted to go.

So you just keep it to yourself.

"If I can't do that, then I'm worthless"

Heather Dupree

*She was a softball catcher in high school who went by the name
of "Hollywood." A black & white yearbook picture—the hotshot
backstop firing down to second with legs planted and lips pursed—
backs up her claim to the name.*

*Heather, 38, grew up in Miami and went to Florida International
University. Her dad worked for Pan Am and her parents relocated
to Atlanta when the company was acquired by Delta. After college,
Heather followed her parents to Georgia.*

*She lives in the city of Marietta. When she first moved to the
area in the 1990s, "there was nothing but cow pastures, and I
was horrified. You had to drive forty minutes to go see a movie."
Marietta has grown up quite a bit since then, particularly after the
1996 Olympics, and it's now part of the massive, looping sprawl
that makes up Atlanta and its suburbs.*

She shares a home in a wooded neighborhood with her partner Leslie, and Leslie's sixth-grade daughter, Gabby, from a previous relationship. Gabby is pushing to wear make-up and has a boyfriend named Andrew. "I call him Bill." Heather smirks. "I do it because you can push Gabby's buttons so easily, so I just do it to drive her nuts. But that's all she talks about. My boyfriend this, my boyfriend that. And I'm like, oh, God: it starts."

I actually went to school for a couple different things; I couldn't figure out what I wanted to do. Originally, I wanted to teach, so I have a minor in Education. And then I decided late that I wanted to get into computers. So I got my Bachelor's in communications with a bunch of computer classes underneath it, and I started doing websites when I was in college.

I got on with a healthcare company. They brought me on as a contractor to rebuild their website. I was with C— for seven years, and in March of 2010 they laid me off. My boss walked back into my office with me and shut the door, and he just started crying. And then I just lost it. I tried to be strong, but I can't actually sit there and watch a man cry without crying. So I was pretty upset. And then I just called Leslie and said, "You've gotta come pick me up."

And she's like, "What's going on?"

I'm like, "You really just need to come pick me up."

She got there, and she thought that they had let my boss go, and that's why I was upset. And I was like, "Nope. That's not really it..." So that's kind of how that went down. And I really didn't even have a chance to, you know, say goodbye to anybody really at that time. They were kind of just, like, "Hey, get your stuff and pack it up."

What I found out later was that same morning they had called him in and said, "Hey, listen. We're going to demote you." They said to him, "We're going to demote you, and we're going to need to let a couple people from the department go, but you have to agree to this demotion." I guess they gave him a 10% salary cut or something like that, and what he had told me a couple months later was that if he would have said, "No, I'm not going to take the demotion. I'll just walk," they would've kept me instead. So I guess he wasn't thinking about that at the time obviously, right? Because he's got his own mortgage and kids and everything else, but we had had that talk a couple weeks later, and he was like, "I just feel like I'm responsible."

And I'm like, "Listen. What's the difference, really?"

And honestly, eventually everybody from that department was let go. So it's not like he saved me. It's like, you gotta do what you've gotta do for yourself and your family. I mean, I don't expect you to throw yourself on the sword for me by any stretch.

So it was the first time I got laid off in the last two years. And then I would say it was about eight weeks before I found another job, and it was a contract position. It was a 90-day contract position. It could have turned into permanent. It did not.

So then I started looking for another job. I think about 30 days afterwards I found a job with a startup. They were sort of in IT, but they built software for mobile devices.

And I was with them for almost a year. And then they could not get funding anymore. So they laid off myself and probably half of my department, and then eventually they sold the business and now everybody's been laid off.

I've got to start from scratch, and thinking about, "God, how's that going to look on my resume?" I worked for someplace for seven years and then now I've only been here 11 months. You know, all those types of things, and you still go back to that place of panic, of here we go again. So we've had basically almost a year to build up our savings, and obviously we're not at where I'd like us to be at for me to be looking for a job again and all those type of things.

That whole optimism in the beginning? You're like, woo-hoo, it's fine, I'll be good, don't worry about it, and you're trying to be strong.

It's just a lot of self-convincing. It'll be fine. Just take a breath. It'll be fine. Don't panic. That type of thing. I'm telling Leslie, "Oh, don't worry. It's fine, honey. I'll find something. Don't worry. How much do we have in savings? Okay, it's cool." And then, you know, when you get to that point of four weeks and you haven't heard anything, you start to get defeated, like what is it going to take? What am I doing wrong?

I would get up the same time every morning. I didn't want to do the whole stay-in-bed-till-noon type of thing, so I would get up every morning at the same time. I would get on the computer, go to all the job sites, check my email, see if I heard from anybody, and then, you know, you can only do that for so long, right? So then it's about ten o'clock, and there's really nothing to do for the rest of the day. So what did I do? I did a bunch of house projects. We had just moved in here not that long before, about six months before that, so you know, started fixing stuff that needed fixing, just trying to keep myself busy. Did a lot of yard work, 'cause I just couldn't fill the day. It's really hard to fill the day. And you're here by yourself.

Gabby's in school, Leslie's at work, and you're just here by yourself, and I used to tell Leslie that I talked to my three friends today: Dr. Oz, Rachel Ray and Ellen. 'Cause those are like the three highlights of my day. Ridiculous. Daytime TV is horrible, by the way.

Obviously, when you get laid off, the rollercoaster of navigating your way through, like I said, trying to be optimistic and then inevitably going, "Oh, God. I'm never going to get a job, and I'm not going to be able to support my family, and this is going to be horrible." And, you know, I think I took that part the hardest. Like, I look at my role as a provider, and when I couldn't do that, I felt like, okay, if I can't do that, then I'm worthless. So as much as I can clean the floors and make dinner, that's really not providing.

So probably another eight, nine weeks before I found something else. It's a company called M—. I've been with them for…just a couple months now.

It's actually going really well. I really like the company. They're part of CC—, but they actually operate like a start-up. So they're really laid back and have a pretty good attitude. So far, so good. I'm still a little gun-shy. Nervous, you know? Twice in two years. You never know what could happen. It's hard to get comfortable. You're like, hmm…I wonder if I'll be here for a while.

Seven years, and then I worked for one place for 90 days, and the next place I worked was, like, 11 months, and you know, a lot of what I was looking for when I was interviewing this last time was longevity, like 'How long have you been here?' and asking people those type of questions, but then again, at the end of the day, you don't know. You have no sense of how long something's going to last. Four or five years? I mean, I would be surprised. I would love it, obviously. You want to stay someplace where you feel comfortable and build relationships with people, but I just don't think corporate America's like that anymore.

"How Many People Can Be Associated With One Person?"

Christine Zika

I'm a genealogist, so I always like anything where history...Where somebody's going to be able to find me, and know about the history of that period of time.

In St. Louis we meet a generous guy named Chris Kuban who offers to help introduce us to folks who have become unemployed. He is really enthusiastic and nice and works in PR so we are suspicious of him. Turns out he's just really nice and enthusiastic and, yes, works in PR so he knows a lot of people and introduces us to several, including Christine who meets us over at Chris's house at the end of the day. Chris is hospitable, producing beers all around and a tour of his place, complete with introductions to his pet turtle. Eventually we all settle in the dining room.

Christine's mostly from St. Louis and the surrounding towns. She is 40 and when she flashes that big smile her eyes retreat—but when she becomes serious they widen, defining her expression. She's married to an electrical engineer. "Apparently he's a genius. I didn't know that when I married him. I thought I was marrying, like, this big goof. And then I got told: 'Your husband's a genius!' Doesn't act like that around me. He's very good at what he does. He works on international projects and whatnot."

Years ago, in a galaxy far, far away, I had an expectation of the life I was going to lead. And that life included being in public relations and communications. Instead, I went into the Army National Guard. After two years in college, I went there, and I served 13 years total having served three deployments at different times. I served in Desert Storm. I also served during Operation Joint Endeavor, which was the Bosnian conflict, and then I also went to Kosovo.

When I came home from Desert Storm, I found myself with only two years of college. Even then— without a degree they didn't want to hire you in public relations and corporate communications, which was my dream. So the next best thing was to go into nonprofit work. They want those skills; they want everything that you have. And so I went into nonprofits because they accepted me fully, and I believed in a lot of the things that I was doing. I worked for several local nonprofits in membership services. I worked public relations and communications, so newsletters and all sorts of the things.

In 2002, I got hired by a local fraternity that helps children. They're not a 501c3, so they're not really accountable to the donors or whatnot. And it is a social, fraternal organization, so they can pretty much do what they want do to. Is it their responsibility to keep me employed? No…I saw my job dissipating for a long period of time.

I was sent away on deployment with the National Guard and when I came back, I realized that I needed to make more money, and at the time, they said, "No, no, no. We love you very much and we want you to stay. We're going to create this position for you." And so they created the position of Office Manager. I oversaw the entire operation, building operations as well as the administrative side.

In the beginning of 2008, the company turned around and said, "We can't give out raises." And my entire staff went into an absolute tizzy. And I said, "Stop, stop." Everybody's starting to face harder times. We had seen a drop in membership from over 5,000 down to 2,700 at the time. I said, "Unless you're going to have income, you've got no place to go." I said, "What you need to be grateful for is the fact that they are actually paying 100% of your health benefits and your dental benefits." And I told them, "Whatever you do, you need to remember that that's a significant amount of money, so you may not have more money in your bank account, but you can go to the doctor, and you can get your teeth taken care of." It's the simplest thing, but nonetheless...

We went about halfway in the year and there were rumors. On a Friday in August, I ended up—all of a sudden, we had board of directors there—and I remember just kind of thinking to myself, "This is a bad day." I went in, I finished the major project for the month that I had to do, and my administrator came out of the board of directors room, looked at me, and you could just see he was totally dejected, and I knew he wasn't the one getting fired. And he walked past my desk, and he said, "They want to see you."

And so...I walked in. The recorder and the president of the board were there, and you have this chair sitting in front. This chair had never been there before, for the entire time that I'd been at the organization. They said, "We're very happy that you're here. However, we can't do this anymore, and we just can't afford you, so we are eliminating your position. We just don't have the revenues." And so the position that they had created for me several years before was now being eliminated. I walked out of there, and I think I was the only person in my world that wasn't surprised. You can't work for an organization and see a decline in membership and not think to yourself, "Something's gotta change." And I was the change.

I just took it. What are you going to do? The decision had been made. You know, you can think about all those things that you want to say when somebody's telling you that you're no longer working there, but there are two things that I've learned over the years. Number one, don't burn bridges. You're talking about people who know people. So why are you going to leave like that? You don't burn bridges, and you just don't take out your anger anymore. Burning bridges and being angry are two different things. You just kind of have to learn to accept some things in this life. There may be things that you don't like necessarily, but you just have to accept them. Now I'm sure my husband would say, "She said that?" (Laughs.) In the outside world, that's what you do. What you do on the inside world is something else.

I'd worked there for seven years. My reputation is what I have. I was a military police person in the Army National Guard. I had a secret clearance. I don't lie, steal or cheat. And they watched over me like a hawk while I cleaned seven years worth of stuff out of a desk. They would not let me touch the computer. They were so afraid that I was going to hurt or harm or delete or do anything to that computer.

If I really wanted to have cheated, I could've come up with ten different ways over seven years to steal money. I could've crashed their system so many times it would've been pathetic. But I didn't do that, because that's not the kind of person I am. But they stood over me while I was cleaning out my desk like I had committed a crime. And the only crime that I committed was the fact that I was in a position that they needed to eliminate.

And I'll tell you what: I try not to think about that moment because I have my administrative assistant, the person that I've trained just bawling because she's so upset that I'm leaving. It took boxes. It took a car. I'd been there for seven years.

I walked out of there and called my husband, and I said, "Well, you remember all that talk of maybe we wouldn't have a job anymore? Somebody's not going to have a job? Well, that person's me."

And he was very, very upset.

And I said, "Don't be upset." You know, I'm one of those very versatile people that can find myself anywhere, and I'm going to find another job. I've always found another job.

So I went home, and I cleaned the house...yelled on the phone a lot. I'm sure that there were several words that were not meant to be recorded. And I think my dog ran and hid too. But when I was done with that part of it, I spent the next week going, "Alright, what am I going to do now? What am I going to do now? What am I going to do now? What am I going to do now?"

And then I kind of started the whole unemployment process, you know, going and applying for it and trying to figure out that system and spending hours on the phone with people that don't answer you. And nobody's got an answer anywhere, so if you've ever called the unemployment office, you just need to go ahead and plan that you're going to spend, like, the whole day on hold. So put the phone on speaker, put it down, and start doing the dishes, because you're going to be there all day.

And so there I was, come December, still didn't have a job. By this point—this is August to December—I had one job interview. I was applying for things that...you know, this-is-below-anything-that-I've-done-but-I-need-to-get-a-job. So they wouldn't even hire me because I had too much experience.

I come from that family. Oh my gosh, you've gotta work. So it wasn't complete Teflon. Not by any stretch. I did pretty much flip out. I flipped out...somewhere around December, right before Christmas, because I couldn't go and buy gifts, and then I flipped out in January.

January came along, and I finally got another interview. I was very excited. I got an interview, and I went to that interview. And I walked out of there, and I said, "I have everything that they need." I have the experience. They did not go into complete shock and awe when I showed them how much I wanted to make. And I went in for my second interview. There were two interviewers. And the one guy loved me. Loved me. Loved everything about me. Loved my experience, loved the fact that we had the same alma mater. I mean, he was very excited. He was my cheerleader. Rah rah rah. And the other guy wouldn't even look at me. And it never even occurred to me until after the interview, and I was kind of going over it in my mind that he didn't look at me.

Well, I happened to know somebody that was working at that company, and after I had gotten the rejection letter…I asked them, "I'm just really kind of curious, who did they hire?"

And he looked at me, and he says, "Well, I will say that she was younger and very bubbly."

And I said, "Oh, so what you have just verified to me is that 40 is a ceiling," and it was at that moment that I realized that there was going to have to be a different path. I didn't know what that path was, but it was going to have to be something, because I don't consider myself to be middle-aged, and I don't consider myself to have hit some sort of ceiling at the age of 40, for crying out loud. But there I was without a job. And I wasn't getting hired. The fact is that I was everything that they needed, and they hired somebody who was significantly younger than me to do a job that I was more than qualified for.

So the next week, I called my mentor, and I said, "Alright, dude. What am I going to do?"

He said, "You need to start a business."

And I said, "You're an idiot." I said, "There is no way I'm starting a business. Have you not caught on to the fact that people are not hiring, let alone me starting a business?"

And he said, "No, no, no. You need to start a business."

The next week, the following week I'm having a conversation with my aunt who says, "We need to start a business," and I said, "Okay, I'm going to tell you like I told the other guy. I want the 9-to-5, I sit at the desk, I get my benefits. I want to fall into what we have now classified as the American Dream: you have a job, and you get benefits."

The next week…You know when karma finally comes down and smacks you in the head and says, "You have no choice. This is what you have to do." So there I was, the very next week, thumbing through the small business journal in St. Louis, and there's this little ad. And the ad says, "Are you a veteran looking to start a business?" And I said, "Why yes, I am." (Laughs.)

I got into a veteran's run program called the Veteran's Business Resource Center that's located here in St. Louis that assists veterans in starting a business or assisting already established businesses either to get to the next level or to sustain their business, to make sure that they are viable.

We went through a six-week program, and they said, "So, you want to start a business. Isn't that sweet?…So, who are you marketing to?"

I said, "Anybody who needs errands.'"

He goes, "Really? Anybody? Are you thinking about this? Can everybody afford you? Probably not."

So, you know, going through that whole process of what it is to start a business. Like I said, I went to college to be in PR. PR is a part of a business. Marketing is a part of a business. I got that down pat. You wanna know my brand? I can tell you my brand: bugles, swoops, stars, a professional personality—I got all that.

Accounts?…I understood those things…but in terms of setting them up? I'm no good at accounting. And then what's a target market? What about your contracts? What about the legalities? And I'm like, "Oh my goodness gracious…You mean I actually have to think about that?"

They really put the hard facts in front of you. They said, "This isn't easy. This isn't just—bam I have an idea isn't this wonderful and here's where we're going to go with it."

The piece de resistance was you had to have a business plan, which I had. My husband had been telling me since January to start making one. So there I was in front of a computer originally going, "I'm going to run errands. I'm going to make $40,000 a year." Never took into account that I needed to spend gas to do those errands. By the end of it, I had this 30-page dissertation that said by year three I was going to make, like, $200,000…I look at that and laugh, because you know, your pie-in-the-sky expectations and the reality of working and getting business, you know, seem to kind of not always go in the same direction. But nonetheless it's going very well.

As a concierge company we come into a business for the employees and do all of their errands. Let us find your daycare. Let us run to the grocery store or pick up your dry cleaning so that you can stay engaged in the workplace, thusly increasing the profitability of you in the workplace, which means that more people get hired. So actually you can look at us of being the savior of the economy. (Laughs.) The number one asset that any employer has is their employee. And the day that they realize that is the day that they're going to put into place these types of benefits, which gives that employee a work-life balance. And once that happens, they become more loyal to the company. Their engagement increases.

Within six months of setting up, I had my first client. A Fortune 100 company hired me to do a job for them. From there, I gained another client. So where everybody was telling me that concierge services was not the right business to be starting in a downed economy, all of a sudden I had people saying, "No, no, no. I need to hire you." And I went from being unemployed, laid off, getting unemployment benefits to having a business where I now employ somebody other than myself, and I am getting business.

It's funny. Everybody's outsourcing. Guess what else they're outsourcing? They're outsourcing their errands. They're outsourcing their grocery shopping. They're outsourcing all that stuff. Busy individuals who are afraid of losing their job who need to work 50 to 60 hours per week need me to be able to do those things so that they can continue to work in the environment that I always wanted to work in.

About a year and a half after Christine had been laid off, she got a call from an old colleague at that office.

They didn't know how to fix the door lock, and he knew I was the only one that did. And we're friends, okay, and I said to him, I said, "Well, the packet of information is…" And I told him where it was.

And he goes, "Oh…"

And he got real quiet, and I knew what he wanted to ask me. And I said, "And my concierge services are $30 an hour, so if you would like me to come and fix it, I'll be more than happy to."

And he said, "Thank you."

And that was the last time he ever called me for anything.

Don't ask me. I'm sorry. It probably sounds way more mean than I mean it to be. It wasn't that I wouldn't help him as an individual but you're not going to fire me in essence—lay me off, call it whatever you're going to do—and then a year and a half later not pay me to do the one thing that apparently I'm the only one in the world who knows how to do. I hope you get a nice locksmith. Other than that, it's $30 an hour concierge services. Make that payable to CZ Concierge. (Laughs.)

My father actually lost his job probably within a year or six months prior to me losing mine, and then the only work that he's been able to find right now is at security. And because he's afraid of his finances, seven weeks after he had open-heart surgery—double bypass and a valve replacement—he made his doctor give him a release so that he could go to work, where he should have twelve weeks of recovery time.

Dale Harris

We meet Christine's dad, Dale, in his apartment in the St. Louis suburb of Hazelwood. He begins by talking about picking up a King snake—"I'm an old farm boy, I pick up or handle anything that grows in the state of Missouri"—an imposing beat to begin on but moments later he's sweetly lamenting the fact that he couldn't bring the snake home to care for it: "…the trauma of taking him out of the wild and trying to feed him was too much for him."

There are several strategically placed digital clocks in his small apartment, as well as two visible firearms. One is pistol tucked into holster on a large belt, hanging off of a hook on his front door. The other is a rifle—displayed on the wall—one of the few items in the place that might qualify as decoration. I can't resist asking about it.

He scratches at his balding head. "That is my phallic symbol," he says.

Mallery, MJ and I all laugh.

"Pardon me." He smirks beneath his gray mustache.

For me…When you're broke, destitute and you're sitting there with no food in the refrigerator, you gotta feel like something, and I know how people…I know my son's been through it, I know Christine's been through it—you get so wrapped up in your despair, depression, that it immobilizes you. And I was there for a while. And I refused to take any kind of medication, I coulda had tons of prozac; I refused to do that. I just felt like I needed something—I should have spent it on food but I didn't, and I bought that. (Eyeing the rifle.) I've never actually regretted it. I look at it. And it's kind of like…it's got a lock on it, it's safe—it would take a jackhammer to get that thing off. I'm not really worried about it going anywhere, it's insured…I guess it's like having a teddy bear, or like a child with one of those binkies, it's just—I don't care how much I spent on it, it just made me feel good that I know it's up there. Made me feel human. To me it was something beautiful to stick up on the wall.

Let's see, I was born in New York City, lived on a farm in Willow Springs Missouri, had a sister born in Las Vegas, then went to Springfield Missouri, St. Louis, and Willow Springs. We moved 18 times before I was 18 years old—seven times in St. Louis alone. My parents were movers. For some reason, they decided "Hey, we could get more money for this house." So as the years went by they actually made quite a bit of money, buying and selling…They did very well for themselves.

I dunno, childhood without some kind of stability, as the old saying goes, makes you insecure. And in a lot of ways it affected my young adulthood, the older years. I think we finally managed to settle in St. Louis when I was in my teens and therefore I was able to finally establish childhood friends that to this very day— guys who I went to high school with—that I still play cards with. Just mostly penny ante poker. I don't think anything's ever gotten over a quarter. Once a month we have a gig where we just sit around and talk about "I remember when…" You know, just a lot of reminiscing. We do that on the first Friday of every month and we've been doing it for some forty-some-odd years now. You gotta keep a hold on some of your past. I figure I'm watching these guys play poker until I die or they're all dead. When I found I had an opportunity to make friends and I got in with this group of guys and we got close, that's it, nothing separates us. Anything happens for any one of them, we're the first to know among each other, and it's a stability. It's good to have something solid. In today's world there's not that much that you could ever rely upon, and I could call upon any one of them right now and they're there.

I'm a bit of a maverick I guess, I'm the jack of all trades and the master of none. After leaving the military when I was 22, I was a Vietnam vet, I started working for what was at that time McDonnell Aircraft, which of course later became McDonnell Douglas, and now it's Boeing. I worked for them for about four years. When I thought about what to do next I figured maybe being a police officer would fill the bill. I enjoyed being a cop. You're never in any one place, each day is always different, you're meeting people, different people, consistently. The guys I worked with there, I'm still in contact with, simply because in that kind of profession, I think you'll find in most law enforcement professions, you're gonna find these are guys you're dependent on to save your life as you would save theirs. They were your backup, they were your support, they were everything to you, they were your family when you weren't at home. I was with them until 79; I went to another department, a little bit bigger...I retired in 1998.

And then from that point I went to A—. In one of my interviews that got me that job at A— they asked me what I was most proud of, some accomplishment, and everybody wants to tout a reward or award or I built this or I created that—the only thing I could think that made me proud to say was: my children.

I was what they call a "computer network associate," combination programming and repair, setting up networks, troubleshooting. I truly enjoyed my job. It took me a while to get used to working in a cubicle having been on the road for as many years as I was, you can well imagine trying to box in a tiger. But I worked for them for four years.

The building I was working at, they started putting on an addition. The addition was off-limits to anyone and everyone in the building except of course for "higher-ups"—your supervisors, building managers. And we couldn't figure out what it was for; it was a rather large addition. And over time we saw them bringing in electronic equipment, routers and servers and you name it, and we kept scratching our heads like what's going on here. And then all of a sudden they were done with the construction and we noticed—and I use the terminology "Indians from India"— were parking and going to the section of the building that we weren't allowed in.

Over a period of time we saw more and more what appeared to be Indians, until finally, word came down that we were going to get laid off—through the grapevine, nothing official.

We were a pretty close group…rumors get around, it's a small building, small cubicles, and you get bored in a cubicle…I've often said cops are the worst gossips in the world but now I'm beginning to realize computer techs are too. (Laughs.) Word spread…

May 15, 2002.

It was through a loudspeaker. They asked everybody to meet in a certain room, rather large room, and then they said, they announced, you have been surplussed. It was 128 of us.

A— started hurting real bad financially. So the new heads decided, we've got to do something here, and they turned around and began bringing in contractors and removing union people so out the door we went and in the door they came. Our section of the building went dark and the other section started handling all the networking.

Lotta people were hurt that day. What am I gonna do with my family—family issues were a big thing. What am I gonna do now for a living? I can't get a job anywhere, nobody wants a computer technician, not when all these contract technicians were out there for half the wages. How can I support my family on $12–$15 an hour? How can I look forward to a retirement now? I'm going to have to sell my home. Yeah, there was a lot of tears, and I don't mean just women—men too.

It damaged not only families, it damaged a lot of these people's parents, they had to help their children. What parent wouldn't help their children? And they were starting to cash in some of their retirement just so their children weren't hurting—who were trying to raise their families. So the effects weren't just somebody out of a job—it was much more than that. You're not only hurting one person, you're hurting the wife, you're hurting the children, you're hurting the wife's parents grandparents, you're hurting the aunts and uncles…how many people can be associated with one person? That's how many people you're hurting.

From that point we were marched, we were asked to leave and return to another smaller building that they had set up for us. According to union contract, they had to give us 60 days to assist us in getting another job. They gave us computers and a server and a router so we could get on the internet, look for jobs...They offered training. In fact, they offered—I think it was through union contract—something like $2500 for either training or equipment to get a new job.

In the little warehouse that we lived in for 60 days, we were allowed to search for a job, we were allowed to call, we had to let them know if we went to an interview, we had to constantly keep them up as to what we were doing.

That seems like it would be a demoralizing atmosphere.

Try the word humiliating. Very humiliating. They brought in some advisors, they would try and get training schedules set up and whatever. And they had good countenance, they had good personalities, they were not being jerks, and in fact, I made friends with one of them, a very nice person...They knew there was gonna be a lot pain, a lot of hurt, a lot of anger—that always happens. But they also brought in professionals to guide everyone through the process...let's not have one of these wars; let's not have a strike where somebody gets hurt. Let's all do this gentle, easy... But no matter how you look at it, being slapped is gonna hurt, if you do it with a boxing glove or with bare knuckles, it's still the same thing.

After 60 days, that was it, they would let us out the front door, locked the door behind us, and we drove home—and tried to do what was best to continue our lives. A lot of us just drove past the building we used to work in and saw that parking lot full of all of these out of state cars...

The one thing A— wanted to do was get rid of the union. All they had left over was five people, and they were union, but virtually no power. We had even tried calling several of the contractors to see if we could get put on the list, and once we mentioned we were US citizens the contractor never even wanted to talk...He'd hang up on us. But if we had called him and said we are not a US citizen, then they wanted to talk to us. In fact, one of the guys did exactly that, he talked with a real funny accent, and he says, "I am not a US citizen," and he got an appointment. He walked into the contractor, they found out he was a US citizen, they almost called the police on him. So yeah that part is what really bothered me—I mean, if A— wanted to make some money to get back to where they were, I've often wondered why they didn't turn around and simply say, folks, we're hurting, would you kindly take a pay cut? To keep a job, to keep seniority—it'd be worth it to take a pay cut. But that was never offered.

I was fortunate to be re-hired by one of their spinoffs, same cubicle, same building, same equipment, and I worked for them up until June of 2007.

And then was laid off again.

How were you notified that time?

A letter. Email. Mr Harris, your last day will be on such and such a day. That was it. No fanfare. It was like a Friday. "Hey guys, see ya later, have a good future." And out the door you went. I could have stayed another week...but I decided to go early because I wanted to get working on my house. I figured the sooner I can get this house sold, the sooner I can make a future for myself, and of course like I say, with the housing bubble burst, and the other issues that developed, my timing couldn't have been any more perfect, my 401K was non-existent, simply because my A— stock just bottomed out. It went from $120 to— oh my gosh—I wanna say to $60? And again I couldn't sell anything.

After the last lay-off, I went looking for a job, couldn't find anything. I had several things working against me: I was 59 ½ years old at that time, I'm sorry, I know age discrimination is illegal, but it is still practiced in full force. Like I say, I couldn't get back into computers, between my age and what I needed in order to live on, I was not a wanted commodity. I kinda had a lot of battles, and a few interviews, and that was about it. I was too old to be a cop again. That's the one government entity that can discriminate intentionally, due to the nature of the business.

So I wound up in security work. I've gone from enforcing a law, now to reporting a law. To the locals. And the sheriff's deputy just think it's so funny because I used to be the one chasing the bad guy, now I'm calling the cops. At least it's feeding my face and that's what I find important.

I had taken my severance money, after I got laid off, and fixed up that house—it looked beautiful. The only problem was, I was in a rather depressed section of North St. Louis County, and the value of my house went from $90,000, down to $29,000. And I couldn't sell it, even at $29,000, nobody was really interested. I couldn't make the payments. I had insurance but that ran out, so I sat on the front porch one day, looked at all the work I'd put into the house, and bawled like a baby. Then called my attorney and said, "That's it, I cannot handle this, I'm walking away from this house." So I did, I declared bankruptcy. It was about three years ago.

You can see all I have is a few reminisces of what I once had...

Dale gestures toward his teddy bear of a rifle.

...but, like I say, at least I feel like that's behind me and I'm going forward on a lower level, but I'm still going forward. It's a small apartment, but at least it's home. And it will be for a while.

BOOK NINE

EVOLUTION

"There is no mystery to this"

Prof. Antonio Avalos

Antonio Avalos is clearly a smart economist, despite the fact that he once paid $21 for eight one-dollar bills. They are framed on the wall of his office at the state university in Fresno, California. The bills are in mint condition, uncut—one sheet of singles shipped directly from the US treasury. Professor Avalos comments on the uncut bills, aptly noting that the treasury department got him to pay more than the face value—and they did less work.

Antonio, 39, originally from Mexico City, has lived in the US for more than sixteen years. "I came here to get my PhD in Economics, I told my dad I'd return in five years, and I never did."

His father worked for the Mexican government as an engineer. His grandfather was a telegraph operator: "And the stories in the family say that he was the first person in Mexico to receive the news of the Hiroshima bombing in the 1940s—my grandfather got sick, you know, he transmitted the news and he got very sick..."

Antonio went to Oklahoma State University and started working at the university here in Fresno seven years ago. This part of California has, for decades, endured some of the highest unemployment and foreclosure rates in the country—along with Reno to the east.

In California the issue for us is the budget deficit because of mismanagement, because of many different things that have to do with politics—but also poor policy making on behalf of the governor's office and others. We are in this mess, I mean, California is one of the states with the highest budget deficits in the country, so as a consequence, we don't have resources to spend money, which is the recipe that has been used at the federal level. And when the government cuts spending, a lot of things go away, including lots of jobs—not just on the government side, but also if the government is not building a road, is not building infrastructure, well, business around the private world cannot operate because they don't have the support of the government.

Nationwide—and perhaps worldwide, but let's focus on the USA—if you look at the numbers, GDP, which is the most important indicator of the size of the economy, it's growing. The problem is that while the economy is growing, employment is not. So, no more jobs are being created, and the question is why?

The simple answer to this question is what in previous years was considered a very positive thing, which is "productivity." Basically that means that we can produce more with less resources—including people. We are growing but when jobs are not being created, it means that productivity translates into: the ones that have jobs work harder, longer, and often receive less pay. That's what we are calling productivity right now. That's not very healthy for the general welfare of the economy because you have a lot less people supporting a lot more people not working.

One of my cousins in Mexico, for years he was a typewriter repairman. Fifteen years ago I told him, "What are you doing? Your job is going to disappear?"

He said, "What are you talking about?"

"Well, look at the computers. You need to start upgrading your skills because eventually you are going to run out of typewriters to repair."

Now he doesn't have a job. And the way I see it—and this is just an example, but it's happening all over the world: the effect of technology, technological improvement, is having this effect. Robotization—if 15–20 years ago you needed ten people to operate this equipment, just screwing in something, eight hours a day, now you can have a robot that can do it, so you get rid of ten people with lower skills and you just hire one engineer that can maintain and operate a machine. The new jobs that I see emerging are in this high-tech world—by high-tech I don't necessarily mean computers, although they are clearly related, but more sophisticated skills. Not just in engineering, but also in economics, in biology, in medicine, in law—all areas of knowledge have been affected by technology. So if you get behind, your skills depreciate. You're going to be less valuable for the labor market and therefore you're going to be displaced. This is why I also see education as an ongoing process. If the students believe that with a college degree, that's it, they are wrong. I mean, I keep reading as I go—with a PhD in economics! Because the things I learned 15 years back—some of them are useless now.

A couple of years ago I was in Cleveland with a friend of mine that works at NASA. He's a mechanical engineer—and he was telling me that in Cleveland they have this very nice hospital industry, similar to the one in Houston for heart surgery…but these guys, to make things cheaper, now they hire a very good physician in India that operates—using a joystick through the internet—on a person in the operating room in Cleveland. Physical presence used to be a big deal—now it's not. He was going to do it with a joystick anyway, they don't get their hands dirty now anymore— what's the difference if he's in the room? You may have a lot of knowledge of medicine, but if you don't get on the technological wave, this physician, although he's a great at his job, wouldn't be able to do what he does. So you need to pair your core skills with other skills that the labor market is demanding from the highly valuable workers.

I spoke of the engineer replacing ten, but behind the engineer, there is a group of people supporting him in these new industries—software, computer. The engineer probably is going to operate the mechanics of the machine. But you need a software, you need the computer, you need an electrician that knows how to connect all the wirings, and so forth. New occupations seem to be displacing the old ones. The problem is that you keep cutting education—how are they going to get there? That's going to be a problem—that's the real problem, and that's a policy issue that I don't think right now they understand very well.

Now, I wish there was a talk, a document, a phrase, an idea that you could share with politicians or CEOs to change their minds, but there isn't. There isn't. Because the way they operate, the way they think, is the result of years—their lives. And how do you change that? It's just not possible. A few, I've seen, they have change of hearts because of a dramatic experience or something, but they are not very many, and unfortunately, not the most powerful people go through or suffer those episodes—they just keep going, because they are protected by all this wealth they have around.

I don't want to sound pessimistic, but the way the world is going, I don't see any bright future for humankind. We have been irresponsible with the use of resources—I'm talking about pollution, and now global warming. One key word is "responsibility," which is the equivalent of the technical word for "sustainability"—we have not been practicing sustainable efforts. Some economists have studied this, there is this "bequest" motive, this trans-generational behavior that we should be following. It's not just "live the moment and leave others to worry later," that's not the right approach I think. Just enjoy the moment, drive a big car, use the gasoline, travel, use planes—we have this value system backwards.

I mean, when was the last time you talked to one of your friends and said, "Hey, what did you do today?"

"Oh, I had a great day, I just took a walk in the woods."

We don't enjoy nature anymore, it's all about computers, gadgets, cars, planes, electronic devices, things like that that are very costly for the environment, are very costly for society, but we don't see it—or we don't want to see it because we are riding and enjoying the moment. So I think there is no mystery to this. To me, it's very clear— humankind, we have been extremely irresponsible, very irresponsible. I'm talking about everybody, not just the business world—policy makers and citizens voting for these guys.

Shape-Shifting

"Sucked into the vortex"
Jenny Elig & Judy Wolf

Jenny plays bass in a band called The Odyssey Favor. "I also play keyboard in another band—I have a 60s organ. His name is Francis 'cause he's like…Francis. That band is called The Pernicious Unicats. I did not name it." Her short bangs rest just above her dark eyebrows. She's 33 and originally from Ohio. Her grandfather was an engineer for the waterworks in Cincinnati; his name is on a plaque at Eden Park. Her grandmother trained in marcelling hair in the 1920s. Jenny's dad "kind of reinvented himself a few times," and when he retired he ran low on cash so he took a job at a liquor store.

"Maybe liquor stores are in our future," says Judy.

Jenny laughs and adds, "We should be so lucky."

The two of them used to work at the same newspaper and were laid off one month before I spoke with them.

Judy, who's 55, had worked at the paper for 24 years. She lives just north of Indianapolis, in Carmel, but hesitates to reveal as much: "It has a bad rap. People think everyone there is rich and condescending. And while I am all of those things...." We all laugh because it's already obvious that Judy is none of those things. Maybe it's the Hawaiian shirt. Maybe it's the flip up sunglass shades. Maybe it's the fact that she's already offered to let Mallery, MJ, and me stay in her house—and that was even before she met us in person—when I was still calling her from St. Louis, mildly harassing her to let me hear her story. She's from Memphis, where her mother was an opera singer who once gave diaphragmatic breathing lessons to a young Elvis Presley. "Six months later my folks are watching Ed Sullivan. The curtain goes up and she says, 'That's that boy who was here with all his little cousins.'"

"Cool," says Jenny. "I'm from Cincinnati where my dad was hit on by Suzi Quatro."

Jenny suggested our current location: Wug Laku's Studio & Garage. It's part of the Circle City Industrial Complex in downtown Indianapolis. This was all unused offices and warehouses until several artists, including Wug, converted it into a collective of workspaces and galleries. There are chefs and painters and sculptures and metallurgists working throughout the attached buildings. The walls of Wug's small gallery space are currently covered with an exhibition of smart phone photography.

Jenny: I just kind of worked my way into the features department for the S—, they had sort of merged everything together. And I ended up writing a weekly style column along with other feature stories. And then I was laid off on June 21st.

Judy: I went to Indiana University. I wanted to be a teacher, high school or junior high. And the second year—my sophomore year—I was visiting a friend at the newsroom at the student paper. And then you get sucked into the vortex.

I found a job at a newspaper in Central Illinois and moved from there to the morning paper in Ft Wayne, Indiana, and was there about six years. And then came down to the S—. I started as a copy editor and I've worked various jobs…page one editor, wire editor, I've edited copy for features, sports, business. I've done some writing in various departments through the years. And I, too, got laid off on the 21st. They laid off roughly 20 percent of the newsroom in one day, which was just stunning to me.

I think circulation is roughly 260,000–250,000. And the rule of thumb in publishing for newspapers…you're supposed to have one editorial staff member for every thousand of circulation. The newsroom at its high point—if I remember correctly, and I was a union official so we try to sort of keep track of that—was about 260 people. And we're down to half that, it's 130. And so when we were at roughly 260, that was a really good proportion for the rule of thumb. But G— evidently chopped off their thumbs at some point. And so they don't believe in rules of thumb. They do believe in profit margins, which are substantially higher for G— than any others. Their profit margins are in the high 20s, percentage-wise.

Why were they laying people off?

Jenny: To keep that profit margin there.

Judy: Yeah.

Jenny: It's kinda sad, especially if you think about how many people they've laid off. I think they had a small round back in 2008, and they got one of my bosses. Then they got Susan and Whitney. (Judy nods.) And then 2009 was the big one. And then there was us.

Judy: I was actually at home, it was a day off. And my former partner had come up and was helping me weed in the front yard, and so we had been out there for a couple of hours, and I came in to a bunch of messages on my phone. There was a message from the managing editor, who said, "I'm trying to get a hold of you, if you could…I'll try again." Sometimes she would call if there was a staffing issue, and my immediate boss couldn't get hold of me. So it didn't seem unusual. Then I got a call from the woman who used to be my cubicle mate who said, "Jenny[1] just called me at home, I was on the list, you have more seniority than I do so I'm hoping you weren't on the list." And then there was another call from Jenny, saying, "I'm still trying to get a hold of you." And I thought, "Ohhh crap." I looked at my ex and I said, "I've just lost my job."

I called her...It felt to me that Jenny was literally reading from a script. "Due to business conditions, you are being..."

This is a woman that...I was at the paper before she got here, and we've always had a really pleasant, cordial professional relationship. At the end of the call, I told her I was sorry she had to make it, because I couldn't imagine making that call.

There's really no reason to say, "How come me?" It was clear to me: although I'd been there more than 24 years and, I think, am a well-respected editor at the paper, it didn't amount to much.

My former partner took me out to lunch. And we took a big legal pad and started making a list of people to call for job leads. I didn't do it immediately but my mid-afternoon I had posted on Facebook. I've really been quite overwhelmed by the response.

I've had people who have called me or sent me an email saying, "You were the last reason that I subscribed to the paper, and I'm cancelling." (Smiles and tilts her head.) I appreciate the support, but I can't encourage that, because I think papers are important.

Jenny: I was out working with our photographer. I was doing a story on shopping districts in Indianapolis. It'd been on the books for a while. And I'd just had a story run 1A, front page, above the fold that got picked up by USA Today, so I was feeling pretty good about myself.

Frank the photographer and I were driving around a couple spots in Indy, and he said, "I heard that layoffs are coming. We heard it late last night, Monday evening." And he said, "We think it's gonna be middle-management." And he had a couple guesses of who it would be.

I said, "Well, you know, we can't really sweat it, it's already decided, whatever happened." So we're going around, it was about lunchtime, and

---

[1]   A second Jenny, not to be confused with present company.

I said, "Let's go back to the office, just kick it for a while, see what's up, get some lunch, and then head back out for our afternoon shoots." And so we did.

I went up, got a sandwich at the cafeteria, came down, was eating it—and everybody was really, really nervous around me. And then I started getting nervous. My cubemate kept getting phone calls from someone else who was just updating her. Like, everybody would get really tense when layoffs are coming, it was the same as two years ago. Every time a phone rings, I'd just tense up.

Judy: An internal ring. An internal ring is one ring, outside is two, and boy, you didn't wanna get one ring.

Jenny: Yeah…and then my phone rang, and it was HR. I just said, "Alright guys, this is it…"

They made me wait 'cause D— was on the phone with someone. And I heard him saying, "I'd much rather deliver this news in person," so he was laying someone else off. I had to sit on a couch in HR with this one HR lady, who I didn't know, 'cause most of our HR staff left. It was all new people.

Finally D— came out and brought me into the office and said, "Well Jenny. I'm sure you have a good idea of why we're talking today."

I looked down at the table—they gave you an envelope that had your information in it. It was only about maybe five pages long. I take it back. Maybe three. So flimsy.

Judy: It was a note that basically said, "You've been laid off for business reasons, you have this amount of severance…" and I love this, "And the employee assistance program is available." It's like, well thank you!

Jenny: That's for the therapists, right?

Judy: Yeah. Talk to counselors and stuff.

Jenny: I didn't wanna go there so they could collect more information or like know how crummy this is that I've been laid off. I didn't wanna talk to them.

I looked down and he hadn't even turned over other people's envelopes, so I could see the names of other people who were waiting to get the axe. And they didn't even know it. And they were people who had been there forever, too. It was just like oh man this is sucky. So I was just looking down at that, and looking at him, and he's saying "Oh well, you're a good person, I'll write you a letter of reference."

I didn't really say much. I was like, I don't care! I don't care what you think, if you think I'm a good person—I know I'm a good person. I just wanted to get out of there. Get out of there before I cried. I really don't like crying in public—I don't like crying in front of people. It's so difficult when you've been at a place five years—24 years...(looking at Judy)...I can't even.

He said, "You can go upstairs and say goodbye to everybody. Do you want to load your stuff up?" I guess what they're supposed to do is have security come and escort you out, so I'm kinda glad they didn't do that. Maybe if they had, maybe then I would have kicked and screamed, "Nooooo!"

Judy: "You can't take me!" (Laughs.)

Jenny: "Do you know who I am?" (Laughs.)

I just went upstairs, and everybody wanted to give me a hug and I just wanted to go home. I went out a back exit. One of my coworkers chased me out and wanted to hug me and I just kinda wanted to go home, call my parents, and drink some wine. Which is what I did. I talked to my former boss, Jackie, who had been laid off in 2009. She said, "don't drink too much."

Judy: Not too much wine.

Jenny: Yeah, "Take it easy." And that was the rest of my night. It was just this thought of, tomorrow I'm gonna get up, it's gonna be Wednesday, and I'm not gonna have anywhere to go. So that was kind of the big thing.

I posted on my Facebook right away, "Thanks to the S— for five great years."

And all of a sudden people are like "Ohhh what's going on!?"

I have a fair amount of friends on there who were, you know, part of my audience. 'Cause that's one thing that I did like, was having a voice and kind of talking to people about style and also just other things. I'm really into pop culture, so Facebook is one way of engaging people. To see that these people really did care and were angry about what happened was heartening. It doesn't fix anything, but it's nice to know that you meant something to some people.

Judy: And it's your community, I mean, it really is—or at least a community. I'm really lucky to have a lot of different communities in the city, but the people at work are who you sit next to, the people that you talk to every day and you update about what everybody's done, your family or your dogs or your cats or your kids. That's a real loss.

Jenny: I've always tried to make sure that I have something outside of work. I volunteer, I'm in a couple bands, I just try and be out in this community, but work is something that you go and do for at least 40 hours a week and then it's just—poof—gone.

Judy: Yeah, and I don't know about you, but I've just had this persistent nausea in my stomach, it's just bizarre. That doesn't happen to me.

Jenny: I just don't have things to break up my day the same way I used to, so I'm just kinda sitting around watching really garbage TV. *Flavor of Love* seasons one and two. And *Toddlers and Tiaras*.

Judy: Oh my god. We need an intervention.

Jenny: I'm gonna start watching that again too.

So I've just been sitting around watching this garbage TV, and eating garbage, and I just, I don't know...

Judy: Mourning.

Jenny: Yeah it really is.

Jenny: I'm sleeping later, I don't really like that.

Judy: There's no routine.

Jenny: Yeah, it varies. Kinda falling asleep when I can.

Judy: Nothing wrong with that.

Jenny: Some days it's really hard to look at it as an opportunity. I'm an optimist but it's difficult to stay optimistic when you're planning out these things which you're gonna do the next day—oh, tomorrow I'm gonna do laundry! And then I'm gonna go to Target and look at stuff! And that becomes what your day consists of.

Judy: Yeah. And my brain isn't working nearly as well. I feel very scattered, and I can get through a day and not feel that I've accomplished anything. And then I think, no, I have applied for jobs. I gotta remind myself. I actually started an excel spreadsheet of what job I applied for, who it's to, when I sent an email, which resume I sent, because—I don't know about you, but my resume was sadly just really out of date—

Jenny: Neglected—

Judy: —yeah, that's a nice way to put it.

Jenny: Before I worked at the S—, I started getting comments from people when I was interviewing, and they were like, "Oh, you jump around too much." And I was like, "Really? Do you know what my career is? I'm a journalist, we jump around." In some ways I think that's better. But then again, just the idea of going in somewhere and starting again is just sort of exhausting.

Judy: It's daunting, at a minimum.

Jenny: Yeah. Because I knew where my desk was. You become resourceful in that community that you have there. I know that so-and-so's gonna have Tylenol if I need it, and I know that my boss is gonna be cranky today because of this...You know all the tricks, and you have a fairly decent idea about office politics. And now we've kinda gotta start again, and maybe in a couple of places, too, you know?

Judy: Although, this has made clear to me that I really need one full time job. And I admire significantly people who cobble together a lot of part time gigs and can make that work, but for me, one of the things I found at the S— —well, all the papers I worked at—I worked really hard at building relationships within the newsroom, and to do that I really need all my focus in addition to obviously doing my job really well. And I don't think I would fare as well or to do as good a job someplace if I was here 15 hours a week, and I was there 20 hours a week—I need a place, a home to go to.

I'm not spending anything, if it doesn't keep the dogs alive, keep me alive, or keep the house in my name, I'm really trying not to spend it. What I'm hoping to do is sack away enough money now so that if I don't have a job after my severance runs out, god forbid, I'll be able to supplement unemployment—which is not real generous in Indiana.

Jenny: I cashed out my 401K so that I can just pay off all my debt, so I can live off unemployment at least for a little while. Just kinda taking it as it comes.

I opted not to take the COBRA. They're taking money out of my check for it, so I have to call and scream at somebody.

Judy: I asked for copies of the pay stubs so I could check stuff like that, 'cause they're not supposed to take that, or parking...

Jenny: They took parking out of mine!—I was like, "Are you kidding me?" 'Cause we had to pay for parking. I'm not paying anything. If they take it out of my check I'll pitch a fit.

Judy: Good for you.

Jenny: Yeah, I'm done.

Judy: A year ago we took 10% pay cuts in order to avoid layoffs, and when that happened—that's a big chunk of change, for anybody—I took in a housemate and I'm now looking at taking in a second housemate because of this. I've been in the house ten years, I've done a lot to it to try and nurse it back to health, and I mean, my preference would be: I get to stay in my house, and I get to stay in my city. And so I'm trying to do reasonable things.

Jenny: I've been selling lots of stuff on eBay so that I can have that stashed away and just get rid of stuff, too. 'Cause when you're home and you've got all that stuff around.

Judy: That's a good idea, I should do that too...

Jenny: Yeah, you feel all the stuff closing in on you, now that you're at home.

Judy: The weight of it, yeah.

Jenny: Now that I'm at home all the time I'm definitely looking around in my apartment more, it's cleaner for the most part.

Judy: I wish mine were...

Jenny: My cats are like, "Why are you here?"

Judy: See, my dogs are so happy, it's like, "Oh gosh, you're home!"

Jenny: They are happy, to be sure...but it's still like, "Well, aren't you gonna leave now?"

Judy: "So we can have our little kittie parties!"

Jenny: Exactly.

We all laugh.

Jenny: There's a song by this band called Quasi that I like an awful lot, the song is called The Happy Prole, and they're singing about having a job, and one of the lines is "paranoid and tired, quit before you're fired, but they've got you in the hole, so you play the happy prole. You need the money so you've got to play it dumb, if you play it long enough, that's just what you become." It's very bitter about this, but very incisive and quite intelligent about really what you go through when you're working. Sometimes work can make you into a different person and you don't necessarily like the person that it makes you into; sometimes you do. There are certain elements of work that I liked an awful lot, and there are certain elements that I didn't really like, and so now that that's really been forcibly removed I'm kind of reconsidering who I am, and trying to—this sounds kind of cheesy, but—just get centered, and figure out, again, who I am and who I want to be.

I've been a little bit more pugnacious than usual, like picking fights—I picked a fight at McDonald's a couple weeks after. It was a Friday and this guy was checking me out and I was like, "Do you have an eye problem? Leave me alone." I don't have anything to lose now. And somebody was like, "Well, he could have shot you." And I was like. "Fine, whatever." So yeah, it's definitely...I'm kind of looking for it, I'm just like, what? WHAT?

Judy: "Do you not see the chip on my shoulder?"

Jenny: Right.

Judy: I guess I'm taking this as God's tap on my shoulder, that...as a copy editor you usually work nights, and it's like, maybe you should find something that lets you have your nights free so you go play with all your friends. And so I'm exploring other things. I know I could get on at some really good papers, but I'm at a point...I don't want to pick up and leave.

Jenny: I have mixed feelings about picking up and leaving, 'cause in five years I feel like I've managed to build community. I've got friends here, I've got people I interact with...I don't wanna move. I don't want to pack up all my stuff. I'm in bands...I have friends here. I've met some of the best people that I've met anywhere, here in Indy. And I'm not quite ready to leave. But it's difficult to stay here, I mean, we've been dropped by the biggest newspaper in Indiana.

I applied for a job at the alternative news weekly here. I'm excited about the prospect of that, working for the little guy again. And then, even though I don't want to—sometimes we do things we don't wanna do—I'll start looking out of state. Or I'll just freelance or try to find some other copy work that I can do. Something dealing with words. I don't wanna go back and do retail, I don't really wanna bartend.

Judy: I'm too short to bartend. (Laughs.) I'm trying to look more expansively. I'm lucky in that I've gotten a couple of freelance gigs for editing that have come in. I sent out a note to all my contacts—I tried to pare it down to people I actually knew. And I sent out a note saying, "I need to throw a big net, but my arms are short, and I can't do it, can't throw that big a net. So I'm asking all of you to help me." And through that, I've gotten a couple of other referrals for freelance. I've figured out through the years in newspapering that I need to do something that's challenging, I need to do something that lets me help others. And it's nice to work with smart people. I don't have to, but it's nice. And so I'm trying to use that as sort of my guiding light in pursuing other stuff.

Jenny: I had an interview on Thursday. It was kind of a conversational interview with four people who work at this paper. And one of the people said, "Why would you want to stay in journalism?"

And I said, "This is what I do." I mean, this is just…It's not desperate, I can do something else, but this is what I went to school for, this is what I know. I've always written, I've always been a writer, and it's just…

Judy: It's in your blood.

Jenny: This is just what I've done since I got out of college, and it just kind of messes with your head.

Judy: There are some jobs that I think are callings, and I think newspapering really is one of those. I think there will always be a need and a place in society for storytellers and storytelling. And I think there is a really legitimate need for—and we call it gate-keeping—for there to be a reliable source of information.

I'm an on-site writing coach at a collegiate writing contest each year here in Indiana, and every now and then you actually find someone in college who thinks Wikipedia is a reliable source, and you just wanna say, "Sweetheart, no. It doesn't work that way."

I don't know if the newspaper going to stay physically in a printed form, I mean, we—we?—the S—will continue because there are a lot of people who are not the most educated consumers of information, and those people especially need someone who will go to bat for them, who will take on government when it makes an error. And newspapers traditionally have provided—have been big enough and economically healthy enough—to be able to do that for people.

Jenny: Every since I was in college—and I graduated pretty much right as the dot-com bubble was bursting, just poof...But we were always getting this reassurance, "Oh, people are always gonna wanna hold this, and having it in their hands, and they want a newspaper!"...I don't think it's true anymore.

Right before I got laid off, my dad started sending messages from his iPad, and he's the main newspaper reader in our house, so—I don't know. I think print is going to go away. Maybe not magazines, and maybe newspapers are going to become a super niche publication, which is what I think that magazines have always been able to do. I mean, I can read not just about cats, I can read about black Persian cats if I want to. There would be a magazine specifically for that. Newspapers—they're trying to be everything to everyone, and that might stop if it stays in print. The world is in the middle of something, and we don't know what it is. As journalists, we're trying to...

Judy: Get a handle...

Jenny: Yeah...describe it and tell people about it—but we don't know what it is, and we don't know what the outcome is gonna be. And it's kind of scary, it's kind of thrilling, too.

Judy: Somebody told me the publisher came down to the newsroom I think the afternoon of the layoffs, and somebody asked her, "Why when other papers are hiring is G— laying people off?"

She said, very simply, "Boards of directors make goals, give goals to the chairman, and goals include profits, and the chairman meets the profits and there you go, and that's just the way it is in the business world."

They've cut the paper down to about as small as it can be without being a post-it note. And a lot of friends of mine through those years have just given me grief about that—and it's hard to defend.

The publisher told the union president the day of the layoffs that we were no longer going to have what we call second-reads, which means: I'm a reporter, I turn in my story, my editor does a first read, and then it goes to the copy desk, where a copy editor reads it and somebody else does a separate read, and then it gets proof-viewed—so it gets four reads. Well, they're now cutting out at least one, if not two, of those reads.

I mean...you want somebody who hasn't been involved—like a reporter has, or an assigning editor—to look at something as if, we always say, "We're the first reader." To say, "Boy, I know you know that going from the first to the second graph makes sense, but I'm getting lost here, so we need some transition, I need more information."

Jenny: I always really appreciated the copy desk for being that—irritating yes—but that level of "Jenny, did you really mean that...?" And it's like, "Huh, no, I guess not."

Judy: To be a copy editor, work with a reporter who just has nailed the story, there's nothing to fix; you can pay me to read that all day long. I'm fine with that. It doesn't happen that often, and that's because, well, because we're human. When I would write stuff, I would just be in terror that I wouldn't get a good copy editor to save my butt before it went into print, 'cause dear lord, that's my name...

We've just dropped a lot of coverage as far as reporters in previous layoffs, and it's really sad. We'd send sports reporters to the Olympics and we would also send a shooter, a photographer, and it's all just kind of grown inward.

Jenny: They sent a photographer and reporter to Iraq in 2007. We had a guy who was going to get a face transplant—

Judy: —in Boston—

Jenny: —and it was going to be difficult to send a reporter to Boston to cover this.

Jenny: And then you have to think, how are they serving the community then? How is the newspaper supposed to serve the community? Is it? It just seems like…The priorities aren't…mine.

Judy: Nor why you got into journalism.

Jenny: Yeah.

Judy: Me too. I'm sure every person has a specific relationship with their work and their field and so it's different, but I think those who go into a field to help others—it's sort of the Don Quixote, you're fighting the windmills, that's a big part of it—I think that makes you especially attuned to how that work interacts with the community. Whether you're fighting windmills by being a public school teacher, or whether you're fighting windmills by being a nurse or a doctor who helps, or a psychiatrist or a psychologist—I think that really gives you a different relationship and that's why you go into it, because you have the skills, and then the position at some point, to be able to help people. I think that is a secondary loss in losing your job as a journalist.

Jenny: A few months ago, the *New York Times* came out with a story about G— board of directors. So we had those two weeks of furloughs and then we found out that because all that money they'd saved, the higher-ups, got million dollar bonuses. I've been sitting around thinking about that at home, like, hmm, I hope they're enjoying all that money.

I think that the community is already angered about it, about the way the paper is, and it's just going to continue to be at least slightly enflamed.

Judy: And the thing is, the S— has consistently made money, and so does G—. And that's the galling thing. Their profits last year were more than half a billion dollars, and the CEO got a $1.75 million dollar bonus for meeting all these goals. But see the point isn't really to make…I mean, you need a healthy paper, and you need to make money. And nobody wants the paper to falter in that area. But you shouldn't have financial people running something that really is a community asset, it really is—it's a much different relationship than anything else has with the community. This is a broad statement, but I really believe it is probably the biggest threat to democracy in this country today because they are not supporting their newspapers. Because of that, the newspapers can't do what newspapers do best, which is bring wrongdoing and things that shouldn't be happening to light, and have enough oomph to put pressure on the legislature—which is six, eight blocks from the newspaper—to fix stuff. And that ultimately is really a threat to how this country works. And that's really sad, it really is.

"You weren't just at the grocery store last night, were ya?"

Doug Messenger

Doug Messenger comes from a long line of Western Iowa farmers. "Some of the worst soil you could think of, but they managed to make it work." He and his siblings, in fact, are the first to leave the farm altogether. His dad began the transition as a farmer-cum-fertilizer salesman-cum-insurance salesman. Doug is not an insurance salesman: "To sell insurance, I might as well just sell plots at a cemetery…I just can't do it—I don't mind selling, I don't mind certain jobs, but that's just one I can't do. Can't sell cars. I'd feel bad if somebody bought a car and comes back two months later and 'you sold me a piece of crap!' 'Yeah. Ok, let's go get you another one.' (Laughs.) I just, I couldn't do it. I just couldn't do it."

His parents are retired in Ames, Iowa. "Dad goes to coffee twice a week, plays bridge twice a week—they're living life. Dad: lay-leader in church, very outgoing type personality—like Richard, me." The Richard he references—the Richard in the highly-sociable column along with Doug and his father—is one Richard Messenger, Doug's older brother, who was, in the previous century, my high school choir teacher and the person who put us in contact for this conversation. Never did I think I would meet Mr. Messenger's brother—who, incidentally, has stolen Mr. Messenger's unflinching eye contact and graceful gesticulations—much less meet him in his own home in West Des Moines, Iowa—much less hear about the day he lost his job—in this case: the days he lost his jobs. This one will require a Selah, maybe two.

Doug, 54, prefers work that gets him moving around: "I would drive everybody nuts if I had to sit at home with no job, 'cause I'd probably be picking up everybody's paper, watering their lawns, mowing—I'm not one just to sit." In January of 1982, looking for work, he moved with his wife to Fort Worth, Texas, for a construction job. "I did drywall for 14 years, and then, after compressing two disks in my back and one in my neck from hanging sheetrock, I finally was convinced by my father-in-law and my wife to go to school. So I did three two-year associate's degrees in three and a half years[1] working full-time. I was carrying 14 hours a semester so I could get it done. So it's been a rough road, but it's been all worth it."

When worked dried up in 1997 he and his wife moved back to Iowa—with two sons—where Doug began a career as a draftsman. He's also known in the YMCA basketball, little league, and soccer circles. Barrel-chested with glasses and a gray mustache, he wears white athletic socks pulled up all the way: he is coach.

When I first started college back in '89 and '90, they could not get enough people to come in to the profession. They could not get enough CAD[2] drafters to come in and meet the demand for architects and engineers… So that's why I fast-tracked so I could get three degrees in five and a half

---

[1] Architectural Technology, Civil Construction Technology, and Construction Management

[2] Computer-Aided Design

years and get out there. I've been working CAD positions ever since, mostly architectural, two engineering firms.

I was residential home designer for seven and a half years. Laid me off due to the economy. Five weeks later I go to work for A—, worked there for 14 months, laid me off due to the economy. Six weeks later, I go to work for the engineer of record, M—. I was there 15 months and they laid me off.

So you were laid off from three positions within a...it sounds like... what was the span of time?
Three and a half years. Just shy of four years.

Tell me about the first one.

I worked for Kevin for seven and a half years. We were a residential homebuilder and I was doing all the home designs, changes, what have you. And we had noticed, oh, probably four or five months before the layoffs came...I was joking with the two other guys in the department that "I'll probably be the first one to go because I've been here the longest." I'd gotten my tenure, so I had full benefits, I had—well, I had everything: 401K, I had it all at seven years. And sure enough, within four months, one of the guys from my department says, "Hey, we need you to go downstairs for a meeting." So I got up and went with John, we went down, we went to the comptroller's office. And I hear the door shut. And I just got that sinking feeling and went dry in my throat, and went, "crap." Sat down in the chair and said, "Ok, this is it, isn't it?"

"Don't take it wrong, it's due to the economy. Here's a letter of recommendation. We're gonna go ahead and pay you for the next three months, we're gonna match all your benefits up for that time frame, don't worry about it."

Took about ten, maybe 15 minutes. Got up, shook their hands, thanked them, took my letter, went upstairs, found a box, packed up. It was one of the things where I felt betrayed, so I just didn't feel like staying around. 'Cause they told me I could stay until the end of the day, take my time...It's like, why? I just felt betrayed, so why would I want to stay, just to sit around here and feel bad the rest of the day—for everybody else to see it?

Everybody was sitting there in shock, going, "Really? Really?"

I just said, "Yeah." I said, "Watch your backs."

I guess I was right, because they found out the next day—some of them later that afternoon. We went from 32 people to 10 in a week.

Hardest thing I had to do was call my wife and tell her I got laid off.

"Oh crap, now what are we gonna do?"

I immediately got on the phone—started calling people I knew, said, "Hey, this is what happened, keep your ears open."

So luckily—that was on a Wednesday or Thursday—by the following Monday I had a job interview and by Thursday I had heard back from one saying, "We're not gonna hire you but we want you to check out this other company; we're calling to let them know you're coming." And that was S—.

So I lucked out. I feel I really lucked out on that job. So then S—, no fault of theirs, they lost three major contracts, and that's what they were banking on to get through the rest of the year, and they lost them, so four of us, they let go that day. This is something that they knew they had to do. And basically it was about one person from each department. So I wasn't alone. I was just the lowest man on the totem pole, that was the only reason.

We were all told individually, they called us in one at a time. It was right after lunch. I walked into the conference room and I saw three people with single manila folders laying on the table. My boss, the HR gal, and then the owners of the company. No blueprints, no job folders, just three manila folders. And they opened them up as soon as I sat down. It's like, been here before. Pretty clear.

"We don't want you to take it wrong."

"Ok, so how am I to take it?"

Did you actually say to them, "How am I supposed to take it?"
Yeah.

And what did they say to that?

"We don't want you to take it the wrong way, it's nothing against you, just something we have to do as a company because we lost these contracts. It's all economy-driven."

I looked at the owner and I said, "Well, are you gonna call me back in three months?"

"No unfortunately this is permanent."

"Ok, what else do I need to do?"

"We need you to sign this departure form."

I scribbled and said, "See ya."

I didn't even wait for them to say anything else, I just walked out.

So Clark, who was my boss so to speak, he came out a couple minutes later, he says, "Doug, come here." So he took me off to the break room and gave me a letter of recommendation. "If you would've just stayed, we would have explained it to you, we realize you're upset."

"Well look, Clark," I said, "I'm not upset, I'm pissed. There's a difference." Plain and simple. No sense mincing words, I just told him the way it was.

I went out, talked to my project manager, and the other CAD drafter. They just really had some bizarre looks on their face, like, total shock, kind of pale, "Did something really happen?"

"Yeah…they just let me go."

"No, crap. What are you gonna do?"

I said, "Find a box." (Laughs.) I mean, I tried to keep a sense of humor about it, because there was no sense in being mad. At that point, what else could go wrong? So I found a box, and everybody helped me out. It was kinda cool, I mean, because everybody was in shock—we knew it was there but we just didn't know who or how many. And they didn't expect it to be me, because I was one of those guys—and I still am—I'm at work 20 minutes early, don't take a break unless I need to, short lunch, first one to volunteer if you need something to get done that night.

And there was more than once when we had contract deadlines coming up to… "Doug, you gonna be around this weekend?" It was more than once, I went out and put a half day here, weekend there, that type of thing. That's always been my work ethic—I don't just work 8–5, see ya, I'm gone. Never have.

Third time I had no idea.

Monday we had our staff meetings at nine o'clock—they call me down at 8:20. And Eric had been out—the other partner—he had been out the week before on vacation, so I thought he was just wanting to get caught up on where I was at on projects, 'cause I had two or three different projects that I was working on with him. John the other partner, I had four or five; AJ I had two. So I had a lot of irons in the fire.

I get down there and sit down and I'm talking to Eric, he's asking questions so I filled him in, next thing I know, John walks in. And they get up and Eric shuts the door, walks over—rolls over a roll of plans—pulls out my file, and goes, "Well, we're terminating your position as of this morning. We'll give you an hour to pack your bags and get outta here."

Deja vu. Yeah, I think I was really in shock, 'cause I saw it, it was right there in my face—it didn't really register, but I knew it was there, I knew it was happening. And I kept looking at both of them and it's like, your lips are moving and I hear what you're saying, but it's just not registering.

No letter of recommendation, no letter stating why, they just told me, we're terminating your position 'cause we no longer feel a need to have a draftsman on board, nothing against you. I just sat there and I just looked at both of them, and Eric goes, "Have you got something to say?"

I said, "Well, Eric, in respect of our friendship, no. Because if I was to really tell you how I felt right now, you wouldn't wanna hear it."

He didn't know what to say. He was sitting there with a big lump in his throat "wha...."

So I just felt like, I'm done, this is it, third time's a charm. I got up and walked out. Short and sweet. And John the other partner, he would not even make eye contact. I've seen the man twice since then—he still won't make eye contact.

When that one came about, just because I felt like I was ambushed, I felt like there was no need even to be cordial. I just went up, grabbed my stuff, laid the key on my desk—"see you guys"—and walked out, and didn't say anything to anybody.

You've got that thick skin, the water's running off your back, it's like, give it to me, I can take anything. Until you see that folder slide out and it's like—bam!—crap, here we go again. So thick skin's only good for so much.

And I've just gotten to the point now, I just don't get my hopes up. You hear about a job—cool. Come home, get your resume, your cover letter out, see what happens. But I don't sit and dwell on it for a week or two if I don't hear from them. 'Cause that's the norm now: "We'll let you know."

Ok, thank you.

Years past, when you went out on an interview, or if you sent your resume out to somebody and you didn't qualify, they'd send you a thank-you. Or a "Sorry we're just not interested at this time" or "We feel…blah blah blah." You don't even get that now. "We'll notify you if we're interested." Well, that's lame. That goes against everything that I was taught. I've always been one where—I get this from my dad and my uncle, from being on the farm—you look somebody in the eye and you give them a firm handshake, that's as good as you get. Well if I go on an interview and I feel I've given somebody an hour of my time, I better get something back. I don't even get emails, phone calls, nothing. You know? So it's really been frustrating, but at the same time, I've been at it for so long it's like second nature.

I went on an interview a few weeks ago. I was just as comfortable as I could be, answered the questions, got along with everybody just fine, felt like everything was great—one call made, said, "Well, you finished number two." I told them, "You know how many times I've heard this in the last year?" So close, that type of thing.

And part of it, I hate to say, is—one, being 54, I've kind of hit the ceiling as far as what I expect for an income, what an employer expects to pay someone, so let's face it, they can hire somebody right out of college, no experience, for pennies on a dollar. So I haven't had an employer come right out and say, "Well, your age…" They just always look at my resume. I read recently where somebody at a job fair said, "Take all your dates off so that they have to talk to you and they have to ask questions."

I've been branching out, talking to other people—I've got quite a good network going now. Retail, some sales—that's about all that is really truly available right now.

I got a paper route. In January started getting up at 2:30 to deliver papers. And a friend of my older son's called me and said, "Hey, we kinda need help at the hardware store, you think you might be interested? It's only gonna be 10–12 hours a week, but it'll be something to help out." So I got down there and I started work in the hardware store and they kept padding a few hours. And then I got on a Hy-Vee. So after about a month and a half of freezing my butt off at 2:30 in the morning, I said, "Enough of the paper route!" Basically within a month, month and a half after I got terminated, I started working two jobs. Both stores I've worked at been 24 hours. I've been lucky and haven't had to work graveyard shifts.

At True Value, which is a hardware store, I am Lawn and Garden Manager. I've gotten to a point that I really kind of like retail…I'm the type of person that—I don't like just to just go into a job and work, I like to work the job so I understand it and I'm comfortable if someone walks up and says, "Hey I need you to do this?"

At Hy-Vee, my main focus is the produce department, where we stock and rotate produce. When we've been slow there, I've been off ordering bakery, learning how to pull orders—how to get a donut order for the next day pulled, get it on trays, get in the freezer. I have been known to go over and eat mistakes. That's why I put my weight back on. (Laughs.) You end up walking a lot. So, I've worn out two pedometers—I walk over five miles a day. My feet are killin' me. Keep joking I'm gonna re-learn how to roller-skate so I can cut down on the amount of steps and pick up the pace, but I've really gotten to the point where I really like working in the grocery store. It's very fast-paced, you get to meet people from every walk of life, you develop some pretty good friendships. I have people come in going, "Weren't you just at the hardware store this morning?" Or they come in the hardware store, "Wait a minute, you weren't just at the grocery store last night, were ya?"

"Yeah."

"Well what's up with that?"

So I tell them a little bit—it's just the way it's gotta be, I gotta work two jobs to make ends meet. And I'm finding at both jobs people are very cordial, very understanding—a lot of people out there are in the same boat. A lot more than I ever thought. I really see people in my situation, of having to work multiple jobs, working out of their comfort zone, just to make ends meet. When this first happened to me, a year or so ago, I felt alone, I really did. As time has gone on and I've heard other people in the last few months comin' up...Not that I'm feeling satisfaction; I'm kinda feeling—well, I can't explain it. It's comforting to know that I'm not alone. I guess the best way to explain it is: I can come home and say, "Guess what? So-and-so came in today, and they're in the same boat, they just lost their job, now they're having to work two jobs." I don't feel good about it, but it makes me feel better knowing that there's somebody else in the boat with me, I'm not paddling the canoe by myself anymore. (Laughs.)

So I work 32 hours at one job, work 20 at the other. True Value wants me to come back on full time this week at 40. So I gotta reschedule everything for Hy-Vee so I can keep my 20 there, so I'll be back to working a 60 hour workweek. And the sad thing about it all is, I'm still not making—even with benefits—half of the yearly income at my last job, at 40 hours a week. Yeah, I'm bitter, but at the same time I'm finding it's a way of life now, and I think it's gonna be that way for probably another year.

I don't wanna say I've become calloused, but I've become pessimistic, I've become leery. The economy, especially here, has been very flat. It just seems like, little by little, more and more companies just go away. The established jobs out there, they're cutting back because they've found they can get more out of less. And I think that's a lot of the mentality right now, it's: "We'll just work everybody harder and not have to hire anybody."

I had a friend, he was the only one left in his department. And he's in construction management, and been there four or five years while they let a couple of the guys over 25–30 years, let them go. Early retirement, whatever you wanna call it. And the newbies that came in didn't have all the experience. Darryl got stuck with five people's jobs to finish up, kind of nurse along...And he kept asking, "Am I gonna get any more help?"

"Oh yeah, oh yeah."

Eight, nine months later, "Am I gonna get help?"

"One of these days."

"Am I gonna get a raise?"

"No, just be glad you got a job."

There's something wrong with that picture. Really, really wrong with that picture. I heard it from people that they feel almost…I mean, people who lost positions, of course coping with that, but they're like, "You know what, on the other hand, yes, I have to figure out things financially, but wow, I wouldn't wanna be one of those people left behind."

I'm thinking, at the age of 54, I'll just do a career change. Six months? Love to be full time, True Value or Hy-Vee— the only problem is retail does not pay. I'm making good money—I mean, Hy-Vee pays $10.15 an hour, True Value doesn't. I get a 10% discount at True Value; Hy-Vee, I don't. I would really like to get in with the company more on a national level, like a Home Depot or a Loewe's, something where I can actually work up the ladder and become a true department manager, people under me and that type of thing; better money. I'm not asking to make the $45,000–50,000 I made at my other jobs—those days are over. But at the same time, I just don't feel like having to work 50–55 hours to make half of what I was, because when you're on your feet all day, dealing with the public, trying to get your job done, and putting up with other people's crap, you don't get paid enough for it. (Laughs.) In all honesty, you don't get paid enough. But I realize that's probably in the cards. The only way I foresee me getting back into construction and doing the CAD work at my age is through one of my contacts saying "We've got somebody we know who can walk in on Monday and sit down and go to work." Yeah, my salary's going to have to be negotiable but I'm not gonna have to go to work for pennies on the dollar.

There's still gonna be need for drafters, but just not in my chosen field. Because a lot of architects and engineers, they're going to 3D third party packages, so they want somebody that can model, just do everything, and not have to worry about somebody else jumping on board to get the job done. What's happened in the last couple years—your professional offices, your engineers, your architects, they're going on to what they call "one hand on." So they get a project, they hand it to one architect and one engineer, and they take it from start and go all the way to the finish. So the days of having a drafter help out—far and few between.

"It didn't feel like it was work"

Liz Laud

My grandfather, he worked for the company Native Lace. I have his watch. It was like a watch he got for 35, 40 years of being at one place. Those days are over. You know what? Today's generation, the average time people spend at a job now? 18 months.

We sit in the Coffee Bean & Tea Leaf in on Beverly Boulevard in West Hollywood. It is not to be confused with the Coffee Bean & Tea Leaf on Beverly Drive, two-and-a-half miles away in Beverly Hills, where MJ & I sat for half an hour, clueless, keeping Liz waiting. Luckily she is a patient Angelino, waiting for us to get over to her, and she's a smart Angelino because this Coffee Bean & Tea Leaf is the one with the parking lot behind the building.

A veteran of radio syndication sales, Liz is in her fifties, and— as she herself notes— comes across much younger, mostly because of the considerable amount of energy she possesses, channeled through a consistently bouncing knee, one intriguing idea or observation after another, and a serious pace for talking. As a speaker, she sprints.

Since becoming unemployed, she's taken on a roommate in her Wilshire Boulevard apartment—a friend who also lost a job. She recently landed freelance work for Big Boy, a big hip-hop radio personality in Los Angeles for nearly two decades.

"Nice man...reached out to me to deal with all of the radio stations that are affiliated with the show. So, you know, I kind of took it as a project."

I'd lived in Manhattan my whole life. I knew nothing but Manhattan. But something happened a couple years after college. I had come out here and I loved it when I came out. And I was like, you know what, this is cool. And when this job opened...I didn't move here with nothing. Because a lot of people come here with big dreams, and they get disappointed and stuff like that. So I came here with a job. All of a sudden making new friends. I like the weather. I like driving everywhere. I got tired of the bus. I got tired of it passing me by, slush coming up and hitting me. I got tired of the winter. I got tired of it. I got mom and dad still on the Upper East Side, living in the same building. My life is here.

I worked for one of the big radio syndication forums. I've always been in the radio business. They were a small company but they started buying everybody else up. As they bought up all these other companies, you had a lot of people doing the same jobs. So as they buy the other companies, they throw people out.

While I was there, I was Head of Affiliate Sales, doing a couple different projects. A lot of us have had a lot of, you know, huge success in the different fields we've been in...People forget one thing with women. When I graduated from college, I graduated in '80, okay? Women were always secretaries. There was no middle management. If you ran any department, you only ran personnel, okay? Oh, don't even think you were running publicity or marketing, because you were doing nothing but taking dictation and answering phones. That's 1980.

I started my career at PolyGram Records, and when I took the secretarial job in the A&R Department for the head of A&R this lady—this is a very interesting story: Rina got promoted from Steve's secretary and got the title Coordinator. It was maybe, like, '80, 81. Rina got put in… must've been like a closet, okay? Not like she moved into an office like these guys who had windows and stuff. A closet with like a little sliver of glass in it with a desk and a phone. She had a door. (Laughs.) And I think back at it, and that was wow, living. And I laugh about it now. But I'm telling you. Women had nothing. I tell friends of mine that are in their 30s now: you don't understand.

I moved from Polygram where I got sick and tired of my whole day dialing the phone and saying "S—'s office." I knew when I answered my own phone at home "S—'s office," it was time to move on. I had to laugh at myself. We were making their out-of-town reservations. We were renting their cars. They never even touched the phone themselves. They would never direct dial. It would be like, "Can you hold for S—?" Nobody picked up the phone themselves. I know it probably sounds bizarre, 'cause it's come full circle and now people think nothing of picking up the phone, you know? And now people are on computers and doing everything. But they would never even dial themselves. Next thing you know, you'd have five people on hold. "Hold for S—, hold for S—, hold for S—," you know?

I went from there to DRI Broadcasting. They had a show called King Biscuit Flower Hour. And it was the first rock radio show of live concerts on radio. And I finally got into sales. And it was my job to sell that show.

How did you manage to break into sales?

I took a job working for this one lady. And she gave me a chance to sell and call all the radio stations around the country. And from then on I was selling syndicated radio shows and running divisions at all these companies from then on. That's how I got out of that secretarial world.

I got into W—. That was the biggest radio company in '86. And then by '90, I was running the radio division. It took a long time to become a vice-president, because they didn't let women become vice-presidents.

I know it sounds really crazy. It took a long time. I didn't get to become a vice-president until, like, '95.

When did you first know you your job might be in danger?

I kind of had a feeling. The bosses always get distant, like you can never reach them. You can kind of see that thing. You're not really hearing from them or whatever. That kind of thing. My boss had called from New York, and he said, "Hey, I want to see you next Tuesday at one or two." A week before, when the boss flies out and says, "I want to see you at a certain time." You know it's not good. You know? They always seem to fly out and fire people.

He was Executive Vice-President. He was a young guy, about 30, or 32, and he was big on letting people go. You know, he was just so happy to be young and rising or whatever. He didn't care, you know? He never made any relationships with any of the employees.

It was after lunch. And I just went into the conference room, and he has a personnel person. And he's like, "We're letting you go."

I kind of felt it was coming, because they were acquiring all these companies. We were under this T— umbrella, which was jingle packages and music production libraries and things. And the company that my company had bought had bought another company for a ton of money. Clearly when they got it, they realized it wasn't worth anywhere near... they realized holy shit, we've got a piece of shit here, you know? This jingle company blows. You know what I mean? It might have been good in 1980, but this isn't 1980 anymore.

They had so many people doing duplicate jobs, and I had just transferred into that little section. They told me they were going to fold it into another area. They were like "Oh, we'll give you a couple months."

It's not like, you know, you're crying or anything. I just said, "Well, what about insurance?"

And they're like, "It's over tonight at midnight." That day. So the personnel person goes, "If you have to see a doctor, I suggest you go today at some point."

I thought it was kind of nervy of her to say, "Well, if something's wrong, you should get there today…" Kind of fuck you.

There's nothing you can say. It's not like it's open for discussion. You're not begging to keep the job. It's not an option.

Right after me, this young guy fired my friend. I found out everyone had gotten blown out. Everybody flew to different offices to get rid of everybody, you know, that did the sales jobs. It was the first time I had ever had to deal with this.

None of us, all of my friends…ever had to deal with insurance. It was just something that came…it was like a no-brainer. You gave no thought to it; never, ever thinking you'd have to deal with that yourself. If people had husbands that were working, they jumped on that plan. But for single people like us, you were on your own. If they accept you within 30 days, you're lucky. They warn you to kind of do some due diligence in a couple months. It's just stuff you learn that you have no clue about. You think like, "Oh, insurance? I want it Friday. I'll apply Thursday." Not happening. They don't always approve people. I got approved, but I got a bunch of friends of mine who didn't get approved, because, god forbid, something was…Oh, you threw your knee out or your back out. All of a sudden, they don't want you.

I had torn my ACL and not known it. So I had to deal with all these surgeons and everything to repair the torn ACL and torn meniscus. This was the coolest thing: Obama had put something in that—right at that time, right after I lost my job—to help people keep insurance. The government picked up 65% of the cost, and you only had to pay 35% of it. So normally this would've cost me mid-fours. Because Obama put this thing in the stimulus that allowed you to pay 35% of whatever your rate was it let people keep their coverage. So that was really very helpful to a lot of us. Then they ended up extending it for six months or five months after the fact. Everybody I know took advantage of it. It allowed people that never could've kept health insurance to keep it.

All my other friends were losing their jobs. My friend Mindy was always in records since the 80s, starting with artist management and stuff like that, and record companies. My friend Eric ran the radio station. My friend Rita ran this big K— here. A bunch of my friends were all with me in radio syndication. They're all offshoots of entertainments. And everybody for the first time in their life found themselves not working. I mean, everybody had worked 20 years straight, 30 years straight. Everybody was turning around, and they were just consolidating and, you know, just letting everyone go. There were a lot of us that had never, ever, ever been out of work before. Ever. And at one point, everyone I knew was out, and nobody had ever been out before. It was like everybody was free during the day, you know?

The first thing I did was I kind of like looked around. All of a sudden I just kind of chilled a little bit. Because first of all, you never had the time. I didn't have like a panic attack like, "Oh my god," kind of thing, probably because I did have money in the bank. You know, that does give you a little bit of whatever, you had severance coming in and you'd get unemployment or whatever. But I think I looked around for the first time, and I'm like, "What am I going to do?" or "What makes me happy?" You know, because you never think like that. You know what? You're on autopilot. And what I find with people, even if they're miserable somewhere, they stay in that miserable job, because not everybody walks from it. So all of a sudden I was trying to think what would make me happy.

You see what happened was it all started a couple years ago when I was out with my dog. And I ordered my sandwich, and they're like, "Hey, dogs aren't welcome here. Why don't you just put your dog in the back of the car?" No way. Once I had had a dog stolen out of a car. I wasn't about to leave a dog in the car. Especially you know how hot it gets. So I'm like, there should be like a Zagat guide or something. I created a website called Dining with Dogs, and it's all dog-friendly restaurants all through Southern California, New York, LA, Chicago, all Southern California, San Diego. I have done New York City. And it's high-end restaurants. There's nothing you can't do these days with pets. It's not like yesteryear. (Laughs.)

I realized that's the thing that made me the happiest. That's something I stumbled into out of the fact that I got tossed out of the Brentwood Country Club. And then having over 100,000 visitors to that site, I'm pretty proud. Because I'm only a person. I'm not a corporation. You know, I can't explain it. That made me so happy in the fact that I couldn't believe

I created something like that, and that all those people were visiting. I'm like, hey, that's pretty cool. And I think when I looked at it, that made me the most happy.

You know, to be honest with you, if I could find a way to monetize it, nothing would make me happier than doing that, nothing would be better than to work for yourself and not kind of feel like, oh my god, I could walk in one day and they don't want me anymore. I mean, I think that's the best thing people do, if they can do something for themselves.

Self-Terminating

"I got big shoulders"
Bob Bendig

When we arrive at the downtown Pittsburg law offices where Bob Bendig has asked to meet, he gathers us in the conference room where he sits behind a slew of printouts about me and this trip across the country. Not only has he taken the time for Google searching and printing but also there are highlighted sections of text and handwritten notes in the margin. He is 51 years old and still does his homework.

His Polish family has been in this city for generations. His father served in the police department for 30 years. His grandfather was the head of the maintenance division at the Gulf Tower, Pittsburgh's signature, pyramid-topped building, looming over the wedge of land where the Allegheny and Monongahela rivers vanish together and reincarnate as the Ohio. "He would take me up there as a kid, and we would go way at the top and right up there, and I remember looking down, you know, as a kid: 'How special I am?—I get to come up here!'" Gulf Oil, which was subsumed in a 1984 merger with Chevron, was the original tenant. In the merger the vast majority of the Gulf employees were laid off or forced to move. Since then the building's vacancy rate has gone as high as 44%. A family of peregrine falcons nests on a ledge near the top of the building.

Bob has a gray head of hair and a great deal of discretion— both, very likely, the result of his chosen career path in private investigation. When we first sit down, he has several questions for me. He wants to know why I'm making this trip, why I'm looking for the stories—he seems quite good—in general—at quickly getting to "why" while most others are still stuck on "what."

He wants to know what else I am hearing from others. I mention a few things that come up again and again—age and loss of loyalty and the disconnect within communities. Suddenly I've said enough and he starts speaking without hesitation.

I lived first in the Pittsburgh south side, and my grandparents…My grandmother was a stay-at-home grandmother. My grandfather worked for Gulf Oil for 30-some years. His work ethic was incredible, and it was like you could set your clock by him. He was up every morning at seven o'clock. Went out to work, five o'clock you could open the door up: Here he was, coming up the sidewalk. He instilled in me what it was like to really put everything you had into a job.

I come from a broken family, my mother and father are divorced since about 12 years old—so I knew early on that I wasn't going to have any type of financial help with going to college and so forth. So at 17, I went into the military. Served active duty in the United States Air Force. I was part of an anti-terrorist team there. I was in the strategic air command, so I was part of missiles—ties into anti-terrorist work. Probably three-quarters of the way through, my commander came and he goes, "Bendig, I'm gonna become the new chief of the investigative branch; I want you to work underneath me." It was a nice honor for him to look at me like that.

So I worked there for several years, helped re-write some regs on background clearances and investigations for clearances. I did background investigations for every level of government employee, from GS18s, colonels, generals, United States marshals...anybody who came through the Midwestern branch had to come through my desk. So I opened up tons of investigation work.

When I was discharged, I immediately went into the United States Air Force reserves. And from there, went into the private sector. Started working for a private security company. Within around six months, I was promoted. From there, I was promoted again to Training Officer, and Assistant Operations Manager. I was very, very overzealous. Enjoyed my work.

You know, we had a lot of large contracts. The company I worked for did a lot of labor disputes. Before you know it, in the mid-eighties, I was doing every labor dispute in Western Pennsylvania. A paper company out of the Midwest—has a paper mill up in Maine—they heard of me; they asked me to come up. I ran a six-month labor dispute up there. It was probably the worst I was ever on.

Upon my return, M— Bank headquarters wanted me to come down and run their entire public safety division. They got into some bad investments, and they knew it was going to be a very tumultuous time. So I agreed to come on as a consultant and run their public safety division. Had 180 officers down there. It got really bad. It was some tough times down there. Here goes a company in existence for, back then, in '87, 110 years without ever laying anybody off. A new CEO was put into place, and they brought in a hatchet guy, and they started having meetings, and every day at five o'clock I was called up to the board of director's room and they said, "Bob, every day at five o'clock, we're gonna call you, and we're gonna let you know what locations throughout the facility we want you to have two plainclothes officers at." And when these individuals came into work, they weren't even allowed to sit down. "Ma'am, we're sorry, you need to gather your belongings and leave." There was a lot that went on down there, and to see the looks in some of those folks' eyes. After 20 years of service, if you didn't meet the cut-off date—you could have 19 years, 363 days— and if it didn't meet that line, you weren't getting retirement. It was heartbreaking.

We had to escort them. My men had to escort them. The reason for that is they didn't want any sabotage, intellectual property transferred, vandalism and so forth. But that kind of went out the window after the first week. People knew that the process was starting; it could be anybody. I'll never forget this one time where this one gentleman was being escorted from one M— Bank center to another M— Bank center, and the guard asked him, "Where's your ID badge?"

I says, "Listen, this guy just lost his job. Just cool it, okay?" From a distance, I witnessed that, and I thought: Wow. That's a pretty profound moment. So those types of things…there were times officers found people dead, I mean suicides.

After they got done laying a lot of people off, they started laying off corporate people who were part of laying those people off, so hold onto everything you have. Don't take anything for granted. And don't take it personal, for real.

After three years, it was the end of my deal there, so I had a friend of mine who owned a big slag company here in Pittsburgh, and he says, "You know, Bendig, you're good at what you do. Why don't you go out on your own?" He goes, "I'll be your first client."

And during that time, I had another guy that worked for a property management company, and he said, "I'll give you the guard contract for this building if you rent office space off of me."

I go, "Wow, that's pretty good; I'll take the deal." You know? And thus I opened up Bendig's Security Services, and started my career in my security field. (Smiles.)

I remember when we opened the doors of that business. It was my brother and I. I remember when I first got my license. I was happy as heck. "Wow. Man, I can't believe this. Now I can operate my own business and do it how I want to do it."

Contract security is a service industry, you're providing a service… what happens is every day you've gotta…(raps three times on conference table)…do a lot of cold-calling. It's a tough business. We had some really good times, and we had some real bad times. In the contract security business, it's all bids. You have to go out and bid. And these companies work on a budget, so they're gonna take a low bid. I've lost contracts because of a nickel an hour. If my bid's $7.50—back then, $7.50 an hour for a minimum-wage guard—if a competitor came in at $7.45, they'd drop you. Reputable companies learned over the years that that's not wise to do, but they were far and few between.

It was very difficult dealing with minimum wage employees, because they didn't make enough money to afford transportation; a lot of them relied on Port Authority. Well, back in the early '90s, we also had an economic downturn. Maybe a week before Christmas, I was talking with my client representative, I says, "Well, listen, you know, I'd like you to make an arrangement for security for the holidays."

He says, "Well, we're not going to need security over the holidays. I'll call you when we get back…"

After the New Year, I'm watching the news: Employees of so-and-so company trying to get back to work, but all of the plants are padlocked.

They stuck me with almost four months of invoices. And four other companies went bankrupt. So it pretty much devastated me, the ripple effect. What I did is I closed my business. In '93 I shut down the big company and worked out of my house. And during that time, there was a lot of personal things going on with my family, I'm having kids and so forth, so I just maintained the home base business and got a house out in Bethel Park—had my daughter in that house. The way things were going, it was just best to keep the business there. I learnt from my past with bidding on contract security, I knew that that wasn't the way I needed to go anymore. So what I did is I found a niche, and I started targeting that investigative area, and I kind of fell into custody investigations, just, like, off-the-cuff.

The downfall of doing private investigative work is this: sometimes clients look at the money versus work thing differently than you do, okay? Just like if you hire an attorney: "Wow, man, $350 bucks an hour? Who gives $350 bucks an hour?" But people don't realize what it takes behind the scenes. Investigators, attorneys, we have a lot of civil procedures, criminal procedures we have to comply with, and if something doesn't get filed on time, an attorney could lose his bar number or be suspended.

An investigator's license could be revoked. So there's a lot of issues, so when you look at $350 an hour, that's because there's so much to navigate when you're dealing with a case, because you have a responsibility to your client, and if you screw up, you're going to be held responsible for that.

I worked in the investigative field until last year, and just like everybody else, we held on. We did everything we possibly could to endure the economy, the way it's affecting everybody. But it was devastating. What we found is the money's just not there, or if it is there with corporations, they're holding tightly on it. My money comes from generating business, working for attorneys, corporations, private people. The stock market's down drastically, you know, and people are getting nervous.

When corporations do have the money, they have millions and millions of dollars, but they don't know how they're going to be affected by privatizing employees having to pay health care, how it's going to affect their budget. When you're dealing with private individuals, people try to budget, but the economy is so uncertain, it's hard to even budget. So ambiguous right now.

Mine was grasping at straws. Mine was—'cause I'm a fighter— probably a lot of it denial. You know, "This can't be happening again." Where do I turn? You know, you use the credit card, balance up as much as you can. You go out and you spin your wheels.

Last year I had to claim bankruptcy. I tried to do the restructuring, just couldn't do it. There's certain criteria to chapter seven, and then to a business restructure, and I didn't meet the criteria because of the revenue just wasn't going to be there to pay my creditors off. So basically I went through that time period, which can be a little bit embarrassing, because that information—when you put your information on a matrix, that's public knowledge. So you have to deal with that a little bit, and then it's a little taxing because there's a lot of hearings you have to go to as far as bankruptcy court goes. And you go over there and you sit with people that are going through the same thing that you're going through. An attorney friend of mine who does bankruptcies: "Man, there's over 6,000 people a week in this country that are claiming bankruptcy." That's a lot of folks claiming bankruptcy.

I was able to survive off the credit cards a lot, but when I knew I can't make these credit card payments this month…that's when I kind of realized that something's gonna have to happen here. And you try to hold on. But you can't hold on for too long, because then you're going to ruin everything. It's difficult to let go. It's difficulty to say, "Hey, I gotta do this bankruptcy thing." But you feel a lot better after it.

The lowest point was probably me having to give my house up. Last year. I had a nice house out in the suburbs. There's a succession of things that have to take place and appeals you can go to, and I pretty much exhausted them all just to buy time. You're hoping while you're going through buying time in the legal process that maybe something will happen. Maybe a job will come through. Maybe the bankruptcy will hold it off…

I have the sheriff's department serve their paperwork and so forth. I knew it was going to happen, so it wasn't a surprise to me. I knew through the process that these things were going to take place, especially in my career field. I've served these types of things, subpoenas and so forth, so I knew, I know what the law is and what has to take place. You try to exhaust what you can, but then you realize that there's only so much you can do.

What goes through your mind is: Are you a failure? You know? Me and my wife are divorced, so I get my kids throughout the summer and every other weekend. My children love that house—my oldest is 22, and I have two teenagers. And you look at how it's going to make an impact on them, how your children are going to look at you. What about people in your neighborhood? You made friends. Now you have to fold up and go somewhere else. How are they thinking of you? You just weren't able to do it right. You weren't successful, not a hard worker. There's all kinds of things that come to mind that you keep thinking: What if they think this?—or what if they think that? And what you have to do is you have to remember that this can happen to anybody.

We see more people moving in with their moms and dads, back in with the family household, and you can only do that for so long too. That happened with me. I went and stayed with my cousin for a while, and that happens to be my mother's sister's daughter. That's my first cousin, we're real close, but after a while, you know you're becoming a burden.

What enabled me to rebound back in '93 through that period of time was the fact that the economy wasn't as bad as it is now. I think we're in uncharted territory right now. The fact is, I don't know how much the American people can shoulder. Just go through your necessities. Putting gas in your car to even get to the grocery store. We have a lot of natural disasters that are happening that are causing our crops to be minimal, so the prices are going up. It's affecting everybody. Personally, I've always preached that what has to happen here—to bring this country back strong—is that the government needs to focus on families. I always believe that strong families make strong communities. I know it sounds like a canned statement, but I'll tell you what: If the families are stronger, then your communities are going to be stronger. The money has to be filtered down to the families. A man is always there for his wife or his children or whatever. And when this happens, you start looking like, "Man, wasn't I good enough?" "Did I do something wrong?" "Didn't I work hard enough?" So those things come to mind too. Fortunately, with me, that's a quickly passing moment. I focus on now we're going to move forward. But I can imagine there's a lot of people out there really get down on themselves because they can't take care of their families anymore, and for the first time in their life they have to go and stand in that welfare line. They may have talked about people being in the welfare line: "Man, I can't believe it. They're getting a free ride." All of a sudden, they're the ones that are in there.

I happen to have an incredible social worker, turned me onto all my VA benefits. Being a veteran, I never took advantage of any of my benefits. My social worker, he says, "Bob, it was just pride." And honestly, I was self-sustaining. I didn't have to worry about welfare. I would never have looked into it, but that's my parachute now.

They're going to help me with getting a new home, 'cause I have the VA loans for a home, and just a bunch of other things that can be afforded to me. So I think if you look for it and don't let anything stop you, don't let anybody tell you you can't do it, don't let anybody throw an obstacle up in front of you, because determination really wins out. If you have determination and you believe inside that you can do it, I'm a living example of that, let me tell you. I really am.

Best thing I've found is write things down. Work to make yourself a checklist. And you might not all of them in that timeline that you wanted to, but you're checking it off, and as you see yourself checking those things off, you become more confident. 'Cause there were times just even getting up in the morning to brush my teeth was tough. It was. But I just kept moving forward. Everyday, I'd find a reason to get up. I found that walking helped me out a lot, because I was getting exercise. I was doing a lot of thinking. And I was engaging people. So when you're out and you're mobile, and you're not held up feeling sorry for yourself, and I hate to say it like that, this "victim spirit" type of thing: You can't do it. Because it's going to drag you down and suck you into that hole. Get out there. Walk. Don't drive. It's too fast. Get out and walk so you engage people. And when you engage people, there's something magic that happens there. Okay? And it really reinforces you, and it keeps you moving. So at the end of the day, you're like, "Wow, man. I never noticed that person before," or "I never noticed that park before," or "I never noticed that business"—even that business!—"I've drove past it so many times, I didn't ever know that was there." So then you find out there's resources out there. And all of a sudden those resources become something you can access, so it really works. It really does. You can't imagine.

You always have to keep looking at it like, "Every day, I've gotta get up with purpose. I gotta find a new challenge to keep working for, because…" If you want to know the truth, I'm happier now than I was a year ago when I had everything, and I know that sounds kind of crazy, but there was a lot of stress back in, a lot of anxiety, a lot of what if's, what happens if I can't come through? What happens if I can't do this? Now that everything's been purged, I'm starting fresh. It's a fresh start with me. It's like, you can see the forest through the trees type of thing. It's more defined.

I'm starting a consulting company, helping other private investigators and security agencies 'cause they call me, they know Bob's been in this business for a long time. So they take a case, but they would call me to help them solve the case.

I know a ton of people that are becoming entrepreneurs. They're opening up their own small businesses. I interact and network on every social networking group you can possibly work on, and I just find it very interesting what's happening out here. There's a lot of good things that come out of bad, it's incredible to see people that are unemployed going into their own niche and helping other people out, you know? I think no matter what you're going through: take your mind off your own problems and help other people. Because once you do that, you're problems will shrink. The way technology exists today, we're becoming less personal. It's like we're almost retreating into ourselves and hiding behind something. You have to engage people one-on-one, because there's something that occurs when you're meeting people face-to-face that can't happen here, or on the telephone, or on your smartphone. It can't.

Seizing

"CEO of me"

Bridgette Lacy

In two weeks she turns 50 and she's thinking of celebrating with 50 lunch dates in the next calendar year—each with a different person. "I like the idea of meeting all the people I didn't have the time to actually see when I was working. (Laughs.) You know, it's not the same thing where you talk to people on the telephone."

We're sitting in her home in Raleigh, where she has just provided sweet teas all around. She lives alone and has a grandmother nearby—"that's why I moved to Raleigh in the first place." Her family is from Lynchburg, Virginia. "My father was a mechanic. He worked for himself. And I kind of think he taught me a lot about working for yourself, you know…my father's people, some of them came from the West Indies and the Islands." She points at pictures of her mother and grandmother on the wall of the living room where we sit—and her grandmother's cabinet below the stairs.

*She speaks frankly and convincingly. Example: "I hate
Facebook...I don't want to know your every thought. I would prefer
your best thoughts. Because people just...(pantomimes typing:) 'I
don't feel good, what should I do?' Get off Facebook and lay down!"*

I graduated from Howard University in 1986 and pretty much got a
job right out of college. I interned at the *Washington Post*, and I think a
month or two later I started at *Sun Bulletin* in Binghamton, then went to
the *Indianapolis Star*, then came to Raleigh. In 2008, the newspaper was
laying off a lot of workers. The writing was clearly on the wall, because
every few months, they were laying people off.

I was part-time. What happened, I came to the *News & Observer* in
1992, but in 1994, I had won a fellowship from the Arts Council to write
fiction, and I had gone to the South of France for three months. It was
wonderful. And I kind of decided when I was on fellowship that I didn't
like the person I was becoming working full-time, you know? Because
when you work for other people, in some ways, they dictate a lot of who
you are, of what work you choose to do, what your emphasis is, what your
priorities are. And so a couple years after I got back, I decided I wanted to
go part-time. And that seemed like a risky decision at the time, but it was
kind of like, you know, I had asked my mother. I had said, "What did you
really want to be?"

And she said, "I wanted to be an actress." And my mom's a bookkeeper.

And I had asked my grandmother. I said, "Grandma, what did you
want to be?"

And she said, "I wanted to be a nurse, but my mother wanted me to
be a teacher."

And I decided I wanted to be what I want to be now—a fiction writer.
I didn't want to have to wait for it. So I went part-time.

Because people, I think, can sometimes try to marginalize your work
or what you do, and I just wanted to be somewhat free to do some of the
things I wanted to do. Just not always be controlled by that place you
work for. And so it's writing fiction, but I freelanced for *Newsweek* at some
point, the *Washington Post*, other publications as well.

Once you make a decision and you walk out on faith, things happen for you that you can't predict. So other opportunities came, I think, based on me making that decision. I would get freelance work, or people would recommend me for sitting on a panel or doing this. I'm one of these people that really believes in saying something out to the universe. Like, I remember one time, I said, "I really need a vacation, Lord," and then a friend of mine was like, "Oh, I know this person who rents a house in Wilmington for $50 for the whole weekend, and I'm going to find somebody, and we'll pay $25 and go to Wilmington for the weekend." (Laughs.) You know, so I kind of believe in really putting that thing out there, and you have to really trust.

So I guess when the *News & Observer* was laying off people—and people were getting unhappy, because people were having to do so much work to maintain the jobs—I kind of wanted to get off the ship on my terms instead of being pushed. I think in part it was somewhat easy, because a person came and recruited me. Like, I was minding my business. They called me on the phone, said, "I love your writing. I was wondering if you'd be interested in this job." So I was recruited by the state government to come and work for them...as the Media Relations Manager for the North Carolina Arts Council.

And it was full-time, and I was used to working part-time, but then there were more benefits and things like that. And I think the other thing is you have to really be flexible in life, and I guess one other part of my story is, in 1999, I was diagnosed with a benign brain tumor, so I had brain surgery. And once you've had a life-altering or changing thing, once again, your priorities are put in front of you. Let me be what I want to be right now. Tomorrow's not really promised. So given all of that, it was easy for me to say let me move and do something a little different. And I knew that I could take the skills of being a journalist to media relations. You know, the writing, the networking. When you've been in a market since 1992—almost 20 years—you really know a lot of people, a lot of resources. So I knew I could take all of that to the next job.

In November the director of the arts council was saying the budget wasn't looking good and that the governor was recommending one position would be cut. The particular department I worked in only had 26 people. The arts, a lot of times, are targeted, because people think of them as extra. They don't think of them as essential. And I was one of the newest hires. Even though I had been there two and a half years, there were people like the director, who had been there 38 years. So the only person newer than me was the webmaster, and I knew they weren't going to lay him off, because nobody else can really do that job.

And I think the other problem was the Executive Director was saying they had never had a Republican legislature, so it was kind of like…that's what you kept hearing, that the cuts were going to be severe compared to other times.

So in November, she told me I might be laid off, and then again in January. And sometimes I'm like, you know, pull the trigger. I hate limbo. I think people get caught up in, "Man, if I do this, or I do this, or I do that… maybe I can prevent this." But it's really not about you when you have massive layoffs. It's really about them.

I'm like, okay, I'm not going to wait. I'm going to start gathering some nuts, you know. So I started trying to get freelance assignments. I started thinking about what else could I do. And again trying to use the skills I had.

Wound up getting laid off in June earlier this year, 2011. I was finally told, I think before Memorial Day weekend. I wasn't surprised.

The Arts Council is under the umbrella of Cultural Resources. So first the Cultural Resources secretary sent out a mass email saying "Based on blah-blah's recommendations, we're going to have to make some cuts, blah blah blah…" Very generic kind of letter. So then that afternoon, my supervisor came to get me and said, "Let's go and talk to Mary in Mary's office." At that point, I was given a letter, and it said basically my position had been eliminated through a reduction in force.

It was funny, because the Executive Director was like, "Wow." You know, I was taking it so calm. I think they expected me to be really, really upset. But really, once you've been diagnosed with a brain tumor and have five-and-a-half hour brain surgery…A couple years ago I had a re-occurrence, so I had radiation. A job layoff is not the end of the world. And I think, too, that's where your worthiness and your value comes in.

I know I'm more than that job. I know I've gotten jobs all my life. I can get another job. Or, I can find work. Because really work and a job are not even necessarily the same thing.

This was one of the largest state government cuts ever, even though it's hard to ascertain numbers. Some people say 30,000, and then you get statements like 5,000. You know? They don't want to put the numbers together, because when you think of state government workers, you're talking about possibly—you know, if you work at a university, that's state government—but they kind of keep the numbers somewhat disjointed so it's hard to get a real sense of the magnitude of the layoff.

I didn't leave until the end of June. I was trying to complete certain things. Again…it's like, I'm a single woman with a brain tumor. You've gotta learn how to quickly do what you need and line up your resources. I was trying to book every doctor's appointment I could think of. I was moving up dental appointments. I was filling prescriptions. I was just like, boom, boom, boom. Trying to get everything ready. I went onto the Employment Security Commission's website, typed in my social security number, seeing how much I would get. So I started putting some stuff together, because I think my journalism training was like, power is information. So let me start arming myself with some information about what I have so I can then start putting together some stuff.

I guess when I went to the unemployment workshop at the Arts Council Cultural Resources, I mean, the workshop was such a sham in some ways. I'll give you an example. We had a guy from the credit union, a little guy. He was supposed to be giving us a workshop on how to live on a reduced income. He says stuff like, "Don't get your hair done. Don't get your nails done." All of this is geared toward women, so I had to do it: I raised my hand. I said, "First of all, I'm kind of wondering why all of this is geared toward women." I said, "Are you telling men give up your mistress?" I mean, if you're going to give crazy advice like that…And the thing was, he wasn't coming with really, I thought, good tidbits. If I have to choose between my mortgage and my credit cards, what should I do? I mean, give me some hands-on things I can do. And throughout the workshop, I would ask questions, and people would go, "Wow. How come you have so much more information than they do?" But you know, as a journalist, that's what I'm used to. I'm used to being able to ask good questions and also find the right people to ask the questions to. And so it really made me think. And there were a lot of men there with their wives too at this workshop, where you could tell the wife was taking notes for the men to try to, you know, once they were unemployed, figure it out. So I kind of thought, there are going to be people out there who need someone to navigate for them, because you're overwhelmed by being laid off. A lot of people are thinking, "Did I do something wrong? Was I good enough?" This, this, this—you're going through that. Then there's a bunch of paperwork—you know, extended COBRA benefits, your retirement-type things, even stuff like get your parking lot thing paid. So you're just bombarded with this stuff.

So I called the Business Editor, who had been one of the Features Editors. She had been my editor. And so I said, "I want to write this unemployment column," and so she said, "Well, write a sample and we'll let you know."

I had written about my brain tumor too, so I had written first-person types of things. And really, throughout my life I have, as a writer, have written about whatever I'm experiencing, and tried to use that to help others, and thinking a lot of what I need to know, they need to know too. So pretty much as soon as I wrote it, and I sent it, they loved it. And readers loved it. And a lot of readers said, "I read you when you were sick. I read you when you left. And I'm so glad you're back." So it was really good kind of getting really back with readers again, now talking about unemployment. I mean, there's so much to write about.

This is no time just to have a high school diploma. And I don't think everybody is meant to go to college, but I'm saying trade school, something else. Because there's been a lot of reports that, for example, African-American men who have a high school diploma or less work less than a year, because it's only seasonal work they can get. So this is no time in the global economy to be slacking. I do stories at Wake Tech[1]. They were telling me they have, for example, a certificate of entrepreneurship.

---

[1]   North Carolina Community College

They were telling me hardly nobody applies for scholarships. There's money out there people are not even getting. Hiding in plain sight!

You almost need to have two occupations. You know, if I was going to college today, I might get a degree in something like hairdressing and then multimedia journalism. You know, something where it's almost recession-proof. And you have a lot of people that only know how to do one thing. And so in North Carolina with these, for example, manufacturing jobs that are going away, you have a manufacturing job and it's going away, and you don't know how to do anything else, it's going to be hard to get other employment. And there are a lot of people who, I think, are illiterate: they know how to do what they do, but if you took that away from them, they don't even know necessarily how to articulate what they did. And so I think that's problematic.

I think you really have to make decisions about what you are willing to do and what you're not willing to do. Because there are a lot of employers that are taking advantage of this current situation. And you know, I kind of kid that I think that your employment package now should come with a burial plot, because a lot of people are trying to kill you on your job. You know, they're working people to death. And it's really sad, because I'm talking to people who are very conscientious workers. They really try to do their best on the job. But they're working unreasonable hours. They're given unreasonable tasks for that time period. And a lot of times, their pay is being cut. They're exhausted from the job, but they're also exhausted from the whole negativity associated now with work, negativity in terms of management, not feeling appreciated, thinking you might get laid off down the line. I mean, there's a lot of mistreatment going on in the workplace, where people don't really feel like they can say anything. So you also have to figure out what you're willing to do and what you're not willing to do. Because I don't think you should have to sacrifice your family and your health just to work.

I think as an African-American woman—I say African-American because I think of the history of African-Americans in this country—I think I always kind of thought of myself as the CEO of me, you know, and that I needed to look out for myself, and that no matter whether you work for somebody or not, I'm going to be the boss of Bridgette. Some of the most disgruntled workers are workers who did sacrifice, they missed the Thanksgivings, they missed the Christmases, they didn't get to certain events in their families. And then when that company cans them, it's like, "I gave up all of this, and this, this and this, and this is what I get?" They get pissed.

And I've never been that kind of person. I'll just say, "No, I ain't doing that." You have to stand up for yourself. And a lot of people think...they almost consider it confrontational to really say what they mean, or to stand up for themselves. You know, it's like, if somebody asked them to do something, for them, almost saying the word "no" is a confrontation for them. And to me, it's not confrontational. I'm just telling you no. You know, I don't take it as that means we have to have a collision. And I kind of think too that relationships—whether they're work or personal—they kind of finish the way they start. If you start making too many compromises early on, and people want to keep putting their foot in your behind, people get mad if they put their foot in your behind every day and then, all of a sudden, you try to take it out. You gotta take it out the first time they put it in there! (Laughs.) That's just the way you need to establish the relationship.

Time can be more valuable than money. And I think one of the things that I am hearing from a lot of workers that have been laid off, they're enjoying their time. Out of all the courses I've taken—I've taken how to live on a reduced income, LinkedIn, the entrepreneur mindset, now I'm taking a planning your business venture—but that entrepreneur class, I was so excited after I left, because I thought, "These people are so bright." On my job, there were really no ideas coming out unless I provided them. I mean, people were so busy on their treadmills. And a lot of these places, they don't want any new ideas. Just do what the hell I told you. They really just want people that are the status quo. And I was kind of realizing, you know, I like learning. I like stretching. And a lot of places, they don't encourage that, and they don't give you time to do that. They just want to keep you on that treadmill. Sometimes we don't know our blessings. One thinks being unemployed or losing your job might be something terrible—and it might be—but it might not be. It might be something else. So I'm leaving room for interpretation.

"It's all on you"

Paul Humphreys

I fell in love with Columbus. I mean, we kind of say we're between Chicago and New York. This is kind of a good place to be for a family, job market, everything.

Originally from Canton, Ohio, he hasn't strayed too far. His mother worked throughout the public school system and "my father was corporate USA." They divorced when Paul was young. His grandparents were factory workers on both sides of the family; his mother's side came from Greece. "Yeah, the craziness is on my mother's side," he says with a smirk and established rhythm: he has said this line before and it's a family favorite.

He is 32 and handsome, with dark eyes, very certain eyebrows, and the defined jaw of a super hero. Just behind the café table were we sit, hot grills await crepe orders. Paul is working the creperie with one other person; they both wear t-shirts and baseball caps, and they are both sweating. We're all sweating because we're outside at a strip mall and the late July sunshine is heavy and wet and perfectly still.

Majority of my work history was in construction sales, residential and commercial. The company I was with, I'd been with them going on four years, and they unfortunately suffered from probably expanding too quickly and at the wrong time. And they went from having I think maybe nine or ten branches throughout the country to having to retract back to about two. So it not only impacted me, but it probably impacted about 50 to 70 employees of theirs over the course of, you know, six months. There were a lot of individuals like myself that were caught off-guard to say the least. At the peak, we had three four-man crews, so 12 crew guys. Rotated in. We were down to two laborers. One of the laborers doubled as a foreman, and then I basically took over all of the operations and all that fun stuff. So we were really down to two people in our Columbus branch. There's a base plus commission type structure, so they cut my base in half. I knew that the company was hurting. I just didn't know to what extent. It got to a point where I would kind of look at my wife—you know, every other Friday—and say, "Hey, the commissions are still being paid and the checks are still being paid, so I'm happy, but something's not adding up here."

My wife and I got married on the last day of April, and went on our honeymoon. On our honeymoon, we went to Italy and Greece, and that's kind of where we had the crepes everyday, and it was street side. And I got back, and I wanted a banana and Nutella crepe, and that's when it started to get the ball rolling for this.

He motions to the café set-up all around, taking it in for a brief moment.

That's kind of where the seed was planted for our concept of a small business with a food cart. That week was really strange. The vice-president who would almost always communicate with me kind of cut off communication. The owner's son, you couldn't communicate with him…So I saw all these things internally collapsing. The appointments started becoming less and less. We had to cut our secretary. I was really doing everything. I was coming into the office. I'd stop in maybe twice a week, when it was my scheduled day to stop in. I had like a 15-minute drive to the office…

I went into the office and it was empty. Completely empty.

I walked in. I kind of took it in…just naturally I went to the back warehouse, because we had been broken in before. So I'm like, "Maybe that happened again." Walked into the back warehouse, because it was a small office space, and then, you know, maybe 3,000 square feet of warehouse space where a lot of our equipment was, our metals, all that stuff, and it was completely empty. There wasn't even a shovel or a vest left. They had come in over the weekend and basically gutted the whole place. It was shocking.

I didn't want to spend any more time there. There was an initial feeling of a lot of deceit and I just wanted to rid myself of it at that point. I would say maybe max I was in there for a minute, a minute and a half. I left my keys and locked up and got in my truck.

Driving home was where there was some reflection and some kind of, like…You know, there's obviously an "Oh, crap."

So I called the vice-president up and just said, "Dave, you know, I've been to the office. I'm kind of interested in why you guys didn't call me."

And there was this…It wasn't even a textbook answer. It was, "Well, we've been meaning to do it. We were going to."

I said, "Well, 'meaning to' and 'going to'—you never did. Why not?"

Didn't really get much of an answer. Because they didn't give me notice, I wanted to make sure that I still had some paychecks coming. That was my biggest concern. They did guarantee that they would keep me on the payroll for X amount of weeks. So that took some of the stress out initially. But there wasn't a severance. It was just, "We'll continue your pay and finish up the jobs and pay you on those commissions for six weeks."

And I said, "That's fine." It's better than nothing.

I felt like at least there was enough operational clues, I guess you could say, of how things were going that I was able to pick up that the shelf life of the business and the branch wasn't going to last, but I never expected to just show up and…I was there on a Friday and then on Wednesday it was completely gutted. When you go and you're with a company, especially a smaller, local company that's family-owned, been in business 25 years, for them to do something like that to you, it kind of felt like a slap in the face. Not to say that if it was a major corporation I would've felt any different, but when you know the owner, you go out to eat with the owner, there's a little bit more of a personal bond there. I would've liked to see it go down a little differently, because I enjoyed the people. I enjoyed the family. And it kind of did burn some bridges because the way they did it.

I was definitely ticked off at the end of the day, because I felt that I enabled them for at least a good 18 months to keep their operation up here based on what I was doing, what I was going out and willing to do for them. I mean, the mileage I put on the car I drive. I was doing probably between 50 to 60,000 miles a year up to Cleveland, down South to the Southeastern part of the state and all the way up to the Northeastern and Northwestern…along with taking the Columbus territory. So I felt like I really enabled them and I would like to see a little bit more appreciation, but I think also there is the belief as a business owner that they were going to be okay, and they weren't being realistic with themselves about the situation.

Even the next morning, though, still kind of woke up and it was like, "Wow. They did that to me." After being very loyal for almost four years, that's how they treated me.

Fortunately, there was something in me internally saying you know, you need to get moving. You need to start looking at other options. I didn't have time to be, like, "Oh, man. Woe is me," and sulk around and say, "Oh, this stinks." I just reacted, and I was forced to react, you know? Two things major after you get married. You look at your spouse and say, "Hey, honey, I lost my job," and, "instead of going back to the corporate world and doing sales, I want to makes crepes on the side of the street."

So that could've been troublesome for some people, but fortunately for us, I feel like our relationship really was strong, so…When I brought the concept of our business to her, it was extremely supportive. Fortunately, she's in a sales position that does well, so she kind of looked at me and said, "Well, you know, do it full-time. Instead of being a side job, do it full-time. I'll support you." It is what it is, and that's life, and we'll figure it out.

Did a search on craigslist for a used crepe cart, and a guy had posted about three, four hours beforehand in New Jersey, and we kind of looked at each other…Everything fell into place. So that's kind of what I mention about just having a burning desire to do this. Drove to New Jersey, picked up a crepe cart, came back and here we are now.

The way you react towards things is really gonna determine the end result. So I look at it as the best thing that could've possibly happened… 'Cause it let me do something I'm passionate about, and it forced me to put all of my focus and attention to it.

August 3rd was the day that I went into the office, and it was empty. August 5th started the business. We were getting ready to start our first event with our new business. And it was a local event, kind of a taste competition, so I went to the kitchen and started mixing some stuff up and just getting prepped for that event. And just figured hey, I got more time now. It won't be as stressful.

It was also kind of coinciding with finding out a month later that my wife was pregnant. Two trips to the grocery store, because I was like, "Well, maybe that brand doesn't work properly." (Laughs.) You know, so we went and got the test and everything, and you know, it was what we wanted, so we were ecstatic.

I may have a different outlook on life, where it's not necessarily what happens to you, it's how you respond to it, and that's how I've always believed. So I felt like I responded pretty well.

I had planned on having her help me on the weekends, but once we found out she was pregnant with the heat and stuff and just the changes a female's going to go through, it just wasn't going to happen.

You can look at things two ways. They kind of hosed me, or I was fortunate that they kept me on the payroll to enable me actually to figure out a game plan for my small business and take that time. You know, most people, when they're starting up a small business, cash flow's limited. But I was able to get six weeks of pay from them, which really enabled me to go out there and operate every day of the week, and put a lot of time and effort into it where, you know, that's one of the biggest things with small businesses. I didn't have to tap into that reserve for that period of time, which I felt fortunate.

March 22nd of this year, our son was born, and that completely lit a fire under me, seeing a little, miniature me out there. Maximus. We call him

Max. So yeah, Greek and Italian. And it's awesome. Best thing in the world. Definitely lit a fire under both of us as far as production.

So it was a very fast…all within pretty much, you know, 15 months. Yeah, our son was born before our one-year anniversary. Kind of put it into perspective. We joke around, if they ever needed someone to do an ad on life comes at you fast, we think we're good candidates for it.

I think the goal I had was within the first three years, to be able to have actual employees. Last year, I did everything by myself for those three months. I relied on family a lot, a lot of volunteer hours from some good friends and family.

I haven't even hit an actual hundred days of being open from last August 5th and operating. So I'm still learning, but my goal is to be able to, within that third year, be able to have employee set-up where we have payroll. We have everything structured like a large business. But at this point it'd be premature.

I think that with your own business, you should have blood, sweat and tears involved in it. It's stressful. If something screws up and you're not ready, or you drop the ball or something, it's your fault. There's no more looking and going, "Well, John should've been on that," or "Mike should've been on that." It's, "I dropped the ball." That would be the worst. The stress involved in knowing that it's all on you.

People who own their own businesses are passionate, so there's no motivation necessary. A lot of people stop and say, "I had your product. It was wonderful. It was great." They really think what you're doing's cool, so there's this positive motivation that comes with it. And it's enjoyable. Overall, it makes me happy.

Because it is your own, I can truly say I work for my family every day, and that's all the motivation I need to, you know, do what I want to do. Plus I don't want to sound like a control freak or anything like that, but it enables you to be able to take it in the direction you want to take it, and at the end of the day if it wasn't a good day, or at the end of the month if it wasn't a good month, you really just need to look at yourself and hold yourself accountable for it.

"Now's your chance"

Nancy Lee

Her great-grandparents came to the US from a town outside the Lithuanian capitol of Vilnius; they were avoiding conscription into the Russian army. The family wound up in Georgetown, eastern Illinois, so small it shared a pastor with neighboring towns; he rode around leading makeshift services, weddings and funerals. The area has "a lot of Lithuanians, and there are a lot of Poles—and there's coal mining." One of Nancy's great-grandfathers worked in the mines; her grandfather worked at a steel mill in Gary, Indiana— as did her father but that only lasted for one day: "That night they went to a bar, my dad watched somebody get knifed to death for their shoes, and he came back to Georgetown." He joined the Air Force and was the first in the family to go to college, eventually becoming a weatherman. Nancy still carries his first name: "Nancy Lee Sherman was my birth name, and I've gotten married a couple times and I just decided to, in 2008 when everything blew up, I just started over completely and dropped everything except my first name and my middle name. And Lee is also my dad's name."

She came to Indianapolis in 1992. We're in the living room of her home in the Springdale neighborhood of the city. A brief summer rain shower has just come and gone outside the windows that look out onto the quiet house-lined street. It's Sunday afternoon and my guess is half the block is taking a nap right about now. Nancy, 53, sits near the fireplace. Her dark red hair provides stark framing for her pale, smooth complexion. She shares the house with her partner, Wug, and if his name sounds familiar it's because this is a name that sticks—and he was hospitable enough to share his studio space when I talked to Jenny Elig and Judy Wolf.

Wug and Nancy have set out a bowl of fresh, ripe cherries. Their home has a balance of modesty and exhibition. They are both artists and they both have bright smiles; their personalities and work fill the home.

Nancy's work history is a mash-up of executive assistant experience at impressive venues like the Indianapolis Museum of Art, and project management in construction. "I really enjoyed working with the architects and doing the whole process, I just really liked that process of collaboration—getting something on paper and then making it happen, come to life."

2008, our jobs started to dry up because the price of steel skyrocketed because China was building so much, so all the steel was going to China; the demand just blew the price out of the water and all of our construction projects started to dry up while people waited for pricing to come down. And it wasn't coming down. And then the thing with the banks started to happen and I could see the writing on the wall.

We had a whole roster of jobs that would come in to your department, and my boss would kind of parse those out to people. And I had a pretty full plate and I had all my projects spread-sheeted out and I had all of the projects that I had out for bid spread-sheeted out. And as my current projects started to wrap up, all of these potential projects, I just kept hearing back, you know, we're not moving on that right now, we're not moving on that right now, we're not moving on that right now.

And the same thing was happening with my co-workers, and just slowly we started to realize that nobody's jobs were kicking off. And things would get shuffled around.

I got called in to the conference room one sunny afternoon and my boss said, "Will you come with me—I wanna talk to you for a minute." I thought, well, don't get all crazy, it's probably fine.

When he opened the door to the conference room and I saw his boss sitting there, I went, "Oh shit," 'cause I knew what was coming. I knew I was getting canned.

It did not take long. The gist of it was, we're really sorry to have to be letting you go, and it is not performance based. I mean he did want to really make sure that I knew that it was not performance based, and that they would do everything that they could to help me find another position. The good thing was—I guess—they kept me on for another 30 days after that, so my boss basically said, "Spend these next 30 days wrapping up your projects, but I want you to look for other work while you're here, on the clock." Because they don't pay vacation, they don't pay severance, I got nothing when I left— zero.

And you know what? Nobody even knew I was getting divorced, and I just kept wanting to scream and shout, "You don't even understand! I'm getting a divorce! I'm gonna be homeless, what am I gonna do with no income?"...I didn't. I was very very polite and well-mannered. I really couldn't...the words wouldn't come out, you know? They were just sort of stuck. My throat just sort of seized up and only niceties...not what I was really thinking.

And how long had you been going through the divorce process?

It had been several months. I'd lost a bunch of weight. One person in my office knew, and that was it. I didn't think it was good to share that. I just didn't want that to take over my work life. It took over every other minute and hour of my personal time and I just wanted to do my job. I didn't want that to be what people thought about when they talked to me.

After they let me go, it was just like a kick in the gut, though. I just was…I was ashamed. I was ashamed that I couldn't do well enough for them to want to keep me. And I just wanted to get out of there. But they gave me the afternoon off and he's like, "You wanna take a couple days off and then come back in, that's cool." So I think I did.

What did you do with the rest of that day?

Cried. Called people. Called a few people and let them know. Called my sisters. They both live in Illinois. They were very supportive, very supportive. And then my little sister, her position was eliminated, whatever that means. I have two sisters and one of the two I believe maybe let my parents know. I don't really know but that wasn't a fun thing.

I think I took like the next day off and then came back in, and it was really weird. It's really weird to be fired and then stay for another 30 days, so that first couple of days after that was really tough. But I got through that month. There just wasn't another position to find. I was my age, I was making all this money, I had a very odd blend of experience—I didn't have ten straight years of classical construction management, I didn't have ten straight years of classic executive assistant…I was making all this money…It was a unique skill-set, and I thought it would be valuable, but it turns out that it wasn't as valuable as I had hoped.

I had already moved out of my home. And I was staying with friends, randomly. My divorce was final the week I got fired, so everything in my life changed. I went to bed. Just hung out in bed for about a month.

It was awful. I just…I so wanted to be OK. I so wanted to just power through it and have everything be OK. And it was so not OK, I mean, it was just not OK. The reality was that I slept until noon most of the time, I didn't wanna do anything, I would clean myself up if I needed to go out for a job interview or meet someone, but the reality was, I just wanted to isolate myself and hide. I was still wounded from the whole experience, and I just…I was embarrassed. I didn't know what I was gonna do with myself. Everything was new, and everything had changed, everything was upside down. I thought I was gonna lose my mind. I just really was very on the edge. Very on the edge, for a while. And my son was upset with me because I'd gotten a divorce, and so I was distanced from him. And as much as my family is loving, when trouble is brewing, they're like, "You know, you need to work through that on your own and just get through it and then when you're ready, you're welcome back to the fold." So I just kind of dealt with it.

I think my experience is probably not uncommon. Your logical mind understands, but your primitive brain has another voice that is there to tear you down, and it's just like an automatic thing in the back of your mind, I'm not good enough, this is shameful, this never should have happened, if I had just been more perfect, if I had just been a better person, or a better employee, none of this would have ever happened. It took me a while to even really get really mad, 'cause I wasn't sure that I deserved to get really mad, and getting really mad kind of helped.

Wug was there for me—I don't know what I would have done if it weren't for him, because it was all OK; no matter how wigged out I was getting, it was all ok. He was kind of my rock.

I'm resilient and stubborn and strong...I mean, my heritage tells me that that's true. My great-grandparents were immigrants from Lithuania—they had nothing. My grandmother went through the great depression with nothing. It's just not that bad having nothing for a while. I had to get over my fear of that; get over my fear of having nothing.

I lived on the north side of town in a very nice neighborhood, $175,000 home, two nice cars, expensive dinners out a lot, the best food, vacations occasionally, and I spent—I bought all my clothes at Banana Republic, you know, it was kind of keeping up with the Joneses type of thing. I was making a lot of money but it really wasn't enough. I was so afraid of letting go of all that, that it was just really weird. But then when I ended up moving in with Wug and he lived in Little Mexico at the time, and I had a real eye-opening experience. There are Mexicans all over. Great people, wonderful people. One morning I woke up and I could hear the roosters crowing in the alley next to our shotgun house and there were little girls next door playing in the dirt, I mean, there was no grass in the yard, they were just playing in the dirt, they were filthy dirty and these filthy little toys that they were playing with, and they were laughing. And I went out there and cried. And Wug said—this is the best thing anybody ever said to me—he said, "How dare you pity them. How dare you. You're judging."

Nancy begins crying and asks for a few moments to gather herself. We sit in silence. I tell her that's a hell of a thing to say to someone— she's right to be grateful for Wug's frankness.

That was like a defining moment. It was just like somebody had dumped a bucket of water on me, it just washed away many years of thinking that I understood, and just not...And I'm a pretty open person, I've felt pretty non-judgmental, but that moment was so eye opening. You never know about people, about their experience, you never know. Those kids, playing in the dirt, they had a roof over their head, they had food coming in the house, they had a mom who was caring for them and a dad who was working. They didn't speak any English, they obviously came from Mexico and I don't know what their experience was like there—I have no idea. So how could I pity them when I didn't even know where they came from?

My mom tells me—even before I have memories of it—that I was drawing and all this other stuff. I've just wanted to create ever since I was little. So probably maybe 15–18 years ago I started making jewelry just by teaching myself how to string beads that I bought, and then I made my own beads out of these polymer clays and I wanted to make my own catches and my own ear wires and my own clasps. So I took a class in metal-smithing for the jewelry maker at our local arts center. And the bead-making, I just never went back to it. I just saw the qualities in the metal, and what you could do with it—those wonderful qualities. The metal-smithing scared me, you know, the torches and doing something wrong with a piece of silver that was expensive. So there was that fear challenge. It was just scary enough to make me really pay attention and be interested and all these many years later, I still feel like there is so much more I can learn about it. And being easily distractible, it's the perfect fit for me, because even if I do this for the rest of my life, I know that I won't even have scratched the surface of all there is to know about it.

I look around, and we have all of our most precious things around us. And our art, that I love, and my dining room table, and it's just like, so simple. So simple what you really need. Good food, we like a bottle of wine, and we love being with our friends and finding ways to be with our friends. Working alone at my bench and creating something from nothing. And then selling to someone who comes into my little studio and watching them leave with it, I mean—gosh—what could be better than that?

It was probably about three or four months after I left my job that I just, I really decided to focus my time, and we set myself up a desk in Wug's office so I—I had a laptop—could do some computer work through there, and I started my website and started to work on that, and started to try to figure out how to do some marketing and get more supplies in and make more things.

Wug and I did this show along with several other people—we met through a social networking place called Smaller Indiana—and we were in this art group, and someone posed a question, "Should we do an art show?" And seven or eight of us formed this little core group and put on the show called Elegant Funk and it was really a great show, I mean, we had hundreds of people come out to the opening. I created two pieces for that show, one was a little sculpture where the tree crashed in on my studio, and another was a pendant, and it was really beautiful, and I sold the pendant, so that was a memorable thing, selling that. And then I've just kind of been selling out of there ever since. But the sculpture I didn't even put up for sale.

The great part is, I like to share knowledge—I like to learn, and then share what I've learned, if I can. And so now I'm teaching and my students just bring me so much…they bring me a lot of joy. They really fill me up, by sharing it just fills me up. So I'm seeing that is going to be part of my future as well.

I've revisited moments from time to time, and it's funny because some of them were pretty recent. And I thought to myself, you know, I'm kind of bitter, I still have bitter thoughts. And it hurts me to see other people around lose their jobs. It makes me feel ill-will towards large corporations, it's just completely changed my whole way of thinking about how people— how humanity, not just me, but humanity—is treated. The downtrodden.

I don't see myself as a victim, I see myself as overcoming this and getting to a good place. But I see so many people who have poured their heart and soul into their companies and their companies just cut them loose. The devastation that you see in people's lives, you're just absolutely blown apart. I'm angry for them too, not just for me. But for them too. It's like, you didn't just do this to me, you did this over and over and over to so many people, just so that you could make your stockholders, this little group of people, really happy. And make this little group of people have a lot more money. God forbid that you should downgrade your own lives a little bit to employ so many extra people. I don't know, it just…It's left me with a very bad taste and I'm not too sure that that will ever go away. My own personal story is one of healing, I think, but the takeaway for me is that there's some things that aren't right that are going on in corporations that have probably gone on for a really long time, but my eyes have just been opened to how people are used and to how things aren't fair. The absolute greed that I see, it's just sickening.

When you think of losing everything, you realize what is worth hanging onto and what isn't. Ending the marriage and losing the job at the same time was sort of like that cataclysmic action where you really…everything is stripped down to brass tacks and you just really figure it out. I had, like, a sack of clothes there for a while. But I had a roof and I never missed a meal, and I had this space around me to just slowly start unpeeling all that stuff, and letting it kind of fall away about who I thought I was, what I thought I needed to get by, what informed me as a human being, and how I related to the rest of the world. And it took…it has taken a long time to start to figure some of this stuff out. It was 2008; it wasn't yesterday. And just like two seconds ago, I'm just starting to figure a couple of things out about what I need and what I don't need. And I think what brings me the most peace at this moment is figuring my way to financial solvency by stripping things out of my life that I don't need or want or don't mean anything to me. I'm one of the lucky ones because I managed to figure things out well enough to hold on to the things that were most precious to me and I just decided the rest of it just really didn't matter. And that included a lot of people.

Usually when you experience some sort of a loss, whatever it might be, a job, or a loved one, or through a divorce, or moving to a new town, you really can be surprised at who sticks and who doesn't. So it was yet another opportunity for me to learn who would stick. And who wouldn't. And I was probably the most devastated by some of the people who didn't stick who I thought would. But the good part is, it really only takes one or two people— that's all it really takes. And if you're lucky enough to have one or two people who will stick with you, you can make it through about anything.

That commercial that's running recently about the woman who has 650 Facebook friends, have you seen that? She's sitting there and she's looking kinda pasty, the white of the computer screen is flickering on her face, and she's saying, "They say when your parents get up there in age they kinda isolate themselves so I made my parents get on Facebook. They've got like 19 friends right now." And it keeps cutting to her parents going out discoing with her friends and taking rides in the mountain with their bikes with their friends and hoopin' it up and laughing and hollering, and they keep cutting back to her sitting there all by herself with the glow of the screen on her face, and she's like, "I've got 650 friends. This is living!" and you're like, woah, not, not so much. So volume doesn't really matter. I know, I get Facebook, it's cool, I love having my 700 Facebook friends, don't get me wrong. But I don't know 'em all.

Interestingly enough, my son just lost his job. Lately we've had a real good conversation, and what I mean by that is, I showed up at his house unannounced and said, "Let me in 'cause we gotta talk." And so I not only broke the ice, I took an axe to it. And I'm like, I gotta get this kid back into my life, no matter what it takes, so I showed up and we've been talking ever since. I was kind of scrambling for the last few years just to manage my own self, and I'm in a better place now to really build a good relationship. I let it go too long, so it's really important for me to have that be where it should be on whatever terms work for him. But you know, if I die tomorrow I don't want that to be a thing where he's like, gosh I wish I could have built a bridge back to my mom. So I'm building the bridge, and it'll happen.

We went swimming together, last night.

Acknowledgments

Thanks goes to:

Colin Robinson who recognized the importance of telling this collective story—and trusted me to go get it.

John Oakes, Crystal Williams, Courtney Andujar and everyone at OR Books.

John Siciliano, who demonstrated early faith in this project—I'm deeply grateful. Shannon Twomey and everyone at Penguin who worked on this book.

Claire Donato and Fernanda Diaz who possess the fastest typing fingers, and sharpest ears in the modern area. I am grateful to have experienced the early text with both of you.

Everyone who helped find the unemployed: Anna Stein, Ruth Adams, Rose Vining, Judith Hug, John McElwee, T Cooper, Richard Messenger, Maureen Reintjes, Bodine Boling, Bodine Boiling, Richard Benjamin, Mark James, Chris Erdman, Clint & Mary Sprague, John & Kate Hayes, Chris Parris-Lamb, Tom Lamb, Linda McNutt, and Cindy Petill.

Tammy & Dana Sparks, for inviting us to stay with them. After one cold call they trusted us enough to open their home and their beer cooler without hesitation or reservation. I await the chance to someday do this for someone else, and I hope to be half as graciously and generous as the Sparks.

Jeff Mitchtell, who was a tireless and generous collaborator in Reno.

CoriDawn Olsen and everyone at the Pioneer Adult Rehabilitation Center in Clearfield, Utah.

Kelley Bernardi and everyone at the S.L.A.T.E. office in downtown St. Louis.

David Greenwalt and Roni Chambers and everyone at the GO! Network.

Mary Loritz at the Columbus Coalition for the Homeless.

Chris Kuban, for going above and beyond.

Professor David Creswell at Carnegie Mellon University, for his insightful perspective.

Ciri Castro who sat down with me despite the fact that he had just put out a fire.

Carey Mann, for allowing us to keep Mallery all summer.

John Tucker, Candy Cheng, Beck Teitel, Katherine Brown, Stephen Fried, and Kevin Coyne for moral and practical support throughout all. And to Sam Freedman for helping me understand what a book is.

Mike Gorrell and Steve Giegerich, two fine reporters who took the time to help me understand their cities.

Wug Laku for use of his studio—and the introduction to Nancy Lee.

Judy Wolf, Skip and Joan Hawkins, Debbie Sheidler and Casey Cahoy, Kevin Lawler & Kay Friesen at Metropolitan Community College in Omaha, and the Muenchow family in Columbus—all of whom provided amazing hospitality and warmth.

MJ and Mallery: we had no idea what we were in for. And I think it will be quite some time before we realize what we experienced. Thank you for sharing it with me.

Paul Thomas, Ruth Pople, James Kelman, Joseph O'Neill, Joshua Furst, Arshia Sattar, Darby Parker, Aileen Silverstone, and John Michener for encouragement across many essential moments. And all of my family for support and love, most of all Shug.

And of course to all the collaborators who shared their experiences, and Tasha—to whom this book is dedicated.